Hiking
Alaska

by
Dean Littlepage

FALCON™
HELENA, MONTANA

A FALCON GUIDE

Falcon is continually expanding its list of recreational guidebooks. All books include detailed descriptions, accurate maps, and all the information necessary for enjoyable trips. You can order extra copies of this book and get information and prices for other Falcon guidebooks by writing Falcon, P.O. Box 1718, Helena, MT 59624 or by calling toll-free 1-800-582-2665. Also, please ask for a free copy of our current catalog.
Visit our web site at http:\\www.falconguide.com

©1997 by Falcon Press Publishing Co., Inc.,
Helena and Billings, Montana.

Printed in the United States of America.

Illustrations by Leslie Reed
Photographs by the author, except as follows:
    Page 18, 19, Helene Feiner
    Page 38, Linda Birtles
    Page 208, Molly McCarthy
    Page 369, Diedra Bohn
Cover photo of Denali National Park by Cliff Riedinger

Library of Congress Cataloging-in-Publication Data

Littlepage, Dean.
    Hiking Alaska / Dean Littlepage.
        p.   cm.
    "Falcon guide."
    ISBN 1-56044-551-3 (pbk.)
    1. Hiking—Alaska—Guidebooks.   2. Alaska—Guidebooks.   I. Title.
GV199.42.A4L58 1997
796.5'1'09798—dc21
                                                        96-53934
                                                            CIP

CAUTION

Outdoor recreational activities are by their very nature potentially hazardous. All participants in such activities must assume the responsibility for their own actions and safety. The information contained in this guidebook cannot replace sound judgment and good decision–making skills, which help reduce risk exposure, nor does the scope of this book allow for disclosure of all the potential hazards and risks involved in such activities.

Learn as much as possible about the outdoor recreational activities in which you participate, prepare for the unexpected, and be cautious. The reward will be a safer and more enjoyable experience.

♻ Text pages printed on recycled paper.

DEDICATION

Yes sir, yes madam,
I entreat you, . . .
stand up straight
like men! like women!
like human beings!
and walk—walk—WALK
upon our sweet and blessed land!

Edward Abbey

Dedicated to everyone who has contributed to the conservation of Alaska's wildlands. To readers, an invitation: enjoy hiking in the state's backcountry, and join in the effort to protect it.

CONTENTS

Acknowledgments viii
Map Legend x
Alaska's Regions xi

HIKING IN ALASKA 1
Regions and Climates 1
Trails and Cabins 3
The Hiking Landscape 5
Wildlife and Fish 7
Insects 8
Plants 8
Hypothermia 10
Stream Crossings 11
The Hiker's Essentials 14
The Three Bears and Other Details 18
Outdoor Ethics/Leave No Trace 24
Hiking with Kids 27
A Word (or Two) for Travelers 28

USIING THIS GUIDE 29
PICK-A-HIKE TABLES 31

SOUTHCENTRAL ALASKA 34
 Map: Trips in Southcentral Alaska 34
 Eastern Kenai 35
  1. Caines Head 36
  2. Exit Glacier 40
  3. Harding Icefield 42
  4. Lost Lake 45
  Fishing the Kenai Backcountry Lakes 48
  5. Ptarmigan Lake 49
  6. Johnson Pass 52
  7. Crescent and Carter Lakes 55
  8. Resurrection Pass 58
  9. Russian Lakes 62
  10. Devil's Pass 66

 Northwest Kenai 68
  11. Fuller Lakes 68
  12. Kenai River 71
  13. Hidden Creek and Skilak Lake 73
  14. Skilak Lookout and Bear Mountain 76
  15. Seven Lakes 78
  16. Captain Cook 81

CONTENTS

Homer 84
   17. Grewingk Valley 85
   18. China Poot Lake and Wosnesenski River 89
   19. Island Peninsula 92
   20. Calvin and Coyle Nature Trail 94

Turnagain Arm 97
   21. Gull Rock 97
   22. Portage Valley 100
   Portage Glacier and Portage Pass 103
   23. Portage Pass 104
   24. Winner Creek 106
   25. Crow Pass 110
   26. Bird Ridge 116
   27. Indian Valley 118
   Chugach State Park 121
   28. Falls Creek 122
   29. McHugh and Rabbit Lakes 125
   30. Turnagain Arm Trail 128

Anchorage 131
   31. Flattop Mountain 131
   32. Ship Lake Pass and Hidden Lake 134
   33. Williwaw Lakes 137
   34. Wolverine Peak 141
   35. Rover's Run 143

Knik Arm 146
   36. South Fork Eagle River 146
   Southcentral's Berry Crop 150
   37. Eagle River Valley 151
   38. Thunder Bird Falls 156
   39. Twin Peaks 158
   40. Bold Peak Valley 161
   41. East Fork Eklutna River 165
   42. Pioneer Ridge 168

Mantanuska and Susitna Valleys 172
   43. Lazy Mountain and Matanuska Peak 173
   44. Little Susitna River 177
   45. Reed Lakes 180
   46. Snowbird Mine and Glacier Pass 183
   47. Independence Mine 186
   48. Red Shirt Lake 189
   49. Lower Troublesome Creek 192
   50. Byers Lake 194
   51. Kesugi Ridge 197

Copper River Basin 202
   52. Tonsina River 203
   53. Worthington Glacier 204

CONTENTS

54. Dixie Pass 206
55. Root Glacier 210
56. Trail and Lost Creeks 213
About the Nabesna Road 218
57. Skookum Volcano 219

Cordova 221
58. Power Creek and Crater Lake 221
59. Haystack Trail 225
Bird Heaven: The Copper River Delta 228
60. McKinley Lake 229
61. Saddlebag Glacier 231
62. Childs Glacier 233

INTERIOR ALASKA 236
Map: Trips in the Interior 236
Denali National Park and Preserve 237
Map: Denali Park and Preserve, Park Road Corridor 238
Fairbanks 242
63. Creamer's Field 242
A Family Named Creamer and a Subarctic Dairy 245
64. Chena River Nature Trail 246
65. Granite Tors 248
66. Angel Rocks 252
67. Chena Dome 256
68. Pinnell Mountain 260
Gold Fever in the Yukon Hills 264
69. Summit Trail 265

Denali Highway 269
70. Landmark Gap Lake 269
71. Maclaren Summit 271

SOUTHEAST ALASKA 273
Map: Trips in Southeast 273
Ketchikan 274
72. Deer Mountain 275
The Southeast Alaska Forests 279
73. Ward Lake Nature Trail 280
74. Perseverance Lake 281
75. Naha River 284

Wrangell 287
76. Rainbow Falls and Institute Creek 288
77. Long Lake 291

Petersburg 292
78. Three Lakes and Ideal Cove 293
79. Ohmer Creek 296
80. Petersburg Lake 298

CONTENTS

Our Friend the Skunk Cabbage 302

Sitka 303
  81. Indian River 304
  82. Sitka National Historic Park 307
  The Ten-Cent Treatise on Totems 310
  83. Starrigavan Bay 311
  84. Harbor Mountain and Gavan Hill 314

Juneau 317
  85. Perseverance Trail and Granite Creek 318
  86. Mount Juneau 321
  87. Dan Moller Trail 324
  88. Mendenhall Glacier Visitor Center Trails 327
  89. West Glacier 331
  90. Montana Creek and Windfall Lake 334
  91. Spaulding and Auke Nu Trails 337
  92. Herbert Glacier 340
  93. Point Bridget 342

Haines 345
  94. Mount Ripinsky and 7 Mile Saddle 345
  95. Mount Riley 348
  96. Seduction Point 352

Skagway 355
  97. Laughton Glacier 355
  98. Chilkoot Pass 358
  The Rush of '98 363
  99. Dewey Lakes 364
  100. Sturgill's Landing 367

OFF THE BEATEN PATH: DISCOVERING WILDERNESS ALASKA 369
  Map 369
  Gates of the Arctic 371
  Arctic National Wildlife Refuge 372
  Wrangell-St. Elias 373
  Katmai 374
  Lake Clark 375
  Kuskokwim Headwaters 376
  White Mountains 376
  Northwest Alaska 377
  Glacier Bay 378

APPENDICES
  1 - Information Sources 379
  2 - Cabin Reservations 382
  3 - Transportation and Outfitting 383
  4 - Further Reading 384
  5 - Sample Backpacking Checklist 386

ABOUT THE AUTHOR 387

ACKNOWLEDGMENTS

Many people contributed in many ways to this guidebook, and here's a big thanks to them all. First, to the many agency people who took the time to provide material, information, maps, and to review drafts:

Chugach National Forest: Pat O'Leary (Seward), Elaine Gross, Cliff Larson, Allison Rein, Sharon Randall, and Chris Roy (Girdwood), Sandy Frost, Dave Zastrow, Dixon Sherman, Pat Green and Bob Behrens (Cordova), and Greg Dixon, Mike Novy and Carol Huber (Anchorage). Tongass National Forest: Marlene Finley, Yvonne Stanley and Ken Crevier (Ketchikan), David Rak and Leslie Murray (Wrangell), Linda Slaght, Brad Hunter and Doug Blanc (Petersburg), Anne Marie LaPalme (Sitka), Nita Nettleton, Rob Morgenthaler, Alroy Deangelis and Joni Packard (Juneau) and Scott Holm (Skagway).

National Park Service: Diane Jung (Anchorage), Sandy Kogl, Jennifer Reed and Lisa Eckert (Denali), Maria Gillett and Glenn Hart (Kenai Fjords), Brian Suderman, Melanie Heacox, Kate Boesser and Lewis Sharman (Glacier Bay), Kim Valentino (Northwest Areas), Jeff Mow (Gates of the Arctic), Susan Savage (Katmai), Clair Roberts (Lake Clark), and Clay Alderson and Cathy Cook (Klondike Gold Rush). Alaska Public Lands Information Centers: Lisa Jodwalis and John Morris. Parks Canada: Dan Verhalle. The National Weather Service provided climate summaries.

U.S. Fish and Wildlife Service: Candace Ward, Doug Palmer, Emily Fiala, and Rick Johnston (Kenai Refuge). U.S. Geological Survey: A.C. Brown. Bureau of Land Management: Janelle Eklund and Jeff Bruney (Anchorage), Kathy Liska and Mike Coffeen (Glennallen), and Lon Kelly, Randy Goodwin and Larry Field (Fairbanks).

Alaska State Parks: Bill Zak (Haines), Bill Garry (Juneau), Darryl Hunt and Mike Lee (Fairbanks), Al Meiners and Dan Amyot (Chugach State Park), Pat Murphy, Mike Goodwin, John Wilber and Dennis Heikes (Mat-Su), Roger McCampbell (Homer), Dave Stephens, Jeff Johnson, Tom Young and Bill Evans (Anchorage), Terry Rude and Jack Sinclair (Kenai), and Rolf Buzzell of the Office of History and Archaeology in Anchorage.

Alaska Department of Fish and Game: Barry Stratton (Anchorage), Pam Tacquard and Herb Melchior (Fairbanks) and Dave Nelson (Soldotna). Alaska Department of Transportation: Laurie Mulcahy. Matanuska-Susitna Borough Recreation Services: Elizabeth Weiant and Warren Templin.

Thanks also to Paul Swift, Allen Traut and Patty Brown (Haines), Lynne Owens (Sitka), Karla Hart (Juneau), Michelle Masden (Ketchikan), Austin Helmers (Palmer), Ann Miller (Hope), Sally Oberstein and Mary Griswold (Kachemak Heritage Land Trust, Homer), Penny Hodges and Jessica Brainard (Center for Alaskan Coastal Studies, Homer), Dan Heitman (Kachmak Bay Water Taxi, Homer), James Larabee (Mountaineering Club of Alaska, Anchorage) and Frankie Barker (Alaska Natural History Association, Anchorage). Then there were all my trail and travel companions: Jeanne, Kevin, Joan, Birt, Linda, Patty, Helene, Cheryl, Clo, Nimbus, Skook, Lelia, Leslie,

Ray, Stefan, Judy, Melanie, Julie, Jim, Bruce, Heidi, Gavin and the "three women" at Dixie Pass.

Finally, special thanks to the generous sponsors of the field work: the Alaska Railroad (Larry Houle), the Alaska Marine Highway System (Linda Mickle), the White Pass and Yukon Route Railroad (Tina Cyr), Glacier Bay Lodge (Gary Sorel and Doug Pryor), Auk Nu Tours (Ellen Cobbs), Alaska Fish Tales (Burl Weller) and Chilkoot Water Charters (Denise and Bud Norman).

MAP LEGEND

State or Other Principal Road	(00)	Day Use Area/Shelter/ Picnic Area	▲
Paved Road		Campground	⋀
Gravel Road		Cabins/Buildings	■
Unimproved Road		Peak	9,782 ft.
Trailhead	◯	Elevation	9,782 ft.
Main Trail(s) /Route(s)		Mine Site	✕ ⤬
Secondary Trail(s)/ Route(s)		Overlook/Point of Interest	◧
Route(s)/Cross Country Trail(s)		Map Orientation	N
Cross Country Trail(s)		Scale	0 0.5 1 Miles
Parking Area	(P)	Glacier	
River/Creek		Wetlands	
Spring			
Intermittent Stream			
Beach/Tidal Flat			

ALASKA'S REGIONS

The top of the Golden Stairs on the Chilkoot Trail.

HIKING IN ALASKA

Alaska—the Midnight Sun in the Arctic, the rain forest along the twisting coastline of the Southeast, the towering peaks and glaciers along the Gulf of Alaska, alpine ridges rolling like ocean waves across the Interior—it's all waiting for hikers to explore.

Alaska's size and diversity aren't easy to comprehend. The name fits; "Alaska" is a corruption of an Aleut word that means "great land." From the forested Southeast to the expansive Arctic plain, the Great Land is a mosaic of forest, glaciers, fjords, islands, mountains, rivers, muskeg, and tundra. The state measures about 1,400 miles north to south and 2,300 miles east to west; it is about a third the size of the entire Lower 48 states.

The Southcentral and Interior regions are the only ones connected by road to the Lower 48. Most of Southeast Alaska's communities are accessible from outside only by air or state ferry. The rest of the state is accessible mainly by air.

REGIONS AND CLIMATES

Southeast Alaska, a land of islands, ocean, mountains and forest, is the southernmost region of the state. The nation's largest national forest, the Tongass, and the largest areas of uncut temperate rain forest in the world are in the Southeast. This is Alaska's mildest and rainiest region.

Hiking a Chugach Mountain ridge near Anchorage.

Southeast is generally drier from south to north (Ketchikan averages 160 inches of rain a year, Skagway just 30), but there is a lot of local variation. May and June are the driest months, but some of the high country, especially in northern Southeast, is not snow-free until late June or early July. The hottest summer days may reach 80 degrees Fahrenheit, but a cloudy day with a high in the 60s is much more common. The low-elevation hiking season is a long one, even year-round in the south if you don't mind hiking in the winter rain. Winter is wet; October usually brings the first major winter storms.

Southcentral Alaska lies north of the Gulf of Alaska, inside the arc of the Alaska and Aleutian Ranges. Southcentral is the home of 70 percent of the state's residents, the most extensive road system, and the most developed hiking trails. Chugach National Forest, on the Kenai Peninsula, and Chugach State Park outside Anchorage are the most popular hiking areas.

Southcentral is also the region with the most natural diversity, with coastal, interior, and transitional forests, fjords and tidewater glaciers, great rivers and major mountain ranges. The climate is transitional too, from the wetter, milder climate of the southern coast to the drier, colder climate of the interior.

During the snow-free season, average rainfall increases gradually from May to September. On average, August and September are the peak precipitation months of the year. In Southcentral's mountains June is "posthole" month, when hikers punch through the snow that lingers at higher elevations. A hot summer day means temperatures in the 70s, rarely above 80 degrees. Autumn begins in late August. Early snow may dust the mountains, but there is usually still plenty of good, if cooler, mountain weather left in September.

Interior Alaska, the largest of Alaska's regions, is the part of the state between the Alaska and Brooks Ranges. The Interior holds many of Alaska's longest rivers and one world-class river, the Yukon. Vast wetlands are home to millions of waterfowl. The best hiking country is in the Alaska Range and in the Yukon-Tanana Uplands near Fairbanks.

Snow melts more quickly in spring in the Interior than in Southcentral, and there is a thunderstorm and forest fire season early in summer. Midsummer can be hot, into the 90s, but the weather cools quickly and significantly by September.

Southwest Alaska runs 1,400 miles down the Alaska Peninsula and the Aleutian Islands, a wet, windblown land of sea and volcano and the home of Katmai National Park and several other conservation areas.

Western Alaska is mainly a tundra zone, stretching north along the Bering Sea from Bristol Bay to Kotzebue Sound. There are millions of acres of seldom-visited preserves and refuges in Western Alaska.

Arctic Alaska lies north of the Arctic Circle, mostly beyond North America's northern tree line, and includes one of the world's great mountain ranges, the Brooks Range. There are several preserves in the Arctic: the Arctic National Wildlife Refuge and four National Park Service areas: Gates of the Arctic, Noatak, Kobuk Valley, and Cape Krusenstern.

The Arctic has twenty-four hours of daylight a day in mid-summer, but the warm weather is short; only in June through September are average daily temperatures above freezing. Like the Interior, the light snow cover melts relatively early, but arctic fronts can blow in from the north with fresh snow anytime in the summer.

TRAILS AND CABINS

Trails. Almost all of the state's developed hiking trails are in three of the six regions of the state—Southcentral, Interior, and Southeast. Anchorage, the Kenai Peninsula, and Juneau are the hiking-trail capitals of Alaska. Many national parks, like Denali, Wrangell-St. Elias, and Gates of the Arctic, are known for cross-country wilderness hiking.

Trails played a big part in the Native history of Alaska and in the settling of the state. On many Alaskan trails hikers can relive experiences of the past hundred years and more. The most famous are the Chilkoot and the Iditarod, but many Alaska trails have a historic or Native cultural connection.

Alaska's hiking trails and routes vary tremendously. There are graded and graveled nature trails, easy frontcountry trails, well-developed backcountry trails, trails on miles of boardwalk, routes that are barely scratched out on the ground or that are marked only with rock cairns, and true wilderness with no trails at all but the ones you sleuth out with map and compass. Alaska's park and forest managers are still building and improving trails; many new trails are planned.

A hike-in cabin along the Southcentral coast.

Cabins. The Forest Service, National Park Service, Bureau of Land Management and the State of Alaska provide rustic cabins for hikers, hunters, anglers, and boaters throughout the state. Typical cabins sleep four to six people; some are larger. Most have bunks, a table, benches or chairs, a few shelves, a wood or fuel-oil stove for heat (the fuel supply is the occupants' responsibility), and an outhouse. The Tongass and Chugach National Forests have the most extensive system of cabins.

The cabins are available through a reservation-and-fee system, and typically are open to reservation six months in advance of intended use. Some of the most popular cabins are available through a lottery. Cabin costs are $25 or more per night, subject to change (See Appendix 2 for reservation information).

There are also trail shelters (no reservation, no fee, first-come, first-served) on some trails in the state. These vary from three-sided shelters to small cabins, and typically are much more rustic than the fee cabins.

Access Roads and Trailheads. Many trails begin from paved highways. A few are on high-elevation, less-developed roads that may be wet, icy, or impassable early or late in the season or after storms. Other trailheads are accessible by boat, train, or plane.

In a few areas, particularly in and near Anchorage and in some areas of the Kenai Peninsula, smash-and-dash auto burglary has unfortunately become a problem. Packs and duffle bags left in plain sight are prime targets

A boardwalk trail outside Wrangell.

A Student Conservation Association Trail Crew at work in the Kenai Mountains.

for thieves. The best prevention is to leave nothing of value in your vehicle. Don't try the ploy of obviously covering up valuable items with a tarp or clothes—they're onto that trick.

THE HIKING LANDSCAPE

Mountain weather, glaciers, the dreaded "brush zone," and wet meadows and muskegs present some unique challenges for Alaska hikers. Alpine ridges and arctic tundra offer hikers little natural protection from the elements, and mountain and arctic weather can change in short order from warm and sunny to howling and raining or snowing. It's vital to carry good clothing and, for backpackers, a tent that will hold up in nasty, windy weather.

Glaciers are the high point of some of Alaska's hikes; in general, hikers without training and glacier-travel equipment should not venture onto glacial ice, which can hide dangerous crevasses and holes.

One of the most important bits of botanical trivia for hikers is the ever-present band of brush between the forest and alpine zones in Southeast and Southcentral. The brush zone, a thick mass of tall grasses, perennials and intertwined shrubs, can make hiking off-trail anything from a challenge to a nightmare.

Wet tundra and muskeg are found all over the state. In Southeast, heavy rainfall is the culprit. As a result, many of Southeast's trails are highly developed, including miles of boardwalk. Long boardwalk hikes can be tough

An alpine brook near Ship Lake Pass.

Battling alders along a river in the Alaska Range.

on knees and hips, especially for those with previous injuries, and board-walks can be slick as slug slime when wet.

In trailless areas, avoiding the wettest meadows and muskegs involves picking routes along stream bottoms and on ridgetops. In remote mountains, especially in the Brooks Range, the cottongrass lumps called tussocks can make hiking very slow and difficult.

WILDLIFE AND FISH

Wildlife. Alaska has the full, natural range of northern wildlife. In the charismatic megafauna department, there are bears and wolves, mountain sheep and goats, moose, black-tailed deer, and caribou. Smaller but no less important mammals like lynx, coyotes, foxes, river otters, mink, martens, wolverines, marmots, pikas, ground squirrels, beavers, lemmings, and voles all inhabit the state as well. Elk and bison are not native, but have been introduced to a few areas.

Humpback and gray whales, orcas, dolphins and porpoises, sea otters, sea lions, and twenty other varieties of marine mammals spend at least part of the year in Alaska's coastal waters. About three hundred species of birds visit or live permanently in Alaska. Roughly one hundred are true sourdoughs, staying through the winter.

Sport and subsistence hunters pursue some of Alaska's wildlife, and use the state's trails to reach hunting areas. Hunting seasons generally begin in early to mid-August.

A freshly-built beaver lodge. Beavers are widespread across Southcentral, Interior, and Southeast Alaska.

Fish. Alaska has more fish, and more kinds of fish, than you can shake a flyrod at. Five species of salmon, rainbow trout and steelhead, char, grayling, Dolly Varden, lake trout, pike, sheefish, and other fishy critters call Alaska's pristine waters home for at least part of the year. Alaska's salmon runs are world class and world famous.

If you plan to fish, be sure to buy a license and read up on the regulations before you wet a line. Even if you don't fish, seeing a run of salmon in a small stream is an unforgettable sight.

INSECTS

One animal that gets attention all out of proportion to its size is Alaska's lovable mosquito. There are twenty-eight species, and they all bite. They can be thick and voracious, especially in the Interior, the Arctic, and in wetlands, lowlands, and forests anywhere. Mid- to late June is the height of mosquito season, though in places they can be annoying until at least the first frosts.

Repellents with DEET or with natural ingredients like citronella offer varying degrees of protection. The chemical DEET is more effective in higher concentrations, but stronger preparations used frequently can make users sick, as the chemical is absorbed through the skin. Be careful using DEET on children; they are especially susceptible to its side effects. Applying it with fingers may mean you eat it with your lunch—not a good idea. If you choose to use DEET, using lower concentrations in stick form and doing all the other things you can do to avoid clouds of mosquitoes is probably the best strategy.

Some hikers consider a head net or a bug jacket necessary gear during peak mosquito season. Clothing makes a difference: light-colored clothing may be less attractive to mosquitoes, and they can't bite through tight-weave clothing. Traveling and camping in open country where there is a breeze, e.g., river bars and open ridges, helps keep them at bay. Some outdoor enthusiasts swear that "mossies" won't gather under a dark or black tarp.

In some years, wasps and hornets are fairly abundant. They typically nest in brush or down, decaying logs. There are also several types of tiny gnats, or "no-see-ums," some of which bite. One type, with a touch of white on its feet, known as a "white sock," can cause significant swelling with its bites.

PLANTS

All the green things. Seeing three dozen species of Alaska wildflowers in a day of June or July hiking is not all that unusual; there are 1,500 species of flowering plants in Alaska. Tundra, the low-growing mix of mosses, lichens, sedges, grasses, and shrubs, is widespread in the mountains (alpine tundra) and beyond northern tree line (arctic tundra).

Trees are easier—this isn't the tropics. Only fifteen Alaska tree species commonly grow taller than 30 feet. The two main types of forest are boreal,

Keep an eye out for cow parsnip on a sunny day. This common Southcentral shrub can be a severe skin irritant in the presence of sunlight.

or northern, forest, the forest of white and black spruce in the Interior, and coastal forests, mainly Sitka spruce and western hemlock, found in Southeast Alaska and the coastal parts of Southcentral. Anyone who needs a botanical challenge can learn a few species of willow. Alaska has thirty-eight different kinds of willows, from small trees to shrubs to creeping dwarf plants.

Wild Berries and Mushrooms. Berries and mushrooms are abundant in Alaska's wilds. Blueberries, salmonberries, huckleberries, and raspberries are favorites among the berries, as are shaggy manes, hedgehogs, and king boletes among the mushrooms. The first rule of berry and mushroom hunting, though, is to know positively what you're looking at before you munch; there are several poisonous berries and mushrooms in the state. See Appendix 4 for references.

Plants to Avoid. There are several poisonous or irritating plants to avoid. Baneberry is a common and poisonous berry, and the poisonous water hemlock and death camas may be confused with other, edible plants. There are several other poisonous plants, so know what you're eating before you put any part of any plant in your mouth.

Cow parsnip, a tall, widespread meadow plant, can cause severe blistering and skin irritation in the presence of sunlight. Burning the plant and breathing the smoke can be very dangerous. Also known by its Russian name, *pootschki*, the plant is absent from the Interior and Arctic, but is abundant in Southcentral and present in the rest of the state. Treat the skin irritation with aloe vera or a vinegar and water solution.

Stinging nettle, which causes relatively minor skin irritation, is found in Southeast and near-coastal Southcentral. Hikers may need to wear long pants and sleeves on some of Southcentral's high meadow hikes to avoid the effects of cow parsnip and nettle.

HYPOTHERMIA

The risk of hypothermia, the decline in body temperature to dangerously low levels, elevates in Alaska's northern climate. Wet summer weather, wind, and cold water all contribute to the risk. Really cold temperatures aren't necessary; a 50-degree rain is just fine for hypothermia.

The best way to deal with hypothermia is to prevent it in the first place. Take along several layers of synthetic clothing, and include a warm hat, neck gaiter, and gloves with a water-resistant shell. Good rain gear and a sleeping bag and tent designed for wet weather are also important. Leave cotton—known in Alaska as "death cloth"—at home. Cotton is not only worthless as insulation when wet, it even contributes to heat loss.

When it is cool, windy or raining, be sure to adjust layers of clothing to avoid sweating. Change into dry clothing when wet, stay hydrated by drinking plenty of water, and snack on high-calorie foods during the hike.

Shivering is the first outward indication of hypothermia. Treat it at that point, before it becomes life-threatening, by getting out of wind and rain, changing to dry clothes, building a fire or warming by a campstove, and drinking warm liquids. Crawling into a sleeping bag with another person is

The poisonous baneberry is usually red, but it also comes in a white form.

Hypothermia weather rolling in over an Alaska Range lake.

the next step. Consult the first aid and medical references in Appendix 4 for more details.

STREAM CROSSINGS

There are bridges across the streams on many of Alaska's trails, but wading is the mode of travel on many cross-country routes and trails. Stream crossings can be very dangerous without preparation and planning. With planning and patience, however, hikers can expand their hiking universes to include the wider wilderness without bridges. A few tips:

• Pick the safest route (see page 12). Consider depth and width of the stream, current strength, and water clarity. Turbid water can hide deep channels, large rocks, and holes.

• Pick the safest time to cross. After a rain or a hot day of glaciers melting upstream, rivers can rise significantly. Glacial rivers are generally lowest in the morning. After a storm and sub-

Crossing a river solo. Even knee-deep water can be difficult if the current is strong.

The "triangle," or "pivot," a very effective stream-crossing technique.

sequent rise in water level, you may have to wait a day or more to cross safely.

• Alaska water is cold, and cold water can quickly rob the body of heat and energy. On all but the simplest crossings, wear your boots. Some hikers change into running shoes or neoprene booties, but boots offer the best protection. For foot comfort later on, bring camp shoes and spare socks. Wear synthetic clothing and rain gear as the air and water temperature and the length and depth of the crossing dictate.

• A heavy pack can actually be a benefit when crossing a stream! The weight will help hold your feet on the bottom in the current. Consider adding rocks to your pack for more stability.

• Unclip the waist strap of your pack and loosen the shoulder straps so you can ditch your pack if you fall. At minimum, pack dry clothes, fire starter, sleeping bag, and camera in bags to keep them dry in case of a spill.

• Cross carefully, one step at a time, testing your footing with each step (especially important in silty, opaque glacial streams). Angle downstream along a riffle or a submerged sand/gravel bar if possible. The current is usually strongest in the middle of the stream, so if it feels strong soon after stepping into the water, it may be best to retreat and find a new crossing.

• If you fall and are swept downstream by the current, slip off your pack and float on your back with your feet downstream. Backpaddling with your arms, position yourself at an angle to the current and ferry to the closest shoreline. Your head should be closest to the shore you're aiming for. Fend off rocks with your feet, but don't stand up too quickly—the danger is that you could lodge a foot between rocks and be pulled under by the current.

• Once across, assess your party's condition. To warm up, change into dry clothes and either get moving or light a stove or build a fire and make hot drinks.

It's a Puzzle: Picking a Route across a Stream.

Safely crossing a stream means taking the time to scout the best route. Before you get your feet wet, sleuth out the current and the shape of the streambed.

• Pick a wide or braided section of the stream ("braided" refers to sections where the stream widens and splits into several channels, a common feature of streams fed by glaciers). The water is likely to be slower and shallower here. Usually the safest crossing on a braided section of river is a line from

Crossing a river in the Brooks Range.

the upstream end of one gravel bar or island to the upstream end of the next bar or island (see illustration on page 14). Look for small, closely-spaced riffles. They indicate shallow water over a relatively smooth bottom.

• Walk upstream and downstream to find the best crossing for all the members of your party. In some cases, you may have to walk upstream above the next tributary to find a safe crossing. In other cases there may not be a safe crossing, and you may have to hike back the way you came.

• Avoid cutbanks and standing waves; they indicate that the water is swift and deep.

• Check depth by tossing in large rocks. If the rock says "ka-thump" when it hits the water, the stream is deep. If you can hear rocks rolling downstream in the current, the water is too swift.

There are several effective techniques for crossing streams.

1. On solo crossings, use a hiking staff or stout stick, held upstream, to create a stable three-point stance. Move only one of the three contact points at a time. You can sidestep across the river, but don't cross your feet until the stream is slow and shallow.

2. Two or more hikers can cross in a line parallel to the current, with the strongest/heaviest member of the party upstream, breaking the force of the water for the other hikers. Downstream members move across in the eddy created by the upstream member and provide support for him/her. The party can walk across the current, side-to-side with arms linked, or face upstream and sidestep across. These "lineup" methods work best when the stream bottom is fairly smooth and of a uniform depth.

A typical braided stream. Dots show what is usually the safest route among the braids, gravel bars and islands.

3. The "triangle" is a slower method, but is very effective in deeper, swifter water. Facing each other, three people grip each other's shoulders or pack straps and work their way across the stream, moving one person, one leg at a time. When it's your turn, check to see that your partners are set before moving. The group may have to pivot back and forth a bit so one of the members doesn't have to step backwards.

THE HIKER'S ESSENTIALS

Preparation is the key to a good hike. Pick a hike within the abilities of all members of your party. Pack gear and supplies based on the trip you're planning. Leave word of your plans with someone who will be responsible for calling for help in the event you are overdue on your return, and check a weather forecast before you leave. It may help you decide whether to add a tarp or another layer of pile to your pack.

One important piece of preparation is to leave city time in the city. Try to adopt wilderness time, and pay attention to what the land, the water and the weather are saying. If you have a plane to catch or a job to get back to, and it's on the other side of an unbridged, raging river, or getting there involves venturing out of a dry tent into a howling storm, you're probably better off letting nature dictate your schedule. There will be other flights and other days to go to work.

The idea of the "Ten Essentials" is widespread and a good general concept, but remember that each trip carries its own requirements. For example, you really don't need a flashlight if you're traveling in 24-hour daylight; fire starter is useless if your entire route is in low-growing, alpine vegetation or rocky tundra; and a short hike on an interpretive trail really doesn't require a map and compass.

Instead, think of the hiking essentials in terms of a checklist, and plan what you bring based on your needs, your party's experience, your route, and the remoteness of the trip. The Ten Essentials for day trips, as usually quoted, include food and water, extra clothing, rain gear, map, compass, matches and fire starter, knife, first-aid kit, flashlight, and sunglasses.

The following section offers some suggestions on hiking gear and supplies not covered in other sections. See the sample backpacking checklist in Appendix 5.

Boots. Lightweight leather or leather/nylon boots work well for most hikes, and running shoes are fine for short, more developed trails like interpretive trails. Some trails, especially in the wet Southeast, call for rubber boots. For hikes involving wet tundra and multiple stream crossings, hikers wear anything from lighter boots to rubber/leather combination boots to rubber boots. Good synthetic or wool socks are a must, and some hikers use waterproof/breathable fabric socks (e.g., Gore-tex) to help keep feet dry.

Pack. Whether it's a day or overnight pack, your "house on your back" should fit comfortably and be capable of carrying the loads you intend to carry. A pack cover, whether of fitted nylon or an improvised garbage bag, helps to keep your pack and its contents dry. Bagging clothes, sleeping bag, camera and other items in plastic bags adds a layer of insurance.

Hiking staff. Whether a recycled ski pole, a cottonwood branch from the side of the trail, or a fancy staff from an outdoor shop, a hiking staff is practically indispensable for crossing streams and is a big help on Alaska's less developed trails and routes, which are often steep or rocky.

Food. Taking along at least a little extra food is a good idea for days that turn out longer than planned, or the rare unintended overnight stay. For multi-day trips, pack ample extra food in case the trail takes longer, a stream is too high to cross, or the plane can't get in to pick you up.

Water. For day trips, carry water from the tap, but for overnight trips, you'll need a water filter or other treatment method. Giardia lamblia is the major health threat from surface water in Alaska. A microscopic protozoan parasite, giardia, can make you really sick, and it is so widespread that no surface water can be considered safe. Filtering and boiling surface water are the best methods of purification; chemicals are less reliable. Be sure the filter you use is rated as giardia-effective.

Many of Alaska's hikes are along silty glacial streams. The silt may clog water filters, so the best advice is to collect water from clear side streams or from small side channels where the silt may have settled. It's also possible to collect silty water in a large container and let it settle out before filtering or boiling it.

Warm clothing. Take layers of synthetic (polypro, capilene, pile, fleece) or wool clothing, socks, hat, and gloves. Cold, wet weather is always a possibility. Leave cotton at home except for the odd t-shirt.

Rain gear. Lightweight, durable rain jackets and pants, either of waterproof or waterproof/breathable fabric, are the optimum rain gear for Alaska. Ponchos and very lightweight nylon rainwear are not recommended. Make sure the seams are either taped or sealed. An umbrella is a good addition to your pack; just don't try to use one in strong or gusty winds.

Map and compass. Topographic maps are absolutely necessary for many of the hikes in this book, especially the minimally-developed trails that traverse high ridges. The most commonly-used USGS maps, at the 1:62,500 scale, were surveyed a generation ago, and in many cases do not show today's trails. Several agency and commercially-made maps are available that show trails and routes; they are listed in the entries for individual hikes.

The magnetic declination, or variance of true north from the magnetic north the compass indicates, is large this near the pole, and makes a signifi-

Filtering lake water. Even Alaska water has to be treated to be safe for drinking.

cant difference in route-finding. Be sure to set the declination (indicated on topographic maps) correctly. See Appendix 4 for references on learning how to use a compass.

First aid. A small first aid kit with supplies for cuts, bruises, bites, and stings should be carried on a hike of any length. Hikers should have at least a rudimentary knowledge of first aid. If you're planning a longer trip, consider the remoteness of the area you plan to visit. In remote areas of the state medical help may be days away.

Injuries involving hypothermia, falls, and cold water are relatively more common in Alaska than elsewhere. The list of supplies to include in your kit depends on the length and remoteness of the trip and the character of the terrain. Consult specialty books; some are listed in Appendix 4.

Signaling devices. In case of an emergency, consider carrying flares; and for more remote trips, a two-way radio. Some folks carry whistles, especially for smaller children, in case members of the party become separated.

Flashlight/headlamp. By late summer and fall, and in Southeast all summer, a light source is needed for multi-day trips and an item to consider for longer day trips. Remember an extra bulb and extra batteries.

Fire starter. Carrying a fire starter—matches, lighters, a bit of candle, and/or a kindling source—is a good emergency measure. These supplies are best carried in a small, waterproof container on your person, not in your pack. Dry fire starter has saved lives after mishaps in water, like a floatplane accident or losing your pack in a fall in a stream.

Camp stove. A small camp stove, with repair parts, is much more reliable than campfires for cooking and warmth on overnight trips, and has less of an impact on the land. Consider taking a small stove on longer, high-country day trips.

Food storage. Carrying food in thick, self-sealing plastic bags is recommended to prevent wildlife problems. For overnight trips, bring rope and nylon bags to hang your food out of reach of bears.

Tent. A two-layer tent with a waterproof fly is the best insurance for dry camping in the rain. Well-built, lightweight tents (3 to 6 pounds) don't sacrifice too many features compared to heavier tents. A freestanding tent may offer more site options, but they still have to be staked out for maximum weatherproofing. Be sure all tent seams are sealed.

Take a ground cloth for keeping the floor of the tent dry and protecting the outer surface from wear. A plastic bag for storing a wet tent fly inside your pack is a good idea, as is a bit of sponge for soaking up water from any leaks. Top off your tent bag with repair materials for the tent body and poles (e.g., duct tape and metal pole sleeves).

Other equipment. Depending on the season, elevation, topography, and type of trip, hikers may need to carry ice axes, crampons, ice creepers, snowshoes, skis, or avalanche transceivers.

THE THREE BEARS AND OTHER DETAILS

Learning and practicing wildlife precautions is simply good sense. Parts of the following section on bears are adapted with permission from the Alaska Natural History Association brochure *Bear Facts*.

Moose are plentiful in Southcentral and the Interior and present but less abundant in other parts of the state. They may look slow and ungainly, but they move quickly and aggressively when perturbed. Cow moose are very protective of their calves. Give any moose a wide berth, and keep dogs under control. If a moose responds aggressively, climb a tree or keep a tree between you and the animal until you are able to move away.

Foxes in the Arctic occasionally contract rabies. Keep your distance if you suspect from its erratic behavior that a fox may be sick.

The Bear Facts

Yes, there are bears, fortunately. Their presence means that we still have real wilderness left. Alaska has all of the three species found in North America: black, grizzly or brown, and polar.

The polar bear, the great white bear of the Arctic pack ice, sticks close to the Arctic coastline and is rarely a concern for hikers. Black and grizzly/brown bears are much more common, though many a hiker goes many a mile without seeing one. Grizzly/brown bears are the most widespread, inhabiting forest, coastline, and tundra. Black bears, the smallest of the three, frequent forests and nearby alpine areas. They are absent from the tundra

Brown bears at nature's cafe, a salmon stream. HELENE FEINER PHOTO.

A brown/grizzly bear, with its distinctive shoulder hump. HELENE FEINER PHOTO.

of western and northern Alaska, from the Kodiak group of islands, and from Admiralty, Baranof, and Chichagof Islands in Southeast.

Browns and grizzlies are the same species living in different environments. A "brown" is a bear that spends at least part of its time along coastal streams feasting on salmon. What Alaskans call "grizzlies" are bears of the Interior and Arctic. They are roughly one-third smaller than the average coastal brown.

Grizzly/browns come in many colors from blond to dark brown. They weigh from 200 to 1,200 pounds and stand 3 to 4 feet at the shoulder. Omnivorous and opportunistic, they eat great quantities of plants and fish, moose, caribou, deer, marmots, and ground squirrels.

Black bears are smaller than grizzly/browns, weighing about 100 to 400 pounds and standing 2 to 3 feet at the shoulder. Usually jet black with a brown muzzle, they also come in brown and cinnamon, and even blue-gray, a color phase of black bears that live near glaciers in northern Southeast Alaska.

How do you tell the difference? Color is not reliable. Grizzly/browns have a dish-shaped face, a rounded head, and a distinct shoulder hump. Blacks have a smaller, more pointed head with a straight facial profile, and no hump. Grizzly front claws are larger, and show up more readily in tracks. A sure way to tell is to measure the upper molar at the back of the bear's mouth, but you probably won't want to get that close.

Bears are potentially dangerous and highly individualistic, so there is no one "cook-book" approach that will work perfectly with every animal in every circumstance. However, with nearly 100,000 grizzly and black bears in Alaska, surprisingly few people have any encounters, much less danger-ous encounters. Bears that are habituated to humans and their food are generally not a problem in Alaska's backcountry. As hikers, it is our respon-sibility to keep it that way.

Bears Don't Like Surprises

Bears generally will avoid humans if we don't sneak up on them. When hiking in bear country, let them know you're there by making plenty of noise. Sing, talk loudly, or clap your hands. A bear bell works too, but a bell may not be loud enough in some cases and it could drive other hikers to mayhem. If you are approaching an area where the lay of the land or veg-etation limits your vision, or the sounds of wind or a nearby stream muffle your own sounds, turn up the volume accordingly.

Other Tips

• Try to avoid brush-choked ravines and alder thickets. If you can't, look for movement in the brush that would give away the presence of a large animal. Even if the area looks safe, make a lot of noise well before you enter.

• If you have a choice, walk with the wind at your back so your scent will get to any bears you can't see before you do.

• If you smell something dead near the trail, don't stop to investigate. Detour, retreat or pass quickly by. It may be a carcass a bear is feeding on, and if the bear is still around, it may defend its food cache aggressively.

• If you see a cub, retreat immediately. Its mother is probably not far away, and she may attack in defense of her cub.

• Before you set up camp, look around possible campsites for animal trails, scat, claw marks on trees, or bear excavations. Move if you find pos-sible evidence of bears. Select a site with good visibility unless wind and weather dictate otherwise, and sleep in a tent.

• Traveling in a group of four to six is optimum for bear safety. (Larger groups are safe as far as bears go, but are hard on the land.) However, if the group is strung out over the trail or otherwise separated, this safety in num-bers doesn't apply.

• Carefully consider whether to take your dog along. Dogs can surprise and excite aggression in bears; your friendly mutt may run back to you with a bruin surprise right on his/her heels.

• Be especially cautious early in the summer when both humans and bears stay at lower elevations while the higher country is still under snow.

Bears are Fussy about Their Personal Space

There is no safe distance for approaching a bear. Studies of bear attacks in parks show that crowding is the most common precipitating event. Bears have a personal space within which they may react aggressively to other creatures. Some bears may feel comfortable at fifty yards, while others have charged people from more than a quarter-mile away. Give them lots of room, especially mothers with young.

Bears are Always Looking for Food

Bears are curious and always on the lookout for a meal. If you attract them to your food, you may be in danger, and afterward the bear may associate humans with food, a dangerous situation for all the hikers who come after you. The first order of business is to keep strong smells, of food and anything else, under control.

• Leave the bacon, sardines, other smelly food, and perfumes at home, and pack all your food and garbage in airtight plastic bags.

• Use bear-resistant food containers in parks that require them, and consider buying your own to use in other areas.

• Clean your pots by eating all the scrapings, and dispose of any wash water well away from camp.

• If you plan meals well, cook conservatively, and eat all the food you cook, you won't have to worry about leftovers. If you have leftovers, carry them out in airtight bags. Animals are likely to find them if you bury them, and it's nearly impossible to completely consume food in a campfire.

• Garbage should be treated like leftovers. Keep the quantity down by planning and by paring down the packaging material. Pack it out in airtight bags.

• In camp, set up separate cooking and sleeping areas 300 feet apart. Cook downwind of your sleeping area and change clothes if you spill food on them.

• If menstruating, use internal tampons rather than napkins, keep clean, and store used tampons in airtight bags for packing out.

• Hang your food and other smelly items like toothpaste out of reach of bears at night, or anytime during the day you're away from camp. Hang food sacks at least 300 feet from your tent, using a line hung from a stout limb or one strung between two trees. About 50 feet of line is usually sufficient. Ideally, your food sack(s) will end up at least 12 feet off the ground, 6 feet from the tree trunk, and 4 feet below a supporting limb.

• In the tundra or where trees are too small to hang food, cache your food in a protected area at least 300 feet from sleeping and cooking areas, placed so that the smells will not carry with the wind (e.g., covered with a tarp, between rocks, in a depression, in brush, buried in river gravel, or in watertight containers under water). Piling pots on your food cache may help; the noise made by an animal intruder trying to get into the food may frighten it away or alert you to the intrusion.

Close Encounters of the Bruin Kind

If, despite all your precautions, you end up with a bruin close by, what next?

1. If it is a surprise encounter, let the bear know you are human and that you're not a threat by speaking to it in a normal voice, as you would to an agitated dog. The bear may show that it feels threatened by growling, huffing, or popping its jaws. It may stand up on its hind legs to try to figure out what you are. Face the bear and don't run. If it is stationary, try a slow, backing, diagonal retreat, preferably moving upwind so the bear can smell you.

*Two ways to
hang food.
The food bags
should end up
twelve feet or
more off the
ground.*

2. If you feel threatened and you're near a good climbing tree, consider climbing it. Be sure the bear is far enough away for you to climb it safely. Stay put until you are certain the bear is gone (worst-case scenario: this could take hours). Depending on the size of the bear, you'll need to be at least 10 feet up to be out of reach.

3. If you've caught a fish and a bear approaches, cut your line. Don't end up fighting a bear over a fish.

4. If a bear approaches you or your campsite slowly and calmly, looking inquisitive, you will need to convince it you're too tough to bother—speak loudly, shout, wave your arms or your coat, stand tall, bang on pots and pans, fire a warning shot from a firearm if you have one. If it continues toward you, be even more aggressive, including throwing rocks and blasting it with cayenne pepper spray. Hold your ground even when the bear gets very close.

5. If a bear gets so close contact is imminent, at the last second drop to the ground and play dead. Keep your pack on your back for protection, and lie flat on your stomach or roll up in the fetal position with arms over your head. Chances are the bear will break off the attack when it no longer perceives a threat. If the bear appears to leave, don't get up immediately; it may be only a short distance away and could renew the attack if it senses your movement.

6. In extremely rare circumstances, attacks by bears, usually black bears, may be predatory. If you suspect a predatory attack, or if the bear is still attacking after 20 to 30 seconds of your playing dead, fight back—with fists, a finger or a stick in the eye, a limb, a rock, a knife, or whatever is available.

Weapons and Bears

Carrying firearms for bear protection should never be used as a substitute for good bear-country behavior. State law allows for self-defense shootings of bears if they attack unprovoked and there is no alternative, but the shooter must turn in the hide and skull to the Alaska Department of Fish and Game. Firearms are illegal in Denali, Katmai, Klondike Gold Rush, and Glacier Bay national parks. On close-in trails near cities and towns, hiker traffic is relatively heavy and firearms pose a significant danger to people.

If you choose to carry a firearm for bear protection, a rifle of .300 or greater caliber or a 12-gauge shotgun using rifled slugs are the best choices. Some people carry heavy handguns such as .44s, but these are difficult to shoot, less effective, and dangerous in inexperienced hands.

A popular alternative is cayenne spray, a defensive spray packaged in a small aerosol can. The spray is effective only at close range, no more than 10 to 25 feet, and is ineffective when used into the wind; in fact, in the wind, it may blow back and incapacitate the user. Be careful not to puncture the can.

Reports of the spray's effectiveness are mixed. It appears to work better against brown bears than black, and in fact many black bears seem to be immune to cayenne's effects, possibly because they produce a protective layer of mucus in their eyes and nasal passages that prevents irritation from the spray.

If you choose to pack a firearm or pepper spray, carry it so that it can be used quickly. Neither are useful if they're buried in your pack.

Don't be Bearanoid

Be cautious but enjoy yourself. With practice, good bear-country behavior becomes automatic. Given the numbers of outdoor enthusiasts and the infrequency of bear encounters, the risk of injury from a bear attack is very low. It's statistically much more dangerous to drive or fly to the start of a hike than it is to actually hike in the wilderness. Bears, in fact, have shown a much greater willingness to coexist with humans than vice-versa.

If you're new to bear country and unsure about the risks, start your hiking career on frontcountry trails where other people travel and gradually work into wilder trips, or team up with experienced bear-country hikers.

OUTDOOR ETHICS/LEAVE NO TRACE

Outdoor ethics for hikers consist of being a good neighbor to your fellow hikers and the wildlife whose homes you are visiting, and minimizing the impact of your visit so others who come after you can experience Alaska's wildlands as you found them.

Plan Your Trip to Minimize its Impact.

1. Limiting group size to six people is best for the land.

Save the tundra a scorch. Flip a flat rock and use it as a stove platform. When finished, return the rock to its original location, lichen side up.

2. Know the regulations and special concerns for the area you're about to visit.

3. Avoid certain areas at times when wet conditions make trails or routes subject to erosion by hikers.

4. Pack items that will help eliminate your impact. Carry a water bag to minimize trips and trampling on the route between your camp and water source, saving stream banks and fish habitat in the process. Bring along a trowel for digging holes for human waste.

Camp and Travel on Durable Surfaces and Sites.

1. Stay on the trail. Use switchbacks, and hike on the established tread even if it is a bit wet. Help out the cash-strapped land manager by moving obstacles from the trail and building small waterbars if water is eroding the trail, and let him or her know about any trail problems you encounter.

2. Choose durable sites for camping or lunch stops. Gravel bars are the least vulnerable to impacts of overuse (and they're better for avoiding mosquitoes and bears, too). Use designated sites where they exist. Select a well-drained tent site well away from water sources. Don't trample vegetation, especially small tree seedlings.

3. When traveling cross-country, choose the most durable surfaces—rock, gravel, dry grasses, or snow—and spread your party out as much as possible to avoid creating pathways. Avoid hiker-made paths near well-used areas, especially where they lead through wet areas or on steep slopes. Pick a better way such as a dry, gently sloping route. Continued use of poorly-located sites and paths can lead to rapid vegetation loss and erosion.

4. Avoid lightly-used sites. Instead of camping on a site that shows faint signs of previous use, choose a well-established site or a pristine site that can stand the impact, such as a gravel bar.

If You Packed it in, Pack it out.

1. Bring along several airtight plastic bags for garbage.

2. Before your trip, remove excess packaging from food and other items you carry you to minimize your garbage and lessen the chance you will accidentally leave garbage behind.

3. Plan meals so you won't have leftovers. If you do, carry them out as you would garbage; don't try burning or burying them.

4. Look around thoroughly before leaving a trail rest stop or campsite to be sure you have everything you brought in.

5. Pack out all fishing line.

Dispose of Waste Properly.

1. Bury human waste in small "catholes" about 6 inches deep and 6 inches in diameter, in inconspicuous spots where other hikers are unlikely to walk or camp. The site should be at least 200 feet (70 to 80 adult steps) from any water source. Carefully remove the topsoil or vegetation mat and recover the hole with it when done. Use toilet paper sparingly, and burn it or pack it out in a plastic bag.

2. Don't use soap of any kind in streams, lakes, or ponds. Dispose of gray water from dishwashing well away from camp and water sources.

3. Fish remains are a natural part of the ecosystem; dispose of them in deep, moving water to minimize the possibility of a bear encounter.

Leave it the Way you Found it.

1. Replace rocks and logs you move from your campsite, and don't tear out clumps of vegetation for your camp.

2. Take care not to burn any tundra with your camp stove.

3. Enjoy the occasional wild edible plant, but don't deplete the population.

4. Leave all cultural artifacts in place. Taking artifacts from public lands is illegal.

5. Respect private property. There are many private parcels of land and cabins in the Alaska backcountry. Respect the wishes of the landowner.

Show Respect for your Human and Animal Neighbors.

1. Respect other hikers' privacy. Pick a campsite out of sight and earshot of other parties, and keep the noise down—let nature's sounds prevail.

2. If you practice catch-and-release fishing, use techniques that harm the fish least. Handle them gently, and hold them in the water while you remove your barbless hook.

3. Avoid certain areas at times when wildlife is sensitive to disturbance, such as ponds and coastlines where birds are nesting.

4. Have your wildlife experiences courtesy of a good pair of binoculars and a long telephoto lens. Don't disturb wildlife for a photograph.

5. Don't feed wildlife, and don't leave food or food scraps behind for them to find.

6. If you take your dog along (where allowed), bring a leash or train it to respond to your voice to avoid disturbing wildlife.

Minimize Impacts from Campfires.

1. Carry a stove. With a good repair kit and knowledge of how to use it, stoves are far more reliable than campfires. Carry enough clothing so you can be comfortably inactive while cooking or hanging around camp.

2. If you have to have a warming fire, use an established ring or fire pan, or build it on a gravel bar or bare earth without a rock ring. Use dead and down wood only.

3. After you've put the fire completely out, remove all unburned trash for packing out, dispose of the ashes, and scatter any remaining wood. On gravel bars, ashes may be buried; scatter the cooled ashes from a fire pan over a large area, well away from camp.

Give Something Back to the Land.

1. Volunteer as a trail or park worker.

2. Join one of Alaska's many conservation groups.

3. Contribute your ideas to park and forest management plans.

HIKING WITH KIDS

As most people who use the outdoors know, time spent in the natural environment is a cornerstone of a physically and mentally healthy life. So start kids early! Even toddlers can appreciate a short trip among the trees and flowers.

1. Let kids be involved. Let them help pick the trip and pack their own gear, clothes, and trail food, to the degree their age and experience allow.

2. Learn about the natural history of the area you're going to visit, and interest them in the little things: feeling spruce needles, smelling cranberries, watching salmon, or deciphering animal tracks.

3. Allow plenty of time to linger at beaver dams, berry patches, birds' nests, moose bedding spots, and stream banks.

4. Practice and pass on to the next generation good low-impact hiking and camping techniques. Make a game of eliminating all traces of your camp or picnic spot.

5. Remember that children have wide ranges in abilities, interests, and stamina, so it's best to tailor your hikes to them as individuals.

For safety's sake, begin to teach self-reliance early. Start by orienting them to the land. For example, orient them to muskeg openings (they're wet, no trees grow there, and it's hot when the sun is out) and stream margins (big trees grow by the water, and it's cooler under the trees by the creek). Move up to using maps, maybe just stick drawings on the ground at first, and a compass.

A young hiker cruising the high country above Sitka.

Eventually they will be able to look out for themselves, but until then, you'll have to help. Avoid areas with large, loose rocks, steep slopes, and cliffs. Teach them about dangerous and poisonous plants, but until they show they understand, don't let them put any wild plant material in their mouths.

Just in case you get separated, have them include survival equipment in what they pack for your hikes, like high-energy snacks and waterproof and warm clothing (a jacket with pockets and a hood is best so they'll have head and hand coverage even if they lose their hats and gloves). Bright clothes are best for visibility.

A whistle is a good idea, if kids are taught they're for use only in emergencies. Three short blasts means "help." Teach them to keep the whistle quiet otherwise, though, because there's nothing like a bunch of munchkins shrieking on whistles to drive other hikers crazy. Keeping them singing and talking is more fun and lets any bears in the neighborhood know you're around.

In general, hikes in this guidebook rated "easy" for difficulty on trails rated "more developed" are good hikes for smaller kids. At the end of each trip entry is a short section labeled "Shorter hikes." These are intermediate destinations on longer hikes, and many of these make good hikes for children. Taking a shorter hike to a public use cabin is a good way to introduce kids to overnight trips.

Try taking hiking breaks with your children on long drives. Between Anchorage and Fairbanks, try Denali State Park, Denali National Park, and Nancy Lakes State Recreation Area (Denali National Park and Trips 48, 49, and 50). Between Anchorage and Seward, there are several trails just off the highway (Trips 4 to 7, 10 and 22), and the Kenai National Wildlife Refuge makes a good break on a trip to Kenai or Homer (Trips 12 to 16).

See the **Pick-a-Hike Tables** for more hiking ideas for families with kids.

A WORD (OR TWO) FOR TRAVELERS

While having a car opens up more hiking opportunities, the state does have many hikes that are easily accessible for travelers and others without their own vehicles. Many hikes begin near city centers or from highways, and are accessible by bus, bicycle, shuttle van, or taxi.

The easiest trailheads for carless travelers to reach are listed in the **Pick-a-Hike Tables**. Details on transportation (where available) are included in some of the hike descriptions.

Don't count on picking up hiking supplies just anywhere in the state. The only cities with outdoor stores with a significant selection of backpacking equipment are in Anchorage, Kenai/Soldotna, Fairbanks, and Juneau. Anchorage and Juneau have rental equipment suppliers. Many other stores in smaller towns, like hardware stores, sell some outdoor equipment and clothing. Maps are available at many Alaska Natural History Association outlets at agency offices and visitor centers, and from outdoor and hardware stores and book shops.

USING THIS GUIDE

The description of each hike in this guide begins with "at-a-glance" information to help you compare trips without reading the entire narrative.

Trip summary describes the length of the trip and the basic geography. For day hikes, most entries indicate the approximate time required for the hike, using three categories as general rules of thumb, based on an average adult hiking pace and decent trail conditions.

Shorter day hikes are, generally, hikes of three hours or less; **half-day hikes**, trips of three to five hours; and **longer hikes**, more than five hours and up to an entire sunset-free day in midsummer. There are options for shorter hikes on most of the longer trips covered; options are listed in **"Shorter hikes"** at the end of the narrative.

Adult hikers in average to decent physical shape on an "average" trail hike about 1.5 to 3 miles per hour (not counting stops of any length). Your pace will also depend on the trail surface and grade and the weight of your pack.

Interpretive trails are trails with signs or brochures that explain the natural or cultural setting. **Loop** trips are hikes where your route takes you back to or very nearly to your starting point without retracing your steps. **Traverses** are trips that lead from one trailhead to another, typically several road miles apart, so that spotting a car or otherwise arranging for transportation between the trailheads is necessary. Most trips are **out-and-back** hikes on one-way trails; if the trip summary doesn't mention a hike type, it is an out-and-back trip.

"Distances" shown are the actual distance of the trail or route. For traverses or loops, this is the entire distance of the trip. Distances shown as one way indicate out-and-back hikes that require covering the trail mileage twice.

"Special features" include natural features, cabins, historic interest, and information like boat or air transportation, and special characteristics of the trail or route.

"Location" is a general location for orientation; directions to the trailhead are given under **"Finding the Trailhead."**

"Difficulty" ratings give a general idea of how strenuous a hike is. The ratings correspond to elevation gain, tempered by the grade, length, and hiking surface.

Easy: can be completed without difficulty by hikers of all abilities.
Moderate: challenging for novices.
Moderately strenuous: may tax even experienced hikers.
Strenuous: quite difficult even for experienced hikers.

"Trail type" refers to the degree of development of the trail. **Accessible** trails are packed and graded and suitable for mobility-impaired people, including those who use wheelchairs. **More developed** trails are planned and constructed trails with some combination of trail structures like bridges or foot logs over streams, switchbacks, steps, bench-cut tread on sideslopes, boardwalk in wet areas, signs, and for the most part, a clear path and even tread. In Alaska, Forest Service trails are most often built to this standard.

Less developed trails may in places have structures like more developed trails, but should be expected to be rougher and slower. While there is a tread to follow in most places, it may be only the tread other hikers have made with their boot soles. Less developed trails are usually maintained less frequently. They are common in Alaska's state parks.

Routes may be marked with rock cairns, wooden posts or fiberglass stakes and follow intermittent sections of tread laid down by hikers' feet, but are rough and may be difficult to follow in places. **Cross-country** refers to travel following a line of geography like a stream or ridgeline without any marking or tread to follow. The word path is used in the text as a general term for any tread hikers can follow on the ground.

"Total elevation gain" is a figure that reflects all the uphill grade on the hike; it is not usually just the elevation of the destination minus the elevation of the trailhead.

"Best season" is the part of the year the hike, **on average**, is substantially free of snow and ice. Early and late-season hikers may still encounter snow on the trail and be caught by snowstorms.

"Maps" lists government and commercial maps that cover the hike. U.S. Geological Survey (USGS) topographic maps are listed at the 1:63,360 scale and, in parentheses, the 1:25,000 scale if available. Many USGS maps were surveyed and printed before today's trails were built, so in some cases the trails are not shown on the topographic maps. Also listed are commonly available commercial maps, e.g., Trails Illustrated maps, and maps, leaflets or brochures provided by the park, forest, or refuge where the trail is located.

The **"manager"** is the park or other agency that manages the trail. For more information on the hike, contact the manager or the Alaska Public Lands Information Center in the region in which the hike is located. Addresses and phone numbers are listed in Appendix 1.

"Key points" is a list of approximate mileages of features like mountain passes, stream crossings, cabins, and trail junctions on the hike.

Some of the directions in the **"Finding the trailhead"** entries utilize Alaska's milepost system of directions. Using mileposts (or miles, as used here, since there are not always physical mileposts) makes simple directions possible once you understand the system. Mileages on the Glenn and Parks Highways begin in Anchorage; the Seward and Sterling Highways in Seward, the Steese in Fairbanks, the Edgerton at the Richardson Highway, the Richardson in Valdez, and Southeast's highways in their respective city centers. *The Milepost* (Vernon Publications, updated annually) is an Alaska highway guide in common use that lists points of interest by highway mile.

Alaska's highways are known by both name and number, and how the names and numbers correspond can be a bit tricky. For example, part of the Seward Highway is Alaska Highway 1 and part is Alaska Highway 8. It is customary to give directions by highway name, but road signs usually show only route numbers. The maps that accompany the hike descriptions show highways by both name and number.

PICK-A-HIKE TABLES

	Shorter Day Hikes	Longer Day or Overnight Hikes	Hikes of Several Days	Hikes to Fee Cabins	Hikes with Trail Shelters
SOUTHCENTRAL Eastern Kenai	2, 7, 9	1, 3, 4, 5, 6, 7, 10	7, 8, 9, 10	1, 7, 8, 9, 10	1, 3
Northwest Kenai	12, 13, 14, 16	11, 12, 13, 15			
Homer	19, 20	17, 18	17, 18	18	
Turnagain Arm	22, 30	21, 23, 24, 25, 26, 27, 28, 29, 30	25, 27	25	
Anchorage	31, 35	32, 33, 34			
Knik Arm	37, 38	36, 37, 39, 40, 41, 42	37, 41		
Matanuska-Susitna Valleys	47, 49, 50	43, 44, 45, 46, 48, 50	51	48, 50	
Copper River	52, 53, 55	55, 57	54, 56		
Cordova	59, 60, 62	58, 61	58	58, 60	58
INTERIOR Fairbanks	63, 64, 66	65, 66, 69	67, 68, 69	69	65, 66, 67, 68
Denali Highway	71	70, 71			
SOUTHEAST Ketchikan	73, 74	72, 75	72	75	72, 73
Wrangell	76, 77	77			76, 77
Petersburg	78, 79	78, 80	80	80	78
Sitka	82, 83	81, 84			84
Juneau	85, 88, 90, 93	85, 86, 87, 88, 89, 90, 91, 92, 93		87, 91, 93	
Haines	95, 96	94, 95, 96			
Skagway	99	97, 99, 100	98	97	99

PICK-A-HIKE TABLES

	Interpretive Hikes	Accessible Trails	Family Hikes	Early/ Late Season Hikes	Best Hikes for Hikers without Cars
SOUTHCENTRAL Eastern Kenai	2	2, 9	1, 2, 5, 7, 9	1, 2	4, 5, 6, 7, 8, 9, 10
Northwest Kenai	16		12, 13, 14, 15, 16	12, 13, 14, 15, 16	11, 12, 15
Homer	19, 20		17, 18, 19, 20	20	17, 18, 19
Turnagain Arm	22	22	21, 22, 24, 27, 30	21, 24, 26, 27, 30	23, 27, 28, 29, 30
Anchorage		31	31, 33, 35	35	35
Knik Arm	37		36, 37, 38	37, 38	
Matanuska-Susitna Valleys	47		47, 48, 49, 50	43, 48, 49, 50	49, 50, 51
Copper River	57		52, 55	52	52, 53, 54, 55
Cordova	59, 62	62	59, 60, 61, 62	59, 60, 61, 62	58
INTERIOR Fairbanks	63, 64	63, 64	63, 64, 69	63, 64	63
Denali Highway			71		
SOUTHEAST Ketchikan	73		73, 74, 75	73, 74, 75	72, 75
Wrangell			76, 77	76, 77	76
Petersburg		79	78, 79	78, 79, 80	80
Sitka	82, 83	82, 83	81, 82, 83	81, 82, 83	81, 82, 83, 84
Juneau	85, 88, 93	88	85, 87, 88, 90, 91, 92, 93	88, 90, 92, 93	85, 86, 87, 88, 89, 90, 91
Haines			95, 96	95, 96	94, 95
Skagway	98		97, 99	99, 100	97, 98, 99, 100

PICK-A-HIKE TABLES

	Coast	Lakes	Alpine	Glaciers	Rain Forest
SOUTHCENTRAL Eastern Kenai	1	4, 5, 6, 7, 8, 9	3, 4, 6, 8, 10	2, 3	1, 4
Northwest Kenai	16	11, 13, 15	11		
Homer	19	17, 18, 20	17, 18	17	18
Turnagain Arm	21, 30	23, 29	25, 26, 27, 28, 29	22, 23, 25	24, 27
Anchorage		32, 33	31, 32, 33, 34		
Knik Arm		36	36, 39, 40, 41, 42	37	
Matanuska-Susitna Valleys		45, 47, 48, 50	43, 44, 45, 46, 47, 51	44, 46	
Copper River			53, 54, 56, 57	53, 55	
Cordova		58, 60, 61	58	61, 62	58, 59, 60, 61
INTERIOR Fairbanks			65, 66, 67, 68, 69		
Denali Highway		70	70, 71		
SOUTHEAST Ketchikan		72, 73, 74, 75	72		72, 73, 74, 75
Wrangell		77			76, 77
Petersburg	78, 80	78, 80			78, 79, 80
Sitka	82, 83		84		81, 82, 83, 84
Juneau	93	90	85, 86, 87	88, 89, 92	90, 91, 92, 93
Haines	95, 96		94		95, 96
Skagway	100	98, 99, 100	98, 99	97	

SOUTHCENTRAL ALASKA

TRIPS IN SOUTHCENTRAL

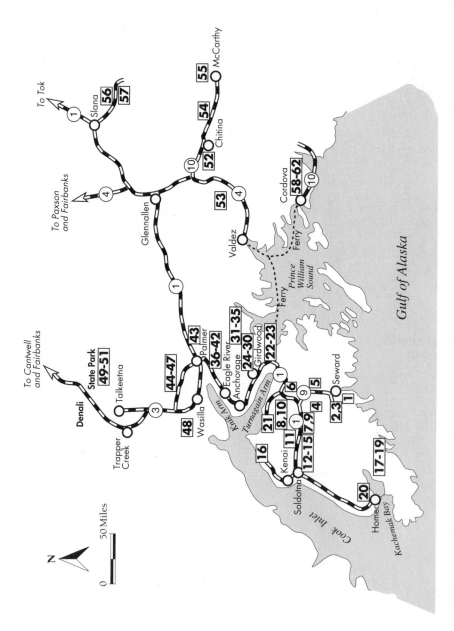

EASTERN KENAI

The eastern Kenai's mountains offer the most extensive overnight and multi-day trail hiking in the state, thanks to the Chugach National Forest's Seward Ranger District. The trails and roadside campgrounds make this a unique recreation area for Alaska, similar to national forests in the Lower 48. Seward is also the headquarters for Kenai Fjords National Park; the only trails in the park are at Exit Glacier (Hikes 2 and 3).

Besides the trails described here, there are short trails to Golden Fin Lake (Seward Highway Mile 12), Grayling and Meridian Lakes (Seward Highway Mile 13), Rainbow Lake (Cooper Lake Road), and Victor Creek (Seward Highway Mile 20). A new trail along the route of the historic Iditarod Trail is partially complete; it begins on Nash Road outside Seward.

The Kenai Mountains also offer experienced cross-country hikers some great ridge running from the Eastern Kenai's higher roads. The best high-ridge access is from Turnagain Pass, Summit Lake, and the Palmer Creek Road outside Hope.

Heaven is a clear-day ridge hike on the Kenai.

Trip summary:	An overnight hike along the coast of Resurrection Bay to Caines Head.
Distance:	North Beach: 4.5 miles one way. Fort McGilvray: 6.5 miles one way.
Special features:	Coastal scenery and wildlife, World War II-era Fort McGilvray, a fee cabin at Derby Cove, beach walking and fishing. The beach section of the hike, 2.5 miles long, is passable only at low tide.
Location:	Two miles south of Seward.
Difficulty:	Moderate.
Trail type:	More developed trail; beach section is an easy-to-follow route.
Total elevation gain:	About 400 feet in and 400 feet out to North Beach; another 600 feet in to Fort McGilvray.
Best season:	Mid-May to early October.
Maps:	USGS Seward A-7 (SW, SE) and Blying Sound D-7; Alaska State Parks brochure *Caines Head State Recreation Area*; Trails Illustrated *Kenai Fjords National Park*.
Manager:	Alaska State Parks, Kenai Area.

Key points:
- 1.5 Tonsina Creek (developed camp area)
- 4.0 Derby Cove (fee cabin)
- 4.25 Alpine Trail junction
- 4.5 North Beach (developed camp area)
- 5.5 Trail fork to South Point (1.5 miles, limited camping)
- 6.5 Fort McGilvray

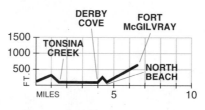

Finding the trailhead: Drive into Seward on the Seward Highway, which becomes Third Avenue as it enters town. Continue south to the end of Third Avenue and at a T intersection take a right (west) onto Lowell Point Road. The gravel road curves south and skirts the west edge of Resurrection Bay; drive two miles from the Third Avenue intersection to the trailhead on the left side of the road.

The hike: This hike along the coastline of Resurrection Bay offers wildlife viewing, scenery, fishing, and historic interest. Caines Head, a state recreation area, is the site of Fort McGilvray, a military garrison built to protect

CAINES HEAD

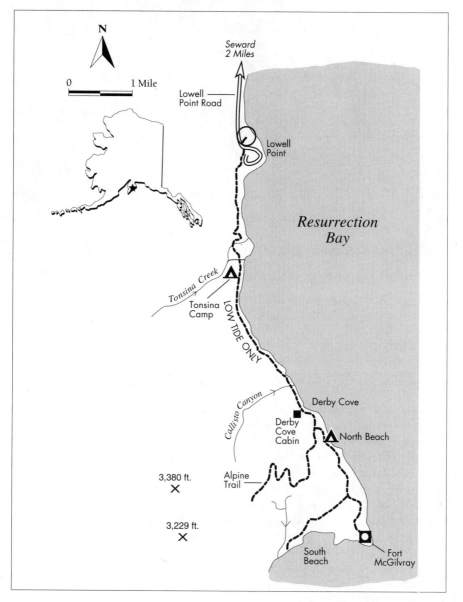

N

0   1 Mile

Seward
2 Miles

Lowell
Point Road

Lowell
Point

*Resurrection
Bay*

Tonsina Creek

Tonsina
Camp

LOW TIDE ONLY

Callisto Canyon

Derby Cove

Derby
Cove
Cabin

North Beach

Alpine
Trail

3,380 ft.
✕

3,229 ft.
✕

South
Beach

Fort
McGilvray

Taking a break on the beach at Derby Cove. LINDA BIRTLES PHOTO.

Seward's harbor during the latter days of World War II. At the north end of the recreation area are a fee cabin at Derby Cove, a backcountry camping area at the entrance to the bay, and South Beach, a remote beach that was the site of the garrison's living quarters.

Seals, sea lions, sea otters, porpoises, and humpback whales cruise the coast, and inner and outer coast birds like guillemots, cormorants, murrelets, scoters, oystercatchers, and harlequin ducks share the waters. Don't forget the rain gear; the coast of the Gulf of Alaska is notoriously wet.

The 2.5 miles between Tonsina Point and Derby Cove is a beach hike that is passable only at low tide. The best plan is to leave the Lowell Point Trailhead an hour before low tide, allowing plenty of time to cover the 1.5 miles between the trailhead and Tonsina Point. Day hiking Caines Head is possible during the long days of summer, but it would be a long day; it's nearly 12 hours between low tides.

From the trailhead, follow Lowell Point Road about 0.1 mile to a marked intersection with a logging road on the right. Follow this side road about 0.3 mile to a Y intersection; take the right fork, and then turn onto the marked trail that angles away to the right in a few feet.

The trail climbs and then drops fairly steeply to Tonsina Point and Tonsina Creek, which has two forks, one at each end of the alluvial fan that makes up the point. Just before the trail hits the beach, there is a camping area with tables and an open-sided shelter. If you don't make the low tide, this is a good place to camp.

The Derby Cove fee cabin is back in the trees at the end of a short trail from the northwest end of the cove; see Appendix 2 for reservation information. The trail over the north point of Caines Head to North Beach starts from the southeast end of Derby Cove. The Alpine Trail, a 2-mile route that climbs to rolling alpine tundra at about 1,500 feet elevation, leads uphill from the North Beach Trail.

North Beach makes a good base camp for exploring the rest of Caines Head; besides plenty of campsites, there are a ranger station and two open-sided shelters in the trees behind the beach.

The trail, actually an old army road, leads south from North Beach to Fort McGilvray and South Beach. In a mile is a Y intersection; to the left one more mile is the fort, and to the right about 1.5 miles is South Beach.

Take a flashlight or headlamp to explore the dark, dripping rooms of the fort, checking carefully for steps and holes. Watch your step, and take care with children.

From the gun platforms on the grassy summit south of the fort's bunkers, hikers can listen to the pounding surf and look out over the islands of Resurrection Bay into the Gulf of Alaska. The army began building the fort to protect Seward, the main supply port for the military in Alaska, after the Japanese attack on the Aleutians in 1943. The rotting pier at North Beach was the landing used for building and supplying the fort. The guns were never fired on an enemy; the Japanese withdrew from the Aleutians, and the military abandoned the fort in 1944.

South Beach is a stony, exposed beach that faces the the wind and weather of the outside of Resurrection Bay. It's more isolated than North Beach, and definitely a rougher boat landing. Remains of the army ghost town, the fort's living quarters, lie back in the woods.

Taking a kayak or motorized raft or skiff to Derby Cove or North Beach makes a good family trip, leaving plenty of energy for exploring Caines Head once you're there.

Campfires are allowed only on the beaches. Please leave all artifacts in place so everyone can enjoy them.

Shorter hikes. Tonsina Creek, 1.5 miles from the trailhead (easy, more developed), makes a good day hike or family camping trip.

Fishing. Hikers can surf fish for Dolly Varden, and starting in late July, for silver salmon.

Trip summary:	Three shorter trails for day hiking near the face of Exit Glacier, the only drive-up glacier in Kenai Fjords National Park.
Distances:	The Lower Loop Trail, to the outwash plain near the face of the glacier: a 0.5-mile loop.
	The Upper Loop Trail, to a viewpoint above the north edge of the glacier: a 1-mile loop.
	The Nature Trail, a loop through the landscape left behind as the glacier retreated: a 0.75-mile loop.
Special features:	Exit Glacier; a shelter with an interpretive display.
Location:	12 miles northwest of Seward.
Difficulty:	Easy.
Total elevation gain:	About 100 feet on the Upper Loop Trail; the Lower Loop Trail and Nature Trail are essentially flat.
Trail type:	Accessible to more developed.
Best season:	Mid-May to early October.
Maps:	USGS Seward A-7 (NW) (trails not shown); Kenai Fjords National Park brochure, Trails Illustrated *Kenai Fjords National Park*.
Manager:	Kenai Fjords National Park.

Finding the trailhead: Three miles north of downtown Seward, turn west off the Seward Highway onto Exit Glacier Road and drive about eight miles to the Exit Glacier area of Kenai Fjords National Park. The trails begin at the parking area at the end of the road.

About 7 miles from the Seward Highway, just before the bridge over Resurrection River, is the Forest Service's Resurrection River Trailhead (see Hike 9).

The hikes: Exit Glacier, the only road-accessible area in Kenai Fjords National Park, is one of the thirty-five glaciers that flow off the 500-square mile Harding Icefield. The glacier is now approximately 3 miles long, but in the past two hundred years, it has extended about eight miles down the Resurrection River valley to near where the Seward Highway is now.

These three short trails introduce visitors to Exit Glacier and the landscape it left behind as it retreated. The first 0.25 mile of the trail system is paved and accessible, leading to an interpretive shelter that features displays about the glacier and the animals that live in the neighborhood. Beyond the shelter, the three forks of the trail system divide. Walking all the trails adds up to roughly 1.5 miles.

There is a seasonal ranger station near the trailhead and a small, tent-only campground nearby. In summer, the park sponsors ranger-led hikes to the glacier.

The **Lower Loop Trail** leads about 0.25 mile beyond the interpretive shelter to the face of the glacier, crossing its outwash plain, the flat gravelly area downstream of the terminus of the ice. A jumble of giant chunks of blue ice looms ahead as you stroll along near the edge. For safety's sake,

EXIT GLACIER

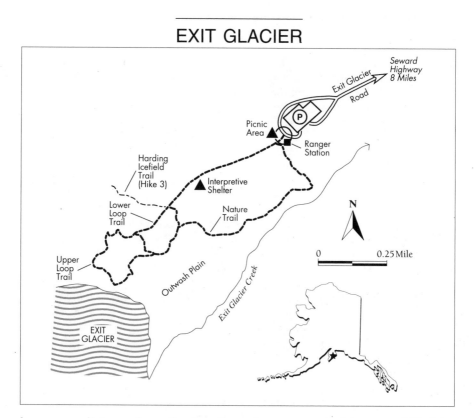

keep your distance from the ice. Several years ago a visitor was killed by falling ice as she posed for a photo.

The **Upper Loop Trail** leads from the interpretive shelter up rock and log steps and over exposed bedrock to a viewpoint above the north edge of the glacier. The reward for the short climb is a view down onto the ice, of a stream issuing out of the glacier, a big melt pool, and ice caves. The trail loops back down to the Lower Loop Trail and the parking area.

The **Nature Trail** forms a 0.75-mile loop from the parking area. Signs explain how plants colonize the raw land left behind as a glacier retreats. Here, natural succession from bare outwash plain to forest moves through stages of brightly-blooming fireweed, alder and willow thickets, cottonwood forest, and finally a "climax" forest of Sitka spruce and western hemlock. Already a few spruce trees are beginning to grow up in the shade of the young cottonwoods along the trail. In time, this will be an evergreen forest.

While exploring the Exit Glacier area, look to the north of the glacier for black bears and mountain goats feeding on the brushy slope. You're more likely to spot animals here early in the summer; they follow the retreating snowline up, feeding on new green growth as it emerges. Look and listen for warblers, magpies, swallows, and golden-crowned sparrows near the trails.

The trail to the Harding Icefield overlook (Hike 3) branches off the trails to Exit Glacier. The Exit Glacier trails are open to foot and wheelchair traffic only, and no pets are allowed.

3   HARDING ICEFIELD

Trip summary:	A longer day hike from Exit Glacier to an overlook of the Harding Icefield.
Distance:	About 4 miles one way.
Special features:	Exit Glacier and the Harding Icefield, great views and wildlife, especially mountain goats. There is an emergency shelter on the trail just below the overlook.
Location:	12 miles northwest of Seward.
Difficulty:	Moderately strenuous.
Trail type:	More developed trail with a few rough, rocky spots; the last 0.75 mile is a less developed trail/marked route.
Total elevation gain:	3,000 feet.
Best season:	July to mid-September, though snow lingers all summer.
Maps:	USGS Seward A-8 (trail not shown); Kenai Fjords National Park brochure; Trails Illustrated *Kenai Fjords National Park.*
Manager:	Kenai Fjords National Park.

Key points:
1.5   Viewpoint, about 1,600 feet elevation.
2.5   Viewpoint, about 2,600 feet elevation.
3.25 End of the constructed/maintained trail.
4.0   Harding Icefield overlook.

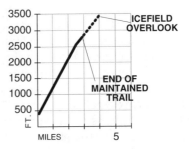

Finding the trailhead: The directions are the same as those to Exit Glacier, Hike 2. From the parking area, follow the paved access trail about 0.25 mile to the interpretive shelter. Just beyond the shelter, turn right onto the Harding Icefield Trail.

The hike: Start early, and pack a camera and plenty of film for this hike to the edge of the Harding Icefield, where dark peaks thrust out of a sea of ice. The trail climbs through forest and brush, alpine wildflower meadows, and finally rock and snow, to the overlook. The switchbacking grade is gradual, courtesy of the Student Conservation Association. The SCA's high school

HARDING ICEFIELD

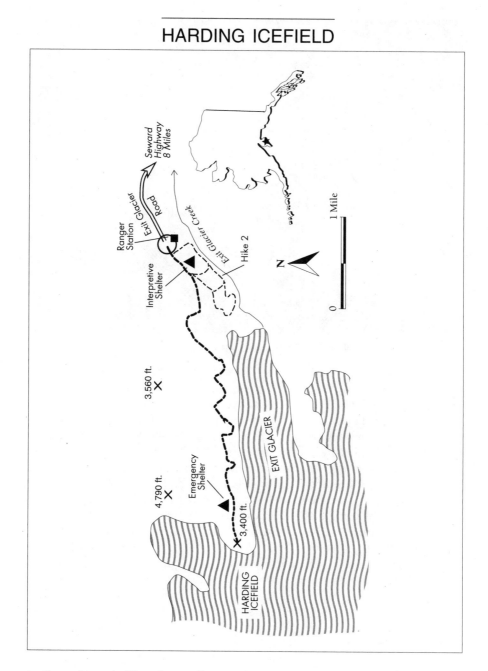

trail workers, hailing from all over the country, have worked for several years to build this spectacular trail.

Fog, rain, and poor visibility are common, and weather can change quickly, so carry warm, waterproof clothes even on sunny days. Be prepared to retreat if bad weather moves in; you probably couldn't see anything anyway. If the weather is decent, be ready to be amazed.

Taking photos from an outcrop above the Harding Icefield.

From the Exit Glacier parking area, pick out the route on the sloping ridge between Exit Glacier and the rocky peaks to the north. The trail crosses a small creek and leads over a rough, rocky stretch where the route crosses a large outcrop. The viewpoint at 1.5 miles is on a brushy knob above treeline; the view at 2.5 miles, in a rocky alpine area, is better.

The last 0.75 mile is an unmaintained route beaten by many feet over snow and loose rock, following a lateral moraine and exposed bedrock above Exit Glacier. There is a shelter below the overlook that is for emergency use only. Camping near the icefield is possible but limited; if you do camp here, please camp on bare rock or snow and not on the sparse, easily-damaged vegetation. Most people will find it better to tent at the small campground back on the park road and carry a lighter day pack up the climb to the icefield. Remember that glacier travel is for the experienced and equipped only.

Mountain goats are fairly common in the high country. Look for black bears, especially earlier in the summer, when they munch on new green plant growth. The trail is for foot traffic only, and no pets are allowed.

If the park budget hasn't been slashed lately, Kenai Fjords staff offer ranger-led hikes to the icefield. Check at the park visitor center in Seward or at the ranger station at Exit Glacier for availability and times.

Shorter hikes. The viewpoints at 1.5 and 2.5 miles make good turnaround points for shorter day hikes. The distance, grade, and the rocky section early in the hike make this a less appealing trail for smaller children.

4   *LOST LAKE*

Trip summary:	A longer day trip or a two to three day hike to a large alpine lake in the Kenai Mountains.
Distance:	7 miles one way to the lake via either the Primrose or Lost Lake trails, or a traverse of 15 miles from one trailhead to the other.
Special features:	Alpine meadows, tundra rambling, fishing.
Location:	12 miles north of Seward.
Difficulty:	Moderate.
Trail type:	Generally more developed; less developed above treeline on the Primrose Trail.
Total elevation gain:	2,000 feet from the Lost Lake Trailhead, 1,700 feet from the Primrose Trailhead.
Best season:	July through September.
Maps:	USGS Seward A-7 (NE) and B-7, Trails Illustrated *Kenai Fjords National Park*.
Manager:	Chugach National Forest, Seward Ranger District.

Key points:

From Seward (Lost Lake Trail)		From Kenai Lake (Primrose Trail)
0.0	Lost Lake Trailhead	15.0
4.0	Clemens Cabin junction	11.0
6.0	High point (2,200 feet)	9.0
7.0	Lost Lake (south end)	8.0
7.5	Lost Creek bridge	7.5
8.0	Lost Lake (north end)	7.0
11.5	Primrose Mine	3.5
13.0	Primrose Falls side trail	2.0
15.0	Primrose Trailhead	0.0

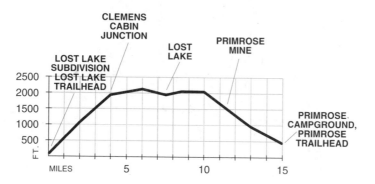

Finding the trailheads:

Lost Lake Trailhead. Five miles north of downtown Seward, turn west off the Seward Highway onto the Lost Lake Subdivision Road. The intersection is 0.3 mile south of the Mormon church and 0.1 mile north of the fire station.

LOST LAKE

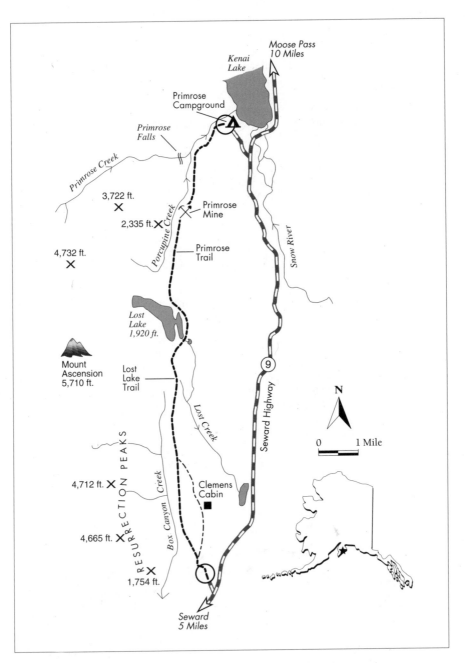

Moose Pass
10 Miles

Kenai
Lake

Primrose
Campground

*Primrose
Falls*

Primrose Creek

3,722 ft.
X

2,335 ft. X

4,732 ft.
X

Porcupine Creek

Primrose
Mine

Primrose
Trail

Snow River

*Lost
Lake
1,920 ft.*

Mount
Ascension
5,710 ft.

Lost
Lake
Trail

Lost Creek

9

Seward Highway

N

0   1 Mile

R E S U R R E C T I O N   P E A K S

4,712 ft. X

4,665 ft. X

X
1,754 ft.

Box Canyon Creek

Clemens
Cabin

1

*Seward
5 Miles*

As road signs indicate, follow the subdivision road 0.2 mile and turn left at an intersection. Follow this road another 0.2 mile and turn right, and the trailhead is 0.1 mile ahead. The location of the trailhead may change if a proposed land exchange goes through, but the trailhead will remain in the subdivision. The current trailhead is on private land; please respect the landowner's privacy.

Primrose Trailhead. Seventeen miles north of Seward and just south of the Snow River bridge at Kenai Lake, turn northwest off the Seward Highway on the road to the Primrose Campground. Drive to the campground entrance, about 1.1 miles from the highway. If you aren't camping in the campground, park in the entrance area, as there is no parking at the trailhead. The trailhead is about 0.2 mile from the carpark, at the back of the campground.

The hike: Lost Lake is an alpine lake two miles long, set at the edge of a huge expanse of alpine country. Long fingers of tundra extend into the lake, and many smaller lakes and ponds dot the low hills to the east of the lake, while to the west, Mount Ascension looms high above.

Good camping, fishing, and miles of alpine rambling are the big draws to Lost Lake. An alpine cross-country route to the west leads across miles of tundra as far as Cooper Lake, and Mount Ascension attracts mountaineers.

The two trails to the lake, the Primrose Trail from Kenai Lake and the Lost Lake Trail from Seward, offer the choices of an out-and-back trip from one of the two trailheads, or a traverse from one trailhead to the other. The Lost Lake Trail is more of a subalpine and alpine trail; the Primrose Trail offers hikers a chance to camp in a developed campground at Primrose Landing on Kenai Lake and do day hikes without driving. Both trails are open to mountain bikes, and to pack and saddle stock after June 30.

Hiking the 15-mile traverse beginning on the Primrose side saves a bit of climbing and offers slightly better views of Resurrection Bay once you're south of Lost Lake. Car shuttle distance between the trailheads is about 15 miles.

The **Lost Lake Trail** is a beauty, with great views of the Kenai Mountains and Resurrection Bay, wildflower meadows, subalpine groves of mountain hemlock, and salmonberries and blueberries for the picking. A side trail at Mile 4 leads 1.5 miles to the Clemens Cabin, a Forest Service fee cabin available under a reservation-and-fee system. See Appendix 2 for reservation information.

At this writing, the Lost Lake Trailhead is in a developing subdivision, and hikers have to follow one of the subdivision roads a short distance. The Forest Service plans to establish a permanent trailhead when a land exchange involving the subdivision owner is complete. Once on the foot path, there are two forks in the first mile. At the first, the hiking trail bears right to avoid a steep, eroded section, rejoining it above. The second is the winter trail to Clemens Cabin, which is steep, wet, and eroded and not recommended for summer travel. The hiking trail bears left.

After two miles in the forest, hikers emerge from the trees on the edge of the V-shaped gorge of Box Canyon Creek, and the glaciated Resurrection Peaks come into view. The brush yields to subalpine meadows by Mile 4, and alpine tundra begins about Mile 5. The first view of Lost Lake is from the 2,200-foot trail summit about Mile 6.

After reaching the south end of the lake, the trail continues as a route marked by a series of posts installed by American Hiking Society volunteers in 1984. The route is a well-beaten path that crosses the lake's outlet creek and skirts the east side of the lake onto the Primrose Trail.

The **Primrose Trail** is a forest trail for 4.5 miles, passing a winter trail on the left about 0.75 mile, a rough side trail to Primrose Falls about Mile 2, and a cabin from the historic Primrose Mine at Mile 3.5. At this writing, the claim-holder has a permit to work the mine and to use an all-terrain vehicle on the trail. The Primrose, a lode (vein) mine for gold, copper, and other metals, had its heyday between the early 1900s and the 1930s, but was never wildly successful. The actual mine was below the trail, along the stream.

Above the forest, the trail follows a 2,100-foot subalpine ridge to Lost Lake. Wedged into nooks and crannies below the ridge are many small lakes and ponds, some with good campsites. This part of the trail can be really wet and slick in rainy weather.

Shorter hikes. On the Primrose Trail, hike 2 miles one way to Primrose Falls or 3.5 miles to the Primrose Mine site. The side trail to Primrose Falls is rough. Be especially careful along the edge of the canyon at the end of path. On the Lost Lake Trail, hiking 2 miles one way leads to views above Box Canyon Creek, and a 4-mile one-way jaunt leads to the subalpine meadows near the Clemens Cabin trail junction. Take a shorter forest hike from either trailhead for berry picking later in the summer.

Fishing. Lost Lake has fair to good fishing for larger rainbow trout.

Fishing the Kenai Backcountry Lakes

Carrying a pack rod on the eastern Kenai trails isn't a bad idea. The mountain lakes are a lot quieter than the lower-elevation, road-accessible streams where anglers often stand shoulder to shoulder, flailing away for salmon. Though the fish aren't as big, the trout and grayling in the high lakes make fine fishing.

There are more than a dozen lakes on the eastern Kenai trails, and all of them have a fishery of some sort. Rainbow trout are the most common fish. Most of the rainbows originated as a hatchery-reared strain from the Swanson River. The Lost and Johnson Lake populations are descended from Pacific Northwest trout. The only lakes with lake trout are the Resurrection Trail lakes—Trout, Juneau, and Swan Lakes.

The grayling lakes are Juneau, Grayling, Crescent, and Bench Lakes. Crescent was stocked in the 1950s, and Crescent Lake grayling were brought in to stock Bench Lake, after the Forest Service diverted glacial Ohio Creek in 1968 to make the lake habitable. A worker, Paul Anderson, died in a blasting accident on the project; there is a small memorial plaque for him north of Bench Lake.

The best fishing in the lakes is soon after the ice goes out in late spring and early summer, and in late summer and fall when temperatures drop again.

5   PTARMIGAN LAKE

Trip summary:	A popular, half-day or longer day hike or an overnight trip to a forested lake in the Kenai Mountains.
Distance:	3.5 miles one way to the west end of Ptarmigan Lake; 7.5 miles to the east end.
Special features:	Camping, wildlife, berries, fishing in the lake and in Ptarmigan Creek; a good family outing.
Location:	23 miles north of Seward.
Difficulty:	Easy to the west (near) end of the lake; moderate to the east (far) end.
Trail type:	More developed.
Total elevation gain:	About 400 feet in and 150 feet out.
Best season:	June through early October.
Maps:	USGS Seward B-7 and B-6; Trails Illustrated *Kenai Fjords National Park.*
Manager:	Chugach National Forest, Seward Ranger District.

Key points:
2.25 Viewpoint and alternate trail junction
3.5   West end of Ptarmigan Lake
7.5   East end of Ptarmigan Lake

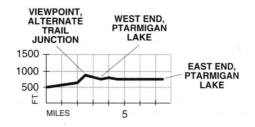

Finding the trailhead: Turn east off the Seward Highway into the Ptarmigan Creek Campground, 23 miles north of Seward and 6 miles south of Moose Pass. Turn right at the fork in the recreation area road to the day use area and drive to the trailhead, a total of about 0.2 mile off the highway.

The hike: A blue-green glacial lake set below the icy summits of Andy Simons Mountain, Ptarmigan Lake makes a fine family backpack trip, a fairly easy hike of 3.5 miles from the trailhead to the west shore of the lake. The trail continues another 4 miles to the east end of the lake.

Camping at the Ptarmigan Creek Campground and day tripping to the lake make a good hike. Though the trail is popular, the long, forested lake still offers decent solitude. Watch and listen for moose, bears, and coyotes in the neighborhood.

The trail follows the Ptarmigan Creek valley to Ptarmigan Lake, staying close by the stream for a bit over a mile. Where the trail veers away from

PTARMIGAN LAKE

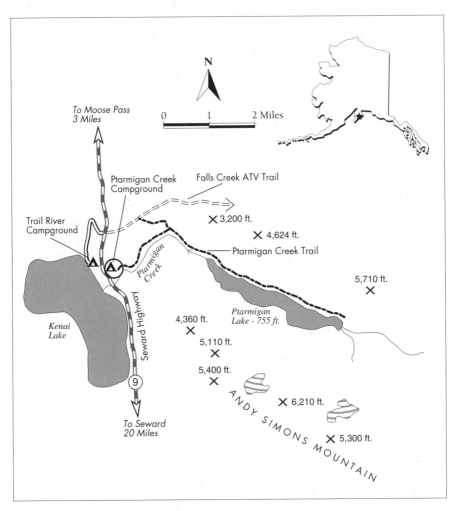

the creek, people fishing can continue cross-country up the creek to more fishing holes. Climbing higher on the north side of the valley, hikers heading for the lake reach a viewpoint on a brushy open slope at about 2.25 miles, with a vista of the creek, forests, and mountains. In another mile the trail drops to the lake, at 750 feet elevation.

The lower end of the lake is thickly forested. At the upper end, the lake opens up a bit, with a view up the valley along the route of the abandoned trail that once crossed Snow River Pass into Paradise Valley. It's a horrific bushwhack now, so taking a float plane trip to one of the Paradise Valley lakes is a better idea these days. To the south of Ptarmigan Lake is Andy Simons Mountain, a good mountaineering peak that's usually approached from the Victor Creek Trail, in the next valley to the south.

Angler at the west end of Ptarmigan Lake.

There is also an alternate trail between the Seward Highway and Mile 2.25 of the trail. The alternate trail may be unsigned; it intersects the main trail at a point where the creek is clearly visible below, and leads about 2.5 miles back to the highway, about half on a forest foot trail and half on the Falls Creek/ATV Trail. This route reaches the highway a mile north of the Ptarmigan Creek Campground, at a point across the road from and just north of the Trail River Campground access road. Until the Department of Transportation builds a shoulder on the busy Seward Highway, it's best to shuttle a vehicle rather than walk the road.

The Ptarmigan Creek Trail is open to mountain bikes and to pack and saddle stock after June 30, but most use of the trail now is by hikers. The lower half of the alternate route is open to all terrain vehicles.

Shorter hikes. Take the Ptarmigan Creek Trail about 2.25 miles one way to the valley viewpoint, or hike and fish along the creek for 1 to 2 miles.

Fishing. The lake has a small population of small Dolly Varden, and Ptarmigan Creek has Dolly Varden and rainbow trout. There are red salmon in the creek beginning in late July, but all salmon fishing is prohibited.

Trip summary:	A popular 2-4 day traverse or a longer, out-and-back day hike to two large lakes and an alpine pass in the Kenai Mountains.	
Distance:	10 miles one way or a 23-mile traverse.	
Special features:	Alpine country, lake fishing, varied scenery.	
Location:	The two trailheads are 32 and 64 miles north of Seward.	
Difficulty:	Moderate.	
Trail type:	More developed.	
Total elevation gain:	About 700 feet from the north, 1,000 feet from the south.	
Best season:	Mid-June through September.	
Maps:	USGS Seward C-6 and C-7; Trails Illustrated *Kenai National Wildlife Refuge.*	
Manager:	Chugach National Forest, Seward Ranger District.	

Key points:

North Trailhead		South Trailhead
0.0	North Trailhead	23.0
2.0	Center Creek bridge	21.0
5.0	Groundhog Creek	18.0
9.5	Bench Lake	13.5
10.0	Johnson Pass	13.0
10.5	Johnson Lake	12.5
16.0	Johnson Creek bridge	7.0
23.0	South Trailhead	0.0

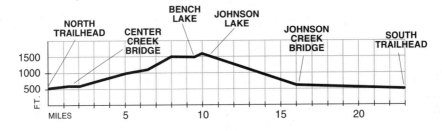

Finding the trailheads: Both trailheads are located off the Seward Highway between Turnagain Pass and Seward. For the north trailhead, turn south onto the signed access road 5 miles south of Turnagain Pass. The south trailhead is 32 miles north of Seward and 0.2 mile west of the Trail Lake Fish Hatchery, on the north side of the highway.

The hike: One of the easier overnight hikes on the Kenai, Johnson Pass makes a good longer family backpack for kids who can carry their own gear. Think of it as a shorter Resurrection Pass hike (Hike 8) without the fee cabins.

JOHNSON PASS

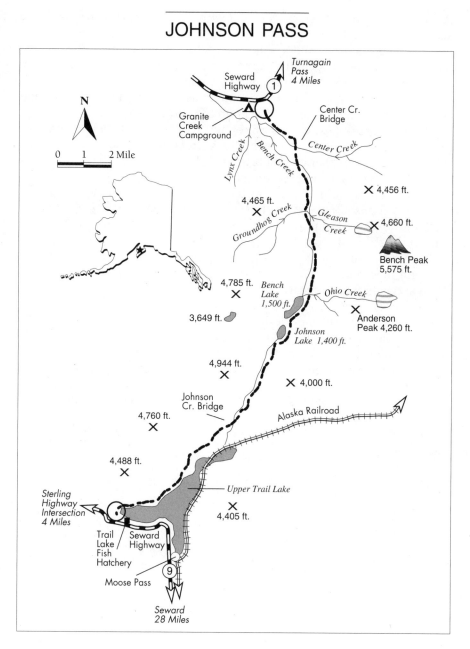

There is good camping and decent fishing at Bench and Johnson Lakes, which are less than a mile apart on opposite sides of gentle, alpine Johnson Pass. Steeper, cross-country hiking into the higher country from Bench Lake is excellent, though best in the first half of the summer before the brushy vegetation has grown up.

The trail over Johnson Pass, originally known as the Sunrise Trail, was one of the Kenai's earliest "highways." Pack trains worked their way over the pass, connecting the port at Seward with the gold-rush towns of Sunrise and Hope. The trail is one of the segments of the historic Iditarod Trail from Alaska's gold rush era, and the hike today still follows some of the original sections of the trail. Groundhog Creek, at about 5 miles, was the site of an early mining operation—the bench-cut wagon road is still visible.

The north trailhead is the more popular, as it's closer to Anchorage and closer by trail to the pass and lakes. From the north, the trail crosses bridges over Center Creek (just over 2 miles) and its tributary Bench Creek (just under 4 miles). Beyond the Bench Creek crossing, the hike cuts through subalpine meadows that can be brushy and overgrown if unmaintained— watch for cow parsnip and stinging nettle.

The two lakes are practically at the same elevation, but Bench Lake is alpine and Johnson Lake is partly subalpine and partly forested. The trail south of the lakes is uniformly forested and rolling; the southern 3.5 miles parallel the shore of Upper Trail Lake.

There are a number of campsites along the trail as well as at the lakes. Bear and moose are fairly common, so exercise reasonable caution. Dall sheep and mountain goats live in the high country.

The trail is open to saddle and pack stock after June 30, but is closed to motorized vehicles during the hiking season. Johnson Pass is one of the more popular mountain biking trails on the Kenai.

Shorter hikes. From the north trailhead, hike just over 2 miles one way to the Center Creek bridge or just under 4 miles to the lower Bench Creek bridge. From the south trailhead, a short walk on the trail through the forest by Upper Trail Lake rates as pleasant, but with no single outstanding destination.

Fishing. Fish for rainbow trout in Johnson Lake and for grayling in Bench Lake.

7 CRESCENT AND CARTER LAKES

Trip summary:	Half-day and longer day hikes or a backpack trip of two to three days to subalpine lakes in the Kenai Mountains.
Distances:	Crescent Creek Trail: 6.5 miles one way to the west end of Crescent Lake.
	Carter Lake Trail: 2 miles one way to Carter Lake and 3.5 miles to the east end of Crescent Lake.
	Crescent Lake Primitive Trail: 8 miles one way, linking the two trailheads for an 18-mile traverse.
Special features:	Subalpine lake and mountain scenery, fishing, two fee cabins.
Location:	35 miles north of Seward.
Difficulty:	Moderate.
Trail type:	Crescent Creek and Carter Lake trails: more developed. Crescent Creek Primitive Trail: less developed.
Total elevation gain:	Crescent Creek Trail: 1,000 feet in, 100 feet out. Carter Lake Trail: 1,000 feet in. Traverse: 1,500 feet from Carter Lake, 1,400 feet from Crescent Creek.
Best season:	Mid-June through September.
Maps:	USGS Seward C-7, B-7, and C-8; Trails Illustrated *Kenai National Wildlife Refuge*.
Manager:	Chugach National Forest, Seward Ranger District.

Key points:

From Crescent Creek		From Carter Lake
0.0	Crescent Creek Trailhead	18.0
3.5	Crescent Creek bridge	14.5
6.5	Crescent Lake (west end)	11.5
	(0.1 to Crescent Lake Cabin)	
11.0	Crescent Saddle Cabin	7.0
14.5	Crescent Lake (east end)	3.5
16.0	Carter Lake	2.0
18.0	Carter Lake Trailhead	0.0

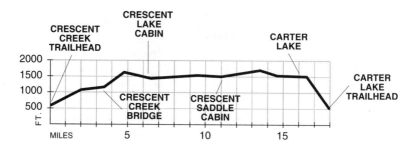

CRESCENT AND CARTER LAKES

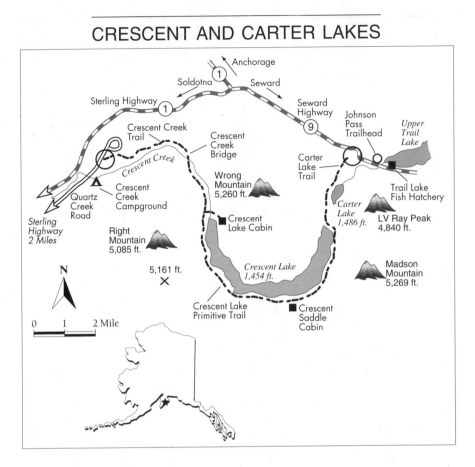

Finding the trailheads:

Crescent Creek Trail. Drive 7 miles west of the Seward/Sterling Highway "Y" junction and turn south onto Quartz Creek Road. Drive about 3.5 miles, past the Crescent Creek Campground, to the parking area on the left (north) side of the road. The trail begins on the south side of the road.

Carter Lake Trail. The trailhead is 33 miles north of Seward on the Seward Highway, on the south side of the road 0.7 mile west of the Trail Lake Fish Hatchery.

The hikes: Crescent Lake, 6 miles long and 0.5 mile wide, wraps around the rocky alpine peaks of Wrong Mountain in a narrow crescent. It's brushy and subalpine at the east end, and partially forested with spruce and cottonwood on the south and west sides. Carter Lake is a smaller subalpine lake set in meadows, brush, and scatterings of weather-beaten mountain hemlocks.

There are good campsites on Carter Lake and the east and west ends of Crescent Lake, with fewer sites on the less developed trail around Crescent Lake. The Crescent Lake fee cabin is on the west end of the lake, and the

Crescent Saddle Cabin is on the south side of the lake about midway on the primitive trail. The cabins may be reserved for a fee (see Appendix 2). Each cabin has a rowboat for cabin occupants.

Carter Lake Trail. The trail begins as a switchbacking, abandoned road bed and climbs 1,000 feet, most of it in the first mile, to Carter Lake. The trail skirts the west edge of the lake, with good camping and fishing spots just off the path. The pass between the two lakes is essentially flat. Near the end of the maintained trail at Crescent Lake, the Crescent Lake Primitive Trail splits off to the left, at the top of an open hill before the lake is completely in view.

Crescent Creek Trail. The path up Crescent Creek cuts over a low divide to join the creek, and then follows it to Crescent Lake. The first bridge, at about 3.5 miles, is just beyond a major avalanche chute, where hardened slabs of snow may linger into the summer.

A second bridge crosses the creek at the mouth of the lake. For the Crescent Lake Cabin, cross the bridge and walk another 0.1 mile. To continue around the lake on the Crescent Lake Primitive Trail, stay on the south side of the creek and don't cross the bridge. There are campsites near the cabin, but the area is heavily used.

Crescent Lake Primitive Trail. The 8-mile trail around the south shore of Crescent Lake is best hiked in early summer and fall. By mid-summer, the trail is passable but thickly overgrown in grasses and shrubs. Expect head-high vegetation in places, and if there has been rain or dew, expect to get soaked. It is a good idea to wear long sleeves and pants since the trail abounds

Crescent Lake from near Crescent Saddle Cabin.

in cow parsnip, which, in the presence of sunlight, may cause skin blisters. There are a few stream crossings. One that could be difficult at high water is a steep, fast-flowing stream between miles 5 and 6 from the Carter Lake Trailhead.

Campsites are limited on the primitive trail, as the shoreline is mostly sloping and brushy. The Crescent Saddle Cabin sits on a partially forested knob above the lake. A historic trail ran through the saddle behind the cabin to Kenai Lake.

The three trails are open to hiking and mountain biking, and after June 30 to pack and saddle stock. The Crescent Lake Primitive Trail is suitable only for hiking.

Shorter hikes. Two good destinations are Carter Lake, 2 miles one way on the Carter Lake Trail, and the Crescent Creek bridge, 3.5 miles one way on the Crescent Creek Trail.

Fishing. Crescent Lake supports grayling; the west end of the lake offers good fishing for large grayling. Carter Lake is stocked with rainbow trout.

---

8   RESURRECTION PASS

Trip summary:	A 3-6 day traverse through the Kenai Mountains over Resurrection Pass, between Hope and Cooper Landing.
Distance:	39 miles.
Special features:	Alpine scenery, lakes and fishing, and a series of fee cabins.
Location:	100 miles south of Anchorage.
Difficulty:	Moderate.
Trail type:	More developed.
Total elevation gain:	About 2,200 feet in either direction.
Best season:	Mid-June through September.
Maps:	USGS Seward B-8, C-8, and D-8; Trails Illustrated *Kenai National Wildlife Refuge.*
Manager:	Chugach National Forest, Seward Ranger District.

Key points:

From Hope		From Cooper Landing
0.0	Hope (north) Trailhead	39.0
7.0	Caribou Creek Cabin	32.0
11.5	Fox Creek Cabin	27.5
14.5	East Creek Cabin	24.5
19.5	Resurrection Pass	19.5
21.5	Devil's Pass Cabin/Trail	17.5
26.0	Swan Lake Cabin	13.0
29.5	Juneau Lake Cabin	9.5

30	Romig Cabin	9.0
32	Trout Lake Cabin/Trail (0.3 mile to cabin)	7.0
35	Juneau Creek Falls	4.0
39	Cooper Landing (south) Trailhead	0.0

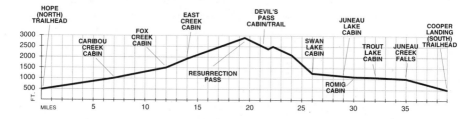

Finding the trailheads:

Hope. Drive 70 miles south of Anchorage and turn northwest onto the Hope Highway. Drive 16.2 miles and turn left (south) on Palmer Creek Road. Take the right fork onto Resurrection Creek Road about 0.6 mile from the Hope Highway, and continue to the signed trailhead, a total of 4 miles from the highway.

Cooper Landing. The marked trailhead is on the north side of the Sterling Highway at Mile 53, about 15.5 miles west of the junction of the Seward and Sterling Highways and 0.2 mile west of the second Kenai River bridge.

The hike: The most popular longer hike on the Kenai, the Resurrection Pass Trail has a string of fee cabins that makes a good 3–6 day cabin-to-cabin hike, if you can reserve the right cabins in advance (see Appendix 2). Plan and make reservations early if you hope to make the trip without pitching a tent. Backpackers with tents have a lot more flexibility. There are many good campsites, some of them marked by the Forest Service.

The Resurrection Pass, Russian Lakes, and Resurrection River trails can be linked for a 71-mile hike from Hope to Exit Glacier outside Seward. See Hike 9.

The southern part of the trail wanders through the Juneau Creek basin, which has three large, forested lakes, all with fair fishing: Trout Lake (7.5 miles from the south trailhead), Juneau Lake (9.5 miles), and Swan Lake (13 miles). Beyond Swan Lake is the switchbacking climb into Juneau Creek's alpine upper valley.

Devil's Pass Cabin is in a treeless zone. Its stove runs on fuel oil, which visitors have to pack in. The Devil's Pass Trail (Hike 10) intersects the Resurrection Trail at the cabin. It leads 10 miles to the Seward Highway, making two other traverses possible using the Resurrection: the 27-mile hike between the Devil's Pass and Cooper Landing trailheads, and the 31-mile trip between the Devil's Pass and Hope trailheads.

It's an alpine hike for about 7 miles between the top of the Swan Lake grade and a point a short distance above American Creek. The trail crosses

RESURRECTION PASS

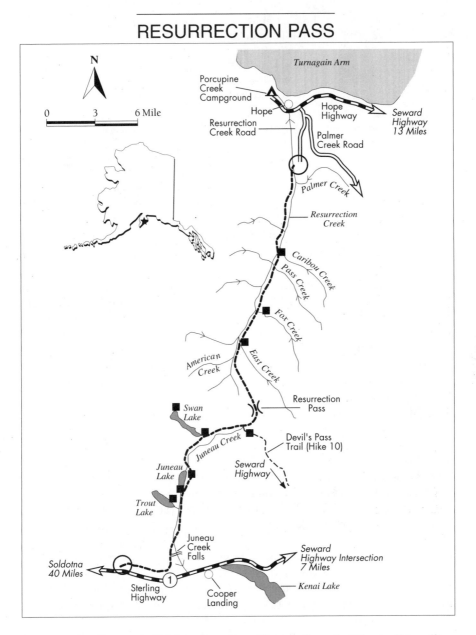

Resurrection Pass at 2,600 feet elevation. The north end of the trail is rolling and forested, with some scenic bluffs above Resurrection Creek between Fox Creek and treeline. The lower end of the north trail threads through a diverse, mixed conifer forest of Sitka and white spruce and its natural hybrid, Lutz spruce. Caribou, Fox, and East Creek cabins and nearby campsites are good destinations from the Hope trailhead.

The Hope end of the trail passes some reminders of the past, like gold dredge tailings and a revegetated mine site. Around 1890 a prospector found

Trailside enterprise, Resurrection Pass Trail. You won't find the Paystreke trading on the New York Stock Exchange.

a couple of small poke's worth of gold on Resurrection Creek. The discovery set off a series of gold stampedes to Cook Inlet later in the decade. The lower part of the trail is on an old mining road, on an easement across mining claims. One of these is the Paystreke Mine, an on-again, off-again tourist mine; it's always interesting to see what the owner has been up to lately.

Resurrection Pass is a National Recreation Trail. It's a very popular mountain bike trail, rated by one magazine as one of the top bike trails in the U.S. Hunters use the trail, especially from the north, for moose and caribou hunting in the fall. It's a popular winter trip as well; many winter visitors reserve cabins and ski the trail. The trail is closed to motorized vehicles from mid-February to the end of November, and to pack and saddle stock until June 30.

There may be some changes coming that will diminish the trail's wilderness character. If, as planned, the Alaska Department of Transportation realigns the Sterling Highway, the new road would cross Juneau Creek above Juneau Falls, shortening the southern end of the trail by more than 4 miles. The Forest Service may also build new logging roads along the north end of the trail.

Fishing. There are rainbow and lake trout, burbot, and whitefish in Trout Lake; the same species plus grayling in Juneau Lake; and lake trout, rainbow trout, and Dolly Varden in Swan Lake. Fish Resurrection Creek for pink salmon and Dolly Varden, and Juneau Creek for Dollies. Check current Alaska Department of Fish and Game Regulations before wetting your line.

Trip summary:	A shorter day or overnight hike to Lower Russian Lake, with a side trip to Russian River Falls; or a 2–3 day traverse through the Russian River drainage via Upper and Lower Russian Lakes.
Distances:	Russian River Falls: 2.3 miles one way. Lower Russian Lake/Barber Cabin: 3.3 miles one way. Russian Lakes traverse: 21.5 miles.
Special features:	Large mountain lakes, fishing, three fee cabins. The falls and Lower Russian Lake are accessible, and also make a fine family hike.
Location:	100 miles south of Anchorage.
Difficulty:	Lower Russian Lake: easy. Russian Lakes traverse: moderate.
Trail type:	More developed. The trails to Russian River Falls and Lower Russian Lake are maintained to a "difficult" level of accessibility.
Total elevation gain:	Lower Russian Lake: about 200 feet in and 150 feet out. Russian Lakes traverse: about 550 feet.
Best season:	June through September.
Maps:	USGS Seward B-8; Trails Illustrated *Kenai National Wildlife Refuge.*
Manager:	Chugach National Forest, Seward Ranger District.

Key points:

Lower Russian Lake (Russian River Trailhead)		Russian Lakes traverse (Cooper Lake Trailhead)	
1.7	Russian River Falls Trail (0.6 mi. to falls)	5.5	Resurrection River Trail
2.6	Barber Cabin Trail	9.5	Upper Russian Lake
3.3	Barber Cabin	12.5	Aspen Flat Cabin
		17.0	Lower Russian Lake
		19.0	Barber Cabin Trail
		21.5	Russian River Trailhead

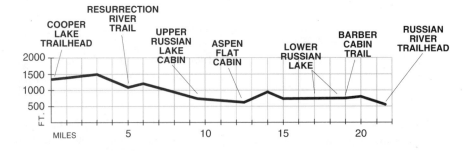

RUSSIAN LAKES

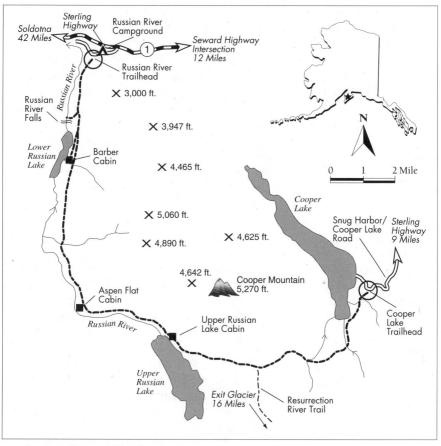

Sterling Highway

Russian River Campground

Soldotna 42 Miles

Seward Highway Intersection 12 Miles

Russian River Trailhead

✗ 3,000 ft.

Russian River

✗ 3,947 ft.

Russian River Falls

Lower Russian Lake

Barber Cabin

✗ 4,465 ft.

✗ 5,060 ft.

✗ 4,890 ft.

✗ 4,625 ft.

Cooper Lake

Snug Harbor/ Cooper Lake Road

Sterling Highway 9 Miles

N

0   1   2 Mile

Aspen Flat Cabin

4,642 ft. ✗

Cooper Mountain 5,270 ft.

Cooper Lake Trailhead

Russian River

Upper Russian Lake Cabin

Upper Russian Lake

Exit Glacier 16 Miles

Resurrection River Trail

Finding the trailheads:

Russian River Trailhead. At Sterling Highway Mile 52.5 (about 5 miles west of the bridge over the mouth of Kenai Lake), turn south onto the road to the Russian River Campground. Continue straight ahead one mile to the trailhead on the left. If the station is open, stop at the campground entrance station for a free trailhead parking permit.

Cooper Lake Trailhead. Turn onto Snug Harbor Road at Mile 48 of the Sterling Highway, 0.1 mile southwest of the bridge over the mouth of Kenai Lake. Drive 11 miles on the gravel Snug Harbor/Cooper Lake Road to the trailhead on the left.

The hikes: The Russian Lakes, two large lakes in the Russian River drainage, offer good campsites, trout fishing, and great scenery. Each lake has a fee cabin with a rowboat for cabin occupants, and there is a third cabin between the lakes at Aspen Flat. A 21.5-mile trail runs along the Russian River valley, connecting the lakes and the river with trailheads on the lower Russian River (elevation 500 feet) and the Cooper Lake Trailhead (elevation 1,300 feet).

The Russian River's two sockeye salmon runs attract gulls, eagles, and yes, bears for the feast, so practice good bear country behavior on the trail when the salmon are in, from mid-summer on.

Hikers have several options for sampling the Russian River backcountry on the Russian Lakes Trail.

Lower Russian Lake and Russian River Falls. From the Russian River Trailhead, it's a popular and easy trip to Russian River Falls and Lower Russian Lake. The trails are maintained to a "difficult" level of wheelchair accessibility, and the Barber cabin on Lower Russian Lake is provided with a ramp and an accessible floatplane dock.

A spur trail leads 0.6 mile from the Lower Russian Trail down Rendezvous Creek to the falls, ending at two viewing decks, one barrier-free, overlooking the rocky cascades and falls. From mid-summer on, visitors may see scores of bright red sockeye salmon milling around in the pools and making great leaps to ascend the falls. The tunnel on the opposite side of the river is a fish pass that the Department of Fish and Game opens only at high water to allow salmon to bypass the falls; under normal conditions they have to do the work themselves.

About 2.6 miles up the Lower Russian Trail is a fork. The wide, gravel trail angling down to the right leads to the lake, the Barber cabin, and campsites along the lake. The narrower trail to the left crosses the open slope above the lake and continues up the Russian River toward Upper Russian Lake and the Cooper Lake Trailhead.

Upper Russian Lake. Upper Russian Lake is a giant body of water, three miles long and up to a mile wide. There is a trail along the lake for only a short distance on the northwest shore, where the cabin and several campsites in groves of cottonwood concentrate most of the recreation use of the lake. The lake's outlet to the Russian River is close by, and for several miles below the outlet the river is popular for rainbow trout fishing.

Upper Russian is 9.5 miles from the Cooper Lake Trailhead and 12 miles from the Russian River Trailhead.

Russian Lakes Traverse. The 21.5-mile, 2-3 day traverse can be done in either direction, but starting at Cooper Lake involves much less climbing. In fact, from south to north the hike is downhill overall, with only a few short sections of climbing.

Except for open slopes near Lower Russian Lake, the entire hike is in forest, making it a good marginal-weather choice over higher-elevation hikes like Resurrection Pass (Hike 8). The forest canopy is open, so tall grasses and brush, including cow parsnip and stinging nettle, grow in profusion. If the trail hasn't been cleared recently, it can be nearly overgrown in brush in places.

Between Cooper Lake and Upper Russian, the trail runs through a wide, forested gap in the Kenai Mountains, crosses an almost imperceptible divide, and descends to Upper Russian Lake at 9.5 miles. There is one signed campsite, at a small lake at about 4.5 miles, and only a few other possible tent sites between the trailhead and the lake. The Resurrection River Trail, at 5.5 miles, leads toward Seward.

Below Upper Russian Lake, the trail stays within about 0.25 mile of the river until Aspen Flat. There it bends away from the river, climbs through low hills and crosses open mountain slopes (an avalanche zone in winter and spring) to Lower Russian Lake. The Aspen Flat cabin is 3 miles below Upper Russian Lake, in forest by the river, at the end of a 0.25-mile spur trail.

Hikers looking for more of an adventure can link the Russian Lakes Trail with the Resurrection Trail, Hike 8, for a 60-mile traverse. The Resurrection Trailhead is 0.5 mile west on the Sterling Highway from the Russian River campground/trailhead road.

Resurrection River Trail. The trail into the Resurrection River valley intersects the Russian Lakes Trail about 4 miles east of the Upper Russian cabin. The trail leads 16 miles to the trailhead on the Exit Glacier Road out of Seward (see Hike 2). The upper Resurrection River is thick with bears and salmon in late summer and fall.

Linking the trail with the Russian Lakes Trail makes a 32-mile hike from Cooper Landing to Exit Glacier, and with the Resurrection Pass Trail, a 71-mile hike from Hope to Exit Glacier. The trail from Exit Glacier to the Resurrection River Cabin, about 6.5 miles one way, is a shorter overnight hike.

Floods in 1996 severely damaged the trail between the Resurrection River cabin and the Russian Lakes Trail. At this writing, the Forest Service is assessing how to rebuild it to avoid flood damage in the future. Check with the Seward office on the condition of the trail before hiking it.

Fishing. The Russian River below the falls is the original home of combat fishing, drawing elbow-to-elbow crowds, but the upper river is much quieter. Fish the upper river and the two lakes for rainbow trout and Dolly Varden. However, no salmon fishing is allowed. Check the regulations.

10 DEVIL'S PASS

Trip summary:	Longer day hikes or a 2 to 4 day backpack up the Devil's Creek valley to Devil's Pass and the Resurrection Trail.
Distance:	10 miles one way, or traverses of 27 and 31 miles connecting with the Resurrection Trail.
Special features:	Alpine scenery, a fee cabin, and traverses connecting with the Resurrection Trail (Hike 8).
Location:	85 miles south of Anchorage.
Difficulty:	Moderate.
Trail type:	More developed.
Total elevation gain:	About 1,500 feet in and 100 feet out to Devil's Pass cabin
Best season:	Mid-June through September.
Maps:	USGS Seward C-7 and C-8; Trails Illustrated *Kenai National Wildlife Refuge*.
Manager:	Chugach National Forest, Seward Ranger District.

Key points:

   0.5   Quartz Creek bridge
   2.0   Beaver Pond Creek
   3.0   Treeline
   6.0   Henry Creek
   8.5   Devil's Pass
   9.0   Devil's Pass Lake
  10.0   Devil's Pass Cabin/Resurrection Trail

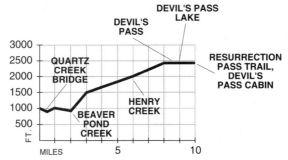

Finding the trailhead: The trailhead is on the west side of the Seward Highway at Mile 39.5, about 2 miles north of the Seward/Sterling Highway junction and 6 miles south of Summit Lake Lodge.

The hike: A gradual climb into high alpine country, the Devil's Pass Trail follows the valley of Devil's Creek into the high valleys and ridges near the Resurrection Pass Trail (Hike 8). The 10-mile trail ends at the Devil's Pass Cabin on the Resurrection, 2 miles south of Resurrection Pass. Connecting with the Resurrection, hikers can continue to the Cooper Landing trailhead (about 27 miles total distance) or to the Hope Trailhead (about 31 miles).

At 2 miles, a marked side trail leads about 0.1 mile to a backcountry campsite the Forest Service calls the Beaver Pond site—with a name like

DEVIL'S PASS

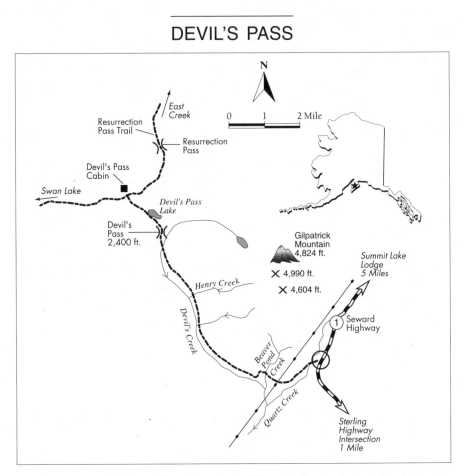

that, be sure to boil or filter the water. There is limited camping between
here and the upper valley, about Mile 8.

Past the treeline at Mile 3 the view of Devil's Creek's deep, v-shaped
valley and Kenai Mountain peaks gets progressively better. Once into the
high country, there is good off-trail hiking to seldom-walked ridges and valleys like Gilpatrick's Mountain and the headwaters of Devil's Creek. The
pass (8.5 miles) and Devil's Pass Lake (9 miles) lie in heavenly high alpine
country. The Devil's Pass Cabin (Mile 10) is one of the Chugach National
Forest's reservation-and-fee shelters (see Appendix 2 for reservation information). If you want to camp nearby, please respect the privacy of people
staying in the cabin and camp well out of sight.

Devil's Pass gets a fair bit of use in conjunction with the Resurrection
Trail, but it's a fine hike in its own right. Mountain bikers' use of the trail is
moderate, and pack and saddle stock are allowed after June 30, though
there is little stock use except during hunting season.

Shorter hikes. The 0.5-mile (one-way) walk to the Quartz Creek bridge is a
short stroll through forest and berry bushes, and hiking three or more miles
up the trail leads into open country with good views.

NORTHWEST KENAI

The most famous natural feature of the northwest part of the Kenai Peninsula is the Kenai River and its amazing fisheries. The section of the Kenai National Wildlife Refuge near where the river emerges from the Kenai Mountains offers good hiking as well; most of the refuge's trails are in the Skilak Lake area, off the Skilak Lake Loop Road. With trails, campgrounds, and lake and stream fishing, the Skilak area makes a good outdoor and family vacation spot.

The refuge also has a few more remote trails. The Surprise and Cottonwood Creek trails, accessible only by boat across the Kenai and Skilak Lake, lead to high country in the Kenai Mountains. The Emma Lake Trail, accessible by boat or floatplane at the roadless end of Tustemena Lake, leads to a trail shelter at the lake and an alpine area beyond.

---

11 FULLER LAKES

Trip summary:	A half-day or overnight hike to two lakes near treeline on the Kenai Refuge, with access to higher country from the lakes.
Distances:	Lower Fuller Lake: 2 miles. Upper Fuller Lake: 3 miles.
Special features:	Lakes, fishing, access to alpine ridge hiking.
Location:	In the Kenai Refuge, 110 miles south of Anchorage.
Difficulty:	Moderate.
Trail type:	More developed to Upper Fuller Lake; less developed to the north end of Upper Fuller Lake.
Total elevation gain:	About 1,400 feet.
Best season:	Early June through September.
Maps:	USGS Kenai B-1 (NE) and C-1 (SE); Trails Illustrated *Kenai National Wildlife Refuge*, Alaska Road and Recreation Map *Kenai Lake and Vicinity*.
Manager:	Kenai National Wildlife Refuge.

Key points:

2   Lower Fuller Lake
3   Upper Fuller Lake
3.5 North end, Upper Fuller Lake

Finding the trailhead: The trailhead is at Mile 57 of the Sterling Highway, 110 miles south of Anchorage and 38 miles east of Soldotna. The trail begins on the north side of the highway, about 2.5 miles west of the Russian River

FULLER LAKES

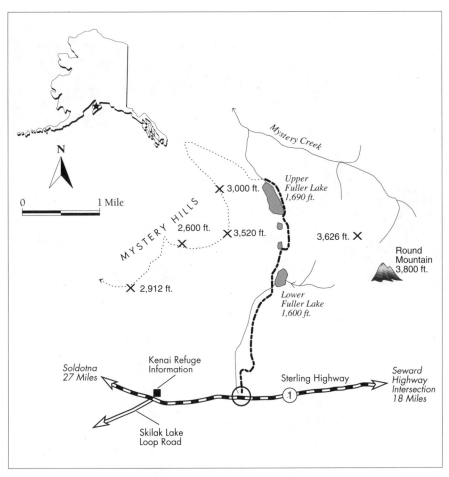

ferry and a mile east of the Kenai Refuge information station and the east junction of the Skilak Lake Loop Road.

The hike: Nestled into subalpine bowls between the alpine summits of Round Mountain and the Mystery Hills, the Fuller Lakes are relatively easy to reach on foot. The trail offers good camping, fishing, and off-trail access to the high country. The entire hike is in the Mystery Creek portion of the Kenai Wilderness.

The hike gains most of its elevation from the trailhead to the lower lake, and then gains only another 100 feet to the upper lake. The lower trail passes through spruce and birch forest with a few beautiful groves of aspen, and switches back by Fuller Creek at one point. Toward the top, there is a fine view back toward Skilak Lake.

Lower Fuller Lake, at about 1,600 feet elevation, is in the last large pocket of timber. Beavers have built a dam at the lake outlet, keeping the water level up.

Upper Fuller Lake and the Kenai Mountains.

The trail crosses the outlet stream and continues along the west side of the lake toward Upper Fuller, passing two smaller ponds on the way.

The upper lake, at 1,690 feet in smaller, scattered white spruce just below treeline, is over a barely discernible divide from the lower lake. The lower lake drains directly to the Kenai, while the upper lake is part of the Mystery Creek watershed. A less developed trail leads above the east shore to the far end of the lake.

There are good campsites at both lakes. Please use a camp stove and avoid building campfires.

Beyond Upper Fuller Lake. Round Mountain and the Mystery Hills are tantalizingly close above Upper Fuller, separated from the lake by a thin strip of mountain hemlock, willow and dwarf birch brush. To go up Round Mountain, you're on your own, but to get to the nearest Mystery Hills ridgeline, there is a well-beaten route to follow that avoids major bushwhacking. At the north end of the lake, continue beyond the maintained trail, crossing the lake's tiny outlet creek, and follow the route that sideslopes up to the west about 1.5 miles to the lower ridgeline. Even if you go only part way, the route has a good view into Mystery Creek.

From the ridgeline, it's possible to traverse the Mystery Hills, finally descending to the Sterling Highway at Mile 61 on the Skyline Trail, a very steep, 1-mile trail. This strenuous, 13-mile traverse follows the ridge's peaks and saddles, gaining over 5,000 feet in elevation.

Fishing. There are grayling in Lower Fuller, and Dolly Varden in Upper Fuller.

Trip summary:	A variety of shorter day, half-day, and overnight hikes on connecting trails along the Kenai River above Skilak Lake.
Distances:	Kenai River East: 2.5 miles one way.
	Kenai River West: 2 miles one way.
	River Loop: a 2.5-mile loop.
	The Kenai River Grand Tour: 6.3 miles total.
Special features:	A forest and river hike, fishing.
Location:	In the Skilak Lake area, east of Soldotna.
Difficulty:	Easy/moderate.
Trail type:	Less developed.
Total elevation gain:	100 to 500 feet, depending on the route chosen.
Best season:	Mid-May through early October.
Maps:	USGS Kenai B-1 (NE); Trails Illustrated *Kenai National Wildlife Refuge*, Alaska Road and Recreation Map *Kenai Lake and Vicinity*.
Manager:	Kenai National Wildlife Refuge.

Finding the trailheads:
Skilak Lake Loop Road directions. This hike and trips 14 to 17 begin on the Skilak Lake Loop Road. The Skilak road forms a 19-mile loop south of the Sterling Highway. The east junction is at Sterling Highway Mile 58, 20 miles west of the Sterling/Seward Highway intersection and 0.1 mile west of the Kenai Refuge information station. The west junction, at Sterling Mile 75, is about 19 miles east of Soldotna and 37 miles west of the Sterling/Seward Highway intersection.

The mileages on the Skilak road given in these directions are measured from the east junction, the most frequently traveled direction.
Kenai River Trail. The two trailheads for the Kenai River Trail are off the Skilak Lake Loop Road at Mile 0.6 (east trailhead to the upper river) and Mile 2.4 (west trailhead to the lower river). Both trailheads are on the south side of the road.

The hikes: The Kenai River Trail meanders along two sections of the river through forests of spruce, aspen, cottonwood, and birch. The hike crosses sections of the 1991 Pothole Lake Fire. It's the only real hiking trail on the entire length of the Kenai, a world-class trout and salmon stream. Scenery, fishing, and late-summer berries are all in good supply. Eagles, waterfowl, terns, and gulls hang out along the river, and bears are fairly common here during the big sockeye salmon runs in June and July.

The Pothole Lake Fire charred 7,900 acres in May, 1991. Now the burn is full of pioneer shrubs that add up to a moose delicatessen. Look for fireweed, wild rose, and raspberries in the burn.

The two trailheads offer a variety of hikes.

KENAI RIVER

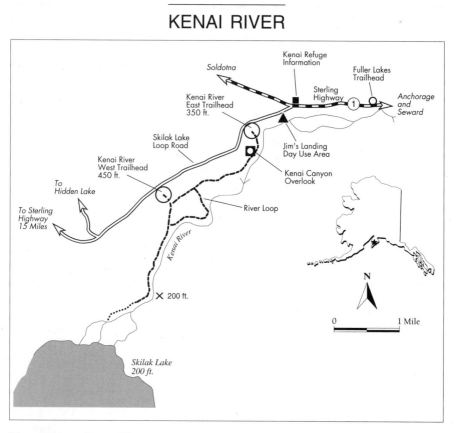

Kenai River East. The East Trail traverses low hills, follows the river briefly, and crosses a section of the 1991 burn before reaching the west trailhead in about 2.5 miles. There is an overlook of the Kenai River Canyon at 0.4 mile. If you plan to hike this section of the trail as a one-way hike with a vehicle shuttle, it saves some elevation gain to start the trip from the west trailhead.

From the east trailhead (elevation about 350 feet), follow an old road bed about 0.2 mile, where it intersects a foot trail to the right. Follow the path up onto the bluff above the river to the canyon overlook in another 0.2 mile. The trail then drops down to the river, here a beautiful green stream flowing smooth over a cobbled bed.

The trail climbs away from the river and crosses the burn. At the junction about 2 miles from the east trailhead, take the right fork for the shortest path to the west trailhead (about 550 feet elevation). Getting back to the east trailhead involves a return trip or a 1.8-mile road walk.

Kenai River West. The West Trail leads down to the Kenai and follows the river to an open cottonwood flat, a good spot for camping and fishing. Beyond the flat, a fishing route continues downriver.

The River Loop. From the west trailhead, hikers can also take the River Loop, a 2.5-mile loop that follows the river a short distance, passing foaming rapids, before returning to the west trailhead.

The Kenai River Grand Tour. To have it all, do the grand tour, about 6.3 miles plus the 1.8-mile road walk if you haven't shuttled a vehicle. Hike out to the river on the West Trail, return to the East Trail via the lower part of the River Loop, and hike out to the east trailhead.

Shorter hikes. Hike about 0.4 mile one way to the Kenai Canyon overlook from the east trailhead. Take care with kids along the edge of the canyon.

Fishing. The Lower Trail offers the best shot at catching fish. Most anglers are after sockeye salmon and rainbow trout, but there are also Dolly Varden and runs of silver salmon (late summer and fall). Sockeye are in the river in June and July, and rainbow and Dolly Varden fishing is good through the summer and fall.

Check the Alaska Department of Fish and Game regulations. The river is usually closed until mid-June to protect spawning fish, and special regulations are in effect.

---

13 HIDDEN CREEK AND SKILAK LAKE

Trip summary:	A shorter day or overnight hike to Skilak Lake, at the mouth of Hidden Creek.
Distance:	1.5 miles one way to Skilak Lake.
Special features:	Lake and mountain scenery, lakeshore camping, fishing.
Location:	East of Soldotna.
Difficulty:	Easy.
Trail type:	Less developed.
Total elevation gain:	Essentially none in, 200 feet out.
Best season:	Mid-May through early October.
Maps:	USGS Kenai B-1 (NW); Trails Illustrated *Kenai National Wildlife Refuge*, Alaska Road and Recreation Map *Kenai Lake and Vicinity*.
Manager:	Kenai National Wildlife Refuge.

Finding the trailhead: The Hidden Creek Trailhead is on the south side of the Skilak Lake Loop Road at Mile 4.7. For directions to the Skilak road, see Hike 12, Kenai River ("Finding the trailhead").

The hike: At 15 miles long and two to four miles wide, Skilak Lake is more than the average puddle; it's the second largest lake on the Kenai Refuge.

HIDDEN CREEK AND SKILAK LAKE

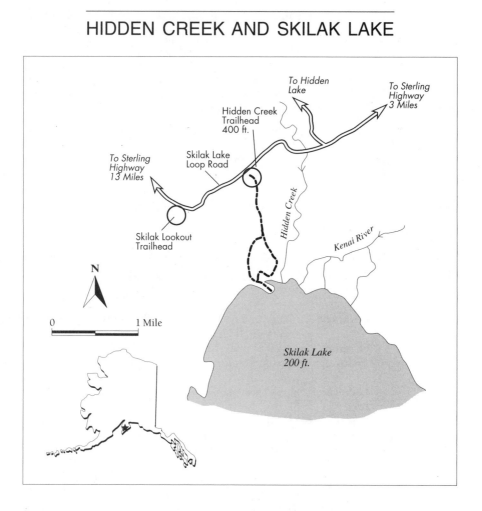

This hike to the lake offers views of the alpine ridges and peaks of the Kenai Mountains, good picnic and camping spots, and fishing.

The trail parallels Hidden Creek to the lake, gradually descending from the car park through thick spruce-birch forest. About a mile into the walk the trail forks—the right fork heads for Skilak Lake, and the left leads to Hidden Creek before circling back to the lake.

Take the right fork for the most direct route to the lake, another 0.5 mile away. The trail reaches the lake on a narrow gravel spit in a small cove, where driftwood lies in huge piles. There are fine campsites on the shore, but tie everything down, because Skilak is notorious for its howling gales. Continuing out onto the spit, the path ends on the beach at the mouth of Hidden Creek. The Kenai River empties into the lake a short distance east.

For a different way back, take the Hidden Creek side trail, to the right as you leave the lakeshore. There is a maze of smaller trails along the creek. When in doubt, stay left to stick with the main trail. In about 0.5 mile the

Skilak Lake near the mouth of the Kenai River and Hidden Creek.

trail loops back to the fork you passed on the way in. From here, take a right, and it's about a mile back to the parking area.

Watch for bears in the area, especially during the red salmon runs in June and July. Though the trail is a bit rooty, this is a good hike and a great destination for taking children along.

Fishing. Most anglers who use the trail cross Hidden Creek to fish the mouth of the Kenai River for rainbow trout and Dolly Varden. Hidden Creek is closed to all salmon fishing. Be sure to check the Alaska Department of Fish and Game regulations before wetting a line; special regulations are in effect here.

Trip summary:	Two shorter day hikes to viewpoints above Skilak Lake
Distance:	Skilak Lookout: 2.5 miles one way. Bear Mountain: 0.8 mile one way.
Special features:	Great views, good hikes for hearty families.
Location:	In the Skilak Lake area, east of Soldotna.
Difficulty:	Moderate.
Trail type:	Less developed.
Total elevation gain:	Skilak Lookout: 750 feet. Bear Mountain: 500 feet.
Best season:	Mid-May through early October.
Maps:	USGS Kenai B-1 (NW); Trails Illustrated *Kenai National Wildlife Refuge*, Alaska Road and Recreation Map *Kenai Lake and Vicinity*.
Manager:	Kenai National Wildlife Refuge.

```
2500                      2500
2000                      2000
1500                      1500
1000                      1000
 500                       500
FT.                       FT.
   MILES          5          MILES          5
      SKILAK                    BEAR
      LOOKOUT                   MOUNTAIN
```

Finding the trailheads: The Skilak Lookout Trailhead is at Mile 5.5 of the Skilak Lake Loop Road. Park on the north side of the road; the trail starts on the south side. The Bear Mountain trailhead is 0.5 mile farther out the Skilak Road at Mile 6. The Trailhead and parking area are on the north side of the road. For directions to the Skilak road, see Hike 12, Kenai River ("Finding the trailhead").

The hikes: The two trails offer fine views of the Skilak Lake country and the Kenai Mountains. Skilak Lookout, directly above the lake, is a longer hike; Bear Mountain is a shorter hike with a good view, but farther from the lake.

Skilak Lookout. The Skilak Lookout Trail is a bit steep, wet, and full of roots in a few places, but it still makes a decent longer family hike. The trip is best done as a day hike, as there are no reliable water and few campsites.

The trail climbs gradually through an open-canopied spruce forest and across open slopes that were scorched by a 1996 forest fire. As the trail nears the rocky peak, it climbs steeply. The view first unfolds to the east and southeast, where the Kenai River and the glacial Skilak River, with its huge delta, enter the lake.

At the top, where the wind will likely be blowing from the southeast (check out the growth of the limbs on the trees at the summit), there is a

SKILAK LOOKOUT/BEAR MOUNTAIN

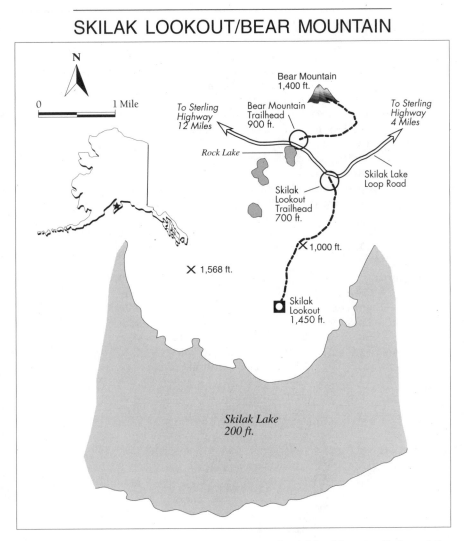

N

0   1 Mile

Bear Mountain
1,400 ft.

*To Sterling
Highway
12 Miles*

Bear Mountain
Trailhead
900 ft.

*To Sterling
Highway
4 Miles*

Rock Lake

Skilak Lake
Loop Road

Skilak
Lookout
Trailhead
700 ft.

X 1,000 ft.

X 1,568 ft.

Skilak
Lookout
1,450 ft.

*Skilak Lake
200 ft.*

180-degree view of the lake, and you can see how big this 15-mile-long lake really is. Alpine ridges of the Kenai Mountains lie to the south of the lake.

Be on bear alert late in the summer when raspberries and mountain ash berries are ripe. Look for moose feeding in the openings, and gray jays in the trees at the summit.

Bear Mountain. The Bear Mountain hike skirts the east flank of its name-sake mountain and climbs steeply, with occasional level stretches as it threads through open forests, brushy sideslopes and alder patches. Rocky ledges and outcrops poke out of the hillside here and there.

A short way from the summit the first view of Skilak Lake and the Skilak River lies to the southeast. On the east summit, the view includes the Kenai River, the Skilak Lake Lookout Peak, and to the southwest, the end of the Kenai Mountain chain and the forested plain of the Kenai Peninsula stretching toward Cook Inlet.

Trip summary:	A half-day or overnight traverse that links four low-elevation lakes on the Kenai Refuge.
Distance:	4.5 miles.
Special features:	Lakes, fishing, wildlife.
Location:	In the Skilak Lake area, east of Soldotna.
Difficulty:	Easy.
Trail type:	Less developed.
Total elevation gain:	About 200 feet.
Best season:	Mid-May through early October.
Maps:	USGS Kenai B-1 (NW), C-1 (SW), and C-2 (SE); Trails Illustrated *Kenai National Wildlife Refuge*, Alaska Road and Recreation Map *Kenai Lake and Vicinity*.
Manager:	Kenai National Wildlife Refuge.

Key points:

From Engineer Lake		From Kelly Lake
0.0	Engineer Lake Trailhead	4.5
1.0	North end, Engineer Lake	3.5
2.5	Hidden Lake spur trail	2.0
3.0	Hikers Lake	1.5
3.5	East end of Kelly Lake	1.0
4.5	Kelly Lake Trailhead	0.0

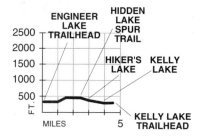

Finding the trailhead: This hike is a traverse between the Sterling Highway at Kelly Lake and the Skilak Lake Loop Road at Engineer Lake.

The access road to **Kelly Lake** is at Sterling Highway Mile 68, between the two junctions of the Skilak Lake Loop Road (seven miles east of the west junction and ten miles west of the east junction). Turn south off the highway and follow the access road about 0.7 mile to Kelly Lake, taking the left fork of the road at about the halfway point. The trail leaves the parking area at the far end, by the boat launch.

Engineer Lake is at the end of a 0.3-mile access road from Mile 9.5 of the Skilak Lake Loop Road, about halfway between its east and west junctions

SEVEN LAKES

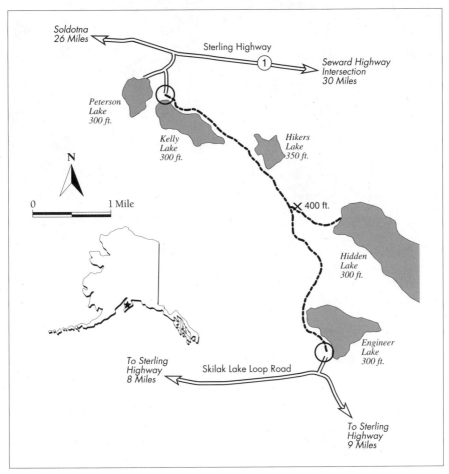

with the Sterling. The trailhead is by the boat launch. For directions to the Skilak road, see Hike 12, Kenai River ("Finding the trailhead").

The hike: Seven Lakes is a lake and lowland trail that reaches the shorelines of four lakes—Engineer, Hidden, Hikers, and Kelly Lakes. Shuttling a car between the trailheads is an easy way to hike this trail if you have two vehicles with your party.

If you're counting, the fifth, sixth, and seventh lakes lie north of the Sterling Highway. Before the Sterling was built, the Skilak road was the highway, and the trail extended down a chain of seven lakes to the East Fork of the Moose River. Now it's no longer maintained north of Kelly Lake and the Sterling Highway, and four lakes are all you get.

It's a flat to rolling walk with wildlife all around—look for moose and beaver and their signs, and signs of bear and wolf. Use your binoculars at

A Kenai Refuge moose, Seven Lakes Trail.

the lakes to pick out loons, scoters, mergansers, terns, cranes, and other waterfowl and shorebirds. Sit quietly by the lakes in early morning or evening and listen for the calls of loons and cranes. There are campsites on Kelly, Hidden, and Engineer Lakes, but Hikers Lake pretty much belongs to the moose.

The country along the lakes is flat with low-growing spruce forest, and the rolling hills between the lakes are covered with stands of bright-green aspens that turn their trademark gold in autumn. Near a meadow north of Engineer Lake, some of the aspens are as much as two feet in diameter. From the low ridge between Hidden and Hikers lakes, the trail overlooks acres of aspens.

The lightly-used, 0.5-mile side trail to the roadless end of Hidden Lake forks off the main trail on a small ridge between Engineer Lake and Hikers Lake. The trail fades as it approaches the lake, but leads across a small stream to a good campsite, which is also accessible by boat from the Hidden Lake Campground at the other end of the lake.

If you're visiting in mid-summer, don't forget the bug dope, and anytime you go, take along binoculars for wildlife viewing.

Shorter hikes. From the south trailhead, hike along Engineer Lake as far as you like, or from the north trailhead, try a short hike on the shoreline of Kelly Lake.

Fishing. Shore fishing is fair in the lakes along the trail. Engineer Lake still may have some hatchery silver salmon from previous stockings, but it is no longer stocked because of the fear that hatchery fish might mix with wild

Kenai silvers lower in the watershed. The most plentiful fish in Hidden Lake are lake trout and kokanee (landlocked salmon); most anglers use boats. There are also rainbows and Dolly Varden in the lake. Kelly Lake has rainbows and a few Dollies. Northern pike, a predatory game fish, have begun to show up in the Seven Lakes area.

16 CAPTAIN COOK

Trip summary:	A half-day hike on a Cook Inlet beach, and a shorter walk on an interpretive trail, in the Captain Cook State Recreation Area.
Distance:	Bishop Creek beach hike: 2.5 miles one way; Yurick Memorial Trail: a 1-mile interpretive loop.
Special features:	Coastal scenery, birds, geology, a short interpretive trail, and two developed campgrounds near the hikes.
Location:	North of Kenai on Cook Inlet.
Difficulty:	Easy.
Trail type:	Beach walk: a route. Yurick Trail: a more developed trail.
Total elevation gain:	Less than 100 feet.
Best season:	Mid-May to early October.
Maps:	USGS Kenai D-3 (SW).
Manager:	Alaska State Parks, Kenai Area.

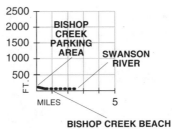

Finding the trailhead: From Soldotna, turn north on the Kenai Spur Highway at Sterling Highway Mile 94.2. Drive about 35 miles to the recreation area entrance.

For the beach hike, drive to the Bishop Creek Campground, 0.3 mile from the entrance. The trail begins in the parking area just off the highway. Bishop Creek is a tent-only camping area.

To get to the campground and the Yurick Trail, drive 3.4 miles past the entrance to the end of pavement at a T intersection. Take the left fork 0.3 mile to the Discovery Campground entrance on the left. The trailhead, on the left, is about fifty feet before you reach the fee station and campground road fork. There are also several spur trails to the Yurick trail from various points in the campground, handy if you're camping there.

CAPTAIN COOK

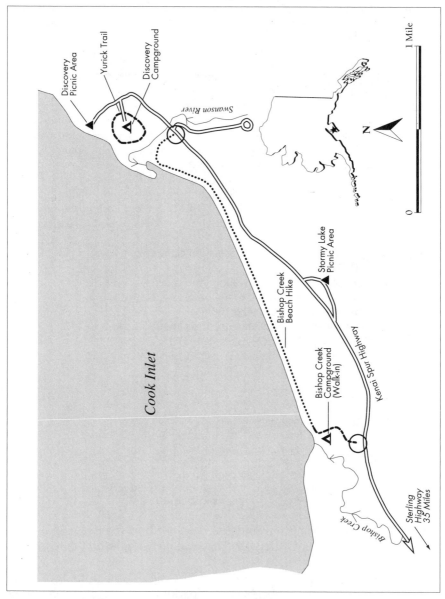

The hikes: Captain Cook is a small state recreation area on the north coast of the Kenai Peninsula. The park fronts on Cook Inlet, at the mouth of the Swanson River. Besides these short hikes, visitors can camp and picnic, boat and fish on Stormy Lake, and cross-country ski in winter.

Bishop Creek Beach Hike. The easiest way to do the park's beach ramble is to walk whatever distance you like from the Bishop Creek Campground and return the same way. It's about 0.2 mile from the Bishop Creek parking

Beach at the mouth of Bishop Creek, Captain Cook State Recreation Area.

area to the coast, and the pristine beach stretches about 2.5 miles from Bishop Creek to the Swanson River.

Just across the river is the Discovery Campground, but unless you like swimming across deep, muddy streams, ending the hike there isn't a terrific option. Instead, either retrace your steps to Bishop Creek or climb the 100-foot bluff by the river and bushwhack back to the park road at the Swanson River bridge, about 0.5 mile from the beach. The latter option makes a 3-mile hike, with a road walk, hitchhike or shuttle of 2.8 miles on the park road back to Bishop Creek.

Parts of the beach may be underwater at the highest tides, approximately 24 feet, so check the tide table at the Bishop Creek bulletin board before setting out. Don't venture out onto the huge mud flats exposed at low tide—these can be as dangerous as quicksand. Also, remember that the tidal range is extremely high on Cook Inlet, and the tide really rushes as the high tide approaches.

Cook Inlet beaches definitely aren't Hawaii. The scenery, solitude, and wildlife make this a different kind of beach experience. By Bishop Creek, the ice-cream peaks of the Chigmit Mountains across Cook Inlet form a backdrop for snarls of driftwood logs resting on the sand, lumps of rocks lying offshore, and flocks of shorebirds working the tidal flats for food. Look for shorebirds like willets and sandpipers, and for gulls, terns, bald eagles, kingfishers, and goldeneyes and other ducks. Beluga whales may be swimming offshore in late summer, and sandhill cranes and trumpeter swans stop here on their spring and fall migrations.

The west end of the beach, near Bishop Creek, is sandy; the east end, closer to the Swanson River, is rockier. There are huge granite boulders, shales, conglomerates, and many kinds of volcanic rocks along the beach, and you might even find an agate or two.

Yurick Memorial Trail. The Yurick Trail is an interpretive trail dedicated to the memory of Maggie Yurick, a long-time state and national park ranger. The trail loops around Discovery Campground, through the forest and along the bluffs above Cook Inlet and the mouth of the Swanson River. A side trail at the northwest corner of the campground leads to a bluff over the inlet, and a fork switches down steeply to the beach at the mouth of the Swanson River.

The trail guide covers the physical shape of the land, its forests and wet-lands, and the lives of the Dena'ina Native people in traditional times. One of the points of interest is a Dena'ina barabara, a partially subterranean ("pit") house site.

HOMER

There are no national parks, forests, or refuges near Homer, but State Parks and two private, non-profit groups manage trails near town and across Kachemak Bay from the city. There are new trails in the works, too, for Kachemak Bay State Park.

The mountains of Kachemak Bay State Park, a wilderness saved by the work of a coalition of community and conservation groups.

Trip summary:	Half-day or longer day hikes or a two to three day backpack to Grewingk Lake and the alpine ridge south of the Grewingk valley.
Distances:	Grewingk Lake: 1.3 or 3.2 miles one way. Alpine Ridge overlook: 2.7 to 6.2 miles one way.
Special features:	A scenic glacial lake, views of Grewingk Glacier, and alpine ridge rambling. The hikes are accessible by boat from Homer, 10 miles away.
Location:	In the Halibut Cove area of Kachemak Bay State Park, across the Bay from Homer.
Trail type:	Less developed trail to route.
Best season:	Grewingk Valley: June to mid-October. Alpine ridge: July through September.
Maps:	USGS Seldovia C-4 (NE and SE) and C-3 (trails not shown); Alaska State Park brochure *Kachemak Bay State Park Trails Guide*; Alaska Road & Recreation Map *Kachemak Bay*.
Manager:	Kachemak Bay State Park.

Key one-way mileages, difficulties, and elevation gains:

Grewingk Lake from Grewingk Glacier Trailhead: 3.2 miles, easy, 200 feet

Grewingk Lake from Saddle Trailhead: 1.3 miles, moderate, 500 feet

Alpine Ridge from Grewingk Glacier Trailhead: 6.2 miles, moderately strenuous, 2,200 feet

Alpine Ridge from Saddle Trailhead: 2.7 miles, moderately strenuous, 2,200 feet

Alpine Ridge from Grewingk Lake: 3.6 miles, moderately strenuous, 2,000 feet

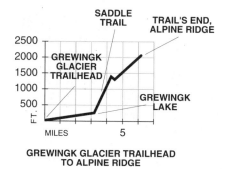

GREWINGK GLACIER TRAILHEAD
TO ALPINE RIDGE

Finding the trailhead: To get to the Grewingk Glacier trails, take a water taxi from the boat harbor on the Homer Spit. The spit is at the end of the Sterling Highway, 230 miles south of Anchorage and about four miles south

GREWINGK GLACIER

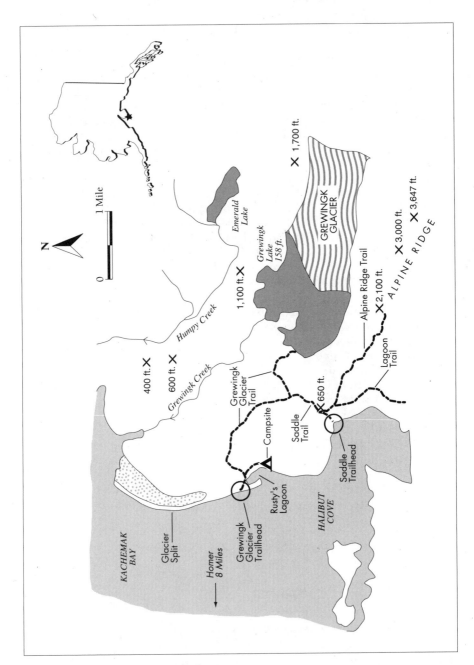

X 1,700 ft.

GREWINGK GLACIER

X 3,000 ft.
X 3,647 ft.

ALPINE RIDGE

Emerald Lake

Grewingk Lake 158 ft.

Alpine Ridge Trail

X 2,100 ft.

1,100 ft. X

Lagoon Trail

N

1 Mile

0

Humpy Creek

400 ft. X X 600 ft.

Grewingk Creek

Grewingk Glacier Trail

X 650 ft.

Campsite

Saddle Trail

Saddle Trailhead

Rusty's Lagoon

HALIBUT COVE

Grewingk Glacier Trailhead

KACHEMAK BAY

Glacier Spit

Homer 8 Miles

A backpack kitchen with a view at Grewingk Lake.

of downtown Homer. See Appendix 3 for water taxi information, or check with the Alaska State Parks office in Homer (location and phone number in Appendix 1) or the Homer Chamber of Commerce Visitor Center for a current list of water taxi operators. It's possible to kayak to the trails, but the crossing from Homer is long and exposed, so it is recommended only for skilled, experienced kayakers in good weather.

The **Grewingk Glacier Trailhead**, at the Glacier Spit landing on the gravelly beach north of Rusty's Lagoon, is 8 miles from Homer. This landing is outside Halibut Cove and open to the weather from the west. In poor weather or in the afternoon after the wind has come up, landing here may be a problem. The spit is a great beach camping area (bring water), There is also a protected, woodsy campsite at the back of Rusty's Lagoon, next to a freshwater stream.

The **Saddle Trailhead**, 10 miles from Homer, is in a small rocky bay inside Halibut Cove. The landing is rocky, but more protected than the Glacier Spit landing.

There are markers visible from the water at each trailhead.

The hikes: Choosing your beginning trailhead is the most complicated thing about this trip. About the easiest way to see the whole area is to backpack to Grewingk Lake by either trail and day hike the Alpine Ridge, leaving by way of the Saddle Trail, but hey, be creative.

One thing to consider is that the Saddle Trail is very steep—it crosses a 400-foot saddle in the first 0.2 mile. As of this writing, the trail just above the landing is extremely eroded and requires some caution. Hiking to Grewingk Lake is shorter but much steeper from here than from the Glacier Spit landing. For a day trip on the alpine ridge, the Saddle Trail is definitely the better choice.

Grewingk Glacier Trail. The trail begins in coastal forest and hugs the south side of the glacier's rocky outwash, passing progressively younger stands of cottonwood and alder until it reaches the lake, where only alder patches and colonizing wildflowers survive. The trail's end is on the gravelly shoreline of the lake, with the glacier in the distance but with no safe access.

The Rusty's Lagoon campsite is about 0.5 mile from the trailhead, about 0.2 mile on the main trail and 0.3 mile on a spur trail to the south. The currently unmaintained Grewingk Glacier Self-Guided Nature Trail, a 1991 Eagle Scout project, is a short loop that leaves the main trail a little less than halfway to the lake. The park may eventually upgrade the walk and reprint the brochure. The Grewingk trail intersects the Saddle Trail in just under 3 miles.

Grewingk Lake. Gaggles of gulls, shorebirds, and icebergs and bergy bits greet hikers on the shore of Grewingk Lake. Wildflowers like dwarf fireweed, yellow oxytrope, and yellow dryas poke out of the gravel beach, and the blue ice of Grewingk Glacier sparkles in the distance at the head of the lake.

If you plan to camp at the lake, look for sheltered tent sites behind the alders near the shore. Please practice low-impact camping and human waste disposal here; use is increasing and the lakeshore could suffer from it. In good weather there may be a fair bit of day use and flightseeing traffic near the lake.

The lake's water is glacial and silty—let it settle before treating it, or snag a piece of the glacial ice near shore to melt for fresh water. There are lots of birds along the shallow edge of the lake, so give your water a good boil.

Alpine Ridge. The climb to the Alpine Ridge overlook is a bit stiff but the view on a good day is fantastic, and wandering out the ridge from the overlook could entertain even an MTV junkie for a whole day. The trail begins in a deep, quiet spruce forest in the saddle between Grewingk Lake and the Saddle Trailhead, with the distant sound of the ocean in the background. Turn east, or uphill, at the junction, and in about 0.2 mile, bear left at the intersection with the Lagoon Trail. Listen for woodpeckers and wood thrushes as you climb.

The climb begins to level out at about 1,400 feet elevation, and the first distant views open. Look up Halibut Cove to the head of the lagoon and more of mountainous Kachemak Bay State Park. Across the cove is the town of Halibut Cove, and the Homer Spit, the cliffs along the northeast end of Kachemak Bay, and the Grewingk Creek valley round out the views.

Above the brush the trail is marked with a few cairns, but the hikers' path is well worn and easy to follow if the trail is snowfree. Find the overlook of the glacier on an alpine knob at 2,100 feet elevation. The knob is the end of the Alpine Ridge Trail, but it could be just the beginning of an alpine adventure. The basin below the peak has some fine meltwater ponds, wild-flowers, and blueberries. The ridge stays broad and fairly gently-sloped for almost four more miles, with fine views of the intricately-crevassed glacier below.

Other trails. The 5.5 mile **Lagoon Trail** connects the Grewingk Glacier Trails with the China Poot Lake/Wosnesenski River Trail (Hike 18) at the head of Halibut Cove Lagoon. The Lagoon Trail is a rough hike, involving about 1,700 feet of elevation gain and a potentially dangerous crossing of glacier-fed Halibut Creek.

The park plans to build new trails north of Grewingk Creek to Humpy Creek and the Emerald Lake area.

18 *CHINA POOT LAKE AND WOSNESENSKI RIVER*

Trip summary:	A two to three day trip to China Poot Lake, Poot Peak and the Wosnesenski River in the Kachemak Bay State Park backcountry.
Distances:	China Poot Lake: 2.5 miles one way. Wosnesenski River: 5 miles one way. South Poot Peak Spur: 6.3 miles one way.
Special features:	Alpine scenery, fishing, and a glacial river. The hikes are accessible by boat from Homer, 13 miles away.
Location:	In the Halibut Cove Lagoon area of Kachemak Bay State Park, across the Bay from Homer.
Difficulty:	China Poot Lake and Wosnesenski River: moderate. South Poot Peak Spur: moderately strenuous.
Trail type:	China Poot Lake/Wosnesenski River Trail: more developed to China Poot Lake, less developed beyond. South Poot Peak Spur Trail: more developed but steep.
Total elevation gain:	China Poot Lake: 600 feet in, 450 feet out. Wosnesenski River: 900 feet in, 650 feet out. South Poot Peak: 2,100 feet in, 500 feet out.
Best season:	June through early October, but the Poot Peak area is best from July through mid-September.
Maps:	USGS Seldovia C-4 (SE) (trails not shown); Alaska State Park brochure *Kachemak Bay State Park Trails Guide*; Alaska Road and Recreation Map *Kachemak Bay*.
Manager:	Kachemak Bay State Park.

Key points:
  0.4   Coalition Trail to China Poot Bay
  2.5   China Poot Lake
  2.8   Poot Peak route junction
  3.8   South Poot Peak Spur Trail junction
  5.0   Wosnesenski River

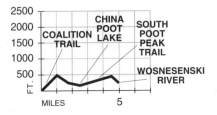

Finding the trailhead: The trailhead is at the dock at the head of Halibut Cove Lagoon, about 13 miles by water from Homer. Take a water taxi from the boat harbor on the Homer Spit, at the end of the Sterling Highway, 230 miles south of Anchorage and about 4 miles south of downtown Homer.

It's possible to kayak to the trailhead, but the crossing from Homer is long and exposed, so is recommended only for skilled, experienced kayakers in good weather. Another possibility is to charter a floatplane in Homer and fly to China Poot Lake.

See Appendix 3 for water taxi information, or check with the Alaska State Parks office in Homer (location and phone number in Appendix 1) or the Homer Chamber of Commerce Visitor Center for a current list of water taxi and air charter operators.

The hikes: The head of Halibut Cove Lagoon may be busy in mid-summer, but decent solitude is just up the trail. Anglers fish for salmon off the dock, and there are three fee cabins at the head of the lagoon (see Appendix 2 for how to reserve one). There are also a ranger station on the bluff above the dock and a camp area on the shore to the west. To find the trail, take the boardwalk to the ranger station, go down the steps past the station into a clearing, and look for the path toward the right side of the clearing.

The **China Poot Lake/Wosnesenski River Trail** begins as a path that climbs and dips through a lush Sitka spruce-hemlock forest with an understory of ferns, devil's club, and blueberries. It intersects the Coalition Trail to China Poot Bay in about 0.4 mile, passes two smaller lakes, and crosses a grassy cottonwood flat before reaching China Poot Lake.

A mountain backdrop lies behind China Poot, a pretty forested lake. Cronin Island, toward the lake's south end, is private. Hanging above the east side of the lake like a big chocolate drop is Poot Peak. There are a few campsites near the lake on Moose Valley Creek, the lake's inlet stream.

From the lake to Wosnesenski River (no, there's no nickname, and locals stumble over the name too), the trail twists along the hilly shorelines of China Poot Lake and the unnamed lake to the south. After climbing a low hill, the trail drops into the wide, braided river valley. The open gravel flats offer good campsites and decent likelihood of a breeze to keep the bugs at bay. The river's course limits exploring on the north side of the valley; crossing the river may not be possible.

The **South Poot Peak Spur Trail** cuts away from the main trail about 3.8 miles from the trailhead, climbs steeply through a gap south of Poot Peak, and emerges onto the peak's southeast shoulder. The country around

90

CHINA POOT LAKE AND WOSNESENSKI RIVER

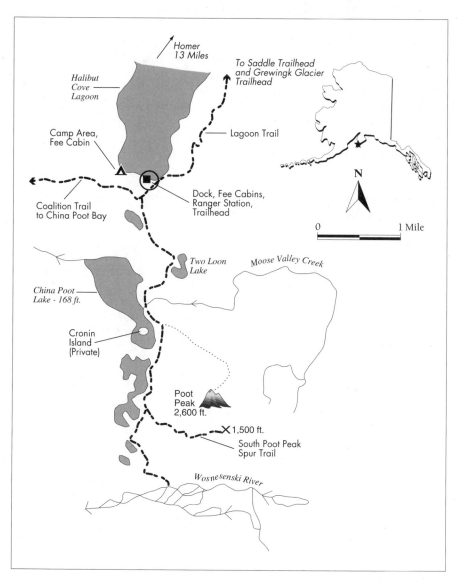

Homer
13 Miles

Halibut
Cove
Lagoon

To Saddle Trailhead
and Grewingk Glacier
Trailhead

Camp Area,
Fee Cabin

Lagoon Trail

Coalition Trail
to China Poot Bay

Dock, Fee Cabins,
Ranger Station,
Trailhead

Two Loon
Lake

Moose Valley Creek

China Poot
Lake - 168 ft.

Cronin
Island
(Private)

Poot
Peak
2,600 ft.

✕ 1,500 ft.

South Poot Peak
Spur Trail

Wosnesenski River

N

0   1 Mile

the peak is a mountain wonderland, with acres of chocolate lilies, forget-me-nots, lupine, columbine, and other flowers and views of glaciers, mountains, and alpine meadows. The constructed trail peters out about 2.5 miles from the trail junction.

A very primitive route leads up from Mile 2.8 of the main trail to the north side of Poot Peak. The route is rough and very steep, more of an eroded gully than a trail. Intermittent cairns mark the route beyond treeline.

It's possible to summit Poot Peak, but the route is very steep over loose scree, rotten rock, and, earlier in the summer, steep snowfields, so only seasoned scramblers should try it. Using this route contributes to serious erosion, so is not recommended.

Shorter hikes. Staying in one of the fee cabins and day hiking the China Poot Lake or Coalition Trails makes a good family trip, and can be combined with salmon fishing in the lagoon.

Fishing. There are rainbow trout in China Poot Lake.

Other trails. The park plans to build a new trail up Moose Valley Creek to connect with the South Poot Peak Spur Trail. These trails would make a loop of about 10 miles around Poot Peak. New fee cabins are planned in Moose Valley and on China Poot Lake.

19 ISLAND PENINSULA

Trip summary:	Shorter day hikes and naturalist programs at the Center for Alaskan Coastal Studies field station on the south coast of Kachemak Bay.
Distances:	A variety of trails, from 0.1 to 2 miles one way.
Special features:	Tidepools, coastal forest, a bog, and a small lake. The CACS station, accessible by boat from Homer, offers tours that include hiking and naturalist programs.
Location:	On Island Peninsula, across Kachemak Bay from Homer.
Difficulty:	Easy to moderate.
Trail type:	Less developed.
Total elevation gain:	Up to 400 feet.
Best season:	Memorial Day to Labor Day. Plan your trip for minus tide days for the best in tidepooling.
Maps:	USGS Seldovia C-4 (SE) (trails not shown); CACS trail description and map.
Manager:	The Center for Alaskan Coastal Studies.

Finding the trailhead: The CACS field station is on the Peterson Bay side of Island Peninsula, about five miles across Kachemak Bay from the Homer Spit. The field station is open to visitors on day tours that include hiking the field station trails and learning about the bay's forest and marine ecology. Booking for the day tour is through the tour operator, and transportation from Homer is by tour boat.

The Center offers overnight tours by special arrangement for school or private groups of ten or more. Contact the Center's business office. Overnight visitors use the cabin at the station, but they have to bring their own food, sleeping bags, and pads.

See Appendix 1 for the addresses and phone numbers of the Center's business office and the tour operator.

ISLAND PENINSULA

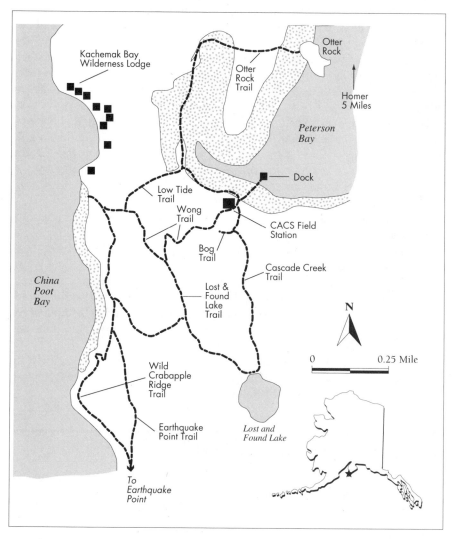

The hikes: The Center for Alaskan Coastal Studies is a local non-profit education group that focuses on the coastal and marine ecology of Kachemak Bay. The group's field station occupies part of Island Peninsula, a small peninsula between Peterson Bay and China Poot Bay, on the south side of Kachemak Bay across from Homer. The peninsula is an island at extreme high tides, when saltwater laps over its narrow connection to the mainland.

The peninsula's spruce/hemlock rain forest and the intertidal zone on Peterson and China Poot bays are the field station's biological high points. On days when there are minus tides, visitors get to explore the beach and the intertidal zone and meet the critters that live there: clams, mussels, sea urchins, sea worms, sea stars, and if you're lucky, an octopus. The field station also has a marine tank for introducing visitors to intertidal fauna when the tides aren't right for tidepooling.

Here is a sampling of the hikes on the peninsula:

Bog Trail: an easy, 0.1 mile walk one way to a boardwalk over a small bog with interesting plant life.

China Poot Bay: an easy, 1-mile hike one way via the Low Tide or Wong Trails to the west side of the peninsula, and the fine tide pools and habitat of China Poot Bay. Naturalists lead group hikes here to view marine life at low tide.

Otter Rock Trail: an easy, lower-tide hike, 1 mile one way, to a gravel spit that looks out on Kachemak Bay. The walk crosses Island Peninsula's lagoon, so keeping an eye on the tide and your watch are important, as the tide may reach the lagoon two hours before high tide.

Lost and Found Lake: an easy 1.5-mile loop on the Cascade Creek, Lost and Found Lake, and Wong trails to a small, forested lake.

Earthquake Point: a moderate hike, 2 miles one way, to a fine viewpoint of the Kachemak coast. The trail is more difficult and passes along some potentially dangerous cliffs, beyond the Wild Crabapple Ridge Trail.

Other CACS trails. CACS has developed a trail system on the Carl Wynn Nature Center property, on the bluff above the east end of Homer. An accessible boardwalk leads to a viewing deck in one of Homer's incredible wildflower meadows, and about two miles of easy trails meander through acres of forest, meadow, and wetland. In late June, these meadows look like gardens of chocolate lilies.

The Wynn Center is open to the public only on guided walks given by Center volunteers. Contact CACS for a schedule. The nature center is on Skyline Drive, east of East Hill Road.

---

20 CALVIN AND COYLE NATURE TRAIL

Trip summary:	A shorter, self-guided interpretive loop trail on a Kachemak Heritage Land Trust preserve.
Distance:	A 0.8-mile loop.
Special features:	A trail brochure on forest ecology and a deck with a view of the Beluga Lake wetlands.
Location:	A mile east of downtown Homer.
Difficulty:	Easy.
Trail type:	More developed.
Total elevation gain:	Essentially none.
Best season:	May through October.
Maps:	USGS Seldovia C-4 (NW) (trail not shown). A trail guide is available at the trailhead, at the land trust office, and at the Fish and Wildlife Service visitor center in Homer (see Appendix 1 for locations).
Manager:	Kachemak Heritage Land Trust.

CALVIN AND COYLE NATURE TRAIL

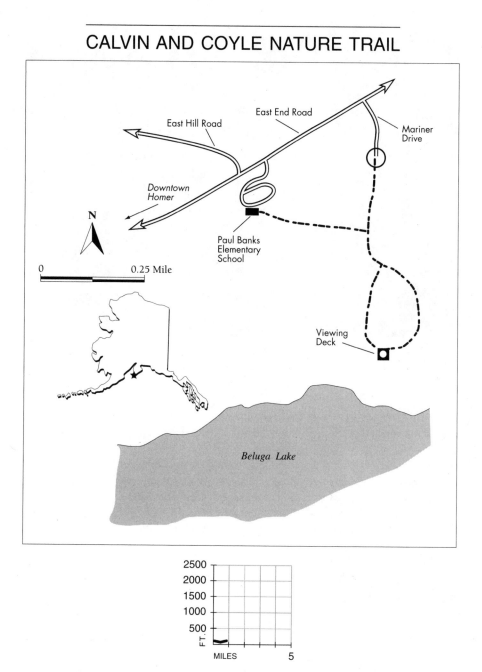

Finding the trailhead: From the corner of Lake Street and Pioneer Avenue in Homer, drive 1.1 miles east on East End Road (the extension of Pioneer Avenue) to Mariner Drive. Turn right (south) and drive 0.1 mile to the trailhead at the end of the road.

Tall lupines in wildflower meadows on the Homestead Trail, near the Reuben Call Memorial.

The hike: This pleasant nature trail, built by volunteers with donated materials, wanders through eleven acres of forest donated to the Kachemak Heritage Land Trust by Dr. Maurice Coyle and D. Bailey Calvin. KHLT is a private, non-profit land trust that serves the Kenai Peninsula.

The trail guide interprets the ecology of this spruce-hemlock coastal forest, including plant succession, forest animals, the Lutz spruce (a natural hybrid of the Sitka and white spruce), and the role of mosses, lichens, and fungi in the forest. If you can never remember the botany rhyme that starts "Sedges have edges...", this guide is for you.

The highlight of the walk is a viewing deck that looks out on the wetlands around the upper end of Beluga Lake, a freshwater lake just above sea level. Swans, other waterfowl, and shorebirds nest here in the snowfree season, and moose winter in the wetlands.

The trail is a little damp here and there, but the wettest places are covered with wood chips for an easy stroll. A connecting trail ties the nature trail to Paul Banks Elementary School, 0.3 mile west.

KHLT, the oldest land trust in Alaska, holds summer programs on the Calvin and Coyle trail, including natural history hikes and birding. Ask the land trust (see Appendix 1) for a summer program guide.

The Homestead Trail. The Homestead Trail, KHLT's first community trail, leads about 6 miles between the hills north of Homer and the Sterling Highway west of town. The most scenic section is the easy one-mile (one way) walk to the Reuben Call Memorial, where meadows thick with wildflowers and views of mountains and ocean combine for a fine short hike. Contact KHLT (see Appendix 1) for its Guide to the Homestead Trail.

To find the Reuben Call section of the trail, drive up West Hill Road from the Sterling Highway west of Homer, turn left on Diamond Ridge Road, and look for the Homestead Trail sign and parking lot two miles ahead on the left (south), opposite Rucksack Drive. Take the trail to the south, or bay, side of the road.

TURNAGAIN ARM

Anchorage's backyard fjord, Turnagain Arm, lies in the basin between the Chugach and Kenai Mountains. Chugach State Park and Chugach National Forest trails lead into the mountains from the Seward Highway and other roads. The mountains along the Arm were the toughest country on the historic Iditarod Trail, back when dog teams and prospectors braved deep snow and avalanches on the winter trail in the early 1900s. Now Southcentral Alaskans are building a commemorative Iditarod Trail in the Girdwood valley.

21   GULL ROCK

Trip summary:	A longer day hike or overnight trip to Gull Rock, along the south coast of Turnagain Arm.
Distance:	5.1 miles one way.
Special features:	Coast and forest scenery; historic interest.
Location:	At the end of the Hope Highway outside Hope.
Difficulty:	Moderate.
Trail type:	More developed.
Total elevation gain:	About 600 feet in each direction.
Best season:	Mid-May to early October.
Maps:	USGS Seward D-8, Trails Illustrated *Kenai National Wildlife Refuge*.
Manager:	Chugach National Forest, Seward Ranger District.

Key points:
2.0   Halfway Island
4.8   Johnson Creek
5.1   Gull Rock

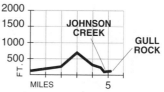

Finding the trailhead: Drive 70 miles south of Anchorage and turn northwest onto the Hope Highway. Drive about 18 miles into the Forest Service's Porcupine Creek Campground at the end of the road. The trailhead is at the far (west) end of the campground.

GULL ROCK

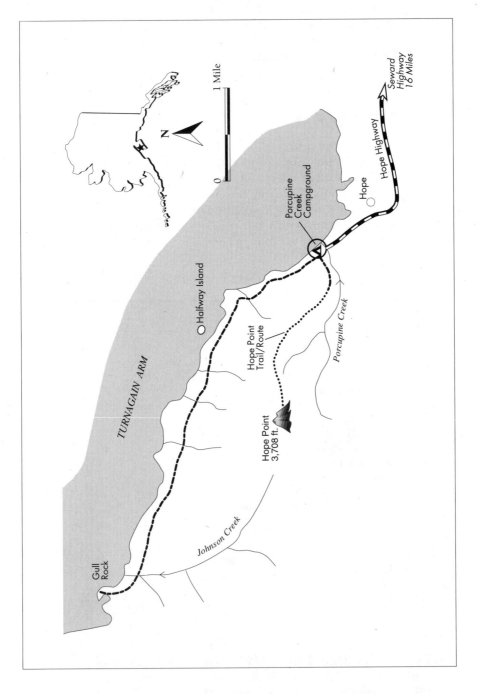

The hike: The Gull Rock Trail crosses the forested slope above Turnagain Arm from the end of the Hope road to Gull Rock, a forested headland that juts out into the Arm. This is one of the earliest hikes to open on the Kenai Peninsula in the spring. The trail follows an old wagon road that used to run along the coast.

The theme for the Gull Rock hike is variety: leaf-carpeted sections of trail through birch woods, bluffs with views of Turnagain Arm, and the Chugach Mountains, small streams running through quiet forest, talus, and tundra slopes, and dark, mossy forests of hemlock and Sitka spruce. The trail crosses several small streams. The only large creek is Johnson Creek, about 0.3 mile from the end of the trail at Gull Rock. Watch for mountain bikes. The trail is popular with bikers, and the narrow trail dips and twists enough that visibility is limited.

About two miles into the hike, catch a glimpse of Halfway Island, a small rock a short way offshore. Most of the last half of the hike is through a forest of mature spruce and hemlock. On the older trees, you can distinguish the hemlock by its furrowed bark from the spruce and its jigsaw-puzzle bark. From a distance, hemlock has a droopy top and the spruce a straight one.

The hike crosses into the Kenai National Wildlife Refuge a few minutes before reaching Johnson Creek. The old stumps along the trail may tip you off that there was once a sawmill nearby—Johnson Creek was the place. The mill cut ties for the Alaska Railroad in the early 1900s.

The sound of a strong wind in the trees may be the first clue that you're nearly to Gull Rock. The wind nearly always blows here, mainly from the

The town of Hope from the Hope Point Trail.

east, as you'll be able to see by the spreading, low-growing spruce trees on the Rock.

When the maintained trail reaches Gull Rock, it forks into several smaller trails. There are a few good campsites in sheltered spots under the trees, but campers will need to carry water from Johnson Creek. Please don't build fires here.

Follow the side trails to explore the headland. The rocky outcrops provide great views over the coast. Look for gulls wheeling in the breeze and listen for the surf crashing on the rocks below. If the tide has retreated, there may be wild ripple patterns in the mudflats. Remember that the mudflats are like quicksand, and don't venture out on them.

Before hiking out, enjoy a moment of peace listening to the birds, the surf, and the wind.

Other hikes. The **Hope Point Trail** is a steep, unmaintained, eroding trail to the alpine ridge above Porcupine Campground and a route to Hope Point (elevation 3,708 feet, about 3 very steep miles one way). The hike begins on the south side of the campground road where it crosses Porcupine Creek, between the entrance sign and fee station. The view of Turnagain Arm from the ridge is fantastic.

Shorter hikes. The first 0.3 mile of the Hope Point Trail is a gentle climb along Porcupine Creek and makes a pleasant short walk. A short hike out the Gull Rock Trail is also a good option for families camping in the campground.

Whether walking one of the trails or just strolling around the campground, be aware of baneberry—a poisonous berry, either red or white—that grows in bushels in the area.

22 *PORTAGE VALLEY*

Trip summary:	Three shorter day hikes in the Portage Valley near Portage Glacier and the Begich, Boggs Visitor Center.
Trails and distances:	Williwaw Trail: 0.5 mile one way to Middle Glacier canyon.
	Moraine Trail: 0.2 mile interpretive loop trail.
	Byron Glacier Trail: 0.8 mile one way to snowfields below the glacier.
Special features:	Portage Valley glaciers and a nature trail.
Location:	11 miles south of Girdwood.
Difficulty:	Easy.
Trail type:	Moraine: accessible to more developed.
	Williwaw: accessible to less developed. Byron Glacier: more developed to less developed.
Total elevation gain:	Moraine and Williwaw: 50 feet.
	Byron Glacier: 100 feet.
Best season:	June through September.
Maps:	USGS Seward D-6 and D-5 (trails not shown); Trails Illustrated *Kenai National Wildlife Refuge*.
Manager:	Chugach National Forest, Glacier Ranger District.

PORTAGE VALLEY

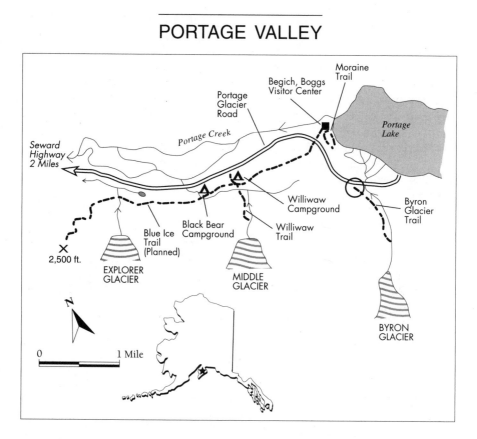

Finding the trailheads: All the trails are on the Portage Glacier Road. Turn east onto the road off the Seward Highway, 11 miles south of Girdwood and 10 miles north of Turnagain Pass.

The **Williwaw Trail** begins in the Williwaw Campground. Drive 4.1 miles up the Portage Glacier Road and turn south into a parking area just beyond the bridge over Williwaw Creek. (To the west of the car park is a salmon-viewing platform — red salmon spawn here from mid-August into September). Park here unless you plan to camp in the Williwaw Campground; there is no trailhead parking in the campground. Walk south from the parking area across a small wooden bridge and continue straight ahead onto a campground spur road. In less than 0.1 mile, at a T intersection with another camp road, look for the trail just across the intersection.

To get to the **Moraine Trail**, drive 5.2 miles on the Portage Glacier Road to the fork at Portage Glacier Lodge, and bear left toward the visitor center. The trail begins past the lodge on the right, next to the restrooms. Park in either the visitor center lot or the lot on the edge of Portage Lake.

The **Byron Glacier Trail** is about 6 miles up Portage Glacier Road. At the fork to the Begich, Boggs Visitor Center, bear right and continue 0.8 mile to a parking area on the right (west). Take the path out of the south end of the parking lot.

101

The hikes: Portage Valley is the most popular visitor destination in Alaska, but don't let that scare you away—this valley's blue ice scenery is outstanding, and most people simply stop at the Begich, Boggs Visitor Center, stare at the ice a bit, and leave. Stick around for a hike or two, and you won't be disappointed. Be ready, though, in case the valley's frequent high winds and pelting, pouring rain strike while you're on the trail.

Williwaw Trail. The 0.5-mile Williwaw Trail leads from the Williwaw Campground to a view of the Middle Glacier canyon. Williwaw used to be a self-guided nature trail. The Forest Service recently abandoned it as an interpretive trail, but plans to reinstall interpretive signing in the future. Signed or not, it's still a decent short walk. The first short section, about 0.1 mile to a view of Middle Glacier from the bank of the Middle Glacier Creek, is suitable for wheelchairs.

The trail then narrows and continues to a bridge over the creek. Two forks of the path (the right is a bit better) meander through a green tunnel of alder and willow, passing a huge erratic boulder carried down by the glacier. The path peters out as it leaves the brush and emerges onto a gravel bar with a view up the lower part of the canyon. The glacier isn't visible from the end of the trail.

Moraine Trail. The Moraine Trail is a short interpretive trail that concentrates on plant succession and the shape of the land after a glacier's retreat. The walk follows the crest of the terminal moraine left by Portage Glacier as it began its current retreat in the early 1900s. (A terminal moraine is a pile of gravel, rocks, and boulders left at the farthest advance of a glacier). The 0.1-mile accessible section of the trail is an out-and-back trip to a good valley viewpoint. From there, steps lead to a higher knob before the trail loops back to the parking area.

Byron Glacier Trail. The Byron Glacier Trail parallels the road a short distance, and then turns up Byron Creek, along its alder and cottonwood-covered bank. The cottonwoods disappear, the alders grow shorter and the air gets cooler as you walk upstream toward the glacier. The path branches and rejoins a few times; just keep heading upvalley.

Continue along the gravel bed to where the creek pours out from under a mass of snow and ice, a permanent field of avalanche snow that has developed fissures and a stream-cut cavern. Wandering onto the snowfield is potentially dangerous because of the cave and fissures. Be aware of the potential for avalanches in the valley into June.

Byron Glacier and Byron Peak are visible up the valley. The Byron is a hanging glacier, so it isn't retreating as fast as Portage Glacier.

Forest Service naturalists lead hikes into the Byron Creek valley during the summer. Check at the visitor center for the schedule.

Other trails. The planned **Blue Ice Trail**, 6 miles long, will run almost the entire length of the Portage Valley. Most of the trail will be relatively level and easy except for a 2-mile spur to the alpine slopes west of the Explorer Glacier, which will involve a moderately strenuous climb to 2,500 feet elevation. Check with the Forest Service in Girdwood or at the visitor center for current information.

Portage Glacier and Portage Pass

The blue ice of Portage Glacier has been in full retreat since about 1914. The glacier is around the bend in Portage Lake now, but 100 years ago there was no lake, and the glacier filled the upper valley. A lobe of the ice ground through Portage Pass, the narrow gap to the north of the upper end of the lake. Had the glacier kept up its grinding a little longer, a saltwater channel might have opened through the pass, and Kenai Peninsula would be Kenai Island.

The pass separated the traditional territories of the Alutiiq and Dena'ina people; the Dena'ina name for the pass meant "where the Alutiiq come." In the 1890s, when the Gold Rush brought the first big influx of whites into the country, steamships docked at the foot of Portage Pass, where Whittier is now, and dropped off prospectors headed for strikes in Hope and Sunrise on Turnagain Arm. They hauled their supplies up the steep east face of the glacier with ropes and pulleys, and walked the beaten trail through Portage Pass to the diggings.

During World War II the military blasted tunnels through the mountains to set up a railroad supply line from Whittier to Anchorage and Fairbanks, and the old trail over the pass became obsolete. Now the only rush through the pass is in January, when skiers do an annual trek to Whittier to watch the Superbowl.

Trip summary:	A half-day or overnight hike to Portage Pass and Portage Lake from the Alaska Railroad stop in Whittier.
Distances:	Portage Glacier viewpoint: 1 mile one way. Portage Lake: 2 miles one way. Getting to the trailhead involves a 1.25-mile road walk from the Whittier railroad stop.
Special features:	Portage Lake and Glacier, alpine scenery, historic interest. Access to the trail is via the Alaska Railroad's Portage-Whittier shuttle train.
Location:	Whittier.
Difficulty:	Moderate.
Trail type:	More developed trail to route.
Total elevation gain:	700 feet to the glacier viewpoint; 700 feet in and 600 out to Portage Lake.
Best season:	July through mid-September.
Maps:	USGS Seward D-5.
Manager:	Chugach National Forest, Glacier Ranger District.

Key points:

0.0   Trailhead (1.25 miles from the Whittier railroad stop)
1.0   Portage Glacier viewpoint
1.5   Divide Lake and Portage Pass
2.0   Portage Lake

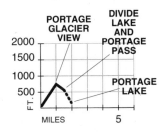

Finding the trailhead: Catch the Alaska Railroad's shuttle train to Whittier at the Portage siding on the Seward Highway, 10 miles south of Girdwood. The shuttle runs several times a day in summer, with a slightly reduced schedule on Wednesdays and Thursdays.

Taking a vehicle on the train shortens the trip by about 1.25 miles one way, but it's not necessary and is a bit expensive. The state is in the process of turning the railroad to Whittier into a combination toll road/railroad. In any case, it will probably still be least expensive to travel to Whittier as a foot passenger on the train. See Appendix 3 for Alaska Railroad information.

The Whittier rail line runs through two tunnels. As it exits the second, look to the right for the trailhead and trail climbing toward Portage Pass. You can't exit the train here, though; the stop is about another 1.25 miles, across from the Whittier small boat harbor. To get back to the trailhead from the train stop, turn left, or west, when you get off the train. Walk (or if

PORTAGE PASS

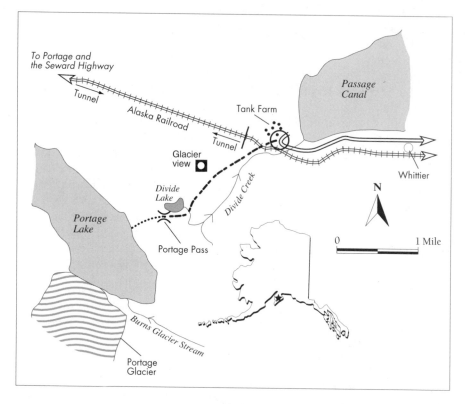

you brought a car, drive) out the lightly-traveled road on the north, or water, side of the tracks, back toward the railroad tunnel.

As the road curves to the right into a tank farm, turn left onto the only road that crosses the tracks. Cross the tracks, turn right immediately, and parallel the tracks about 200 feet to a berm. If you have a car, park here. The trail starts beyond the berm.

The hike: Portage Pass is a hike into history (see **Portage Glacier and Portage Pass**). It's also about the least expensive way to get a good view of Portage Glacier, since the train ticket is more of a bargain than the Portage Lake boat tour, which leaves from the end of the Portage Glacier Road. Once you're at the trailhead, this hike is just a mile to a viewpoint of the glacier and another mile to a point on upper Portage Lake directly across from Portage Glacier.

The trail, an old road bed, is wide and easy to follow as far as Divide Lake, a small lake at the elevation of Portage Pass. From Divide Lake to Portage Lake, the hike is partially an alder bushwhack, partially a clear route following small cairns and streambeds. It's easy in the alders to lose the route momentarily, but even if you do, it is not a very difficult hike. Hikers should make plenty of noise through this section to let any bears in the neighborhood know of their presence. The Forest Service has plans to build a real trail down to Portage Lake.

At the glacier viewpoint (750 feet elevation) look out on the crevassed, jumbled face of Portage Glacier. Bear right on a branch route to a knob with a better view. This viewpoint, a good destination for a shorter hike, should not deter you from the real highlight of this jaunt, Portage Lake and its glacial landscape.

The trail curls around to the left from the viewpoint and drops to Divide Lake and Portage Pass, 550 feet elevation, where the low-key route-finding begins. The trail peters out, and the rough route continues down to the beach at Portage Lake. The view is fantastic on a good day, and good campsites and plenty of places to explore abound. Walking to the Burns Glacier outlet stream through the jumble of glacial rocks and boulders is a good side hike. This land has only very recently been exposed by the glacier's retreat.

Be prepared for weather; Portage Pass is a wind and storm tunnel. Whittier is one of the wettest places in Alaska, and much of its weather blows through the pass to Portage. The pass can have 20 feet of snow in winter, so it may take until July for it all to melt.

24 *WINNER CREEK*

Trip summary:	A half-day hike to Winner Creek Gorge, or a longer day or overnight hike into the upper Winner Creek basin.
Distances:	Winner Creek Gorge: 2.5 miles one way. Upper Winner Creek basin: 3 miles or more one way.
Special features:	A gorge on lower Winner Creek and a subalpine basin in upper Winner Creek.
Location:	In the Girdwood valley, near Alyeska Ski Resort.
Difficulty:	Winner Creek Gorge: easy. Upper Winner Creek: moderate.
Trail type:	More developed trail to Winner Creek; less developed trail to Winner Creek Gorge; less developed trail/route in upper Winner Creek.
Total elevation gain:	About 300 feet in and 200 feet out to Winner Creek Gorge, and 500 feet in and 100 feet out to subalpine country in upper Winner Creek.
Best season:	June through September.
Maps:	USGS Seward D-6 (trail not shown); Trails Illustrated *Kenai National Wildlife Refuge*; Alaska Road & Recreation Map *Anchorage and Vicinity*.
Manager:	Chugach National Forest, Glacier Ranger District.

WINNER CREEK

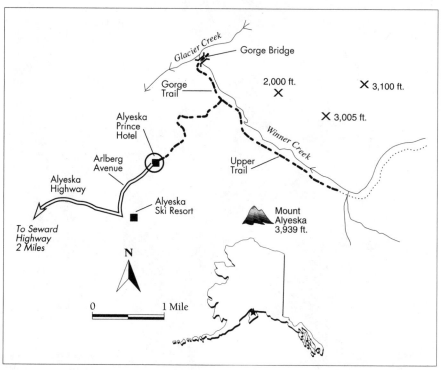

Key points:

Gorge trail		Upper basin trail	
1.5	Winner Creek	1.5	Winner Creek
2.5	Winner Creek Gorge	2.0	Historic cabin
		3.0	Upper Winner Creek basin

WINNER CREEK GORGE

Finding the trailhead: Drive 35 miles south of Anchorage on the Seward Highway to the Alyeska Highway junction. Turn east toward Alyeska and Girdwood and drive 3 miles, past the Girdwood townsite, to a T intersection in front of Alyeska Resort. Turn left onto Arlberg Avenue, following signs to the Alyeska Prince Hotel. In a mile, pass the hotel entrance, follow the road as it loops back to the left, and park in the visitor area by the shuttle bus stop.

Winner Creek Gorge, just above its confluence with Glacier Creek.

Here's the way the hotel designers want you to walk to the trailhead. Across the road from the shuttle bus stop, find a bike trail with a sign for the Winner Creek Trail. Take this trail, following the signs, past two intersections and through an underpass, about 0.25 mile in all, into an opening with a chairlift. Take a hard left onto a gravel path into the trees, wind past the hotel's pond and back entrance, and finally cross under the resort's tram line to the trailhead, maybe another 0.2 mile.

Yes, it is nearly half a mile to the trailhead this way. The much shorter alternative? Just walk around the north end of the hotel, the end with the tram terminal, following the access road and the edge of the forest until you reach the trailhead.

The hike: It's never been easy to *find* the Winner Creek Trail, but once you've found it, it's hard to stay away. It is a fine trail, winding through the northernmost patch of Pacific Coast forest, the spruce-hemlock forest that extends south to Oregon. The narrow, crashing gorge at the mouth of the creek and the alpine basin in its upper reaches make Winner Creek a great hike.

Hikers can see it all in one long day, see the upper and lower parts of the creek on different days, or overnight in the upper basin. The trail to the gorge, though relatively short, is not a good trail for smaller children at this writing; it is rough for the last mile, and the narrow bridge over the gorge and nearby cliffs could be dangerous.

Think of this hike in three sections: the access trail to the creek from the hotel; the gorge, or lower, trail; and the upper trail into Winner Creek's alpine basin.

The Access Trail. The old-growth forest helps hikers make a quick transition from the bustling extravagance of the hotel to the quiet of the trail. Big Sitka spruce, hemlocks, ferns, tall devil's club, blueberry bushes, and equisetum, the fern-like horsetail, line the trail, and bridges and boardwalks cover the many small creeks, seeps, and bogs. Parts of the trail may be wet after a rain, which is fairly likely, this being a pocket of rain forest.

At about 1.5 miles, the trail passes a pretty meadow, climbs a low rise and drops down to the bluff above Winner Creek. It T's into the trail that runs up and down the creek. Go left, downstream, to the gorge, or right, upstream, to the upper basin.

The Gorge Trail. The lower trail to the gorge follows the bluff above the creek about a mile to a narrow bridge over the gorge. Below, foaming through its narrow bedrock channel, the stream sends spray up over the bridge. The confluence of the three major streams in the Girdwood valley—Glacier, Winner, and Crow Creeks—is a few hundred feet below the bridge. Rough, unmaintained tracks, not recommended for casual hiking, run downstream on both sides of the bridge toward Glacier Creek. The trail leading to the left just before the final descent to the bridge leads back to Girdwood's airstrip.

The Upper Trail. About 0.5 mile upstream of the intersection with the access trail are the tumbled-down remains of a miner's cabin, reputed to have belonged to a local sourdough named Axel Lindblad, who prospected along Turnagain Arm starting in the 1890s. Lindblad pioneered the Winner Creek Trail, and had some other major adventures. He fell into a creek in winter and lost his fingers to frostbite, but carved out a slot between his thumb and what was left of his index finger so he could use a knife, fork, and pen. Lindblad also lost an ear in a fight with another prospector.

About a mile beyond the cabin, upper Winner Creek's lush meadows, groves of cottonwood, and scattered stands of spruce and mountain hemlock begin. Mount Alyeska, 3,939 feet elevation, is nearly straight up to the south. These steep slopes can avalanche when there is a snow load, as the chutes and debris near the trail show. Continue on the trail/route up the valley as time and inclination allow.

The Forest Service and the Girdwood Trails Committee are planning to upgrade and extend the trail.

Shorter hikes. A short, out-and-back walk on the access trail from the hotel is a good option for sampling Alaska's northernmost rain forest and picking a few blueberries in season. The forest is a kid's paradise.

25 CROW PASS

Trip summary:	A longer day or overnight hike to Crow Pass, or a two to four day traverse through the Chugach Mountains over the pass to Eagle River.
Distances:	Crow Pass: 3.5 miles one way. Traverse: 24 miles.
Special features:	An alpine pass and mountain glaciers, mining and Iditarod Trail history, wildlife, mountaineering, and one of Southcentral Alaska's classic alpine traverses.
Location:	7 miles north of Girdwood.
Difficulty:	Moderately strenuous.
Trail type:	More developed to Crow Pass; less developed north of the pass.
Total elevation gain:	Crow Pass: about 2,000 feet. Traverse: from Crow Pass: 2,000 feet; from Eagle River: 3,100 feet.
Best season:	Late June through mid-September.
Maps:	USGS Anchorage A-6 and A-7 (NE); Alaska Road & Recreation Map *Anchorage and Vicinity*; Alaska State Parks leaflet *Historic Iditarod/Crow Pass Trail*.
Manager:	Chugach National Forest, Glacier Ranger District, and Chugach State Park.

Key points:

From Crow Pass		From Eagle River
0.0	Crow Pass Trailhead	24.0
1.7	Monarch Mine	22.3
3.0	Fee cabin	21.0
3.5	Crow Pass	20.5
5.5	Clear Creek	18.5
6.0	Raven Gorge	18.0
7.5	Turbid Creek	16.5
12.0	Eagle River ford	12.0
13.0	Thunder Gorge	11.0
15.5	Twin Falls	8.5
19.0	Heritage Falls	5.0
20.0	The Perch	4.0
21.0	Echo Bend	3.0
24.0	Eagle River Trailhead	0.0

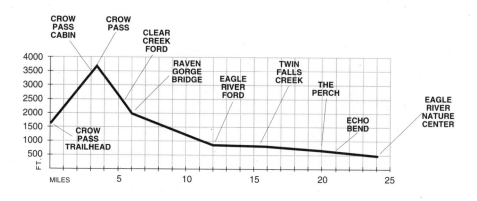

Finding the trailhead: The trail begins at the end of the Crow Creek Road outside Girdwood. To get there, drive 35 miles south of Anchorage and turn east onto the Alyeska Highway. Drive 1.9 miles, turn left (north) on Crow Creek Road, and follow it 7 miles to the trailhead. The road is often rough, but is passable during the snow-free season.

For directions to the Eagle River Trailhead, see Hike 37, Eagle River Valley.

The hike: Glaciers, waterfalls, wildflowers, and mining ruins spice up the hike to Crow Pass, the highest point on the historic Iditarod Trail and one of the most scenic day hikes in Southcentral Alaska. Backpackers can continue over the pass to the Eagle River Nature Center on a 24-mile traverse through the Chugach Mountains.

Arctic ground squirrels, marmots, and mountain goats inhabit the high country near Crow Pass, and bears, moose, and Dall sheep are frequently spotted too, especially on the Eagle River side of the pass. Eagle River, in fact, has a significant bear population. Salmonberries and blueberries can be a trail prize for hikers later in summer.

CROW PASS

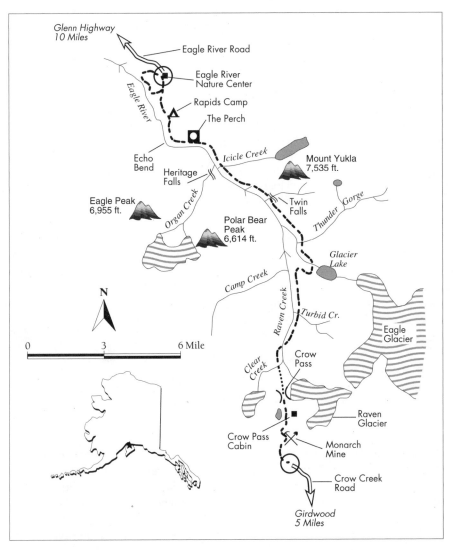

The trail is relatively snowfree by late June, though the Crystal Lake basin and the area north of Crow Pass hold snow well into July. Some snow usually stays on the trail north of the pass all summer.

The mining history starts even before you reach the trailhead—the Crow Creek and Girdwood Mines, both just off Crow Creek Road, were two of the earliest mining claims in this part of the state. The Monarch Mine, 1.7 miles up the trail, was a lode (vein) mine active until 1938. After the turn of the 20th century, hundreds of prospectors heading for other parts of the state on the Iditarod Trail passed the Monarch's undiscovered vein without knowing it. The vein was finally discovered in 1909.

Crow Pass Trail. The trail starts in the brush zone above treeline, and climbs steadily up the old Monarch Mine road. Pieces and parts of tram cable, a boiler, an ore-crushing mill, and a compressor mark the site of the mine. At the mine's height, the miners had built a bunkhouse, cookhouse, and blacksmith shop here. They hacked the ore out of the mountains above the trail.

Beyond the mine, the trail starts a series of switchbacks, and a short, rough side trail leads to Crow Creek's cascades. A second trail, steeper than the main trail, cuts away from the switchbacks not far above the creek's lower cascades. This is an alternate trail toward the pass that avoids some snow-covered sidehilling on the main trail early in the summer.

At 3 miles and 3,500 feet elevation is the Crystal Lake basin and the Crow Pass fee cabin, available under a reservation-and-fee system (see Appendix 2 for information). At Crow Pass, 0.5 mile farther and 500 feet higher, the main event is a view of Raven Glacier. For side trips, plenty of peaks and ridges are nearby. The crevassed glacier can be dangerous; don't travel on it unless properly trained and equipped.

Some hikers, apparently lulled by how short a hike this is, walk in little more than shorts, t-shirts and running shoes, betting on good weather and

Berry hunters in the alpine country of Raven Creek, on the Crow Pass Traverse.

Raven Gorge bridge, Crow Pass traverse.

taking a chance on ending up wet, cold, miserable, and maybe hypothermic. Come prepared with warm clothes and rain gear.

The Crow Pass-Eagle River traverse. The trail continues from Crow Pass down Raven Creek and Eagle River about 20.5 more miles to the Eagle River Nature Center. Campsites for larger parties are fairly limited in the Raven Creek valley between Crow Pass and Eagle River, but the Eagle River valley has loads of campsites of all sizes. See Hike 37, Eagle River Valley. About ten miles of the 24-mile traverse are above treeline.

Following rock cairns is necessary through the glacial rubble just north of the pass. Often steep snow slopes in this area can be difficult if the snow is hard-packed. Climb or descend to get around them if necessary. The trip also involves two stream fords, one at Clear Creek, Mile 5.5, and one at a marked ford across Eagle River, Mile 12. Extra foot gear is worth carrying.

Some of the highlights of the traverse are Raven Glacier and the glacially-sculpted terrain below it; Raven Gorge, where water blasts through a rock arch in a tight bedrock canyon; Eagle River's upper valley and Glacier Lake; and the many side canyons, waterfalls, mountain walls, and glaciers of Eagle River. Several strenuous cross-country hikes are possible from the trail, including high passes to the west of Raven Creek.

Shorter hikes. The hike to the ruins of the Monarch Mine, 1.7 miles one way, involves 1,000 feet of climbing and leads to beautiful alpine country.

Trip summary:	A half-day or longer hike to the crest of Bird Ridge, overlooking Turnagain Arm.
Distance:	About 1 mile one way to alpine views; about 3 miles to Peak 3,505.
Special features:	A very steep trail; fine views of Turnagain Arm.
Location:	25 miles south of downtown Anchorage.
Difficulty:	Moderately strenuous to strenuous.
Trail type:	Less developed trail/route.
Total elevation gain:	3,450 feet to Peak 3,505.
Best season:	Mid-May to early October.
Maps:	USGS Seward D-7 (NW) and Anchorage A-7; Alaska Road & Recreation Map *Anchorage and Vicinity.*
Manager:	Chugach State Park.

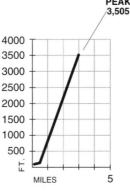

Finding the trailhead: The trailhead is 25 miles south of downtown Anchorage on the north side of the Seward Highway. It is 0.9 mile east of the Indian Creek bridge, and 0.6 mile west of the Bird Creek bridge.

The hike: The hike up Bird Ridge offers a chance to see the Anchorage area's first mountain wildflowers of the year, and leads to sweeping views of alpine mountains, green valleys, and shimmering Turnagain Arm. The trail climbs the ridge between Indian and Bird Creeks; the ridge is steep and south-facing, so it melts early in spring.

Locals use the Bird Ridge Trail as a tune-up hike early in the year. It's an extremely steep trail, so consider taking a staff or ski pole, and be ready for sore quads the next day if this is your first hike of the year. If snowfields still linger on the ridge, there is usually a trail of packed snow to follow. The ridge is exposed and usually windy, so even if the weather is good at the trailhead, pack a hat, gloves, and warm and windproof clothing.

To begin the hike follow the paved trail out of the parking lot. After about 0.2 mile of pavement and elevated boardwalk, turn left, uphill, at the

BIRD RIDGE

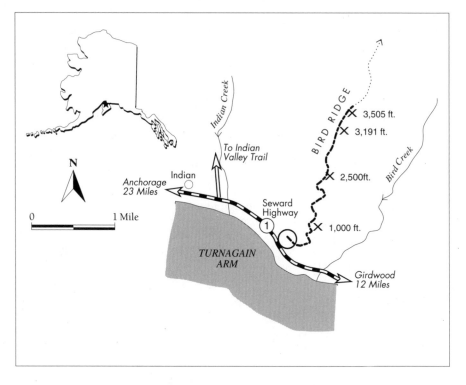

restroom. Climb about 0.1 mile to a maintenance road. Turn right and continue about another 0.1 mile, until you reach a point where you can see into the next valley, Bird Creek. Look for the ridge trail cutting uphill to the left.

The trail climbs steeply. At roughly 1,000 feet elevation, it leaves the spruce forest and opens to views of Turnagain Arm and the Bird Creek valley. After another stretch of climbing, the trail breaks out into the rocks and boulders of the alpine ridge.

The first high point with a 360-degree view is Peak 3,505, about three miles from the trailhead. Looking west, the valley of Indian Creek appears (Hike 27), with the powerline heading over Powerline Pass toward the Glen Alps Trailhead in the distance. Looking east yields a view up the valley of Penguin Creek, and south are Turnagain Arm and the Kenai Mountains. To the north lies a jumble of wild peaks in the heart of the Chugach Mountains.

For a much longer ridge run, keep walking to the Bird Ridge Overlook, elevation 4,650 feet and about four miles beyond Peak 3,505. The peak overlooks the east fork of upper Ship Creek.

Trip summary:	A longer day or overnight hike up Indian Creek to Indian Pass and the upper Ship Creek valley, or a two to three day traverse between either Glen Alps or Ship Creek and Indian Creek.
Distances:	Indian Pass: 6 miles one way. Glen Alps-Indian traverse: 15 miles. Ship Creek-Indian traverse: 20 miles.
Special features:	A forest walk on lower Indian Creek; subalpine and alpine country; two traverses of the Chugach Mountains.
Location:	25 miles south of Anchorage.
Difficulty:	Moderately strenuous.
Trail type:	Less developed.
Total elevation gain:	2,100 feet up Indian valley to the pass.
Best season:	June through September.
Maps:	USGS Seward D-7 (NW) and Anchorage A-7; Alaska Road & Recreation Map *Anchorage and Vicinity*.
Manager:	Chugach State Park.

Key points:

Indian Valley Trail

0.2 Powerline Trail junction
1.0 Lower Indian Creek bridge
4.0 Three forks of Indian Creek
6.0 Indian Pass

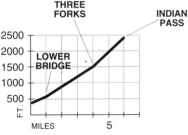

Finding the trailhead: Drive to Indian, 25 miles south of Anchorage, and turn north at the Turnagain House restaurant, 0.1 mile west of the Indian Creek crossing. Drive 0.5 mile to a fork in the road, and bear right another 0.5 mile to the trailhead. The park has moved the trailhead a bit closer to the highway to make room for the long-term cleanup of a 1993 fuel spill.

The hikes: The Indian Creek Trail features lush coastal forest, mountain meadows, and subalpine Indian Pass. Spruce forest alternates with alder brush patches and healthy crops of tall grasses and devil's club—some of the devil's club leaves are almost big enough to use as an umbrella.

For longer trips, hikers can continue through the pass into the upper Ship Creek valley and explore its three headwater forks. Really adventurous hikers can do a 20-mile, mostly cross-country traverse between lower Ship Creek and the Indian Creek Trailhead. There's also a 15-mile traverse between Glen Alps and Indian Creek via Ship Lake Pass.

Indian Creek figures largely in the history of Chugach State Park. Anchorage citizens objected to a timber sale proposed for the valley by the Alaska Department of Natural Resources, and the Alaska Legislature responded with a law creating the half-million acre park in 1970.

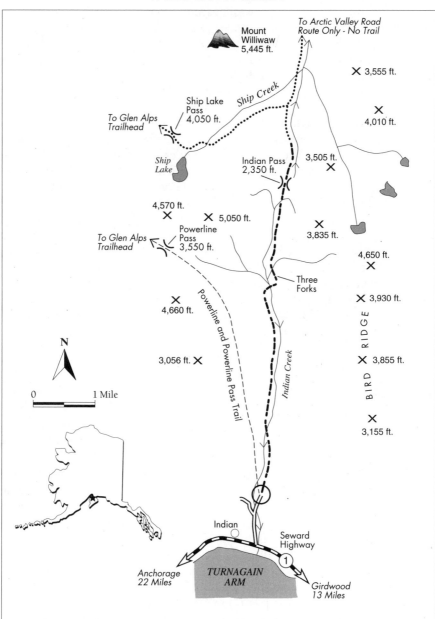

Mount Williwaw 5,445 ft.

To Arctic Valley Road Route Only - No Trail

X 3,555 ft.

Ship Creek

Ship Lake Pass 4,050 ft.

To Glen Alps Trailhead

X 4,010 ft.

Ship Lake

Indian Pass 2,350 ft.

3,505 ft. X

X 3,835 ft.

4,570 ft. X

X 5,050 ft.

Powerline Pass 3,550 ft.

To Glen Alps Trailhead

4,650 ft. X

Three Forks

X 3,930 ft.

X 4,660 ft.

Powerline and Powerline Pass Trail

3,056 ft. X

Indian Creek

BIRD RIDGE

X 3,855 ft.

X 3,155 ft.

N

0   1 Mile

Indian

Seward Highway

1

Anchorage 22 Miles

TURNAGAIN ARM

Girdwood 13 Miles

Indian Creek. The Indian Creek Trail intersects the Powerline Trail, which leads to the South Fork of Campbell Creek and the Glen Alps Trailhead, about 0.2 mile from the trailhead. The lower section of the Indian Trail stays close by the stream.

At the three forks, the trail crosses to the east side of the creek and climbs into the high meadows of the upper valley. By late summer, ferns, shrubs, and grasses may thickly overhang this part of the infrequently maintained trail. There are, however, bridges on all the creek crossings.

At broad, rolling Indian Pass, 6 miles from the trailhead at 2,350 feet elevation, alpine tundra mixes with patches of stunted mountain hemlock. There are a few spots flat enough to set up camp among the gnarled hemlocks. Beyond the pass, the trail becomes intermittent, but the open country makes for easy hiking into the valley of Ship Creek. From Indian Pass, explore the headwater forks of Indian Creek or the three main headwater forks of Ship Creek near the pass.

Ship Lake and the Glen Alps-Indian Traverse. Ship Lake is about 3.5 cross-country miles west of Indian Pass. The lake is a good destination in itself, and it's on the route of the traverse over Ship Lake Pass between the Indian Creek Trailhead and the Glen Alps Trailhead, a moderately strenuous jaunt of 15 miles. Start the traverse at Glen Alps (see Hike 32), for the least elevation gain, 2,000 feet versus 4,000 feet from Indian Creek.

Ship Creek-Indian Creek. The traverse between Ship and Indian Creeks is most often done on skis between February and early April, but it makes a very adventurous, mainly cross-country summer hike as well. If you do it, do it for the adventure. If exploring Ship Creek's high country is your objective, it's much easier to go in on the Indian Creek Trail.

The best idea is to start from Ship Creek, since this direction is much less of a climb (1,200 feet vs. 3,100 feet from Indian). The Ship Creek Trailhead is at Mile 6.5 of Arctic Valley Road, on Fort Richardson, north of Anchorage. Take the Arctic Valley exit from the Glenn Highway at Mile 6.1 (northbound) or 7.5 (southbound). The trailhead is at a pullout on the right side of Arctic Valley Road, directly across from an intersection with a gated military road. There are normally no restrictions on private use of Arctic Valley Road.

The trail on the Ship Creek side runs 2 miles to the valley floor and another 3 miles along the creek. Horses have badly mucked up the trail in the valley bottom. The trail eventually fades into the forest, and there are only hints of a trail to follow until higher in the valley.

Wade the creek to the west side of the valley well below the North Fork. Crossing earlier in the summer or after rain may be difficult or impossible because of high water. The only way to go seriously wrong on this hike is to stay too long on the east side of Ship Creek and mistakenly wander up the North Fork instead of staying in the main valley.

Stay high to avoid brush after crossing to the west side. Eventually the valley opens up and a good game trail appears; follow it and several route markers up the center headwater fork to Indian Pass and the connection with the Indian Creek Trail. The trip is a slow 20 miles. It can be done in a very long day, but taking two or three days is a good idea. This is a good wildlife trip; black bears, moose, and beaver are common in the Ship Creek valley.

Shorter hikes. The best shorter hikes are on the Indian Creek Trail: 1 mile one way to the lower bridge, 4 miles-plus to the three forks area and the first big meadows, or any distance in between for a good forest hike. The lower valley makes a good family outing.

The Chugach Mountains and Cook Inlet, Chugach State Park's spectacular setting.

Chugach State Park

Out Anchorage's back door is the third-largest state park in the country, smaller only than western Alaska's Wood-Tikchik State Park and California's Anza-Borrego desert park. Chugach is what Anchorage folks are referring to when they joke that the city is only a half-hour from Alaska.

From coast to lush forest to mountain peak and glacier, Chugach's half a million acres (about 800 square miles) stretch along 60 miles of the western end of the Chugach Mountains, possibly America's least-known major mountain range. Bears, wolves, Dall sheep, lynx, wolverines, and armies of moose call the park's wilderness home, and some of these animals—mainly moose and bears—frequently wander into town.

The park includes fifteen major watersheds, seventy lakes, fifty glaciers, and thirteen peaks over 7,000 feet, not a mean feat considering the boundaries aren't far above sea level. The park lies on a biological crossroads between the temperate coastal forest to the south and the boreal forest to the north. Sitka spruce and western and mountain hemlock, trees that grace the forests south to Oregon, reach their northern limits in the park.

Much of the interior of the park is trailless, and there are a number of great cross-country routes through its high passes and alpine valleys.

28   *FALLS CREEK*

Trip summary: A half-day or longer day hike or an overnight trip into the upper basin of Falls Creek.

Distances: Falls Creek basin: 2 miles one way.
Headwater lake: 2.5 miles one way.

Special features: Alpine scenery, wildlife, cross-country hiking from the end of the trail, and Chugach Range peaks. A steep trail.

Location: 20 miles south of Anchorage.

Difficulty: Moderately strenuous to strenuous.

Trail type: Less developed trail/route.

Total elevation gain: From 2,500 feet in the basin to 3,800 feet on the ridge above.

Best season: Late June to mid-September.

Maps: USGS Seward D-7 (NW) and Anchorage A-7; Alaska Road & Recreation Map *Anchorage and Vicinity.*

Manager: Chugach State Park.

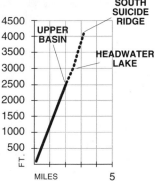

Finding the trailhead: Drive 20 miles south of Anchorage on the Seward Highway. The trailhead is on the north side of the highway, just east of Milepost 106, or 2.7 miles west of Indian Creek and 1 mile east of the Windy Corner trailhead for the Turnagain Arm Trail. Look for the highway turnout by the beautiful, cascading creek.

The hike: A steep hike to a high tundra basin, the trail threads its way up the narrow Falls Creek valley into some of the highest peaks along Turnagain Arm. Wildflowers, berries in season, Dall sheep, and high points for mountain views are all good reasons to visit Falls Creek. Indianhouse Mountain (4350 feet) and South Suicide Peak (5,005 feet) are the high peaks above the valley.

Distances are about 2 miles to the end of the beaten trail, another 0.5 mile to the small headwater lake, and another 0.5 mile to the great views at the crest of the ridge to the north. Once on the ridge, South Suicide Peak's

FALLS CREEK

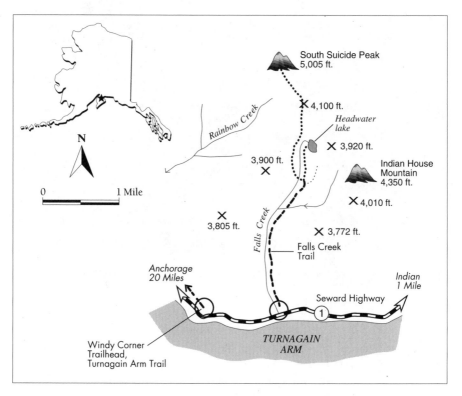

summit is about another mile, and is a non-technical but very challenging trip, with a total elevation gain of almost 5,000 feet.

The trail is steep and brushy, especially in the alder brush zone about a mile into the hike. The trail is infrequently maintained, and has two potentially confusing spots in the first 0.5 mile. Take a switchback to the right where a left fork stays low along the creek, and a bit higher, take the path to the left in a small rocky opening. Allow most of a summer day for this seemingly short hike, as the trail is rough, steep, and slow.

At about 1.5 miles and 2,000 feet elevation, the small sparkling stream jumps in short falls and cascades down the mountainside through wildflower meadows. After crossing the east fork of the creek, the path climbs the ridge between the forks and disappears. Head left, cross country, into the upper basin clearly visible to the west.

In another 0.5 mile, this high tundra valley takes a sharp turn to the east to its headwater lake, a good destination at just below 3,000 feet elevation. The best views are on the ridgeline to the north, another 800-foot climb. A flat area a little east of a direct line to South Suicide Peak overlooks the Indian Creek valley; bearing west of the peak leads to views down Rainbow Creek.

Subalpine meadows on the Falls Creek Trail.

Most people day hike Falls Creek. There are good campsites in the upper basin, but the trail is a steep haul with an overnight pack. In late summer, the berries come out: blueberries, cranberries, crowberries, watermelon berries, salmonberries, and the poisonous baneberry.

Shorter hikes. Any hike into Falls Creek is a steep hike. Hiking the 1.5 miles to the first wildflower meadows is a good half-day trip with a 2,000-foot elevation gain.

Trip summary:	A longer day hike or backpack to two alpine lakes in the Chugach Mountains.
Distance:	6.5 miles one way.
Special features:	Alpine tundra, mountain lakes, access to cross-country hiking.
Location:	15 miles south of Anchorage.
Difficulty:	Moderately strenuous.
Trail type:	More developed trail for the first mile; less developed trail to the upper valley; a route beyond.
Total elevation gain:	About 3,200 feet in and 200 feet out.
Best season:	Mid-June through September.
Maps:	USGS Anchorage A-7 and A-8 (SE); Alaska Road & Recreation Map *Anchorage and Vicinity*.
Manager:	Chugach State Park.

Key points:
1.0   Table Rock side path
4.5   Upper McHugh Creek valley
6.0   Routes divide to Rabbit and McHugh Lakes

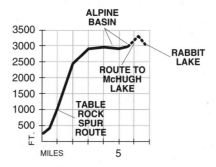

Finding the trailhead: Drive to the McHugh Creek Picnic Area 15 miles south of Anchorage, at Mile 111.8 of the Seward Highway. From the south, the picnic area is around a sharp bend in the road and is not visible until you're there. The Mile 112 marker on the northeast side of the road is a warning the picnic area is coming up.

The trailhead is at the end of the upper parking lot; pass up a right fork that leads to the mid-level parking area. The road is too steep for large vehicles or vehicles with trailers, so park these in the lower parking area just off the highway.

The hike: The "new" trail to Rabbit and McHugh Lakes follows the McHugh Creek valley upstream from Turnagain Arm. The original trail, which ran up the Rabbit Creek valley in South Anchorage, was blocked by a private landowner, and the State's attempt failed to regain legal public access over the long-used Rabbit Creek Trail.

MCHUGH AND RABBIT LAKES

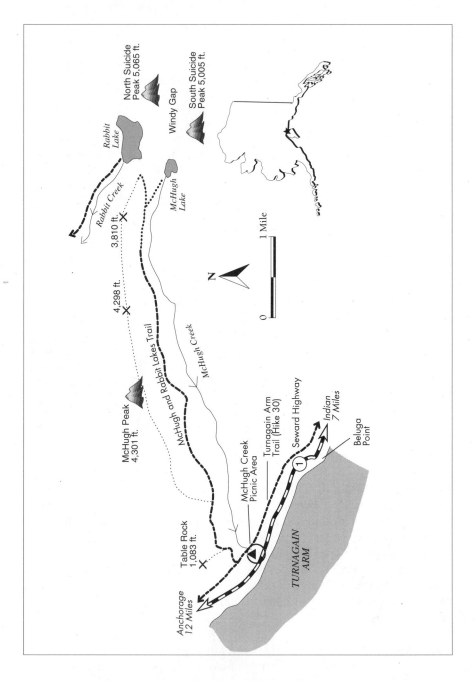

North Suicide Peak 5,065 ft.

Windy Gap

South Suicide Peak 5,005 ft.

Rabbit Lake

Rabbit Creek

McHugh Lake

3,810 ft.

4,298 ft.

McHugh Peak 4,301 ft.

McHugh and Rabbit Lakes Trail

McHugh Creek

N

0   1 Mile

McHugh Creek Picnic Area

Turnagain Arm Trail (Hike 30)

Seward Highway

Indian 7 Miles

Beluga Point

Table Rock 1,083 ft.

Anchorage 12 Miles

TURNAGAIN ARM

A fairly steep hike for the first 3 miles, the McHugh Trail leads through forest, meadow, and brush into alpine tundra below the craggy Suicide Peaks. Great views and McHugh Creek's high alpine basin are highlights of the hike. Moose, Dall sheep, grouse, ptarmigan, and bear frequent this wild valley. Two mountain runners were killed by a grizzly on the trail in 1995, so use caution here. The bear is believed to have been feeding on a carcass just off the trail in the alder brush.

Take the Turnagain Arm Trail out of the upper parking area at the McHugh picnic area. At the T in 0.1 mile, turn left toward Potter Creek. In another 0.2 mile, turn right, uphill, onto the McHugh/Rabbit Lakes Trail. About a mile from the trailhead, at the end of a series of switchbacks, is a short, steep side path to the top of Table Rock, elevation 1,083 feet. Table Rock makes a good picnic and sunbathing spot on a sunny day, with great views of Turnagain Arm, Cook Inlet, and the Kenai Peninsula.

Past Table Rock, the trail swings over onto the steep sidehill above McHugh Creek. On the right in another few minutes is another open outcrop, this time with a view of the McHugh valley and the Arm. About 2 miles into the hike, just beyond the last switchbacks in the trees, is a steep side trail that leads up to the McHugh Peak ridgeline. Once on the ridgeline, hikers are about 2 miles from McHugh Peak, elevation 4,301 feet.

Most of the climb is in the first 3 miles of the hike. By 4.5 miles the trail reaches a level alpine valley with scattered, low-growing mountain hemlock and willows and countless tiny blueberry and crowberry bushes. Camping possibilities are good here and near the lakes.

About Mile 5.5, the trail becomes an intermittent path marked by cairns. Near the head of the valley, stay low to find McHugh Lake. Climb over the low ridge to the northeast, a glacial moraine, to find the much larger Rabbit Lake, at the head of the Rabbit Creek valley. North and South Suicide Peaks rise in dark cliffs above the lakes, with the aptly-named Windy Pass between them.

Other hikes: Glen Alps-Turnagain Arm. Hike between Glen Alps and McHugh by hiking the Powerline Trail from Glen Alps and crossing Ptarmigan Pass, elevation 3,600 feet, into the Rabbit Creek valley about 2.5 miles downstream from Rabbit Lake. Take the old Rabbit Creek Trail to the lake and continue down McHugh Creek to the picnic area and Turnagain Arm. (See Hike 31 for directions to Glen Alps.) Chugach State Park also has plans to build a trail from Glen Alps to Rabbit Lake on the Rabbit Creek side of the Flattop Peak ridge, avoiding the private land on lower Rabbit Creek.

McHugh Peak ridgeline. From the moraine between McHugh and Rabbit lakes, hike west onto the McHugh Peak ridgeline. Travel out the ridge a short way and then backtrack to the trail for the trip out, or even hike all the way back to the trailhead via the ridge. Continue along the ridge past McHugh Peak and eventually drop down to Mile 2 of the trail. This alternative hike back to the trailhead is long and hard.

Shorter hikes. Table Rock, an outcrop with a view, is 1 mile one way and an 800-foot climb.

Trip summary:	A variety of shorter to longer day hikes on a Chugach State Park trail above Turnagain Arm.
Distances:	1.9 to 9.4 miles. Four trailheads split the 9.4-mile trail into 3 sections.
Special features:	Forest and coastal scenery; an early and late season hike.
Location:	Ten miles south of downtown Anchorage.
Difficulty:	Easy to moderate, depending on the section hiked.
Total elevation gain:	About 200 to 800 feet, depending on the section hiked, or about 1,400 feet for the entire trail.
Trail type:	More developed.
Best season:	May to mid-October.
Maps:	USGS Anchorage A-8 (SE), Seward D-8 (NE), and Seward D-7 (NE and NW); Alaska Road & Recreation Map *Anchorage and Vicinity*; and Alaska State Parks brochure *Turnagain Arm Trail*.
Manager:	Chugach State Park.

Key points:

From Potter		From Windy Corner
0.0	Potter Creek Trailhead	9.4
3.3	McHugh Creek Trailhead	6.1
7.5	Rainbow Trailhead	1.9
9.4	Windy Corner Trailhead	0.0

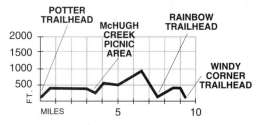

Finding the trailheads: All four trailheads are just a few miles south of Anchorage on the Seward Highway. The nearest to Anchorage is the Potter Trailhead, about ten miles south of downtown Anchorage and just south of the south end of Potter's Marsh. Turn east into the parking area, which is across the highway from and 0.1 mile south of the Potter Historic Site and Chugach State Park headquarters.

The other three trailheads are the McHugh Creek Picnic Area, 3.3 miles beyond Potter; Rainbow, 3.4 miles beyond McHugh; and Windy Corner, 1.7 miles beyond Rainbow.

Rainbow and Windy are immediately off the highway. The McHugh trailheads are in the McHugh Creek Picnic Area, up the steep picnic area road. The road is too steep for large vehicles or vehicles with trailers, so park these in the lower parking area just off the highway. To hike to the southeast

TURNAGAIN ARM TRAIL

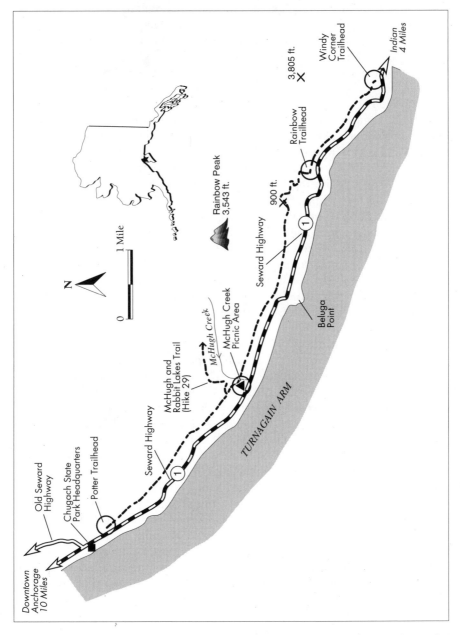

toward Rainbow, take the right fork in the road and begin the trip from the mid-level parking area. To hike northwest toward Potter Creek, pass the right fork in the road and continue straight ahead into the upper parking area.

The hike: The Turnagain Arm Trail crosses a steep southwest slope that receives lots of spring sunshine, and is one of the first trails near Anchorage to melt in the spring. Winding along the slope above the Arm, the trail follows the route of a wagon road used to supply railroad construction camps when crews were building this section of the Alaska Railroad in 1915–18. The hike offers great views of the Arm, the Kenai Mountains, and the peaks of the Chugach Range. The grade of the trail is gentle overall, but there are steep sections near each of the trailheads.

Spruce grouse, songbirds, moose, and even the occasional bear frequent the trail. In late summer, look for beluga whales, the small white whales that swim up the Arm to feed when salmon are running.

Weather along the Arm is usually mild, but there is nearly always a wind. Fires are prohibited here, and the trail is closed to mountain bikes.

Potter Creek-McHugh Creek. The section between Potter and McHugh is the most-developed and most-traveled section of the trail, and is a good trail for families and beginning hikers. This section's high point is about 400 feet. Mainly a forest hike, this section does have one good viewpoint on a rock outcrop about 2 miles from Potter. The first 0.5 mile is highly developed, wide and graded. The park unfortunately wiped out some rare violets and ferns when it surfaced this section of the trail.

About Mile 3, or 0.3 mile west of McHugh, is an intersection with the McHugh Creek-Rabbit Lake Trail (Hike 29). At McHugh, short feeder trails connect the Turnagain Arm Trail with the picnic area. The west feeder trail leads to the upper parking lot, and the east feeder trail leads to the mid-level lot.

McHugh Creek-Rainbow. The McHugh-Rainbow section is the longest and steepest part of the trail, with a high point of 900 feet near Rainbow. Starting the hike from McHugh avoids the steep climb from Rainbow, the steepest on the trail. Crossing McHugh Creek on a bridge, the trail passes scree, rocky slopes, rock ledges, and patches of forest on the way to Rainbow. About 1.8 miles east of McHugh, a steep side trail descends to the highway at Beluga Point, highway Mile 110.

Rainbow-Windy Corner. The trail between Rainbow and Windy is rocky and open, with stands of small aspen trees. It runs relatively close above the highway, and has some of the best views along the trail. This is the shortest section at 1.9 miles, and has a high point of about 400 feet. Dall sheep like the rocks above the highway at Windy Corner, so look for sheep as you walk the few hundred yards closest to Windy Corner.

Shorter hikes. The first 0.5 mile of the trail from Potter is graded and gravel-surfaced, with interpretive signs. An accessible trail leads 0.1 mile one way from the McHugh Creek Picnic Area's upper parking lot to two Turnagain Arm overlooks.

The McHugh overlook is a good spot for viewing the Turnagain Arm bore tide, a wall of water up to five feet high traveling as much as ten miles an hour up the Arm on the incoming tide. Turnagain Arm and Knik Arm of Cook Inlet are the only places in the U.S. with bore tides; the 30-foot range in the tides and the shape and length of the Arm contribute to the generation of the tidal bore. Look for the bore tide at McHugh Creek about an hour after predicted Anchorage low tides.

ANCHORAGE

Anchorage, Alaska's largest city, may also be Alaska's best-kept outdoor secret. Behind the city, Chugach State Park may be the finest local wilderness park on the planet. Within the city, multiple use trails like the Coastal Trail and the Kincaid Park trails attract hundreds of thousands of visitors, and Far North Bicentennial Park, a minimally-developed, 5,000-acre city park, still hosts salmon, coyote, moose, bears, and even the occasional lynx.

---

31 FLATTOP MOUNTAIN

Trip summary:	Shorter to half-day hikes in a popular, scenic alpine area above Anchorage.
Distances:	Flattop Trail: 1.5 miles one way.
	Blueberry Loop Trail: a 1-mile loop.
	Anchorage Overlook Trail: 0.1 mile one way (accessible).
Special features:	Awesome views, an accessible trail, and the most-visited mountaintop in Alaska. The last pitch of the climb to Flattop is a bit rough and requires special care.
Location:	In the Glen Alps area in south Anchorage.
Difficulty:	Flattop: moderate; short but steep.
	Blueberry Loop and Anchorage Overlook: easy.
Total elevation gain:	Flattop: 1,350 feet.
	Blueberry Loop: 400 feet.
	Anchorage Overlook: 50 feet.
Trail type:	Flattop: mainly more developed; less developed on the final pitch.
	Blueberry Loop: more developed.
	Anchorage Overlook: accessible.
Best season:	June through September.
Maps:	USGS Anchorage A-8 (SE); Alaska Road & Recreation Map *Anchorage and Vicinity*.
Manager:	Chugach State Park.

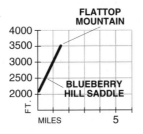

Finding the trailhead: Drive about 6.5 miles south of downtown Anchorage on the New Seward Highway, and exit east toward the Chugach Mountains

FLATTOP

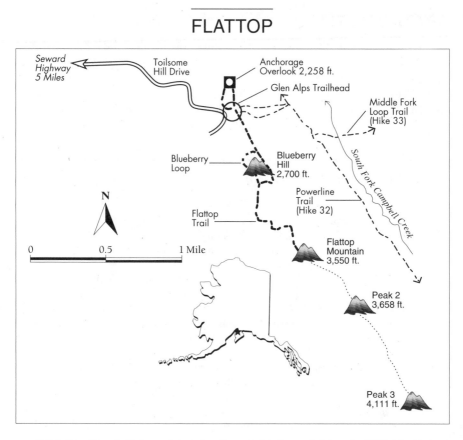

on O'Malley Road. Drive about 4 miles and take a right onto Hillside Drive, just before O'Malley takes a sharp turn to the left. In another mile, turn uphill (left) off Hillside Drive onto Upper Huffman Road, and drive 0.7 mile to a three-way intersection. Here, go right onto the steeply-climbing Toilsome Hill Drive. Follow Toilsome Hill just under two more miles to the Glen Alps parking area and trailhead on the left.

The hikes: Flattop Mountain. The trail to Flattop, a flat summit on the edge of the rugged Chugach Mountains, is a popular hike to great views of the Chugach Mountains, the Kenai Peninsula, Cook Inlet, Anchorage, and the Alaska and Aleutian Ranges. On summer weekends and evenings after work, scores of Anchorage residents visit the Glen Alps entrance to Chugach State Park for short hikes, berry picking, or the steep hike to the top of Flattop.

Just because Flattop is close to the city and only a short hike doesn't mean that the usual precautions for venturing into Alaska's mountains don't apply. Decent boots with good traction and foul weather clothes are musts, and a hiking staff for the steep descent is a good idea. The last pitch to the peak on the rocky northwest ridge is steep and a bit exposed, and requires care, especially descending. If there is still snow on this pitch, it can be dangerous without an ice axe. Late spring avalanches are not uncommon.

That said, Flattop is a great destination, and you can camp on top if you carry your own water. There is even an Anchorage tradition, started by the Alaska Mountaineering Club, of spending the nights of the summer and winter solstices on the summit.

To find the trail, climb the stairs on the southeast (mountain) side of the parking area. The first intersection with the Blueberry Loop Trail is just ahead. Blueberry Hill is the nearby tundra knob, and Flattop the rocky peak beyond.

In the saddle behind Blueberry Hill, the Flattop Trail leads to the Rabbit Creek side of the ridge, and the Blueberry Loop peels off to the right, back toward the parking area. The Flattop Trail then climbs in switchbacks to the base of the peak. The last few hundred feet to the top are steep and rocky and require special care.

The top invites a bit of wandering to see all the views from this 3,550-foot peak, and there are rock outcrops to hide behind if the weather turns nasty. Experienced hikers can continue out the ridge to the southeast on the route to Peak 2 and Peak 3. When descending Flattop, look for the post marking the route down, and be very cautious on the steep, rocky section just below the summit.

Blueberry Loop Trail. The loop trail around Blueberry Hill, elevation 2,700 feet, involves much less climbing and provides good views. This trail is a good one for families or casual hikers looking for a great viewpoint and a place to stalk the wild blueberry.

Anchorage Overlook Trail. The overlook trail leads from the north end of the parking area to a viewpoint overlooking Anchorage and Cook Inlet. Two short paths, one paved and one gravel, climb gently to the overlook, at elevation 2,258 feet.

All three trails are closed to bicycles and to motorized travel.

Trip summary:	Longer day or overnight hikes in the South Fork Campbell Creek drainage to Ship Lake Pass and Hidden Lake.
Distances:	Ship Lake Pass: 5.5 miles one way.
	Hidden Lake: 4.5 miles.
Special features:	High alpine scenery, unbridged stream crossings.
Location:	In the Glen Alps area in south Anchorage.
Difficulty:	Moderate.
Trail type:	More developed trail to the South Fork Campbell Creek crossing; less developed trail/route beyond.
Total elevation gain:	1,800 feet to Ship Lake Pass; 1,500 feet to Hidden Lake.
Best season:	June through September.
Maps:	USGS Anchorage A-8 (SE) and Anchorage A-7; Alaska Road and Recreation Map *Anchorage and Vicinity*.
Manager:	Chugach State Park.

Key points:

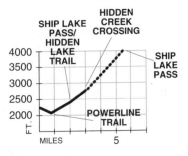

0.4	Powerline Trail
2.0	Hidden Lake/Ship Lake Pass Trail
3.0	Trail fork at Hidden Lake Creek
5.5	Ship Lake Pass

Finding the trailhead: The trailhead is located at the Glen Alps entrance to Chugach State Park. See Flattop Mountain (Hike 31) for directions.

The hike: Three-quarters of Chugach State Park is above treeline, and this walk from Glen Alps is a fine way to sample the Chugach's alpine country. This hike is good all summer, but fall, from late August to mid-September, may be its finest season, when the gnarled mountain hemlocks are still green, the blueberry and bearberry have turned fiery red, and the willows, birches, and mountain ash have gone gold.

Take one of the two parallel trails from the Glen Alps parking area to the Powerline Trail. They both begin just to the left of the stairs leading to Flattop Mountain. The trail to the left is a foot trail, and the one on the right is open to mountain bikes. Mountain bikes are also allowed on the Powerline Trail.

The Powerline Trail is just what it sounds like, an access road along the powerline that runs up the South Fork of Campbell Creek over, you guessed it, Powerline Pass. Turn right (southeast) onto the trail. Ship Lake Pass is at the head of the large tributary valley visible north of the South Fork.

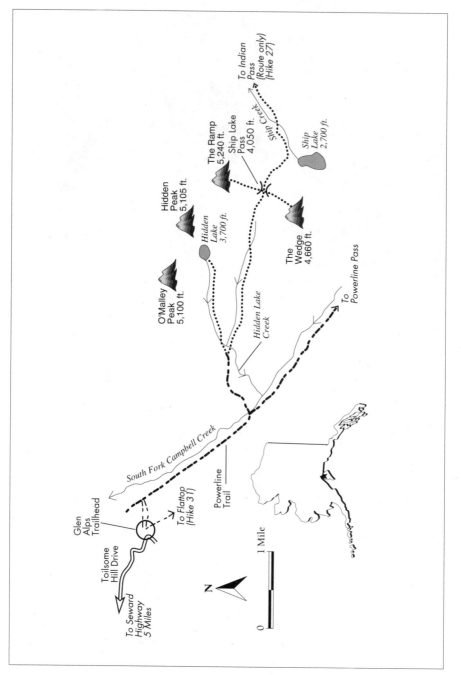

Ship Lake from Ship Lake Pass.

The junction with the trail toward Ship Lake Pass and Hidden Lake, about two miles from Glen Alps, is signed and obvious (at this writing, it is signed as the Hidden Lake Trail). Turn east onto the trail, a jeep trail that leads to a ford of the South Fork. About 0.1 mile past the crossing, the trail bears left as a narrower, eroded footpath that climbs through mountain hemlock into alpine tundra.

In another mile, the Ship Lake Pass and Hidden Lake trails divide at an unsigned, fairly confusing junction by Hidden Lake Creek. To head for the pass, bear right across the creek at one of two crossings. Intermittent, beaten paths wind up both sides of the sparkling alpine stream that flows out of the pass. For Hidden Lake, don't cross Hidden Lake Creek here; continue to another creek crossing above the confluence of the Ship Pass Creek, cross here and head up the low ridge on the south side of Hidden Lake Creek.

The paths to both destinations eventually peter out, but the routes are obvious in the wide-open tundra. Finding the way up the broad valley to Ship Lake Pass (4,050 feet) is easy, wandering where you will along the creek or higher up the slope. At the pass, linger a while over the views of Ship Lake and the wild Chugach Mountains. For even better views, take a side trip to The Ramp (5,240 feet) to the left (north), or The Wedge (4,660 feet) to the right (south) of the pass. Each peak is a bit less than a mile from the pass.

Hidden Lake, a small tarn in a rock-strewn bowl below Hidden Peak, is a slightly shorter destination from Glen Alps, at 4.5 miles and 3,700 feet elevation. To take in both the pass and the lake on the same trip, sidehill west from the pass along the slope below The Ramp. Hiking a contour about 300 feet below the pass intersects the Hidden Creek valley at the lake's elevation.

Dall sheep are common; also look for Alaska's "torrent ducks," harlequin ducks, navigating the foaming streams like expert kayakers. There is good camping near Ship Lake Pass Creek—bring a stove and fuel, as no fires are allowed, and there isn't any wood anyway. Snow remains near the pass into the early summer. Use caution traveling then; slipping while walking on hardened snow can result in uncontrolled slides, and late-season avalanches are possible under the right conditions.

The Glen Alps-Indian Creek traverse. Linking the Ship Lake Pass hike with the Indian Valley hike (see Hike 27) makes a fine two-pass traverse of about 15 miles.

Shorter hikes. For an easy walk from Glen Alps, take the Powerline Trail, which hikers share with mountain bikers, up to 5 miles one way up the South Fork Campbell Creek valley.

33 WILLIWAW LAKES

Trip summary:	A longer day or overnight trip to Williwaw Lakes, at the headwaters of the Middle Fork of Campbell Creek.
Distance:	5 miles one way to lower Williwaw Lakes.
Special features:	Alpine scenery, wildlife, lakes. There are several alternate trips on the trails to Williwaw Lakes; see "other hikes" below.
Location:	In the Glen Alps area in south Anchorage.
Difficulty:	Moderate.
Trail type:	More developed trail the first mile; less developed trail the next 3 miles; an alpine route the last mile and beyond.
Total elevation gain:	Lower lakes: 600 feet in, 200 feet out. Upper lake: 1,200 feet in, 200 feet out.
Best season:	June through September.
Maps:	USGS Anchorage A-8 (SE, NE) and A-7; Alaska Road and Recreation Map *Anchorage and Vicinity.*
Manager:	Chugach State Park.

Key points:

0.4	Powerline Trail
0.5	Middle Fork Loop Trail
0.8	South Fork Campbell Creek bridge
1.0	Junction with "The Ballpark" route
2.0	Williwaw Lakes Trail
5.0	Lower Williwaw Lakes
6.0	Upper Williwaw Lakes

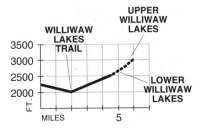

Finding the trailhead: The trailhead is located at the Glen Alps entrance to Chugach State Park. See Flattop Mountain (Hike 31) for directions.

The hike: The upper Middle Fork of Campbell Creek is a jewel of an alpine valley, so close to the heart of Anchorage that it's possible to do a wilderness day hike among Dall sheep and get back to the city in time for an off-Broadway play. Bands of sheep roam the valley and ridges, and Williwaw Lakes, a series of shallow alpine lakes below 5,445-foot Mount Williwaw, lie at the head of the valley.

There are two ways to get to the Williwaw Lakes Trail, which officially begins near the point where the Middle Fork Loop Trail crosses the Middle Fork: from Prospect Heights Trailhead (see Hike 34), or, a mile shorter, less of a climb, and the hike described here, from Glen Alps. Hikers doing the Middle Fork-North Fork loop described below, though, should begin at Prospect Heights.

From the Glen Alps parking area, take one of the two parallel trails to the left of the stairs leading to Flattop Mountain. The trail to the left is for foot traffic only, and the one on the right is open to mountain bikes. Hike about 0.4 mile and turn right on the Powerline Trail, continue 0.1 mile, and turn left on the Middle Fork Loop Trail. Descend the trail, cross the bridge over the South Fork of Campbell Creek, and in another 0.1 mile, turn left at the junction with the route to The Ballpark (unsigned at this writing). From here, it's another mile to the junction of the Middle Fork Trail with the Williwaw Lakes Trail.

Between the South Fork bridge and the curve in the Middle Fork valley at about Mile 2.5 of the hike, there are a few wet spots in the trail. The park is planning to plank the wettest sections. About 0.8 mile past the South Fork bridge, the trail crosses a tiny creek on stones in an open-canopy stand of white spruce; the trail has dropped below tree line briefly.

As the Middle Fork trail nears the intersection with the Williwaw Lakes Trail, look down over the toy city of Anchorage, with its miniature skyscrapers and subdivisions. Mount Susitna, the Sleeping Lady, and farther away, the snowy Aleutian Range form the backdrop.

Turn right onto the Williwaw Trail, and follow the Middle Fork valley around a bend to the east, where Mount Williwaw comes into view. The hike cuts through the stunted mountain hemlock that marks tree limit in the Chugach, and in the last mile below Williwaw Lakes, emerges into alpine

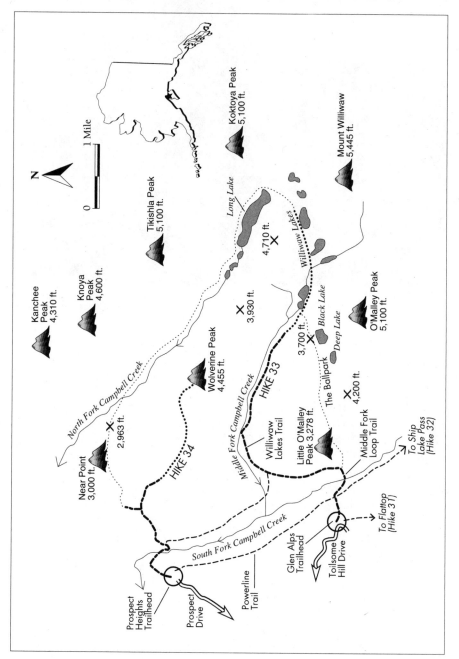

tundra as the trail grows fainter. The lower lake is at 2,600 feet elevation. The chain of lakes tops out at 3,250 feet, the farthest a bit over a mile away. There is good camping at the lakes; don't forget the camp stove.

Williwaw Lakes and Mount Williwaw.

Other hikes: Black Lake. From the lower lake take a side trip to Black Lake, in a hanging valley about a mile to the southwest and 300 feet above the Middle Fork valley. Climb up toward the obvious drainage on the mountainside above the lower lake.

Return via The Ballpark. For new scenery on the hike back to Glen Alps, try the high route (no developed trail) to Black Lake, Deep Lake, The Ballpark, and the South Fork of Campbell Creek. The route, a bit over 4 miles long, stays above treeline the entire trip.

Hiking it requires negotiating a steep section of loose boulders and talus between Black Lake and the 3,700-foot pass that leads to Deep Lake and The Ballpark. The route crosses The Ballpark, a big, flat expanse of rocky tundra, and begins the descent into the South Fork valley south of Little O'Malley Peak. You'll need a map and compass for this trip, especially in marginal weather.

Mount Williwaw. The challenging summit route to Mount Williwaw, the peak atop the vertical wall above the lakes, starts up the drainage to the right of the peak and climbs the south ridge. There is no avoiding one section of free climbing with considerable exposure, so only experienced backcountry scramblers should try it.

Long Lake Loop. Another trip, probably best done as a 2-3 day hike but possible as a very long day trip, links the Middle and North Fork of Campbell Creek valleys through the pass above the upper Williwaw Lake. This 18-mile jaunt is a gem of a hike that passes nearly a dozen alpine lakes and ponds. The largest is mile-long Long Lake, near the head of the North Fork.

The trip is best hiked from the Prospect Heights Trailhead. From Williwaw Lakes, cross the obvious pass left of Mount Williwaw to Long Lake and the North Fork valley, follow the North Fork downstream, pick your route toward Near Point (climbing to the 2,750-foot pass southeast of the point is the shortest), and intersect the Near Point/Wolverine Bowl Trail for the hike back to Prospect Heights. Take along a topographic map and your route-finding skills for this trip.

Shorter hikes. A stroll out the Powerline Trail, down to the South Fork of Campbell Creek, and out the subalpine trail to the Middle Fork bridge makes a fine shorter or family hike.

---

34 *WOLVERINE PEAK*

Trip summary:	A longer day hike to the summit of Wolverine Peak, a 4,455-foot landmark summit above south Anchorage.
Distance:	5.5 miles one way to the summit.
Special features:	Great views of Anchorage and Campbell Creek. The first 2 miles of the trail are open to mountain bikes.
Location:	Prospect Heights Trailhead above Anchorage.
Difficulty:	Moderately strenuous.
Trail type:	More developed trail for 2 miles; less developed trail for 0.6 mile; and a well-traveled alpine route beyond.
Total elevation gain:	3,450 feet in, 100 feet out.
Best season:	June through September.
Maps:	USGS Anchorage A-8 (NE) and A-7; Alaska Road and Recreation Map *Anchorage and Vicinity*.
Manager:	Chugach State Park.

See Map on Page 139

Key points:

1.0	Middle Fork Campbell Creek
1.3	Middle Fork Loop Trail junction
2.0	Wolverine Peak Trail
2.6	Tundra viewpoint
5.5	Wolverine Peak

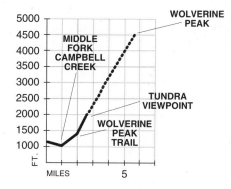

Finding the trailhead: Drive about 6.5 miles south of downtown Anchorage on the New Seward Highway, and exit east toward the Chugach Mountains on O'Malley Road. Drive about 4 miles to a sharp left curve in the road. Follow the curve and take the immediate right turn onto Upper O'Malley Road.

In about 0.5 mile, turn left at a T intersection onto Prospect Drive. In another mile, bear left where Prospect Drive intersects Sidorof Lane, and continue 0.1 mile to the Prospect Heights parking area on the right. The trailhead for this hike is at the far end of the parking area.

The hike: Wolverine Peak, the triangular peak at the far point of two alpine ridges above south Anchorage, is a well-known local landmark. The peak offers a fine overlook of the upper North and Middle Fork Campbell Creek valleys and a view of some of Chugach State Park's rugged inner peaks. The peak got its name from wolverine tracks once found on the summit ridge.

This trip is so close to town many people do it after work on long summer days. The first 2 miles of the trail, an old homestead road along the lower slopes of the Chugach Mountains, is open to mountain bikes; it's possible to ride the first 2 miles and hike the rest of the way.

From the trailhead, bear left at the powerline in 0.1 mile and continue to the bridge across the Middle Fork of Campbell Creek, about a mile from the parking area. After a switchback, the wide trail passes a junction with the Middle Fork Loop Trail at 1.3 miles. Just beyond a small stream, at about Mile 2 and 1,300 feet elevation, take the narrower trail to the right, the Wolverine Peak Trail, and follow it uphill through the thickest part of the Chugach brush zone.

At 2.6 miles, a flat patch of tundra with a fine view to the west makes a nice rest stop or a destination for a shorter hike. If continuing to the peak, climb to the ridge to the right, leaving the brush behind, and follow the crest as it curves left and up to intersect Wolverine's northwest summit ridge. A few snow patches linger near the summit into the early summer, but the route and the peak generally melt off quite early. The wild view to the east is worth the climb, and it's not a bad view toward Anchorage and across Cook Inlet, either.

Shorter hikes. Hike out to the end of the old homestead road, at a small knob below Near Point, about 2.5 miles one way. The summit of Near Point is another 1.5 mile on a less developed trail/route. The hike to the first patch of tundra on the Wolverine Peak Trail, about 2.6 miles one way, is a shorter trip with a view.

35 ROVER'S RUN

Trip summary:	A shorter day to half-day hike in the forest near the South Fork of Campbell Creek in Anchorage.
Distances:	2.5 miles one way or a 6-mile loop.
Special features:	Salmon runs, wildlife, and a pristine creek in the heart of Anchorage.
Location:	Far North Bicentennial Park, in southeast Anchorage.
Difficulty:	Easy.
Trail type:	More developed.
Total elevation gain:	200 feet.
Best season:	Mid-May to mid-October.
Maps:	USGS Anchorage A-8 (NE); Bureau of Land Management/Municipality of Anchorage *Far North Bicentennial Park and Campbell Tract Trails*.
Manager:	Municipality of Anchorage, Parks and Recreation; U.S. Bureau of Land Management.

Finding the trailhead: The hike begins at one of two trailheads on Campbell Airstrip Road in Anchorage. From north of Anchorage, take the Muldoon Road south exit off the Glenn Highway, about 4.5 miles northeast of downtown. Follow Muldoon Road and its extension, Tudor Road, a total of 4 miles from the highway, and turn left (south) at the traffic light at Campbell Airstrip Road.

From downtown Anchorage or south of Anchorage, take the Tudor Road exit east from the New Seward Highway. Tudor is about 3 miles south of downtown. Drive about 3 miles to Campbell Airstrip Road and turn right. The Anchorage People Mover bus #75 runs to the corner of Tudor and Campbell Airstip Road.

The two trailheads are at Mile 1 (the Buckner Trailhead) and Mile 2.3 (the South Bivouac Trailhead), as measured from Tudor Road. Either trailhead will do — the hike connects the two trailheads. The hike is downhill from Mile 2.3 to Mile 1, but it's so nearly flat it really doesn't matter which way you walk.

Warning. Trailhead crime, mainly of the smash, grab, and dash variety, is unfortunately a problem in Bicentennial Park. Leave nothing of value in your car that may invite thieves.

ROVER'S RUN

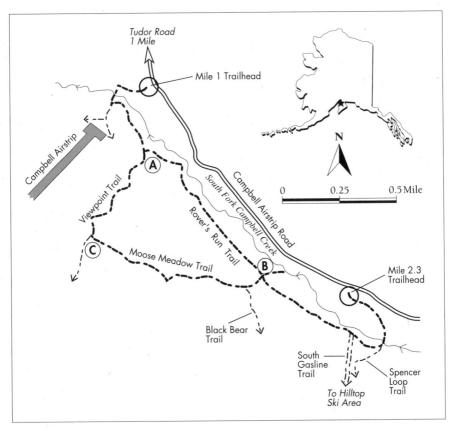

The hike: Far North Bicentennial Park, Anchorage's crown jewel, is 5,000 acres of forests, streams, and wetlands on the edge of the city. Salmon, bears, moose, coyotes, lynx, goshawks, and other wilderness wildlife frequent the park and adjoining BLM land. Far-sighted citizens got these former military lands dedicated as a park in 1976, and citizen groups still reassemble from time to time to fight the latest development threat to this last piece of the real Alaska in Anchorage.

Known mainly as a winter park for skiing, sled dog training, and racing, and skijoring (skiing while being pulled by one or more dogs in harness), summer brings visitors too: hikers, runners, mountain bikers, and horseback riders. Other summer visitors are salmon (a king run in mid-summer and a silver run in fall) and the creatures that like salmon best, black and brown bears. Don't assume you won't run across a bear this close to the city. Moose are common in the park.

Rover's Run Trail was built in the late 1980s by the local skijoring club. It's a non-motorized, multiple-use trail; you may see bikers, runners, and horseback riders as well as other hikers.

Hiking the 2.5-mile version of this trip requires two vehicles. Other possibilities are to walk out and back to your starting point, making a 5-mile round trip, or to do the return via the Moose Meadow Trail, a 6-mile loop.

To hike from the Mile 1 trailhead, park by the vehicle barrier in the pullout, step over the barrier, and walk down the graveled trail to the right. Continue over the steel bridge that spans Campbell Creek and, in the opening beyond the bridge, turn left onto the Viewpoint Trail, a wide trail leading into the trees. (BLM plans to build a second bridge over the creek to separate winter foot and dogsled traffic; when built, take this bridge for a small shortcut.)

Cross an abandoned road in about 200 feet, and continue about 0.2 mile more, turning left at a skijoring sign (intersection A on the map) onto the Rover's Run Trail. Rover's Run is a narrower path that parallels the creek through spruce and birch woods and cranberry bushes. Here, thrush songs and the sounds of the creek begin to drown out the noise of the city.

At a four-way intersection (B), the Rover's Run Trail is straight ahead. To the left is a green tunnel to the creek, 0.1 mile away. The Rover's Run Trail continues through open woods and crosses the South Gasline Trail. To the right, uphill, is Hilltop Ski Area and Abbott Road. In another 0.1 mile the trail merges with the Spencer Loop Trail. Bear left and then left again to a bridge across Campbell Creek, and hike up to the Mile 2.3 trailhead.

Turn around at the bridge if you're returning to the Mile 1 trailhead. Back at intersection B, continue straight ahead on the Rover's Run Trail to return the way you came. To take the Moose Meadow Trail, turn left here. In another 0.1 mile, pass the intersection with the Black Bear Trail, which eventually ties in with the Hillside Ski Trails and Service High School. Just a few feet to the left is a small bridge over the pretty headwater spring of Little Campbell Creek.

Continue on the Moose Meadow Trail to the top of a small rocky hill, intersection C. Turn right onto the wider Viewpoint Trail and stay on it as it bends and twists back to intersection A. Bear left and retrace your steps across the bridge to the Mile 1 trailhead.

Bicentennial Park is open for day use only, closing at 11 pm.

Fishing. The creek is closed to all salmon fishing, but is open to fishing for rainbows and Dolly Varden, which are most plentiful in the fall. At this writing, rainbows are catch-and-release only, and special tackle restrictions are in effect, so check the regulations before you go.

KNIK ARM

Eagle River, Eklutna River, and Knik River flow into Knik Arm, the north arm of Cook Inlet. The trails into the mountains in these watersheds make some of the finest hikes in Southcentral Alaska. The Eagle River Nature Center and Eklutna Lake are two of the most popular local outdoor destinations. The recreation area at Eklutna Lake includes trails, a campground and a picnic area.

36   SOUTH FORK EAGLE RIVER

Trip summary:	A longer day or overnight hike following the alpine South Fork valley to Eagle and Symphony Lakes.
Distance:	Eagle and Symphony Lakes: 5.5 miles one way.
Special features:	Alpine and mountain scenery, off-trail hiking, and mountaineering.
Location:	8 miles southeast of Eagle River.
Difficulty:	Moderate.
Trail type:	Less developed, with some boulder-hopping in the last mile.
Total elevation gain:	About 1,000 feet in, 200 feet out.
Best season:	Mid-June through September.
Maps:	USGS Anchorage A-7 (NW, NE); Alaska Road and Recreation Map *Anchorage and Vicinity*.
Manager:	Chugach State Park.

Key points:

2.0   South Fork bridge
4.5   Eagle Lake outlet stream
5.5   Trail's end between Eagle and Symphony Lakes

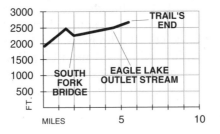

Finding the trailhead: Take the Eagle River Loop/Hiland Road exit off the Glenn Highway, a mile south of Eagle River and 11 miles north of downtown Anchorage. Go east, toward the mountains, and turn right at the traffic light at Hiland Road in 0.2 mile. Drive 7.3 miles on Hiland Road and turn right at a Chugach State Park sign on South Creek Road. Turn right on West River Drive in 0.3 mile, and in another 0.1 mile turn left into the trailhead parking area.

SOUTH FORK EAGLE RIVER

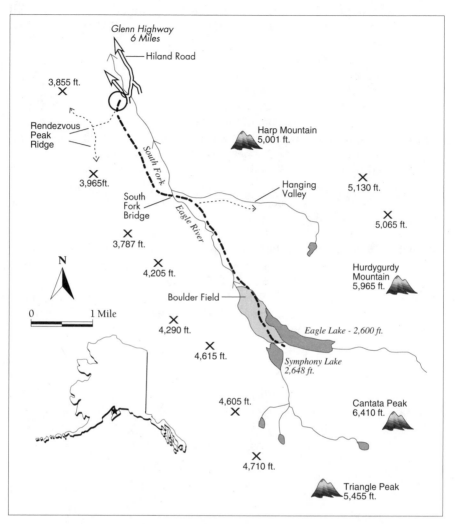

Glenn Highway
6 Miles

Hiland Road

3,855 ft.
X

Rendezvous
Peak
Ridge

South Fork

Harp Mountain
5,001 ft.

X
3,965ft.

South
Fork
Bridge

Eagle River

Hanging
Valley

X
5,130 ft.

X
5,065 ft.

X
3,787 ft.

N

X
4,205 ft.

Boulder Field

0   1 Mile

Hurdygurdy
Mountain
5,965 ft.

X
4,290 ft.

Eagle Lake - 2,600 ft.

X
4,615 ft.

Symphony Lake
2,648 ft.

4,605 ft.
X

Cantata Peak
6,410 ft.

X
4,710 ft.

Triangle Peak
5,455 ft.

The hike: The trailhead, just below treeline at 1,900 feet, is at the edge of a subalpine subdivision with a short summer and a longer avalanche season. For about the first mile, the trail is in sight of subdivision homes as it traverses the slope west of the South Fork of Eagle River. The first section of the trail has been routed high on the west side of the valley to avoid private land in the valley bottom.

The hike begins on a boardwalk through spruce forest, but quickly climbs above this last patch of spruce. Listen for magpies and golden-crowned sparrows as you hike across the slope, passing patches of willow and dwarf birch and small, densely clustered mountain hemlocks. At 2 miles, the trail descends to the valley bottom and crosses the South Fork on a bridge. Look

147

for the hanging side valley east of the bridge, which makes a good cross-country hike; see below.

The trail is a bit wet in places between the bridge and Eagle Lake. A small seasonal bridge crosses the lake's outlet stream and leads onto a massive medial moraine (a rock pile that forms between two lobes of a glacier), which fills the valley between the lakes. Then it's boulder-hopping time, with cairns marking the way up the rocky moraine toward a high point between Eagle and Symphony Lakes.

Hike to the strange structure on the spine of the moraine, an old, partially-completed cabin, and take in the view of Eagle and Symphony Lakes, their valleys, and Cantata and Triangle Peaks above. The rough trail continues a bit farther on the long ridge between the lakes. There are campsites on the ridge and by the lakes. Symphony Lake has better drinking water, with fewer glaciers in its watershed. If you have time, take extra days to explore more of the South Fork drainage. Experienced mountaineers can tackle some of the rugged peaks above the lakes.

Other hikes: Rendezvous Peak Ridge. A hiker-beaten track peels off uphill to the west a few minutes past the trailhead, leading to a 2,850-foot saddle on the ridge between the South Fork and Ship Creek. You can hike the ridge south, with its ups and downs, all the way to the lakes, or a bit over 2 miles north to Rendezvous Peak, from where hikers can descend to Arctic Valley Ski Area and Arctic Valley Road. If you want to head toward

South Fork Eagle River bridge.

Low-bush cranberries.

the lakes on the ridgetop, an alternate way to gain the ridge is to climb to the saddle above the trail just before it descends to the river, a little less than 2 miles from the trailhead.

South Fork hanging valley. The high valley on the east side of the South Fork above the foot bridge at Mile 2 makes a fine cross-country hike. Once across the bridge, walk on the trail until it turns south toward Eagle Lake, and climb the slope into the hanging valley. It's about 3 miles to the lake on one of the headwater forks, and about 4 miles to the 5,000-foot ridge overlooking Eagle River, the next large valley to the east.

Eagle and Symphony Lake valleys. From the end of the trail, explore the valleys above Eagle and Symphony lakes. The trailless Eagle Lake valley runs back to the falls below Flute Glacier, but is easier to explore on skis in winter. The Symphony Lake valley, also trailless, leads back to some smaller tarns. Due south of Symphony Lake and about 1,700 feet higher is a plateau that overlooks the North Fork of Ship Creek.

Shorter hikes. Hike as far as the South Fork bridge, 2 miles one way, for a shorter day trip with alpine views, a pretty stream and berry picking in season.

Southcentral's Berry Crop

The South Fork of Eagle River and other Southcentral trails are good places to stock up on wild berries in August and September. Blueberries, raspberries, and salmonberries are local favorites. Watermelon berries make a tasty trail snack, and berry lovers also gather currants, nagoonberries, rose hips, crowberries, and low-bush and high-bush cranberries. The musky scent of the red-leafed high-bush cranberry is the smell of the Southcentral woods in fall.

The rest of the crop—bearberry, timberberry, mountain ash, elderberry, Devil's club, soapberry, and a few others vary in edibility and are better admired than eaten. Baneberry, a common red berry, is extremely poisonous. Baneberry also comes in a striking white form known as porcelain berry.

Most of the common berries are red or orange. The berries' riot of color, mixed with the lush green of late summer, makes berry time a colorful season to be on the trail.

Trip summary:	A variety of day and multi-day hikes in Eagle River's glacial valley from Eagle River Nature Center.
Distances:	Rodak Nature Trail: a 0.6-mile interpretive loop trail.
	Albert Loop Trail: a 3.2-mile loop to Eagle River and back to the nature center.
	Eagle River Trail: 12 miles one way to the head of the valley; day hikes to a 3-day backpack.
	Crow Pass Traverse: a 24-mile traverse between Eagle River and Girdwood over Crow Pass; a 2 to 4 day backpack or a killer day hike.
Special features:	A glacier-carved valley, wildlife, mountaineering, an interpretive trail, and one of Southcentral Alaska's classic alpine traverses.
Location:	12 miles southeast of Eagle River.
Difficulty:	Rodak and Albert Loop: easy.
	Eagle River: easy to moderate, depending on the distance hiked.
	Crow Pass: moderately strenuous.
Trail type:	Rodak and Albert Loop: more developed.
	Eagle River: More developed near the nature center, and less developed, with a few rough, steep sections, beyond.
	Crow Pass: less developed south of Crow Pass, more developed north.
Total elevation gain:	Rodak and Albert Loop: 150 feet.
	Eagle River: up to 500 feet.
	Crow Pass: 3,100 feet from Eagle River, 2,000 feet from Girdwood.
Best season:	Valley trails: Mid-May to mid-October. Traverse: Late June through September.
Maps:	USGS Anchorage A-7 (NE), Anchorage A-6; Alaska Road and Recreation Map *Anchorage and Vicinity*; Alaska State Parks leaflet *Historic Iditarod/Crow Pass Trail*.
Manager:	Chugach State Park.

Key points:

Eagle River Trail

0.05   Rodak Nature Trail and Albert Loop junction (to viewing deck)
0.3   Second Rodak Nature Trail junction
0.7   Four Corners (Albert Loop junction)
1.7   Rapids Camp
3.0   Echo Bend
4.0   The Perch
5.0   Heritage Falls
5.2   Icicle Creek
8.5   Twin Falls
11.0   Thunder Gorge
12.0   Ford Site (12 miles to Crow Pass Trailhead - see Hike 25)
12.3   Glacier Lake (head of Eagle River Valley)

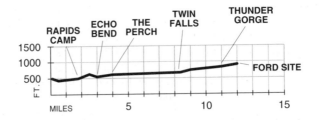

Finding the trailhead: Take the Eagle River exit off the Glenn Highway, 13 miles north of Anchorage. Turn east, take a right turn onto Eagle River Road, and drive 12 miles to the end of the road at the Eagle River Nature Center. The trailhead for all the trails is behind the nature center.

For directions to the Crow Pass Trailhead outside Girdwood, see Hike 25, Crow Pass.

The hikes: The Eagle River Nature Center is a homey log cabin with maps and displays, books for sale, binoculars and spotting scopes set up for scanning the ridges for sheep, and a "do-touch" exhibit for kids of all ages. The private, non-profit "Friends" group that runs the center also schedules nature programs and walks throughout the summer. Pick up the map of the nearby trails in the center or at the trailhead behind the building.

Head for the back of the visitor center to start your hike. A view of Polar Bear Peak and the remnant glacier hanging from its summit greet you as you head down the trail. It's not hard to imagine the valley under a wall of ice 4,000 feet thick, as it was at the height of glaciation a few thousand years back. A lot more recently, the trail between here and Girdwood over Crow Pass was part of the historic Iditarod Trail, the famous gold rush-era trail between Seward, Iditarod, and Nome.

Rodak Nature Trail. The 0.6-mile Rodak trail forks right at a signed junction in a hundred yards. Interpretive signs along the trail explain glacial geology, forest ecology, the salmon life cycle, and northern seasons. The trail loops down to a large viewing deck built over a spring-fed stream that

EAGLE RIVER VALLEY

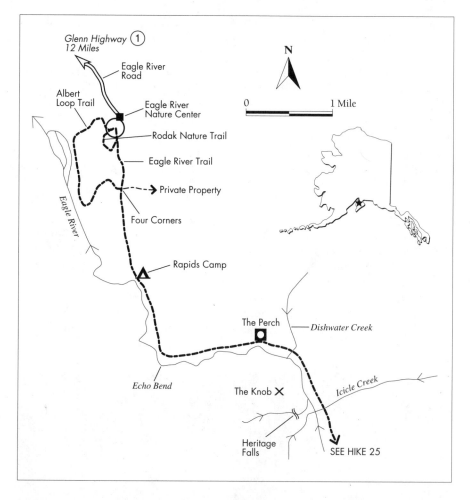

Glenn Highway ① 12 Miles

Eagle River Road

Albert Loop Trail

Eagle River Nature Center

Rodak Nature Trail

Eagle River Trail

Private Property

Four Corners

Eagle River

N

0   1 Mile

Rapids Camp

The Perch

Dishwater Creek

Echo Bend

The Knob ✕

Icicle Creek

Heritage Falls

SEE HIKE 25

flows through a wet meadow. There are small salmon runs in the stream in late summer. The springs that feed the stream flow out of a rocky glacial moraine a mile up the valley.

The beaver-made ponds and dams along the stream are changing the local ecology from forest to wetland. Only in recent years have goldeneyes, mallards, snipe, and other waterfowl begun using this part of the valley. From the deck, enjoy the great view up the valley, and look for water ouzels bobbing at the water's edge. There may be a mink nearby, or a bald eagle flying up the river.

To complete the Rodak loop, continue on the trail to the second junction with the Eagle River Trail, and turn left to return to the nature center.

Albert Loop Trail. The loop follows the Eagle River Trail for 0.7 mile through a bottomland forest of spruce, birch, and cottonwood to the Four Corners trail junction. Turn right at the junction, and hike down the trail to the gravel bars along Eagle River. An alternate trail cuts through the forest and avoids the river.

Posts mark the trail along the valley bottom downstream, and a sign marks where the trail reenters the forest. It winds back toward the nature center, crossing five bridges, each one over a small stream, on the way.

The loop trail may be occasionally flooded, courtesy of those same dam-building beavers that make the Rodak Trail a good wildlife hike. The park plans to keep it open, but it's a good idea to check on conditions at the center.

Eagle River Trail. The trail up Eagle River meanders along the valley floor 12 miles to the head of the valley. Peaks rise to 7,000 feet above the valley, and the many vertical mountain walls, hanging valleys, glaciers and water-falls make this a Yosemite without the crowds.

Moose, black bear, and the occasional grizzly frequent Eagle River Valley. Moose can often be seen near the visitor center, and there is a healthy popu-lation of black bears in the valley, especially in spring and early summer, so use good bear country practices when hiking and camping. There is a large Dall sheep population in the upper reaches of the valley, with a permit-only sheep-hunting season in August and September.

With as many as 50 species of wildflowers, good mushroom hunting, side canyons to explore, and challenging mountaineering access (experienced and equipped climbers only) to peaks like Polar Bear and Mount Yukla,

Crossing the swinging bridge over Icicle Creek, Eagle River Valley.

154

Eagle River Valley and Polar Bear Peak.

there is plenty to keep valley visitors busy. Look for animal tracks on the sand bars along the river.

There are good campsites practically everywhere, in the forest and on the river's gravel bars. The river is glacial, so it's heavy with silt after the glacier begins to melt in the summer heat. Clear water options are to carry water from the nearest side stream, find a small side channel on the river with clearer water, or let pots of river water partially settle out before using it. Don't forget to boil or filter all drinking water.

Fires are allowed only in the fire grates at several of the more popular campsites, but save the wood and bring a stove. It's not a great idea to camp near the fire grates, as there may be lingering food odors that can attract bears.

Twelve miles up the valley is a marked ford site, the safest crossing for hikers heading for Raven Creek and Crow Pass. The ford is normally passable, but after periods of rain or glacier melt during hot weather, it may be more difficult or unsafe. The crossing is wide and the water is cold, so an extra pair of shoes and socks is a good idea.

The glacier lake at the head of the valley is about 0.3 mile upstream (southeast) from the ford site, accessible from either side of the river. There is no trail but the walking is easy through the cottonwoods along the river's wide gravel bar.

The trail, especially in the upper part of the valley, is rough and a bit slow in places.

Crow Pass traverse. The 24-mile hike over Crow Pass is usually walked in the opposite direction, from Crow Creek Trailhead outside Girdwood to the nature center. Some Crow Pass aficionados, though, like the hike better from Eagle River to Girdwood, as the trip builds up to the highlight of Crow Pass more gradually. Come prepared for stormy weather, and be prepared to be amazed no matter which way you walk it. See Hike 25, Crow Pass.

Shorter hikes. The Rodak and Albert loop trails are very popular, as is the out-and-back hike to Four Corners on the Eagle River Trail (0.7 mile one way). These trails and the nature center are great for kids.

Good longer day hikes are to Rapids Camp (1.7 miles one way), where a side trail descends to the bank of the river's rocky canyon; Echo Bend (3 miles one way), a forested flat by the river; the Perch (4 miles one way), a rocky outcrop with a great view up the valley; or Heritage Falls (5 miles one way), a waterfall across the river from the trail. All these destinations are generally easy hikes.

Fishing. There are a few Dolly Varden in the river, but the fishing isn't the best in the cloudy glacial water.

---

38 *THUNDER BIRD FALLS*

Trip summary:	A shorter day hike to Thunder Bird Falls along the Eklutna River gorge.
Distance:	1 mile one way.
Special features:	A gorge and waterfall.
Location:	25 miles north of Anchorage.
Difficulty:	Easy.
Trail type:	More developed.
Total elevation gain:	About 200 feet in and 100 feet out.
Best season:	May to mid-October.
Maps:	USGS Anchorage B-7 (NE).
Manager:	Chugach State Park.

Key points:

0.3 Gorge viewing deck
0.8 Falls viewing deck
1.0 Base of falls

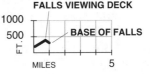

Finding the trailhead: From the south, take the "Thunderbird" Falls exit off the Glenn Highway, 25 miles north of downtown Anchorage. (There are two spellings for the name of the creek and the falls; the USGS, the name authority, uses two words.) The exit leads in only one direction, east. Drive about 0.4 mile to the marked trailhead on the right side of the road, just before the bridge over the Eklutna River.

Coming from the north, take the Eklutna exit 26 miles north of Anchorage and turn right (south) onto the Old Glenn Highway. Continue about 0.6

THUNDER BIRD FALLS

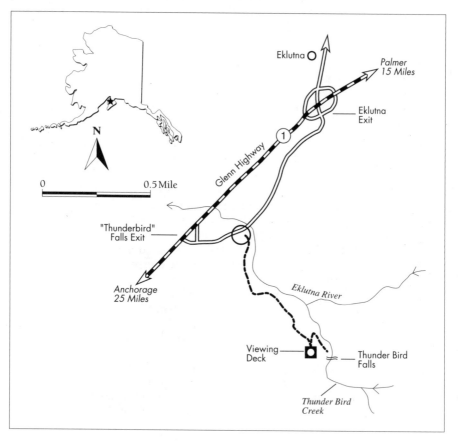

mile to the parking area on the left, just after crossing the Eklutna River bridge.

When leaving Thunder Bird Falls, remember that the "Thunderbird" Falls freeway entrance is for northbound traffic only. Drive to the Eklutna interchange to enter the freeway southbound.

The hike: A short, scenic trail through spruce and birch forest, this highly developed trail leads along the Eklutna River Gorge to a crashing waterfall on Thunder Bird Creek, a tributary of the Eklutna. The trail is limited to foot traffic only, and no camping is allowed.

The first part of the hike follows the lip of the Eklutna gorge on a narrow right-of-way between the river and a housing subdivision. The viewing deck in 0.3 mile offers the best view into the gorge. Please don't approach the edge on the old side trails, for your safety and to let the old trail scars heal.

Near the falls is a trail intersection—continue straight ahead to the best view of the falls, about 100 yards away on a long, sturdy boardwalk built over the face of a cliff. The boardwalk is about the elevation of the top of the falls. To walk to the base of the falls, go downhill at the trail junction. This trail is a bit steep at first, but levels out at the elevation of the creek.

In the canyon bottom, spray from the falls keeps the vegetation wet and lush. This is a good place to teach any kids along what devil's club, the tall plant with huge leaves, is. Also be alert for a glimpse or sound of a water ouzel near the falls. There is no good view of the falls from here because of a sharp bend in the creek. The steep, slick rock faces here are dangerous; don't try climbing them.

39 TWIN PEAKS

Trip summary:	Half-day or longer day hikes or an overnight trip from Eklutna Lake to the alpine Twin Peaks area and East Twin Pass.
Distances:	Twin Peaks Trail: 2.5 miles one way. East Twin Pass: 4 miles one way.
Special features:	Alpine meadows and wildflowers, abundant Dall sheep. There is a day use fee.
Location:	In the Eklutna Lake area, 35 miles north of Anchorage.
Difficulty:	Moderate to the end of the Twin Peaks Trail; strenuous to East Twin Pass.
Trail type:	Twin Peaks Trail: more developed trail. Twin Peaks basin and East Twin Pass: route/cross-country.
Total elevation gain:	About 1,800 feet in to the end of the maintained trail; about 3,600 feet in and 100 out to East Twin Pass.
Best season:	Mid-June through September.
Maps:	USGS Anchorage B-6 (NW); Alaska State Parks brochure *Eklutna Lake*.
Manager:	Chugach State Park.

Key points:
  1.5 Viewpoint
  2.5 End of the Twin Peaks Trail
  4.0 East Twin Pass

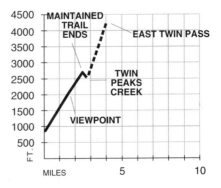

TWIN PEAKS

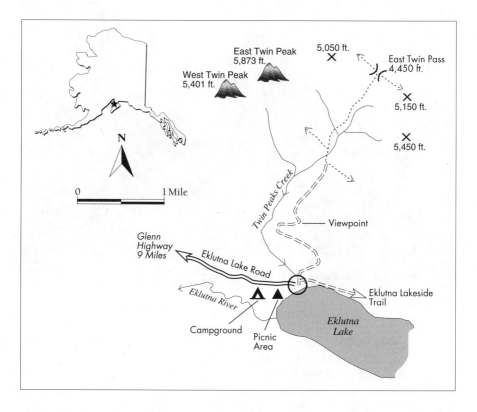

Finding the trailhead: Take the Eklutna exit off the Glenn Highway, 26 miles north of Anchorage and 16 miles south of Palmer. Exit east, follow the access road as it curves to the south for about 0.4 mile, and turn left (east) onto the Eklutna Lake Road. Follow it about 10 miles to the Eklutna Lake Recreation Area. Trailhead parking is at the end of the road, past the turn-offs for the campground and picnic area. The trailhead is on the northeast side of the parking area.

From the trailhead, walk across Twin Peaks Creek to an intersection in 100 feet. The Eklutna Lakeside Trail, which is open to bicycles and 4 days a week to all-terrain vehicles, is to the right. Turn left for the Twin Peaks Trail.

The hike: The 2.5-mile Twin Peaks Trail (actually an abandoned road that's recently been recleared) climbs to the alpine slopes below the craggy summits of Twin Peaks. The maintained trail ends at a good viewpoint, and unmaintained hiking routes branch off to different destinations. East Twin Pass, 1.5 miles farther, is a high gap on the prominent ridge east of the Twin Peaks. East Twin Pass is a full-day hike.

Near Twin Peaks, the mountain slopes are alive with wildflowers, small bright streams tumble over their rocky beds, and bands of Dall sheep graze

Twin Peaks.

here and there. Hikers may see arctic ground squirrels and ptarmigan on the tundra, and golden eagles riding the currents above.

The hike climbs via switchbacks through mixed forest and brush. At about 1.5 miles is a vista of Eklutna Lake and Bold Peak. The maintained trail ends at about 2,700 feet elevation, with views of Twin Peaks and the green alpine slopes below East Twin. Look for sheep on these slopes; large bands of ewes and lambs use the area all summer. There may also be a few, usually solitary, rams.

There are several possibilities for extending your hike. A steep hiker's route sidehills down to cross Twin Peaks (or Thachkatnu) Creek and divides into a route to the slopes below East Twin Peak and one to East Twin Pass. Another route leads uphill to the right from the end of the trail, and climbs steeply, about another mile and 800 feet of elevation, to an overlook of Eklutna Lake and its valley.

The route toward East Twin Peak meanders across alpine slopes below the peak. Look for sheep on the slopes. The peak is climbable but very challenging. There are loose rock and steep scree to negotiate, and the route is complicated and not easy to find from here. Another, longer approach to the peak is from East Twin Pass via the main ridge.

The hike to East Twin Pass bears right after the Twin Peaks Creek crossing. After crossing the tributary creek that enters from the left, or northwest, pick out East Twin Pass to the northeast. The pass, elevation 4,450 feet, is the low point in the main ridge at the top of the gully directly ahead.

The path peters out, but the pass is obvious. The route crosses a major sheep trail or two in the final climb.

To the north of East Twin Pass are massive Pioneer Peak, the Matanuska River, and Palmer. Hiking up to the peaks on either side of the pass nets even better views, and possibly a chance to look down on Dall sheep! The peak to the northwest (5,050 feet) looks out over most of the Mat Valley, and the rocky peak to the southeast (5,150 feet) looks out over the Valley and also has a view east toward Bold, Bashful, and Baleful Peaks, the highest part of Chugach State Park. Eklutna Lake isn't visible until farther out the ridge, on Peak 5,450, but the view is fantastic.

Most people day hike the Twin Peaks area, but there are possible camp-sites along the forks of Twin Peaks Creek beyond the end of the maintained trail. The trail is open only to foot traffic.

Shorter hikes. It's a fairly steep haul, but the hike to the first full view of Eklutna Lake, about 1.5 miles from the trailhead, makes a decent shorter hike.

40 BOLD PEAK VALLEY

Trip summary:	A longer day or overnight trip from Eklutna Lake to the high valley below Bold Peak and a lookout point on Bold Peak ridge.
Distances:	Head of Bold Peak Valley: 4 miles one way.
	Bold Peak ridge overlook: 3.5 miles one way. Hike, bike, or ATV to the trailhead, 5 additional miles one way, on the Eklutna Lakeside Trail.
Special features:	Alpine tundra; massive, snowcapped Bold Peak; views of Eklutna Lake and Glacier; and mountaineering.
Location:	In the Eklutna Lake area, 35 miles north of Anchorage.
Difficulty:	Bold Peak Valley: moderately strenuous.
	Bold Peak ridge overlook: strenuous.
Trail type:	More developed trail for the first 2.5 miles; a route beyond.
Total elevation gain:	End of developed trail: 2,500 feet.
	Head of Bold Peak Valley: 2,800 feet.
	Bold Peak ridge overlook: 3,600 feet.
Best season:	Late June through September.
Maps:	USGS Anchorage B-6; Alaska State Parks brochure *Eklutna Lake*.
Manager:	Chugach State Park.

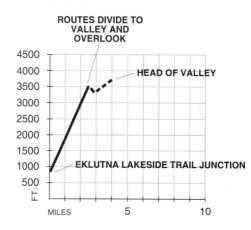

ROUTES DIVIDE TO
VALLEY AND
OVERLOOK

HEAD OF VALLEY

EKLUTNA LAKESIDE TRAIL JUNCTION

4500
4000
3500
3000
2500
2000
1500
1000
500

FT.

MILES   5   10

Finding the trailhead: The trailhead is on the left side of the Eklutna Lakeside Trail at Mile 5.1, just beyond the Bold Creek bridge. For directions to Eklutna Lake and the Lakeside Trail, see Hike 39, Twin Peaks, "Finding the trailhead."

The hike: Mountain wildflowers, views of milky-blue Eklutna Lake, the massive, glacially-carved Bold Peak, and one of the best views there is of the Chugach Mountains lie up the trail to Bold Peak Valley. The steep hike and brushy trail are worth the effort.

Dusk settling over Eklutna Lake.

162

BOLD PEAK VALLEY

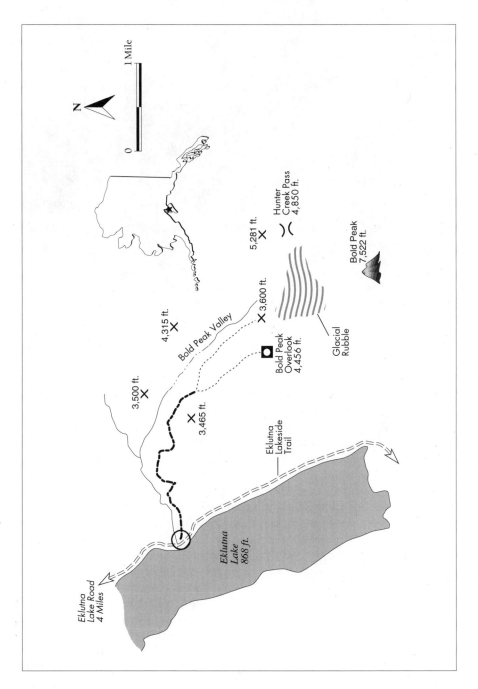

N

0   1 Mile

Hunter
Creek Pass
4,850 ft.

5,281 ft.

Bold Peak
7,522 ft.

4,315 ft.
X

X 3,600 ft.

Bold Peak Valley

Glacial
Rubble

Bold Peak
Overlook
4,456 ft.

3,500 ft.
X

X
3,465 ft.

Ekluma
Lakeside
Trail

Ekluna Lake
868 ft.

Ekluna
Lake Road
4 Miles

Bold Peak Valley and Bold Peak.

Mountain biking the first 5 miles of the Eklutna Lakeside Trail to the Bold Peak Trailhead cuts at least 2 hours off the round trip hike, and makes a day hike to Bold Peak possible. The Lakeside Trail is an easy mountain bike trip on a gravel road that is closed to cars and trucks but open to all-terrain vehicles from Sunday to Wednesday of each week. If you don't bike or take an ATV, the trip is a 9-mile hike one way. You'll have to leave your bike or ATV near the trailhead; the Bold Peak Trail is suitable for and open only to foot traffic. Bringing a bike chain and lock is a good move for security and peace of mind.

The steep, abandoned road that serves as the first 2.5 miles of the Bold Peak trail parallels Bold Creek, climbing through aspen, birch, and brushy slopes to a 3,400-foot tundra knob. At this writing, the trail is overgrown with a swath of alder above treeline, but is passable.

Two routes divide on the knob. The lower is a path that leads to the head of the valley at Bold Peak's glacial moraine. The higher, a path that eventually peters out, leads onto Bold Peak's northwest ridge to the overlook.

Bold Peak Valley. A camp in the upper valley makes a good base for exploring the area, including the convoluted geography at the head of the valley. Bold Creek flows only a short distance out of the moraine before disappearing for about a mile, so choose a campsite with water in mind. Hikers should leave the peak to experienced mountaineers, but a stiff climb leads to some fine ridge-running on either side of the valley. Hunter Creek Pass, the 4,850-foot notch to the left of Bold Peak's glacial rubble, is the best legal access to Hunter Creek, a wild, rarely-visited valley.

Bold Peak Overlook. The higher route from Knob 3,400 leads up another 1,000 feet in a little over a mile to the overlook on Bold Peak ridge. The route is easy enough to follow—just hike up to the ridge and follow it toward Bold Peak until the view bowls you over, and you've found Point 4,456. The vertical face of Bold Peak looks close enough to reach out and touch. Eklutna Lake, River, and Glacier are spread out below, and rugged, dark peaks hog the skyline to the south. All in all, not bad for a day hike.

Shorter hikes. The views of Eklutna Lake and Bold Peak from the 3,400-foot knob at Mile 2.5 make a good shorter destination.

---

41 EAST FORK EKLUTNA RIVER

Trip summary:	A half-day or longer day trip, or a backpack of two or three days, up the East Fork of Eklutna River.
Distances:	Tulchina Falls: 2.5 miles one way.
	Trail's end: 6 miles one way, with another 3 cross-country miles to the head of the valley. Hike, bike or ATV to the trailhead, 10 additional miles one way, on the Eklutna Lakeside Trail.
Special features:	A narrow mountain valley, hanging valleys and waterfalls, Dall sheep and mountain goats, and access for mountaineering and hunting.
Location:	35 miles north of Anchorage.
Difficulty:	Tulchina Falls: easy.
	Beyond Tulchina Falls: moderate to moderately strenuous.
Total elevation gain:	Tulchina Falls: 200 feet.
	Trail's end: 900 feet in and 300 feet out.
Trail type:	Less developed trail to Tulchina Falls; less developed trail/route beyond.
Best season:	Mid-June through September.
Maps:	USGS Anchorage B-6, A-6, and A-5; Alaska State Parks brochure *Eklutna Lake*.
Manager:	Chugach State Park.

Key points:
  2.5   Tulchina Falls
  4.5   High point, 2,000 feet
  6.0   Route ends

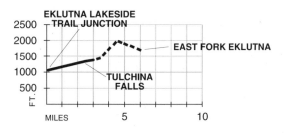

EAST FORK EKLUTNA RIVER

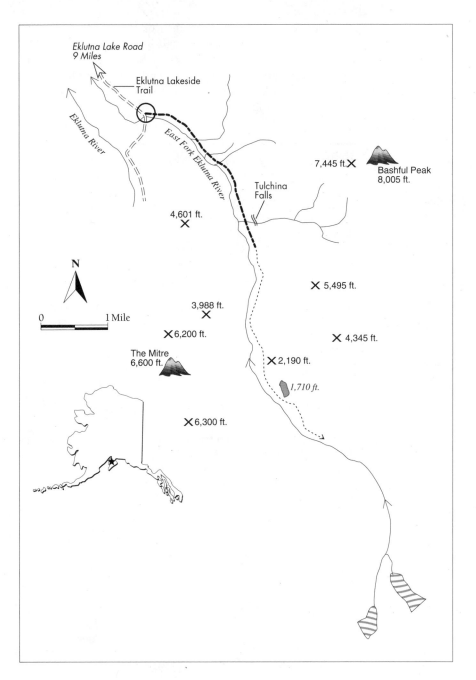

Eklutna Lake Road
9 Miles

Eklutna Lakeside
Trail

Eklutna River

East Fork Eklutna River

7,445 ft.✗

Bashful Peak
8,005 ft.

Tulchina
Falls

4,601 ft.
✗

N

0   1 Mile

3,988 ft.
✗

✗6,200 ft.

The Mitre
6,600 ft.

✗ 5,495 ft.

✗ 4,345 ft.

✗ 2,190 ft.

1,710 ft.

✗6,300 ft.

Finding the trailhead: The East Fork Trailhead is on the left (northeast) side of the Eklutna Lakeside Trail at Mile 10.2, just before the trail crosses the bridge over the East Fork. For directions to Eklutna Lake and the Lakeside Trail, see Hike 39, Twin Peaks ("Finding the trailhead").

The hike. The East Fork of the Eklutna River is a small, swift glacial stream sandwiched between mountain walls. To the west is The Mitre, a vertical-walled massif at 6,600 feet elevation, and to the east are Chugach State Park's highest peaks, topped by Bashful Peak at 8,005 feet. Total relief from the canyon floor to the summits above is over a vertical mile. Waterfalls tumble from the heights to meet the river, and hikers may spot Dall sheep and mountain goats high on the mountain walls.

Since the trailhead is over 10 miles from the parking area via the Eklutna Lakeside Trail, it's best to ride a mountain bike to the trailhead, or use an ATV on open days, normally Sunday-Wednesday of each week. The Lakeside Trail is an easy mountain bike trip on a gravel road that is closed to cars and trucks. Using a bicycle instead of hiking the Lakeside Trail cuts about 6 hours off the round trip. You'll have to leave the bike or ATV near the trailhead; the East Fork trail is suitable and open only for foot traffic. Bringing a bike chain and lock is a good move for security and peace of mind.

A maintained trail runs up the river the 2.5 miles to Tulchina Falls, and a rougher, unmarked and unmaintained trail/route continues another 3.5 miles into the upper East Fork Eklutna valley. Beyond Tulchina Creek, be prepared to find your own way.

The upper valley, East Fork Eklutna River.

Tulchina Falls, which leaps and crashes its way into the East Fork valley through a narrow rock slot, is an easy walk. A side trail leads to the base of the falls, where the spray keeps the nearby vegetation perpetually wet. There is also a double falls above the trail about Mile 1.5, though there is no easy route to the base of the falls.

Near Mile 3.5, a section of the trail briefly follows a gravel bar along the river. A very rough track continues near the river, but a better path climbs the slope toward Knob 2,190, several hundred feet above the river, and cuts across an open bench away from the river. Look carefully for the point where this path leaves the river; the knob and the slope leading to it are fairly obvious. The trail's high point, at about 2,000 feet elevation, is just below the summit of the knob.

This route peters out about 6 miles from the trailhead, still about 3 miles from the head of the valley. Travel beyond is cross country. The upper valley is alpine, with waterfalls and glaciers hanging from the mountainsides.

There are a number of good places to camp. The best are at Tulchina Falls and on the gravel bars a bit beyond Tulchina Falls, and in the upper valley, if you make it that far.

There is a permit-only hunting season for moose and sheep in the Eklutna Valley, including the East Fork, in September.

Shorter hikes. Tulchina Falls, 2.5 miles one way, makes a good half-day trip if you ride a mountain bike along the Lakeside Trail to the trailhead.

42   *PIONEER RIDGE*

Trip summary:	A longer day hike or possible overnight on a steep trail to the shoulder of Pioneer Peak, a prominent Chugach Range peak.
Distance:	5.5 miles one way.
Special features:	Great views, high country access.
Location:	40 miles north of Anchorage.
Difficulty:	Strenuous.
Trail type:	More developed trail lower to an alpine route above, marked only with fiberglass stakes.
Total elevation gain:	5,100 feet.
Best season:	Late June through September.
Maps:	USGS Anchorage C-6 (SE) and B-6.
Manager:	Matanuska-Susitna Borough Parks and Recreation Division, Alaska Division of Land.

Key points:
2.5   Brushline
4.7   4,600-foot rest area
5.5   Ridge summit, 5,300 feet

PIONEER RIDGE

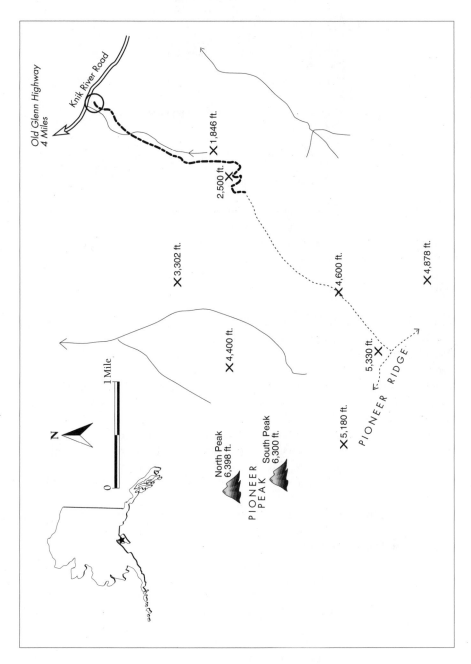

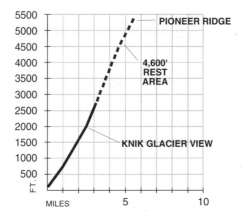

Finding the trailhead: Turn east from the Glenn Highway onto the Old Glenn Highway, 12 miles south of Palmer and 30 miles north of Anchorage. Drive about 8.5 miles to Knik River Road, which continues straight ahead on the south side of the Knik River as the Old Glenn curves north to cross a bridge over the river. Take Knik River Road about 4 miles to the marked trailhead on the right.

The hike: A long, steady, uphill hike, the Pioneer Ridge Trail climbs to a spectacular view of Knik Glacier, and higher up, of the Matanuska Valley, Pioneer Peak, and the Chugach Range. The 5,300-foot shoulder of Pioneer Peak is the highest point hikers can reach on a trail in Southcentral Alaska. The peak is near-vertical on the north, or Palmer side, but this hike is via the seldom-seen east side of the mountain, where a steep but passable feeder ridge leads up.

With few flat places to recoup your energy, expect a slow hike; breaking a mile an hour is a good pace going up. Plan on a full summer day, and pack food and water accordingly. Camping is possible in the high country, with some water available from snow and snow-melt ponds around 5,000 feet elevation.

Above treeline, much of the trail is marked with orange or red fiberglass stakes. Higher up the ridge, the trail is not obvious on the ground, so pay attention to the route; clouds and mist often obscure the higher elevations and could make finding the way down difficult if the weather gets too thick.

Four picnic tables—two not far above brushline, one in a flat area at 4,600 feet, and one on Pioneer Ridge—lend an oddly civilized touch to the hike. Colony High School Junior ROTCers carried the materials for the tables up the trail on their backs.

On a sunny day, the view of the Knik Glacier and the Chugach at about 2.5 miles is incredible. Look for Mounts Palmer, Gannett, Goode, and even Marcus Baker, the highest point in the Chugach Mountains, on the skyline. Pioneer Peak is not visible until higher up the trail.

Knik Glacier and the Chugach Mountains from the Pioneer Ridge Trail.

At 4,600 feet, voila! Another unlikely picnic table appears, just right for a rest in a really scenic spot before the final 700-foot climb. The view here includes the ridge and both of Pioneer Peak's summits.

The last push to Pioneer Ridge is worth the extra effort. Views of the steep country around Goat Creek open up, and the ridgeline toward Pioneer Peak makes a good walk if you haven't had enough yet. The south peak, which experienced hiker/scramblers can summit, is still about 2 miles away and 1,000 feet higher. The north summit, 6,398 feet, is a technical climb and not for hiker/scramblers.

At this writing, a line of markers extends out the ridge to the southeast, leading nowhere in particular. This ridgeline, though, makes a long ramble over to Eklutna Lake possible, curling around Goat Creek and eventually tying in with the Twin Peaks (Hike 39) or Bold Peak Valley (Hike 40) Trails. This trailless trip is only for experienced backcountry travelers with route-finding skills.

Look for raptors, nesting migratory birds, arctic ground squirrels, and Dall sheep in the high country, and be alert for moose and bears on the hike. There may be a bit of stinging nettle on and near the trail.

Shorter hikes. Take the trail about 2.5 miles to the first viewpoint of Knik Glacier, still a demanding hike that climbs about 2,000 feet.

MATANUSKA AND SUSITNA VALLEYS

North of Anchorage are the Matanuska and Susitna Rivers, by far the two largest of Cook Inlet's rivers. The Talkeetna Mountains, north of the Matanuska and east of the Susitna, are a rugged range with a few hiking trails, mainly in the Little Susitna-Hatcher Pass area. Farther north, off the Parks Highway in the Susitna watershed, is fine hiking country in Denali State Park.

Besides the hikes described here, there are several hikes into the Talkeetnas from the Glenn Highway northeast of Palmer that combine all-terrain vehicle, foot, and game trails and cross-country hiking. Try Kings River, Boulder Creek, Pinochle/Hicks Creek, or Squaw Creek.

A Talkeetna Mountains outhouse with a view.

43 LAZY MOUNTAIN AND MATANUSKA PEAK

Trip summary: Hikes to peaks in the Chugach Mountain front outside Palmer: a half-day hike to the top of Lazy Mountain, or a longer day or overnight hike to McRoberts Creek basin and Matanuska Peak.

Distances: Lazy Mountain Trail: 2.5 miles one way (allow at least 4 hours round trip). Matanuska Peak Trail: 6 miles one way (allow at least 10 hours round trip).

Special features: Chugach Range ridges and peaks, views, wildflower meadows in McRoberts Creek basin.

Location: Four miles east of Palmer.

Difficulty: Lazy Mountain Trail: moderately strenuous. Matanuska Peak Trail: to McRoberts Creek basin, moderately strenuous; to Matanuska Peak, strenuous.

Trail type: Less developed, steep trails/routes. Matanuska Peak Trail is extremely brushy lower, and steep and difficult near the peak.

Total elevation gain: Lazy Mountain Trail: about 3,000 feet. Matanuska Peak Trail: about 2,000 feet to McRoberts Creek basin and 5,800 feet to Matanuska Peak.

Best season: Lazy Mountain: mid-May through September. Matanuska Peak: mid-June through mid-September.

Maps: USGS Anchorage C-6 (SE).

Manager: Matanuska-Susitna Borough.

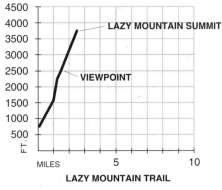

Finding the trailheads: Lazy Mountain Trail. Drive to Palmer on the Glenn Highway and turn right, or east, onto West Arctic Avenue/Old Glenn Highway, the second traffic light in Palmer driving north from Anchorage. Follow Arctic Avenue east, toward the mountains, about 2.3 miles through town and across the Matanuska River bridge, then curving south, to Clark-Wolverine Road.

LAZY MOUNTAIN AND MATANUSKA PEAK

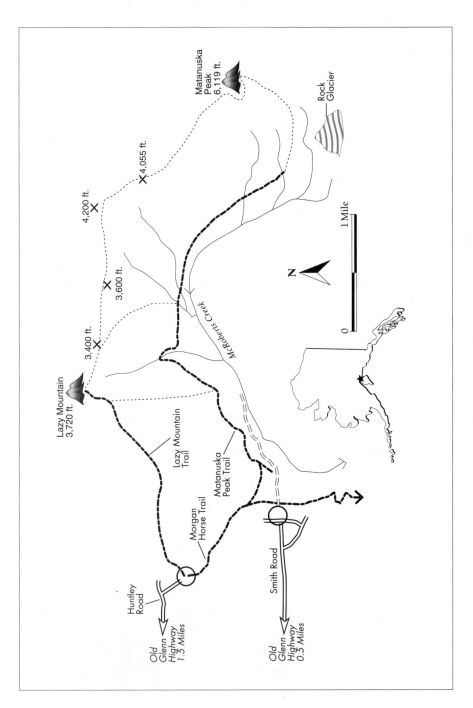

Turn left (east) and follow Clark-Wolverine Road 0.7 mile to Huntley Road. Turn right on Huntley, following a sign for the Lazy Mountain Recreation Area, and in another mile, bear right at a fork in the road. Pass a gate and drive downhill 0.2 mile into the parking area. This parking area and trailhead are a day-use area only.

Matanuska Peak Trail. Follow the Lazy Mountain Trailhead directions as far as Clark-Wolverine Road. Continue south on the Old Glenn Highway to Smith Road, 0.4 mile south of Clark-Wolverine Road. Turn east onto Smith Road and follow it 1.5 miles, straight ahead, to a sharp right bend in the road; the name changes at the bend to Harmony Avenue. The trailhead is directly ahead at the bend. There is limited parking here, so be sure to park out of the path of traffic.

The hikes: Lazy Mountain and Matanuska Peak are easily visible east of Palmer on a clear day. Lazy Mountain is the rounded peak nearest town, and Mat Peak is the prominent, rocky peak behind. A trail leads to each peak, and it's possible to connect the two trails for a very long high country adventure just a stone's throw from Palmer.

These trails are a bit rough. Lazy Mountain is extremely steep in one section (don't forget the hiking staff). The lower 2.5 miles of the Mat Peak Trail are so thick with tall grasses and cow parsnip by late summer that if it's wet even with dew, you'll be soaked to the neck. Wear long pants and bring rain gear. Watch for cow parsnip and stinging nettle on both trails.

The Mat Peak Trail (and the Lazy Mountain Trail, if you hike off-trail) leads into the alpine basin of McRoberts Creek, a fine day hike or overnight destination if you're not up for the stiff climb to the Mat Peak summit. Allow at least 10 hours (12 is better) for the entire trip if you climb the peak.

Lazy Mountain. The obvious, wide trail at the end of the parking lot is the Morgan Horse Trail. To head for Lazy Mountain, instead take the narrow footpath that begins on the uphill side of the lot at the far end. Immediately out of the lot, bear right, and in another fork in about 0.5 mile, bear right again to avoid a brushy section.

The climb is nearly unrelenting, and part of it is steep in the extreme. The first bump with a view, about 1.5 miles and 2,500 feet elevation, is a good destination—there is even a picnic table for relaxing and having lunch.

The peak is still a mile and three more bumps away. The grade moderates and the views improve as the trail climbs into low-growing alpine vegetation. The very top is narrow and rocky with a drop on both sides, so be careful, especially with any children who have managed to get this far. The view at the top is terrific. Matanuska Peak is out the ridge to the east, the Matanuska River below separates the Chugach and Talkeetna Mountains, and Pioneer Peak dominates the view to the south across the Knik River.

McRoberts Creek and Matanuska Peak. From the Mat Peak Trailhead, follow the dirt road that serves as the beginning of the trail for 0.4 mile. Just past an iron gate, trails peel off left and right on the uphill, or left, side of the road. Bear uphill on the right-hand trail. (If you reach a second gate, you've gone too far.) Just above, the trail curves right and then left, avoiding a side trail back down to the road. Climb a steep hill for 0.3 mile, and bear right at the top of the hill. All the confusing side trails are behind you now; in a couple of minutes, in a grassy aspen flat, the peak is clearly visible ahead.

At 2.5 miles, the trail crosses a small perennial stream that flows down from the Lazy Mountain ridge. Once out of this draw, tall meadow vegetation is less of a problem, and soon it's forgotten as you ramble along on a well-beaten alpine path in the McRoberts Creek basin. Once in the basin, the route is marked with wood and fiberglass stakes all the way to the peak.

At about 3 miles, a side route to the left, or north, leads to Lazy Mountain. In another mile, on an alpine flat above McRoberts Creek, is another picnic table. This spot, 4 miles one way from the trailhead, is a good destination. Beyond the table, the route crosses a gulch and begins the steep climb northeast to the peak, about 2,300 feet above. Higher up the summit ridge there are scree and loose rock to negotiate, and the final pitch is up a steep boulder field; be careful here.

There is a great view west and south back to Palmer, the Matanuska River and the Mat Valley, but the real draw of the peak is the view into the inner Chugach, undoubtedly one of the wildest mountain views within ten miles of a latte shop on earth.

Loop trips. Really energetic hikers can try a very long loop, about 13 miles and 7,400 feet elevation gain, connecting the two trails via the ridge between Lazy Mountain and Matanuska Peak. Pick the route up or down Mat Peak carefully. The safest section of the mountain just below the peak is the south/southwest side, requiring a traverse to get to or from the ridge, which trends northeast from Mat Peak.

A second loop is the route between Lazy Mountain and Mile 3 of the Mat Peak Trail, approximately a 9-mile loop. For an even shorter loop, about 7 miles, take the south ridge of Lazy Mountain about a mile downhill to Mile 1.5 of the Mat Peak Trail.

Trip summary:	A longer day hike or 2–3 day backpack on the Gold Mint Trail. The hike follows the upper Little Susitna River to the Mint Glacier Valley in the Talkeetna Mountains.
Distance:	8 miles one way to the Mint Glacier Valley.
Special features:	A rugged mountain and glacier landscape, mountaineering access.
Location:	16 miles north of Palmer.
Difficulty:	Moderately strenuous.
Trail type:	More developed trail lower to a well-beaten route above.
Total elevation gain:	About 1,200 feet to the head of the lower Little Susitna Valley and 2,500 feet to Mint Glacier Valley.
Best season:	Mid-June through September for the lower valley, July through mid-September for the Mint Glacier Valley.
Maps:	USGS Anchorage D-6.
Manager:	Alaska State Parks, Matanuska-Susitna Area.

Key points:
  1.5 Lower valley viewpoint
  3.5 View of the head of the Little Susitna River
  7.0 Head of lower valley
  8.0 Mint Glacier Valley

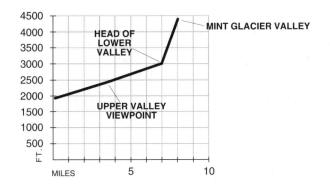

Finding the trailhead: Drive north of Palmer on the Glenn Highway to Fishhook-Willow Road, which is about 44 miles north of Anchorage and 2 miles north of the Palmer-Wasilla Highway intersection in Palmer. Turn west toward Hatcher Pass, and drive 14 miles to the parking area on the right, across from the Motherlode Lodge and just before the road curves sharply to the left.

LITTLE SUSITNA RIVER

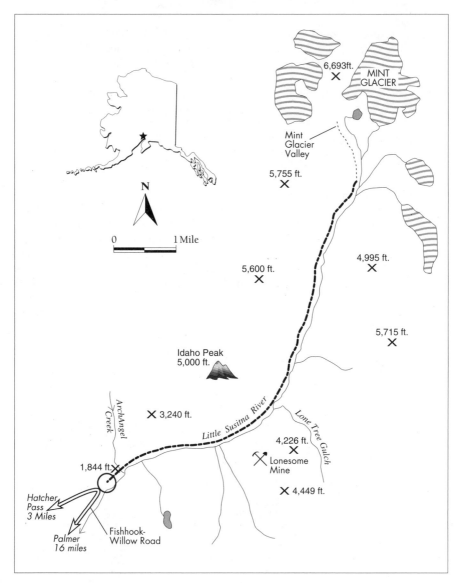

The hike: Following the valley of the upper Little Susitna River, the Gold Mint Trail leads to the headwaters of the river in the high basin below the Mint Glacier. The glacier has sliced up and left behind an awesome landscape of serrated peaks and waterfalls. The area is popular with mountaineers, and there is good off-trail hiking as well. This high country is the big attraction of this hike; there are really no great intermediate destinations on the Little Su.

Heading up the last pitch to Mint Glacier Valley.

The lower portion of the trail cuts through alder thickets with limited views. The first good view is about 1.5 miles from the trailhead, in a meadow on a low hill. At about 2.5 miles, look for the single building still standing from the Lonesome Mine, across the river and a bit east of the double drainage that enters the Little Su from the south. (The USGS map shows the trail crossing the river to the Lonesome Mine, but the trail now stays on the north side of the river.)

The mine, worked in the 1930s, was unique for the area in that it produced more silver than gold. Avalanches and fires have finished off most of the mine buildings.

At 3.5 miles, the trail turns the corner to the north, with a distant view of the peaks, glaciers, and waterfalls at the head of the river. The trail deteriorates as it leads north; expect it to be wet and brushy. After about 4 miles, the hike is alongside the foaming, tumbling, bouldery stream. There are a few possible campsites in this stretch.

At about 7 miles and 3,000 feet elevation, the broad valley of the Little Su ends. The track becomes much fainter as it climbs toward the Mint Valley; follow rock cairns through the rocky tundra. A second route curls around the left side of the steep dome ahead, but stay right, in sight of the steep course of the river, for the most direct route to the upper basin. The 4,300-foot basin is starkly beautiful. Dark spires, boulder slides, and remnant glaciers fill the view.

Good campsites are limited in the lower valley, but there is decent camping in the upper basin. Weather is always a consideration this high in the Talkeetnas, so be prepared to wait out a storm if you want to be assured of a chance to explore the high country. Hikers could easily spend several days exploring here.

There is a Mountaineering Club of Alaska hut in the upper basin. Contact the club for information (see Appendix 1). The Club built and maintains the hut, so users are encouraged to join the club to share in the expense of maintaining it. MCA also works on conservation issues, sponsors classes and a schedule of hikes and climbs, and holds monthly meetings with hiking and mountaineering programs.

Shorter hikes. Hike 1.5 to 3.5 miles one way for views that give tastes of the rest of the valley.

45   *REED LAKES*

Trip summary:	A half-day or longer day trip or overnight hike to two lakes in alpine country in the Talkeetna Mountains.
Distances:	Lower Reed Lake: 3 miles one way. Upper Reed Lake: 4 miles one way.
Special features:	Glacial lakes, the rugged Talkeetna Mountains, rock-climbing areas.
Location:	19 miles north of Palmer.
Difficulty:	Moderate.
Trail type:	More developed trail for the first 1.5 miles; a well-beaten route the rest of the way.
Total elevation gain:	1,300 feet to the lower lake, 1,800 to the upper lake.
Best season:	July to mid-September.
Maps:	USGS Anchorage D-6.
Manager:	Alaska State Parks, Matanuska-Susitna Area.

Key points:
1.5   Snowbird Mine Trail (Hike 46)
2.5   Upper Reed Creek valley
3.0   Lower Reed Lake
4.0   Upper Reed Lake

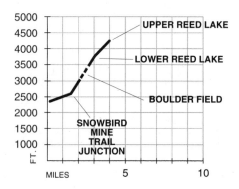

REED LAKES
SNOWBIRD MINE AND GLACIER PASS

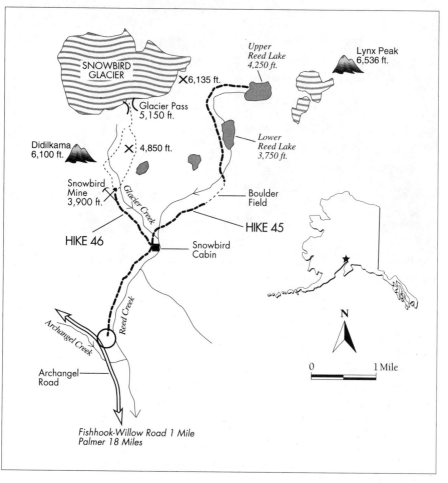

Finding the trailhead: Drive north of Palmer on the Glenn Highway to Fishhook-Willow Road, which is about 2 miles north of the Palmer-Wasilla Highway intersection in Palmer. Turn west toward Hatcher Pass, and drive 14.6 miles to Archangel Road. The intersection is about 0.8 mile beyond the sharp left curve where the Fishhook Road begins to climb steeply. Turn right onto Archangel Road and continue about 2.3 miles to the trailhead on the right, 0.2 mile beyond the bridge over Archangel Creek. Going is slow on the rough road, but the scenery is spectacular.

The hike: An annual pilgrimage for many Anchorage and Mat-Su hikers, the Reed Lakes Trail leads into the heart of the Talkeetna Mountains, a wild land of jagged granite peaks, rock walls, blocky boulders, glaciers, and cirque lakes. The trail makes a great long day hike, but there are plenty of good

Waterfall above Lower Reed Lake.

campsites near the lakes and on the benches above them. Rock climbers use the trail to get to good climbing areas.

Look for alpine wildflowers, tundra-nesting birds, arctic ground squirrels, and marmots, and if energy allows, scramble up to the ridges and peaks near the lakes. If it's sunny, dare your hiking partners to a swim in Upper Reed Lake and see how cold an unfrozen lake can be.

The trail is wide and easy for the first 1.5 miles, following an old road to the site of Snowbird Mine Village, but is much rougher beyond, including some boulder-hopping to get into the upper valley of Reed Creek. Past the Snowbird Cabin, a dilapidated remnant of Snowbird Village, the trail is entirely hiker-made, with no construction or maintenance. Just past the cabin is the junction with the Snowbird Mine Trail (Hike 46), which may be unmarked. Here, the Reed Lakes Trail crosses Glacier and Reed creeks to the east side of the valley. Both creeks are bridged.

Beyond the crossing, the trail climbs toward the upper valley of Reed Creek. At the top of the pitch, the trail more or less disappears as it crosses a massive field of granite boulders that chokes the narrow valley. This boulder-hop is challenging for the older, the younger, and the canine. A slightly less challenging option is to cross the valley at the beginning of the boulder field to a hiker's path on the other side, which avoids some of the bouldering. In either case, the trail eventually ends up on the west side of the creek and emerges into the upper valley with its meandering, pooling stream and meadows.

The entire east side of this valley is one big boulder slide, and azure Lower Reed Lake is near the end of the slide, at 3,750 feet. Upstream, the creek pours over two rock ledges. Around the bend to the right, 500 feet higher and a mile farther, is the upper lake, which lies at the head of the drainage below Lynx Peak, a 6,536-foot peak. There's good cross-country hiking and scrambling above the upper lake toward the Kashwitna River drainage to the north and the Little Susitna River (Hike 44) to the southeast.

The trail is closed to motor vehicles, but the first 1.5 miles are open to and suitable for mountain bikes. This is a popular trail on good summer weekends.

Shorter hikes: Hike about 2 miles to a lower valley view, 2.5 miles into the upper valley with its pretty stream, or 3 miles to Lower Reed Lake. Two miles on the trail is about the limit for smaller children because of the boulder field described above.

46 SNOWBIRD MINE AND GLACIER PASS

Trip summary:	A half-day or longer day trip or overnight hike to the Snowbird Mine, Glacier Pass, and the Snowbird Glacier in the Talkeetna Mountains.
Distances:	Snowbird Mine: 2.5 miles one way. Glacier Pass: 4 miles one way.
Special features:	Mine ruins, Talkeetna Mountains scenery, the Snowbird Glacier.
Location:	19 miles north of Palmer.
Difficulty:	Moderate to the Snowbird Mine, moderately strenuous to Glacier Pass.
Trail type:	More developed trail below; less developed trail to the Snowbird Mine; a route/cross-country hike from the mine to Glacier Pass.
Total elevation gain:	1,500 feet to the Snowbird Mine, 2,700 feet to Glacier Pass.
Best season:	July through mid-September.
Maps:	USGS Anchorage D-6.
Manager:	Alaska State Parks, Matanuska-Susitna Area.

See Map on Page 181

Key points:

1.5	Snowbird Mine/Reed Lakes junction
2.5	Snowbird Mine
4.0	Glacier Pass

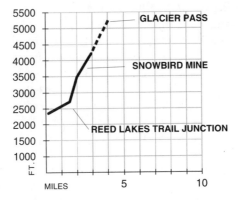

Finding the trailhead: The directions to the trailhead are the same as to the Reed Lakes Trail, Hike 45.

The hike: The Snowbird Trail climbs into the high country of the Talkeetnas to the ruins of the Snowbird Mine, and a route continues up Glacier Creek to Glacier Pass and the Snowbird Glacier, which fills the high basin north of the pass. The granite peaks, alpine wildflowers, mine ruins, and the glacier make this a diverse and beautiful hike.

Take the Reed Lakes Trail 1.5 miles to the Snowbird Cabin, all that's left of the Snowbird Mine Village. Turn left, uphill, at the Y in the trail just past the cabin. There is no sign at the Y at this writing. A steep path follows cable lines from the mine into Glacier Creek's hanging valley. The trail more or less peters out at the upper end of the mine.

The old cable towers are on the first level of the hanging valley; climb to the next level to see more of the ruins. The Snowbird's ore came from the mountainside to the south. The mine was prospected in the 1920s, developed in the 1940s, and closed in 1950.

The Glacier Creek valley above the mine is magical: a small, bubbling mountain brook flows through alpine meadows with granite boulders lying around in giant heaps. Glacier Pass is directly above to the north, but the granite dome ahead blocks the view. The hike to the pass is essentially a cross-country trip, so carry a map and compass—don't forget that the weather can change and visibility can disappear quickly at this elevation.

The most-traveled route is to the left of the dome, ascending the creek, but either side will do. Taking the route to the right means passing near the pretty tarn in the basin east of the creek. In either direction, getting onto the pass ridge as soon as possible makes the easiest walking. Allow two hours or more for the one-way trip from the mine to the pass; although it's only about 1.5 miles, it's slow going.

The 5,150-foot pass looks out over the Snowbird Glacier. The glacier, a little bigger than a square mile, survives in a north-facing basin protected from the sun by high peaks like 6,100-foot Didilkama. In late summer, when all the snow is melted and you can see the surface of the glacier, it is relatively

184

Ruins of the Snowbird Mine.

safe to venture out onto the ice, but be wary of a few crevasses and holes. The meltwater cuts channels all along the surface and then drops in free fall down several deep holes in the ice. To be safe, stay off the steeper ice slopes unless you've brought crampons.

Shorter hikes. The steep, 2.5 mile-hike to the Snowbird Mine makes a great trip.

Trip summary:	Shorter day hikes in the Independence Mine State Historical Park in the Talkeetna Mountains.
Distances:	•The Hard Rock Trail, 0.5 mile one way, an easy walking tour through a partially-restored mining camp.
	•The Gold Cord Lake Trail, 0.5 mile one way, a hike to an alpine lake.
	•The Gold Cord Mine Trail, 1 mile one way, a hike to two historic mines.
Special features:	Mining history, alpine tundra, wildflowers, and rugged mountains. There is a day use fee.
Location:	20 miles north of Palmer.
Difficulty:	Hard Rock Trail: easy; Gold Cord Lake Trail and Gold Cord Mine Trail: moderate.
Trail type:	Hard Rock Trail: more developed. Gold Cord Lake and Gold Cord Mine trails: less developed.
Total elevation gain:	Hard Rock Trail: 100 feet; Gold Cord Lake and Gold Cord Mine trails: 600 feet.
Best season:	Mid-June to mid-September.
Maps:	USGS Anchorage D-7, Alaska State Parks brochure *Independence Mine State Historical Park*, Alaska Road and Recreation Map *Matanuska Valley*.
Manager:	Alaska State Parks, Matanuska-Susitna Area.

Gold Cord Lake in June.

INDEPENDENCE MINE

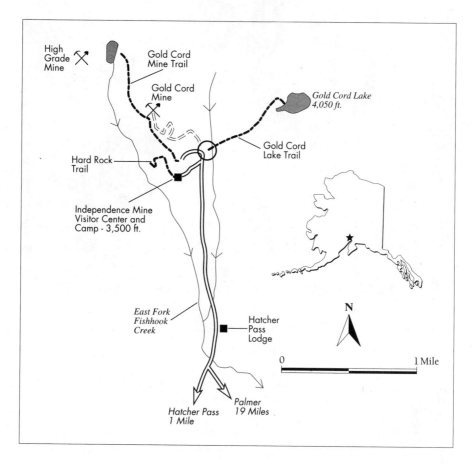

Finding the trailhead: Drive north of Palmer on the Glenn Highway to Fishhook-Willow Road, which is 2 miles north of the Palmer-Wasilla Highway intersection in Palmer. Turn west toward Hatcher Pass, and drive 17.3 miles to Gold Cord Road. The last three miles beyond the Motherlode Lodge are fairly steep. At Gold Cord Road, continue straight ahead as the road over Hatcher Pass bears left. Drive past the Hatcher Pass Lodge on the right to the park entrance station. The parking area is a mile beyond the entrance station on the left, below the red-roofed visitor center.

The hikes: The Independence Mine State Historical Park commemorates the Alaska Pacific Consolidated Mining Company gold mines near Hatcher Pass, the second-richest lode (vein) mines in Alaska's history. The park's trails are all alpine hikes, beginning at 3,500 feet elevation. Hikers can explore acres of alpine tundra and check out the wildflowers that are out in force by late June or early July.

Independence Mine State Historical Park.

The Independence Mine walking tour begins at the visitor center, the restored manager's house that was built in 1939. Inside are displays about the mine's glory days in the late 1930s and early 1940s. Outside, an accessible walkway with interpretive signs leads to the camp's old bunkhouses, a warehouse, commissary, and mess hall.

Hard Rock Trail. Beyond the first cluster of buildings in the restored mining camp, the Hard Rock Trail winds at an easy grade up to the mine's shops, mill complex, and the tunnel portal that carried water down to the processing area. Return to the visitor center by the same route, or find the steeper, narrower trail that heads uphill from near the portal. This rougher trail crosses the creek above the portal and loops back behind the mill to the lower cluster of buildings by the mess hall.

Gold Cord Lake Trail. The hike to Gold Cord Lake starts beyond and below the visitor center parking area, at the road closure gate on Gold Cord Road. A small sign marks the trail, which leads to the northeast toward an obvious, high basin. The trail climbs gently across the high tundra. The small holes all around are burrows of arctic ground squirrels.

Most of the climb to the lake is in the last 0.1 mile, and is nearly straight up. The lake may hold ice until July. A waterfall slides down a rock face at the far end, and there are great views back to the Chugach Mountains to the southeast.

Gold Cord Mine Trail. This hike to the northwest of the visitor center begins as an unmarked, fairly steep trail from the upper parking area. For a more gradual climb, follow the switchbacking Gold Cord Road, now closed to vehicles, up to the Gold Cord Mine buildings. The trail joins the dirt road at the buildings. Just beyond the Gold Cord camp, take the left fork in the road gently uphill to the High Grade Mine cabin and to the small tarn near the head of Fishhook Creek. Take some time to explore the old mining trails in the rocky tundra, and enjoy the view across the Matanuska Valley to the Chugach Mountains.

The visitor center is open daily from June to Labor Day, and on weekends from Labor Day until mid-September. Take care around the collapsing buildings and mine structures, and please don't disturb the privately-owned Gold Cord and High Grade Mine buildings.

48 RED SHIRT LAKE

Trip summary:	A half-day or overnight hike in the Nancy Lake area from South Rolly Lake Campground to Red Shirt Lake.
Distance:	3 miles one way.
Special features:	A large lake, fishing, camping, fee cabins, and rental canoes.
Location:	In the Nancy Lakes State Recreation Area, 25 miles north of Wasilla.
Difficulty:	Moderate.
Trail type:	More developed.
Total elevation gain:	About 500 feet each way.
Best season:	Mid-May to mid-October.
Maps:	USGS Tyonek C-1 (NE); Alaska Road and Recreation Map *Matanuska Valley*; Alaska State Park brochures *Summer Guide to Nancy Lake State Recreation Area* and *Nancy Lake State Recreation Area Fee Cabins*.
Manager:	Alaska State Parks, Matanuska-Susitna Area.

Finding the trailhead: Drive to the Nancy Lake Parkway intersection at Mile 67.3 of the George Parks Highway. The intersection is 25 miles north of Main Street in Wasilla and about 2 miles south of Willow. Turn southwest (left if coming from Wasilla) and drive 6.6 miles to the end of the maintained road. The Red Shirt Lake Trailhead is on the right, opposite the entrance to the South Rolly Lake Campground.

RED SHIRT LAKE

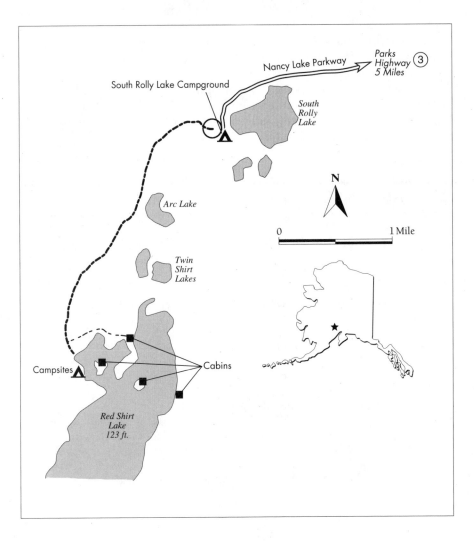

The hike: Nancy Lakes State Recreation Area is a low-elevation, lake-dotted park with fair to good fishing early and late in the summer. The park's main attraction is its Lynx Lake Canoe Trail, but canoeless hikers can walk three miles to one of the largest lakes, Red Shirt Lake, elevation 36 feet, from the end of the Nancy Lake Parkway.

The trail winds along the ridge west of a chain of lakes (South Rolly, Arc, Twin Shirt, and Red Shirt Lakes), passing through an open birch forest that is lush with tall grasses, ferns, devil's club, and wildflowers. The grade is gentle, with many short ups and downs. Along the trail are carpets of white-flowered dwarf dogwood, roses, geraniums, patches of red elderberry and alder, fireweed, and high-bush cranberry.

There is a small backcountry camping area at the end of the trail, along the northwest edge of the lake. The ground is sloping and the understory thick, so the leveled sites here make the best camping. Undeveloped trails continue near the lakeshore, but the lake is brushy, and the best exploring and fishing is by canoe. Hikers can make arrangements to use rental canoes stored by a concessionaire at the lake; see Appendix 3 for information. Carrying your own canoe is possible, but a major grunt.

There are four fee cabins, available by reservation for a nightly rental fee, at the north end of the lake. All are within a mile of the trail, but three are only accessible, and all are best reached, by boat. The only cabin that's foot-accessible is Cabin #2, about 0.75 mile around the lakeshore from the camp area. There is no trail, but it's possible to bushwhack around the lake with the canoe rental fee as motivation. The earlier in summer you go, the easier the bushwhack. See Appendix 2 for cabin rental information.

There is a day use fee to get into the park. There are private lands on the lakeshore to avoid, and watch out for the hordes of mosquitoes in midsummer—they munch hikers like hors d'oeurves.

Fishing. The best fishing is soon after the ice goes out (average ice-out is in mid-May), and in the fall after the weather cools. Northern pike are becoming the most abundant fish in the lake. The pike is native to Interior Alaska, but not here—pike fishing fans illegally introduced the fish into the Susitna Valley in the 1950s. Pike are aggressive predators, and they are wiping out rainbow trout and salmon in Susitna Valley lakes. There are rainbows, silver and red salmon, and Dolly Varden in Red Shirt Lake, but they are on the decline.

More about Nancy Lakes. The Nancy Lake area also has four fee cabins on Nancy Lake, all about a 0.5-mile walk one way from the trailhead at Mile 1.8 of the Nancy Lake Parkway. There is a new fee cabin at Bald Lake, a 0.25-mile walk from the trailhead at Nancy Lake Parkway Mile 2.5. The Tulik Nature Trail, shown on the park brochure, has been abandoned, but park staff plan to build a new nature trail near the South Rolly Lake Campground.

Trip summary:	A shorter day hike following lower Troublesome Creek to the Chulitna River.
Distance:	0.5 mile one way.
Special features:	A braided glacial river, fishing and salmon viewing on Troublesome Creek, and a small roadside campground. On clear days, there is a dramatic view of Denali from the end of the trail.
Location:	The south end of Denali State Park.
Difficulty:	Easy.
Trail type:	Less developed.
Total elevation gain:	Essentially none.
Best season:	Late May through September.
Maps:	USGS Talkeetna C-1 (trail not shown).
Manager:	Denali State Park.

Finding the trailhead: The trail begins at the Lower Troublesome Creek recreation site in Denali State Park, at Mile 137 of the Parks Highway, about 38 miles north of the Talkeetna spur road. The recreation site is 4.5 miles north of the Chulitna River bridge and 10 miles south of the Byers Lake Campground. The parking area, picnic and camping areas, and the trail are on the west side of the highway. Look for the trailhead at the south end of the parking area.

The hike: The trail follows the south edge of Troublesome Creek to its confluence with the Chulitna River, ending on a gravel bar where the clearwater stream flows into the deep, fast, silty Chulitna.

On a clear day, hikers can look across the river to the glaciated peaks of the Alaska Range. By mid-July, fireweed is in bloom on the river flat, and the salmon are in. King salmon run up the creek in July, and you can often spot numbers of the big salmon resting in pools in the creek. Other salmon runs are silvers in August and September, chum from July to September, and pinks late in the summer of even-numbered years. If it's a nice day, try just relaxing on the creek's banks and gravel bars.

The forest along the trail is a bottomland forest with hybrid trees of black cottonwood and balsam poplar. An interpretive sign at the "granddaddy cottonwood" in the first part of the walk explains the hybridization of the two species.

Besides the trail to the river, the Troublesome Creek recreation site has a covered picnic shelter and a small campground (fee), with tent sites back in the forest. The site is just off the highway, so expect traffic noise if camping here.

LOWER TROUBLESOME CREEK

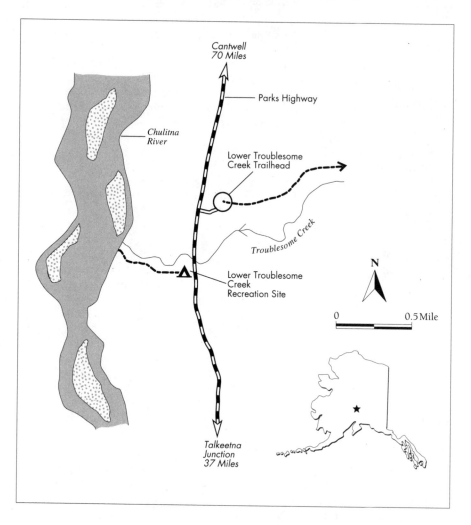

Fishing. There are several places along the trail to detour to Troublesome Creek for fishing for rainbow trout, grayling, and Dolly Varden. The creek is closed to king salmon fishing, but open for other salmon species.

Trip summary:	A half-day hike or possible overnight on a loop trail around Byers Lake.
Distance:	4.1 miles on the trail, plus a 0.5-mile road walk to complete the loop.
Special features:	Two fee cabins, backcountry campsites, fishing.
Location:	In Denali State Park, 48 miles north of Talkeetna and 63 miles south of Cantwell.
Difficulty:	Easy.
Trail type:	More developed.
Total elevation gain:	Less than 100 feet.
Best season:	Late May through September.
Maps:	USGS Talkeetna C-1 (trail not shown); Alaska State Parks brochure *Denali State Park*.
Manager:	Denali State Park.

Key points:

From the campground		From the picnic area
0.0	Campground trailhead	4.1
1.0	Inlet stream bridge	3.1
1.3	Cascade Trail junction	2.8
1.8	Lakeshore Camp	2.3
3.1	Outlet stream bridge	1.0
3.8	Trail to Cabin #2 (0.2 mi.)	0.3
4.1	Picnic area trailhead	0.0

Finding the trailhead: The trailhead is in Denali State Park at Mile 147 of the Parks Highway, in the Byers Lake Campground. Turn east off the Parks about 14 miles north of the Chulitna River bridge and 17 miles south of the Little Coal Creek Trailhead. To hike the trail clockwise as described here, drive 0.6 mile from the highway to the boat launch area on the right and park. Walk 0.2 mile on the campground road to the beginning of the foot trail, at the entrance to the Dogwood Loop.

If you are headed to the walk-in fee cabin or want to walk the trail counterclockwise, park in the picnic area 0.3 mile from the highway on the right side of the campground road. Walk around the road barrier at the end of the parking area to start the hike.

Whichever direction you take the loop, it takes an extra 0.5 mile of road walking to return to your vehicle, in addition to the 4.1-mile trail.

The hike: The easy hike around Byers Lake makes a good day trip, but there are also a walk-in fee cabin (Cabin #2) and a backcountry camping area, the Lakeshore Camp, for overnighters. Day hiking the lake while staying in the Byers Lake Campground or in the fee cabin on the campground

BYERS LAKE

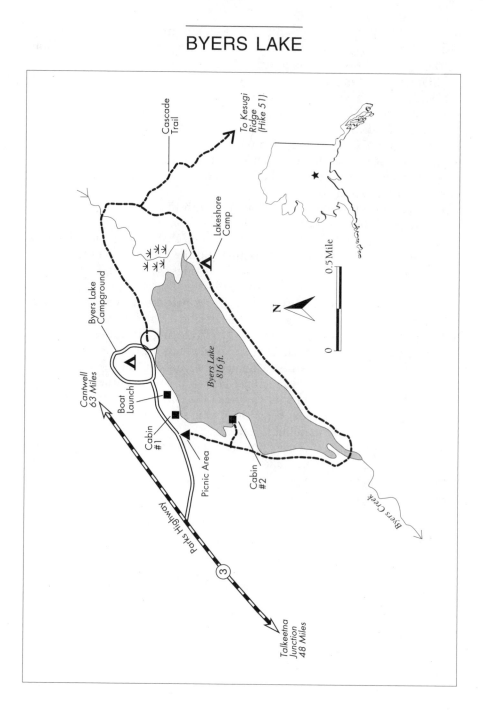

To Kesugi Ridge (Hike 51)

Cascade Trail

Lakeshore Camp

Byers Lake Campground

0.5 Mile

N

0

Byers Lake 816 ft.

Cantwell 63 Miles

Boat Launch

Cabin #1

Picnic Area

Cabin #2

Byers Creek

Parks Highway

3

Talkeetna Junction 48 Miles

road (Cabin #1) is a good option too. The cabins are available by making a reservation and paying the fee in advance; see Appendix 2 for information.

The trail is close to campground civilization, but it's wilder than you might imagine. Look for nesting swans and their young (called cygnets) and the beavers that have set up housekeeping near the lake. Pick blueberries and cranberries in season, and enjoy the small sand beaches when the lake level is low. Find wildflowers like wild iris, dogwood, twinflower, and spirea. By mid-August, smell pungent high-bush cranberries, Southcentral Alaska's musky odor of fall, in the air. Check out the bridges on the trail—a long, springy suspension bridge over the inlet stream and a massive gabion-piling bridge over the outlet stream.

Hiking the trail clockwise, the junction with the Cascade Trail is about 1.4 miles from the campground trailhead. A 0.3-mile side trip on this trail leads to a foaming, 100-foot cascade on a creek that drops from the alpine ridge above. It's about 2.5 *very steep* miles up the Cascade Trail to the first lake on Kesugi Ridge, Mini-Skinny Lake. The ridge is a fine alpine area with many small peaks and tarns. See Hike 51.

At 1.8 miles is Lakeshore Camp, with its half-dozen tent sites, picnic tables, outhouses, and a food cache for bear safety. The trail on the east side of the lake is entirely on the shoreline. After crossing the outlet stream, the trail continues around the edge of the lake and joins a closed road; Cabin #2 is 0.2 mile away to the east. At Mile 4.1 the trail ends at the picnic area. Walk another 0.3 mile back to the boat launch if you've parked there.

Shorter hikes. Hike a mile one way from the campground to the suspension bridge over Byers Creek. From the picnic area, stroll about 0.5 mile to the cabin or 1 mile to the outlet stream.

Fishing. There are rainbow trout, grayling, Dolly Varden, and a small population of lake trout in Byers Lake, but fishing is better from a canoe than from the trail. No gasoline-powered boats are allowed on the lake, and the area is closed to all salmon fishing.

Trip summary:	A 2 to 4 day alpine traverse of Kesugi Ridge in Denali State Park, between Little Coal Creek and Byers Lake.
Distance:	A 27.5-mile traverse.
Special features:	A long alpine ridge ramble, Denali and Alaska Range views.
Location:	In Denali State Park, about halfway between Talkeetna and Cantwell.
Difficulty:	Strenuous.
Trail type:	More developed trail approaches to the ridge; a marked route across the ridge.
Total elevation gain:	About 5,400 feet north to south and 6,000 feet south to north.
Best season:	Mid-June through mid-September.
Maps:	USGS Talkeetna Mountains D-6 and C-6 and Talkeetna C-1 (trail not shown); bring the USGS maps and copy the maps posted on park bulletin boards.
Manager:	Denali State Park.

Key points:

From Little Coal Creek		From Byers Lake
0.0	Little Coal Creek Trailhead	27.5
3.0	North Fork Birdhouse	24.5
4.0	Hike's high point, 3,500 feet	23.5
8.0	Eight-Mile Divide	19.5
10.0	Stonehenge Hill	17.5
13.5	Ermine Hill Trail junction	14.0
15.0	Ridge route's low point, 1,500 feet	12.5
17.5	Skinny Lake	10.0
19.0	Point Golog	8.5
22.0	Whimbrel Hill	5.5
23.5	Mini-Skinny Lake	4.0
24.0	Troublesome Creek Trail junction	3.5
26.0	The Cascades	1.5
27.5	Byers Lake Trailhead	0.0

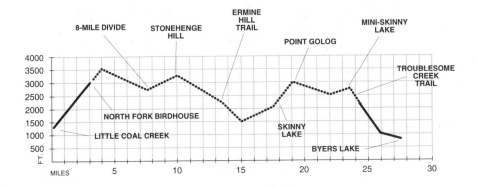

Finding the trailheads: The north trailhead, Little Coal Creek, is at Mile 164 of the Parks Highway, about 65 miles north of the Talkeetna spur road and 46 miles south of Cantwell. Turn east onto the marked access road to the trailhead.

The Byers Lake Campground, the south trailhead, is at Parks Highway Mile 147, 17 miles south of Little Coal Creek and about 14 miles north of the Chulitna River bridge. Turn east off the Parks Highway into the Byers Lake Campground, and drive 0.6 mile to the boat launch area on the right. Park here; there is no parking area at the trailhead. The trailhead is 0.2 mile ahead on the campground road, at the entrance to the campground's Dogwood Loop.

The hike: Kesugi Ridge, a long alpine ridge across the Chulitna River basin from the Alaska Range and Mount McKinley (Denali), makes a fine 2-4 day backpack. It can be done in 2 days, but plan on 3 or 4 or more to make the most of the trip. It's a glorious 20+ miles of alpine hiking in "real Sound of Music country;" as the park bulletin board says, and yeah, it is possible to go bounding around singing "Edelweiss" up there.

Many Alaskans think of this as the Curry Ridge hike, but Curry is the next ridge south. Kesugi, 2,500 to 4,700 feet elevation, is a big block of earth between the Chulitna and Susitna River valleys that's been raised by the same faulting that produced the Alaska Range and Denali. *Kesugi* means "the ancient one" in the Dena'ina Athabaskan language.

The hike is challenging. Besides the climb to the ridge, there are several ups and downs of hundreds of feet while on the ridge. Above treeline, the hike is a marked route, sometimes a beaten path across the tundra and sometimes just a series of cairns to follow. Don't start without topo maps with the route drawn in. Copy it from the maps on bulletin boards at Byers Lake, Little Coal Creek, or the alternative trailhead at Troublesome Creek.

Lousy weather, cold winds, and bad visibility are common. Try the traverse only if you are confident of your route-finding ability, your gear, and your ability to deal with nasty alpine weather. Otherwise, sampling the high country on an out-and-back hike from either trailhead is a good option.

KESUGI RIDGE

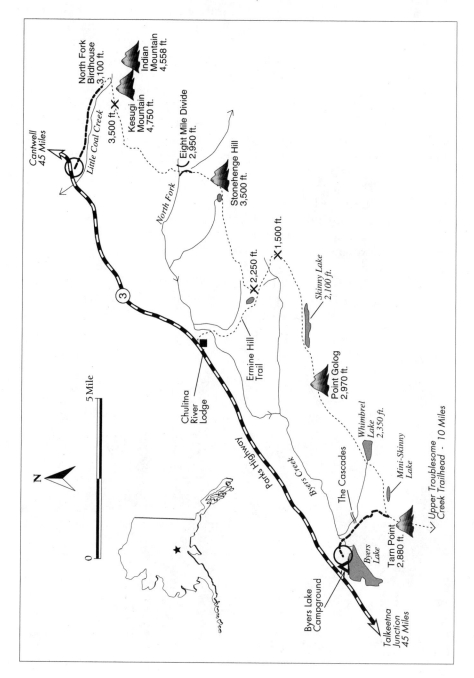

It's faster and easier to treeline from Little Coal Creek than from Byers Lake. The Ermine Hill Trail, which descends from the Kesugi route to the Parks Highway at Mile 156.4, 0.2 mile north of the Chulitna River Lodge, is a bad-weather bail-off point halfway along the ridge. Following is a brief trail log from north to south. The first mileage figure is the distance from Little Coal Creek; the second, from Byers Lake.

Mile 3/24.5. The North Fork Birdhouse, about 3 miles in and 3,100 feet elevation, an expanse of rolling alpine tundra with sweeping views and great wildflowers. Camping here and hiking to the highest part of Kesugi Ridge (Indian Mountain, 4,558 feet and Kesugi Mountain, 4,750 feet) makes a challenging trip; a map posted at the North Fork crossing shows the easiest routes to the peaks. The ridge route stays lower, on a 3,000-foot bench below the higher peaks.

Mile 4/23.5. The trail's high point, about 3,500 feet.

Mile 7.5/20. North Fork Byers Creek crossing, about 2,900 feet.

Mile 8/19.5. 8-Mile Divide, 2,950 feet, where the trail joins the Susitna - Chulitna River divide from the north.

Mile 10/17.5. Stonehenge Hill, a stony hill littered with bedroom-sized chunks of granite, at 3,300 feet. 10-Mile Tarn is just to the west.

Mile 13.5/14. Junction with the Ermine Hill Trail, the bad-weather escape route, in a 2,250-foot saddle. It's about 3 miles to the Parks Highway.

Hiking Kesugi Ridge, with Denali in the distance.

Skinny Lake, Kesugi Ridge hike.

Mile 15/12.5. A forested valley bottom, the low point of the ridge route at about 1,500 feet. The path here is brushy and steep. Make plenty of noise to dissuade bears.

Mile 17.5/10. Skinny Lake, 2,100 feet, in a narrow basin that's protected enough to shelter a few spruce trees. Set among long, low granite ridges, the lake and its brushy, sloping shoreline offer few good campsites.

Mile 19/8.5. Point Golog, 2,970 feet, a rocky point with a panoramic view, completely circled by alpine lakes and ponds.

Mile 22/5.5. Whimbrel Hill, 2,500 feet, a good birding spot. Swampy Whimbrel Lake is below to the east.

Mile 23.5/4. Mini-Skinny Lake, 2,700 feet. Good camping, and a good hike from Byers Lake.

Mile 24/3.5. Trail junction, about 2,500 feet. To the left, or south, is Tarn Point (2,880 feet, about 0.8 mile) and the Troublesome Creek Trailhead (12 miles). (See information on the Troublesome Creek Trail below under "other hikes.") The route to the right (north) leads to Byers Lake down an extremely steep trail.

Mile 26/1.5. The Cascades, a foaming whitewater drop of 100 feet in the creek that drains Whimbrel Lake.

Mile 27.5/0. Byers Lake Trailhead.

Other hikes. Hike between Little Coal Creek and the Troublesome Creek Trailhead, Mile 137.6 of the Parks Highway, for a 36-mile traverse; or hike between Troublesome and Byers Lake, a 15-mile traverse.

Troublesome-Byers is less of an alpine hike, so is a decent marginal-weather substitute for Kesugi Ridge. The Troublesome Trail, though, is troublesome because of bears feeding on salmon in the creek. The park closes the first 5.5 miles of the trail every year from mid-July to early September to keep bears and hikers apart.

Shorter hikes. The hike from Little Coal Creek to treeline (about 2 miles one way) or to the North Fork Birdhouse (3 miles one way) samples the high country, and the Birdhouse make a good short backpack. Mini-Skinny Lake, 4 miles from the Byers Lake side, makes a good long day hike or overnight.

COPPER RIVER BASIN

The Copper River is a great river inside a relatively small watershed, but it's what's in the watershed that counts. The Copper drains the wild, mountainous corner of the state where the Wrangell, St. Elias, and Chugach Mountains and outliers of the Alaska Range all meet, a land of Dall sheep, glaciers, jagged peaks, and volcanoes. The heart of the Copper country is Wrangell-St. Elias National Park and Preserve, the biggest national park in the country at 13 million acres.

Park trails described here are a few of the hikes accessible from the **McCarthy and Nabesna Roads**, near the central and northern parts of the park/preserve respectively. Most of the park is remote, accessible only by air, mainly from McCarthy, Glennallen, and Nabesna. For a description of the park's fly-in backcountry, see *Off the Beaten Path*.

McCarthy is a tiny, isolated town that's lately become a tourist destination. In general, hiking is fairly limited in the McCarthy area and along the McCarthy Road; most of the land is privately-owned. Road-accessible hiking is better from the Nabesna Road.

Other McCarthy area hikes are the **Nugget Creek Trail** (also a mountain bike trail), accessible from Mile 14 of the McCarthy Road, and the **McCarthy Creek route to Nikolai Pass**, beginning in McCarthy. The park also plans to build a day-hiking trail into the Crystalline Hills near Mile 40 of the road. Stop in at the park visitor center at Copper Center, 9 miles south of Glennallen, or at the Chitina Ranger Station for current information before heading for McCarthy.

Other hikes on the Nabesna Road are the **Caribou Creek route** into the Mentasta Mountains at Mile 19.5, and the **Big Grayling-Soda Lake Trail/route**, which begins at the Lost Creek Trailhead, Mile 31. Check in at the Slana Ranger Station for more information.

Valdez, south of the Copper River on Prince William Sound, is in an incredible mountain-and-fjord setting, but has almost no hiking. If you're desperate, try the walk on a trail and power project road to Solomon Lake from Dayville Road, or take a hike on Mineral Creek Road north of town.

Trip summary:	A shorter day hike to a lookout point on a bluff above the Tonsina River.
Distance:	1.5 miles one way.
Special features:	A surprisingly scenic spot.
Location:	45 miles southeast of Glennallen.
Difficulty:	Easy.
Trail type:	Less developed.
Total elevation gain:	None in, 300 feet out.
Best season:	June through September.
Maps:	USGS Valdez C-3 (trail not shown).
Manager:	Bureau of Land Management, Glennallen District.

Finding the trailhead: Drive about 32 miles south of Glennallen on the Richardson Highway and turn east onto the Edgerton Highway, the road to Chitina and McCarthy. (The intersection is about 86 miles north of Valdez.) Drive 12.3 miles to the trailhead in a small pullout on the south side of the road. The trail sign and register are barely visible from the highway.

TONSINA RIVER

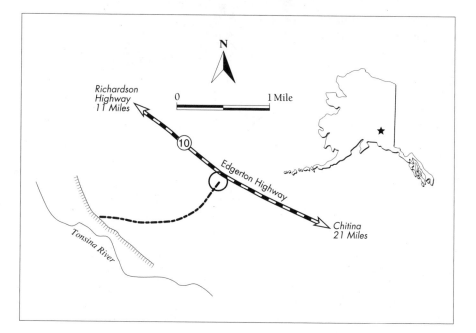

The hike: The Tonsina River Trail is a short, pleasant forest walk that ends on a bluff overlooking the Tonsina River. The change in vegetation on the dry, sandy river bluff is dramatic; stands of aspen and dryland plants like grasses and sagebrush replace the spruce and cottonwood forest of the rest of the hike.

Look and listen for hawks near the bluffs, and look for the channel across the main part of the river that's been made into a small lake, courtesy of some industrious beavers. Across the river are alpine ridges of the Chugach Mountains. The Tonsina flows into Prince William Sound by way of the Copper River, which it joins a few miles to the east.

The forest is low and protected, so it can be mosquito-infested in mid-summer, but the bluff is often breezy and relatively bug-free. Soapberry, the common shrub along the trail, is a favorite berry of bears.

53 WORTHINGTON GLACIER

Trip summary:	A shorter day hike that climbs Worthington Ridge and overlooks Worthington Glacier, a roadside glacier north of Valdez.
Distance:	1 mile one way.
Special features:	Worthington Glacier. The hike is a bit exposed and potentially dangerous in places on the narrow ridge.
Location:	33 miles north of Valdez.
Difficulty:	Moderate.
Trail type:	Less developed trail/route.
Total elevation gain:	1,200 feet.
Best season:	Late June through mid-September.
Maps:	USGS Valdez A-5 (trail not shown).
Manager:	Alaska State Parks, Matanuska-Susitna Area.

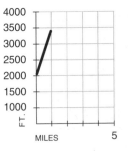

Finding the trailhead: The Worthington Glacier State Recreation Site is immediately off the Richardson Highway, about 33 miles north of Valdez and 2.7 miles north of Thompson Pass. Turn west into the recreation area. A short access road leads to the parking area, a viewing shelter and the trailhead.

WORTHINGTON GLACIER

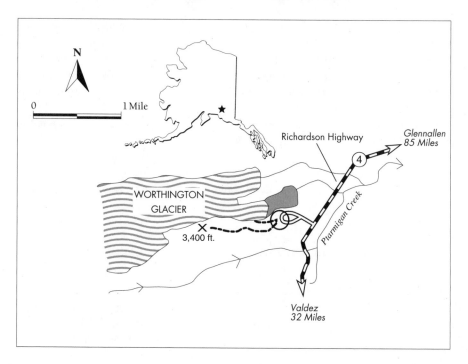

The hike: Another of Alaska's fine crop of drive-up glaciers, Worthington has the distinction of being three miles down the road from the state's snowiest weather-recording station, Thompson Pass, where 81 feet fell in the winter of 1952-53. Clouds billowing over the peaks behind the glacier may give you an idea why it's here.

The glacier falls four miles from its source to its terminus at the lake below the recreation site's viewing shelter. The lake's dam is a terminal moraine, the mass of rock and gravel that accumulates at the toe of a glacier, that is less than 100 years old. Worthington has retreated about 1,000 feet in the last century or so, much less than many of Alaska's glaciers.

To get a better look, take the path that climbs out of the south side of the parking area to the left. The hike is only a mile one way, but is not totally easy, and is not a good one for smaller children. The requirements for hiking to the overlook are good knees and good boot sole traction, and a staff or ski pole is a good idea for better footing coming down.

The trail is steep with poor footing in places until it reaches the top of the lateral moraine south of the glacier. In several places on the foot-wide trail on the moraine, there is considerable exposure, with steep, hard-packed scree slopes on one or both sides. This is not a spot for people who have problems with heights or exposure, and a fall here could be serious. Near the end of the hike on a 3,400-foot point, the trail is very narrow and exposed and beginning to crumble away. Below the peak, though, is a broader slope that's good for sitting a while, looking into the glacier's crevasses from above, eating lunch and taking photos.

On the moraine, the contrast between the blue ice in the valley to the north and the green alpine meadows and small mountain brook in the valley to the south could hardly be more striking. The trail briefly curls away from the glacier to the south side of the moraine through sloping wildflower meadows, where columbine, valerian, and geranium bloom in red, white, and blue at summer's height.

Other trails. State Parks is planning a short interpretive loop trail near the face of the glacier. It will be partially accessible.

---

54   DIXIE PASS

Trip summary:	A 2–4 day hike following Strelna Creek to Dixie Pass, a 5,150-foot alpine pass in the Wrangell Mountains.
Distance:	10.5 miles one way.
Special features:	Mountain scenery, challenging hiking. The hike is a collection of constructed trail, game trails, and creek-bottom walking with multiple stream crossings.
Location:	80 miles southeast of Glennallen.
Difficulty:	Strenuous.
Trail type:	Less developed trail for 5 miles; a route the rest of the way.
Total elevation gain:	About 3,700 feet in, 200 feet out.
Best season:	Late June to early September.
Maps:	USGS Valdez C-1 and McCarthy C-8.
Manager:	Wrangell-St. Elias National Park and Preserve.

Key points:

2.0   Strelna Creek
5.0   Confluence of the east and west forks of Strelna Creek
8.0   Strelna Creek canyon
9.0   Alpine meadows
10.5   Dixie Pass

DIXIE PASS

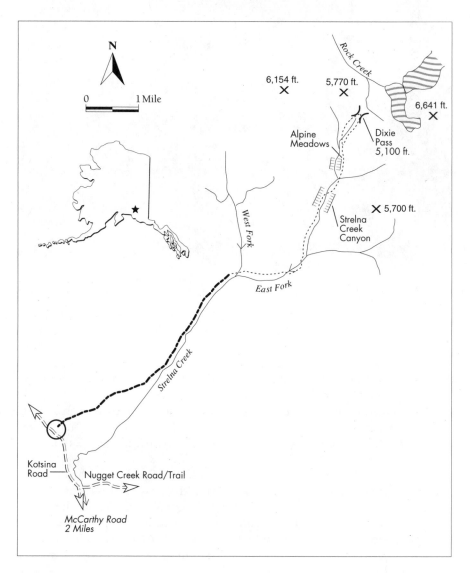

Finding the trailhead: The trailhead is on the McCarthy Road, between Chitina (say it *Chit' na*) and McCarthy. To find the McCarthy Road, turn east onto the Edgerton Highway from the Richardson Highway about 32 miles south of Glennallen and 86 miles north of Valdez. Take the Edgerton to Chitina, about 33 miles, and continue through town and over the Copper River bridge onto the rough gravel road toward McCarthy.

From the bridge, drive about 14 miles and turn left (north) onto the Kotsina-Nugget Creek Road, across the McCarthy Road from the west end of the Strelna grass airstrip. The intersection may be unmarked.

Loving the wildflowers near Dixie Pass. MOLLY MCCARTHY PHOTO.

From the McCarthy Road, the trailhead is 3.9 miles over the fairly rough dirt/gravel Kotsina-Nugget Creek Road. Consider parking low-clearance vehicles at Mile 2.6, where the Nugget Creek road/trail forks right across Strelna Creek. With a higher-clearance vehicle, continue straight ahead on the Kotsina branch of the road to the trailhead. At this writing, most vehicles can make it to the trailhead, but the road is subject to runoff and erosion.

The trailhead is unmarked, but is fairly obvious. It's directly across from a small clearing on the left side of the road. Park in the clearing and follow the narrow trail into the forest on the north, or right, side of the road.

The hike: The hike to Dixie Pass follows Strelna Creek to its headwaters, climbing to the 5,150-foot alpine pass. From the pass are fine views of the Strelna Creek drainage and the Chugach Mountains to the south. To the north, a cluster of jagged, glacier-carved Wrangell Mountain peaks lies across the headwaters of Rock Creek, which flows out of a massive rock glacier. In good weather the snow-covered volcanic summits of the Wrangells are visible in the distance.

It's possible to camp at the pass, with water from the stream or snowbanks just to the east. The weather in the pass, though, is chancy; wind and rain can blow in from the coast by way of the Copper River canyon. It's a good idea to take a little extra food and fuel in case the weather prevents reaching the pass or seeing the view for a day or two. There is good gravel bar camping all along Strelna Creek, and it's possible to drop down into the Rock Creek basin, north of the pass at 4,500 feet elevation, to camp and explore. The descent from the Rock Creek basin to the Kotsina River is rugged and not recommended.

The route is straightforward, following Strelna Creek to the pass, but it is rough in places and has a few potentially tricky spots. Take topo maps. The first five miles, to the confluence of the east and west forks of the creek, are on a decent trail, but beyond the confluence the hike is a route up Strelna Creek. Following is a brief trail log:

Mile 2. A small gravel bar, elevation 2,000 feet, on Strelna Creek where the creek enters the foothills.

Mile 5. Confluence of the east and west forks of Strelna Creek. The trail becomes harder to follow; here hikers have to cross the west fork and follow the east fork toward the pass. The only way to go wrong here is to follow the west fork instead of the east. Anticipate the crossing by looking for the west fork valley, visible through the trees as you approach. Continue northeast and stay low, near the creek, until reaching the west fork — it is a smaller stream than the east, or main stem. Cross the west fork near the confluence, a relatively easy crossing.

Now the fun begins. A discernible hiking route continues on the north side of the east fork; pick it up about 100 feet above the confluence, and stay near the creek until you're on the established route.

Mile 6. Cliffs on the north side of the creek. Cross to the southeast, or right bank as you travel upstream. It may be necessary to cross and recross the creek a few times here; pick a good route for the water level. In 0.5 mile or so, the best route is again on the northwest (left) side.

Mile 7. A large tributary stream (USGS quad map McCarthy C-8, Section 22, NE quarter). The route continues along the left side of the main (left, or north) fork, which is now smaller and easier to cross. Only a few trees remain at this elevation (about 3,100 feet), and the brush is low enough to see the mountains all around.

Mile 8. A short section of canyon, good for getting your feet wet again. There's an S-turn with a pool and rock ledge to negotiate, not difficult at lower water. Alternatively, climb around the canyon on the east (right) side. The valley widens again above the canyon, and the right side is the better for walking. In another half-mile, at a stream confluence at 3,700 feet elevation, take the obvious path up the ridge between the two forks. The stream on the left heads toward the pass but enters an impassable gorge just above.

Mile 9. Alpine meadows at the top of the climb from the forks, with the first view of Dixie Pass, the high gap straight ahead. Monkshood, forget-me-nots, fireweed, bluebells, cow parsnip, paintbrush, and other wildflowers bloom here in mid-summer. The trail may disappear momentarily; contour along at the same elevation until you find it again, eventually dropping down into the creek again, well above the gorge.

Mile 9.5. A choice of routes below the pass, which is close and easily visible now. The east route climbs a gently sloping tundra ridge between the pass creek and its last tributary. Meet a beaten path on the slope above and follow it to the pass. The west route climbs left of the pass creek and ascends to the pass on a path with one set of switchbacks.

Mile 10.5. Dixie Pass, elevation 5,150 feet. Peak 5,770 to the west has a fine view.

Hikers may encounter bears anywhere along the route. Also look for moose at the lower elevations, and Dall sheep higher up.

55 ROOT GLACIER

Trip summary:	A shorter day, half-day, or overnight trip along the edge of the Root Glacier, north of Kennicott.
Distances:	1.5 miles one way to campsites above the Root Glacier; 4.5 miles one way to a view of the Stairway Icefall.
Special features:	The historic Kennecott Mine, Root Glacier, the Stairway Icefall, and views of the Wrangell Mountains. The lower section is a good family hike. If camping, use the bearproof food bins provided by the Park Service.
Location:	4.5 miles north of McCarthy.
Difficulty:	Lower trail: easy. Upper trail: moderate.
Trail type:	Lower trail: more developed. Upper trail: less developed, infrequently maintained.
Total elevation gain:	Root Glacier campsites: 200 feet. Stairway Icefall view: 800 feet.
Best season:	June through mid-September.
Maps:	USGS McCarthy C-6 and B-6; Trails Illustrated *Wrangell-St. Elias National Park and Preserve.*
Manager:	Wrangell-St. Elias National Park and Preserve.

Key points:
- 0.5 Bonanza Creek
- 1.0 Jumbo Creek
- 1.5 Campsites
- 4.5 Stairway Icefall viewpoint

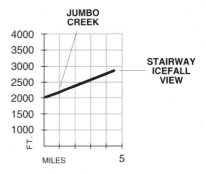

Finding the trailhead: The hike begins at the historic Kennecott Mine, 4.5 miles outside McCarthy. Visitors can drive as far as the bank of the Kennicott River across from McCarthy. (Yes, there are two spellings: one for the river and settlement, one for the mine.) There is no vehicle bridge into the town, so the only way to the trailhead is on foot or by bicycle or shuttle van.

Turn east onto the Edgerton Highway from the Richardson Highway about 32 miles south of Glennallen and 86 miles north of Valdez. Take the Edgerton

ROOT GLACIER

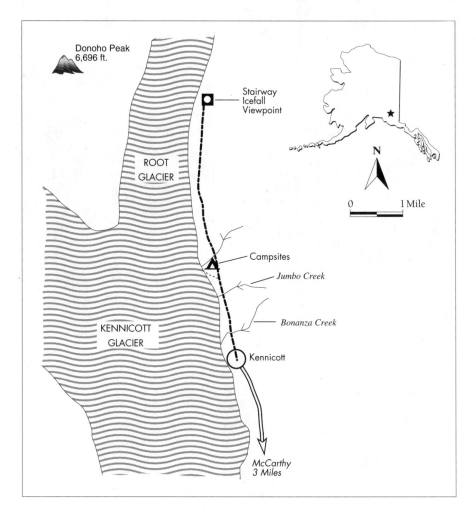

Donoho Peak
6,696 ft.

Stairway
Icefall
Viewpoint

ROOT
GLACIER

N

0   1 Mile

Campsites

Jumbo Creek

KENNICOTT
GLACIER

Bonanza Creek

Kennicott

McCarthy
3 Miles

to Chitina, about 33 miles, and continue through town and over the Copper River bridge onto the rough gravel road toward McCarthy. It's 59 miles of rough gravel road from the Copper River bridge outside Chitina to the end of the road at the Kennicott River. Allow about 2.5 hours for the trip. (There is also public transportation to the end of the road.)

Cross the river on foot (a bridge is scheduled to be built to replace the old tram in 1997), and walk the gravel road to the McCarthy/Kennicott intersection, about a mile east of the river crossing. From here, either walk the 4.5 miles to Kennicott or stroll into McCarthy and catch the shuttle van. If you've brought a mountain bicycle with you, this is a good place to use it. Rental bikes are usually available in McCarthy.

Kennecott Mine, the trailhead for the Root Glacier hike, with the snowy mass of Mount Blackburn, 16,390 feet, in the distance.

There are no campgrounds in McCarthy, but there is a private parking/camping area (fee required) at the end of the McCarthy Road. There is undeveloped National Park Service land along a side road to the north about 0.75 mile before the end of the road. Check with the Park Service at Copper Center or Chitina for current status, and if you camp there, please keep the area clean. There are public toilets at the end of the road.

The hike: This hike along the edge of the Kennicott and Root Glaciers begins in Kennicott, the site of the ore mill and mining settlement that worked the incredibly rich copper deposits on Bonanza Ridge to the east. The ore, some of it as rich as 70-80 percent copper, brought a 1910s construction and mining boom to this remote corner of Alaska. The road through Kennicott, the first section of the hike, is on the route of the old Copper River and Northwestern Railway. The railway connected the mine to Cordova from 1911 until the mine's closure in 1938.

The road out of Kennicott becomes a foot trail after the first 0.5 mile, following above the rubbly Kennicott Glacier. Donoho Peak separates the Root and Kennicott glaciers ahead, and if it's a clear day, the snowy mass of Mount Blackburn, one of the park's feature volcanoes at 16,390 feet, is visible to the left of Donoho. Spruce and willow grow on the slope above the trail, but gradually disappear as the trail heads up the valley.

The hike crosses private land until just before Jumbo Creek, so please stay on the trail. Jumbo Creek, at one mile, flows down a steep, narrow bed and disappears under the glacier. In about another 0.5 mile are campsites with secure food storage and, a bit farther, an outhouse. There have been several incidents of bears getting into campers' unsecured food, so please use the storage bins. This is a fragile, popular area, so please use a camp stove, camp at existing sites, and keep the area clean.

The first clean ice, the bottom of the Root Glacier, is just below the camp area. At about 1.25 miles is a spur path that leads about 0.25 mile down to the snout of the glacier. Hike onto the glacier at your own risk. Ice conditions can change from year to year, and crampons may be necessary. Slick ice combined with deep holes and fissures can be really dangerous. For adventurous hikers looking for a longer trip, crossing the glacier on crampons makes the Donoho Peak ridge accessible.

The trail becomes rougher and brushier as it leads up the valley, and the last section follows the edge of the glacier's steep-sided lateral moraine. The end of the trail is a fine destination—a terrific view of the Stairway Icefall, plunging 5,000 feet from the heights of the Wrangell Mountains. An old cable line stretches up the steep talus slope and cliffs toward the site of the Erie Mine, one of the mines that fed the Kennecott mill. If you haven't had enough yet, it's possible to scramble a few more miles farther out along the rocky margin of the glacier.

56 TRAIL AND LOST CREEKS

Trip summary:	A 2–4 day loop hike over a high pass in the Mentasta Mountains, following the Trail and Lost Creek valleys.
Distance:	About 21 miles, plus about 1.4 miles of road walking between the two trailheads.
Special features:	Alpine meadows and canyons, a 6,000-foot pass, Dall sheep. The hike is an undeveloped route following creek beds, ATV tracks, and game trails; map-reading and route-finding skills are essential.
Location:	30 miles east of Slana off the Nabesna Road.
Difficulty:	Strenuous.
Trail type:	Lower half: a route. Upper half: cross-country.
Total elevation gain:	About 2,900 feet.
Best season:	July to early September.
Maps:	USGS Nabesna C-5; Trails Illustrated *Wrangell-St. Elias National Park and Preserve.*
Manager:	Wrangell-St. Elias National Park and Preserve.

Key points:

- 3.5 Trail Creek narrows
- 7.0 Trail Creek/pass fork confluence
- 9.0 Rubble canyon of pass fork
- 10.0 Trail Creek/Lost Creek pass
- 14.0 Lost Creek valley widens
- 21.0 Lost Creek Trailhead

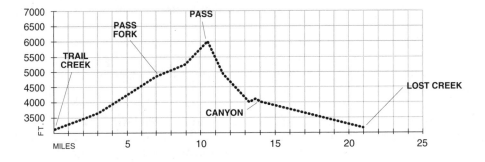

Finding the trailhead: The hike begins on the Nabesna Road—see "About the Nabesna Road," below. Trail Creek, the beginning of the hike as described here, is at about Mile 29.8 of the road. The creek is signed, but there is no trailhead sign. The Lost Creek parking area is at about Mile 31.2 of the road, 0.1 mile east of Lost Creek on the north side of the road.

The hike: This high-country hike connects Trail and Lost Creeks over a 6,000-foot pass. The pass is in spectacular alpine country below craggy, 8,147-foot Noyes Mountain, the crest of the Mentasta Mountains, and above an ice-cored, rock-covered glacier. The hike loops around a striking, unnamed, brown and white-layered mountain visible north of the Nabesna Road, following the valleys of the two creeks.

The trip is challenging but rewarding. Hikers could spend several days exploring the side valleys and ridges on either side of the pass. Dall sheep are abundant on the slopes and ridges.

There is camping almost anywhere on the lower stretches of the creeks. Of the upper valleys, camping is better on upper Trail Creek. Lost Creek's upper basin on the east side of the pass is probably the best high-elevation camping. Trail Creek is more of a valley hike, and Lost Creek more of a canyon hike.

The lower sections of the hike follow the gravel streambeds of the two creeks, occasionally following all-terrain vehicle tracks and game trails. In places where the creeks swing over against their banks, hikers must either cross or continue up on the bank in the forest. Creek levels vary depending on snowmelt and recent rains.

TRAIL AND LOST CREEKS

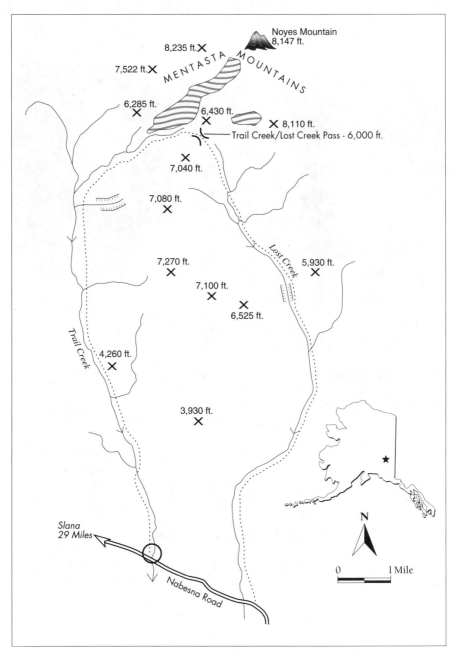

Noyes Mountain
8,147 ft.

8,235 ft. ✗

7,522 ft. ✗

MENTASTA MOUNTAINS

6,285 ft.
✗

6,430 ft.
✗

✗ 8,110 ft.
Trail Creek/Lost Creek Pass - 6,000 ft.

✗
7,040 ft.

7,080 ft.
✗

7,270 ft.
✗

Lost Creek

5,930 ft.
✗

7,100 ft.
✗

✗
6,525 ft.

Trail Creek

4,260 ft.
✗

3,930 ft.
✗

Slana
29 Miles

Nabesna Road

N

0   1 Mile

A rainy day on upper Trail Creek.

Following is a brief hike log, starting up Trail Creek and ending on lower Lost Creek:

Mile 2. Trail Creek's valley begins to narrow in the Mentasta foothills. Below, the easiest walking is on the west side, but above, the east side is easier.

Mile 3.5. The landmark rimrock Point 4,260 is above to the right. Turning a corner, the hike passes the last large grove of spruce trees at about 3,800 feet elevation.

Mile 5.5. The easiest route climbs up to and crosses a tundra bench on ATV tracks and game trails. Willow and dwarf birch brush gradually disappear as the hike gains elevation. Staying high until the pass fork is recommended.

Mile 7. The fork of Trail Creek that leads to the pass into Lost Creek flows in from the right, or east. Consult your topographic map to be sure you're heading up the correct fork. A running stream issues out of a slot canyon on the right, and beyond is a flat stretch of tundra; the next valley, a large, obvious one, is the pass fork. Follow the stream, or cut across the tundra bench. The creek is the more obvious route, but experienced cross-country hikers can try a higher cross-country route, with some ups and downs, south of the pass fork's canyon.

Mile 9. The pass fork canyon narrows and the stream may disappear for a bit as it enters a rock-rubble canyon and turns right (south) toward the pass. Follow the canyon from here if you've taken the high route this far.

Mile 10. The stream narrows to a slot; climb around (the left is best) if you can't get through. Above the slot is a rocky bowl, with the pass above to the right. Once in the pass, climb up to Peak 6,430 for the best view.

Mile 11. Lost Creek's upper canyon cascades down 600 vertical feet over the next 0.5 mile. The canyon is passable, but it could be an impossible route at high water, requiring a difficult hike around it.

Mile 11.5. At the bottom of the canyon, at a confluence with a stream from the east, aufeis, or shelf ice, lingers in the stream bottom all summer. Below the upper canyon, the best traveling is on the east, or left, side of the stream all the way to the trailhead. There are places just below that require climbing, wading the creek, or picking your way along the left bank at lower water levels.

Mile 14. Lost Creek's impassable lower canyon: climb about 200 feet to the alpine bench on the east side. A good animal path crosses the top, and the route eventually drops back to the creek below the canyon.

Miles 15 to 21. At the bottom of the lower canyon, the Lost Creek valley widens and the first spruce trees appear. Follow the creek's gravel bed, either crossing or following moose trails on the bank where necessary, to the hike's end at the Nabesna Road. About 2 miles from the road, a well-traveled, muddy ATV trail leads east to Big Grayling Lake.

About the Nabesna Road

The Nabesna Road is a remote, gravel, dead-end road that begins at Slana, on the Glenn Highway/Tok Cutoff about 62 miles south of Tok and 60 miles north of Gakona. Devil's Mountain Lodge is at the end of the Nabesna Road in 43 miles. The road follows the upper Copper River and Jack Creek valleys, sandwiched between the Mentasta and Wrangell Mountains in Wrangell-St. Elias National Park and Preserve. A couple of small, Alaska-style lodges are the only services on the road; there is no gasoline or vehicle repair.

The road is generally passable for passenger cars, but there are several stream fords on the upper half of the road. These fords can become swift and deep during periods of snowmelt and rain, and may become uncrossable. Check conditions at the Slana Ranger Station before setting out, and be prepared with extra food and cooking fuel in case heavy rains strand you and your vehicle until the creek levels drop again—it's happened before.

There are a number of all-terrain vehicle and foot routes into the mountains from the road. The relatively high elevation, about 3,000 feet in the road's upper reaches, means there is only a narrow strip of forest and brush between the road and treeline. Stream gravel beds make the best hiking routes into the high country.

Established routes are open to ATVs with a Park Service permit. ATVers use the trails mainly during sheep hunting season, beginning in early- to mid-August. To avoid most of the motorized traffic, hike before the season or avoid weekends during the season. The hikes described here are not normally heavy-use ATV areas.

57   SKOOKUM VOLCANO

Trip summary:	A half-day or longer day hike to an extinct, eroded volcano in the Wrangell Mountains. Hikers can loop back to the Nabesna Road over a 4,850-foot pass.
Distances:	Trail into the volcano canyon: 1.5 miles.
	Loop hike: 5 miles plus about 1.4 miles on the road.
Special features:	Alpine hiking, striking volcanic geology, Dall sheep. The park plans to print an interpretive brochure.
Location:	37 miles east of Slana on the Nabesna Road.
Difficulty:	Trail hike: moderate.
	Loop hike: moderately strenuous.
Trail type:	Less developed trail into the canyon; the loop hike is cross-country.
Total elevation gain:	Trail: 900 feet.
	Loop hike: 1,900 feet.
Best season:	Late June to early September.
Maps:	USGS Nabesna B-5; Trails Illustrated *Wrangell-St. Elias National Park and Preserve*.
Manager:	Wrangell-St. Elias National Park and Preserve.

Key points:
Loop hike
1.5   Trail's end in volcano canyon
2.5   Pass
5.0   Nabesna Road

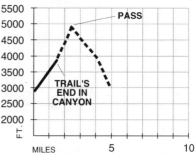

Finding the trailhead: The trailhead is in a pullout on the south side of the Nabesna Road at Mile 36.9. See *About the Nabesna Road* above for directions. If you're hiking the loop, the streambed the route follows reaches the road in a small pullout at about Mile 38.3.

The hike: A new trail scheduled for construction in 1997, the Skookum Volcano Trail is a short hop into the domain of an extinct volcano, the Skookum Creek Volcano, which roared to life between 2 and 3 million years ago and went dormant in more recent times. Erosion has revealed the inside of the volcano, and gives us a glimpse of what the inner life of the more recently active volcanoes in the Wrangell Mountains must be like.

The hike begins in the forest just northeast of the unnamed small creek the hike follows. The trail joins the creek's gravel bed in less than a mile and enters the canyon at treeline at about 3,400 feet elevation. It stays with the creek until the marked trail ends at 1.5 miles, just after taking a left fork in the stream. This left fork leads to the unnamed pass to the south, the route of the 5-mile loop hike. From the end of the trail, the loop hike's direction is fairly obvious, but there are no route markers.

SKOOKUM VOLCANO

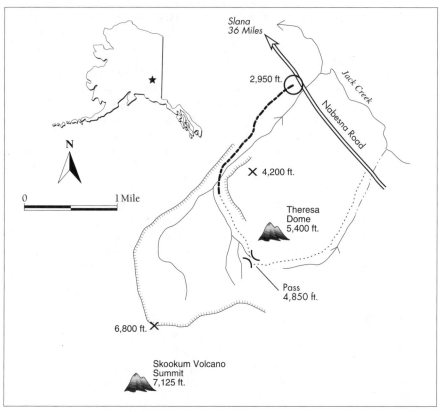

To hike the loop, continue up the left fork another mile, climbing steeply in places, heading for the west edge of the massive cliffs ahead. Take two left forks in the stream to stay on the most direct line to the pass. Once over the pass, 4,850 feet elevation, drop down to the rocky creek below and follow it east and north back to the Nabesna Road. Staying in the creek bed avoids thick brush. Once on the road, you're about 1.4 miles from the starting point.

Another possible cross-country destination is the 4,200-foot alpine shoulder of Theresa Dome, the obvious dome the loop hike circles. Wade the creek near the mouth of the canyon and climb up the long, green slope east of the canyon. The view from the shoulder is worth the climb. It's also possible to continue to the top of the dome (5,400 feet) and complete the loop from there.

The area is a geological fantasyland. Massive, flat-lying lava flows form cliffs to the west and south of the main canyon. Theresa Dome is a cinder cone that still has its original shape. Light-colored volcanic ash forms strange, curlicue towers above the pass. Harder bumps of rock, andesite dikes, protrude from deep layers of ash, and huge pyroclastic boulders, volcanic bombs made of welded-together chunks of rock, lie in the western stream bed.

In the animal realm, look for Dall sheep, arctic ground squirrels, and pika.

CORDOVA

Cordova, in eastern Prince William Sound, is accessible only by state ferry or air, and isn't yet an RV or cruise ship destination. The 48-mile Copper River Highway east of town is the access road to a fine vacation of hiking, camping, fishing, and wildlife watching. Bring your best rain gear; eastern Prince William Sound can be wet.

58 POWER CREEK AND CRATER LAKE

Trip summary:	A variety of day and overnight hikes on the Power Creek/Crater Lake trail system.
Distances:	Crater Lake: 2.4 miles one way.
	Power Creek Cabin: 4.2 miles one way.
	Mount Eyak ridge traverse: 12 miles between the Power Creek and Crater Lake trailheads.
Special features:	Scenery, alpine rambling, and a fee cabin. Hikers need to be experienced in route finding before tackling the Mount Eyak ridge traverse. There is a shelter on the ridge traverse.
Location:	The two trailheads are 2 and 7 miles northeast of Cordova.
Difficulty:	Crater Lake and Power Creek: moderate.
	Traverse: moderately strenuous.
Trail type:	Crater Lake and Power Creek: more developed trail.
	Traverse: a ridgetop route.
Total elevation gain:	Crater Lake: 1,500 feet.
	Power Creek: 700 feet.
	Traverse: about 3,000 feet.
Best season:	Late June through September.
Maps:	USGS Cordova C-5 (trails not shown); Forest Service leaflets *Crater Lake Trail* and *Power Creek Trail*; Trails Illustrated *Prince William Sound East*.
Manager:	Chugach National Forest, Cordova Ranger District.

Key points:

Power Creek Trail

1.0	Ohman Falls
2.3	Alice Smith Cutoff
4.2	Power Creek Cabin

Crater Lake Trail

1.0	Overlook
2.4	Crater Lake

Power Creek to Crater Lake Trailhead

1.0	Ohman Falls
2.3	Alice Smith Cutoff
4.3	Mount Eyak ridge
6.5	Shelter
9.6	Crater Lake
12.0	Crater Lake Trailhead

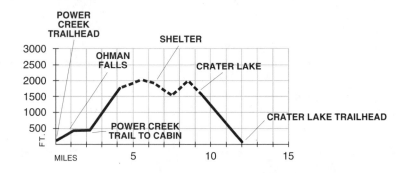

Finding the trailhead: Both trailheads are on Power Creek Road, the extension of Cordova's Lake Avenue. From 1st Avenue and Browning in downtown Cordova, drive 0.2 mile and take a hard left onto 2nd Avenue. Drive another 0.1 mile to the second right, which is Lake Avenue. The corner may be unsigned; Lake is the street with the small shingled church on the southwest corner.

Turn right (east) onto Lake Avenue and continue past the city airstrip and floatplane base, a total of about 2 miles from downtown, to the city-owned Skater's Cabin. Park on the right side of the road by the cabin and walk across the road to the Crater Lake Trailhead.

For the Power Creek Trail, keep driving past Skater's Cabin to the end of the road, about another 5.5 miles past the Crater Lake Trail.

The hikes: The Power/Crater trail system leads into spectacular country, traversing rain forest, the glacial Power Creek valley, mountain meadows, and alpine Mount Eyak ridge and Crater Lake. Hikers can day hike or camp at Crater Lake, day hike up Power Creek, rent the Power Creek Cabin for an overnight hike, or spend two or more days on the Eyak traverse. The diversity of terrain and vegetation on these hikes is outstanding.

Crater Lake Trail. This 2.4-mile hike begins as a climb through western hemlock forest above Eyak Lake—look for blueberries and black slugs. At about a mile a short side trail leads to an overlook of the lake and the surrounding country. When crossing an open muskeg on log corduroy, look for the blue-ribbon sized skunk cabbage.

At Crater Lake, wildflower meadows, rocky promontories, and gravel beaches make a pretty setting for a ramble along the shore. There are a few protected campsites near the lake. A steep hike up the ridge to the southwest and south leads to the top of Mount Eyak.

The Mount Eyak ridge route to Power Creek cuts away from the lake and heads north along the ridge. The traverse may be a bit easier beginning on the Power Creek side—the longest climb on the traverse is on a developed trail from Power Creek, instead of the steep, sometimes slick route above Crater Lake.

POWER CREEK AND CRATER LAKE

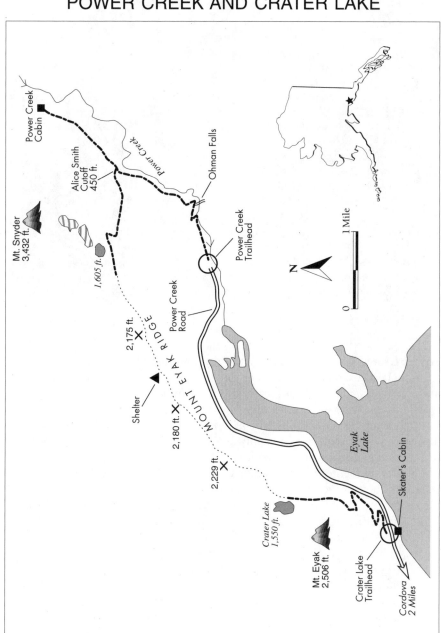

Power Creek Cabin

Alice Smith Cutoff 450 ft.

Power Creek

Ohman Falls

Power Creek Trailhead

Mt. Snyder 3,432 ft.

1,605 ft.

2,175 ft.

Shelter

2,180 ft.

2,229 ft.

MOUNT EYAK RIDGE

Power Creek Road

Crater Lake 1,550 ft.

Mt. Eyak 2,506 ft.

Crater Lake Trailhead

Eyak Lake

Skater's Cabin

Cordova 2 Miles

N

0   1 Mile

Power Creek Cabin.

Power Creek Trail. There aren't any dull moments at the beginning of the 4.3-mile Power Creek hike. A deep gorge encloses thundering Ohman Falls (not "oh, man"; it's named after a hydropower pioneer named Oscar Ohman). Smaller, snow-fed waterfalls slide down the valley walls as the trail cuts through a jungle of salmonberry and ferns. Above the falls, the trail runs through a wide basin known locally as Surprise Valley, with its wide, braided stream and sandbars.

The trail cuts into the rock ledge at the west edge of the valley as it passes a series of beaver dams, ponds, and lodges. Look for major beaver architecture and nesting waterfowl, swans included, along this section of the creek. At 2.3 miles the hike reaches the Alice Smith Cutoff to Mount Eyak ridge and the traverse to Crater Lake.

The trail ends at the cabin, a big cedar shelter with a rain catchment barrel—there is no surface water close by. (Remember to boil or filter the barrel water just as you would surface water.) Try counting all the waterfalls on the steep mountain slopes on both sides of the valley.

The cabin is available through the Forest Service's reservation-and-fee system (see Appendix 2).

Mount Eyak ridge traverse. The 12-mile traverse makes a great 2 or 3 day hike. The hike is probably a bit longer than the stated distance. The Forest Service's 5.5-mile estimate of the length of the ridge is accurate, but the route is not a straight line on the ridgetop; it dips back and forth on either side of the ridge.

Hikers must carry a map and compass and must be experienced in route finding to hike the traverse. The weather and visibility in Prince William Sound's mountains are subject to change on about ten seconds' notice. The cairns that mark the route along the ridge may be very difficult to follow when clouds close in. In good weather, though, the views are simply amazing.

From Mile 2.3 of the Power Creek Trail, take the Alice Smith Cutoff west and up about 1,200 feet to the ridgetop, passing through a mossy, bouldery forest, a steep, brushy slope, and subalpine stands of mountain hemlock. The trail first touches the ridgeline at about 1,700 feet elevation. Look north across a high lake basin and mountain glaciers to Snyder Mountain, elevation 3,432 feet, and scan the area for mountain goats.

A bare but enclosed shelter (no reservation, no fee) sits on the north side of the ridge at about 1,900 feet elevation, a little over 2 miles away. There are snow patches and runoff for water nearby, though these may dwindle by late summer. In about another 2.5 miles the route begins to drop steeply into the Crater Lake basin. Take care to find the right route before descending. Just above the lake, find the Crater Lake Trail and hike the 2.4 miles to the trailhead.

Shorter hikes. The 1-mile hike, one way, to Ohman Falls on the Power Creek Trail is the best easy hike on this trail system.

Fishing. There are stocked rainbow trout in Crater Lake.

59 HAYSTACK TRAIL

Trip summary:	A shorter day trip on an interpretive trail through the forest at the edge of the Copper River Delta.
Distance:	0.8 mile one way.
Special features:	Forest scenery and an interpretive trail.
Location:	20 miles east of Cordova.
Difficulty:	Easy.
Trail type:	More developed.
Total elevation gain:	About 150 feet in, 50 feet out.
Best season:	May through October.
Maps:	USGS Cordova B-4 (trail not shown); Forest Service leaflet *Haystack Trail*; Trails Illustrated *Prince William Sound East*.
Manager:	Chugach National Forest, Cordova Ranger District.

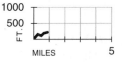

HAYSTACK TRAIL

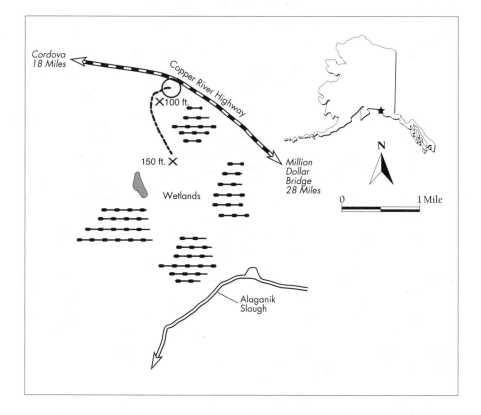

Finding the trailhead: The Haystack Trailhead is 19 miles east of Cordova on the Copper River Highway, on the south side of the road.

The hike: The Haystack Trail is an out-and-back interpretive trail that climbs a low double knob at the edge of the Copper River Delta. Steps and board-walk lead through a mossy Sitka spruce and hemlock forest, some of it old growth and some second growth. In the early 1900s, railroaders cut some of the timber here for ties for the Copper River and Northwestern Railway, the line that connected the rich Kennecott Copper Mine near McCarthy with the port at Cordova.

The knob is the haystack, a glacier-carved chunk of granite left like a stack of grass in a field after haying when rivers of ice ground across Alaska thousands of years ago. The haystack is an island of forest, a higher and drier environment than the wetlands of the delta below. Interpretive signs explain its ecology. Look also for the bright tags on trees by the trail that mark songbird census points. Migratory songbirds are generally in decline, and information from these points is fed into an Americas-wide data net-work to keep tabs on their numbers.

Overlook at the end of the Haystack Trail.

The overlook at the end of the trail is at the edge of a high cliff, with a pole fence erected at the edge—parents should be cautious with small children here. The part of the delta known locally as Goose Grass Flats is below, through the trees. Look for dusky Canada geese during the summer and a variety of waterfowl during spring migration. With binoculars, you might be lucky enough to spot a moose or bear out on the delta, or a bald eagle soaring above.

Bird Heaven: The Copper River Delta

The Copper River, the fourth largest river in Alaska, carries megatons of sediment out of the Wrangell, Alaska, and Chugach mountain ranges and dumps it, 700,000 acres worth, on the coast of Prince William Sound east of Cordova. The river's delta is the largest wetland on North America's Pacific Coast.

Twenty million shorebirds and waterfowl take a migration break or nest on the delta. The late April/early May arrival of shorebirds, about 6 million of them, is the biggest gathering of its kind anywhere in the Americas. Cordova celebrates with a shorebird festival the first week of May. The fall return of the birds is less concentrated, spread out from July through September.

The entire population of dusky Canada geese and the largest concentration of trumpeter swans anywhere, about 10 percent of the world's population, stay in the delta through the summer. Waterfowl like mallards, pintails, bufflehead, scaup, and white-fronted geese also nest here, and bald eagles are everywhere, like robins in suburbia.

For a closer look at the Copper River Delta, try the 0.1-mile Pete Isleib Memorial Boardwalk at the end of the Alaganik Slough Road at Mile 17 of the Copper River Highway. Named for the Cordova fisherman and ornithologist who studied the importance of the delta for migratory birds, the accessible boardwalk, with an enclosed viewing blind and an elevated deck, is a great spot for birding and drinking in the scenery of the delta and the Chugach Mountains.

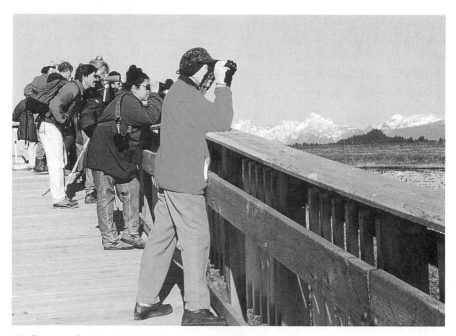

Birding on the Pete Isleib Memorial Boardwalk, Copper River Delta.
U.S. FOREST SERVICE PHOTO.

60   MCKINLEY LAKE

Trip summary:	A shorter day or overnight hike to McKinley Lake and the McKinley Lake fee cabin.
Distances:	McKinley Lake Cabin: 2.2 miles one way.
Special features:	Fishing, spawning salmon, a historic mine, and two fee cabins.
Location:	21 miles east of Cordova.
Difficulty:	Easy.
Trail type:	More developed.
Total elevation gain:	About 150 feet in and 100 feet out.
Best season:	May through October.
Maps:	USGS Cordova B-4; Forest Service leaflet *McKinley Lake-Pipeline Lakes Trail System*; Trails Illustrated *Prince William Sound East*.
Manager:	Chugach National Forest, Cordova Ranger District.

Key points:

0.05 McKinley Trail Cabin
1.0   South end of McKinley Lake
1.2   Pipeline Lakes Trail junction
2.2   McKinley Lake Cabin
2.4   Lucky Strike Mine

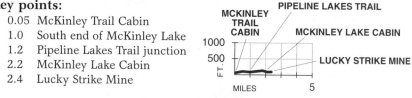

Finding the trailhead: The McKinley Lake Trailhead is on the north side of the Copper River Highway, about 21.6 miles east of Cordova.

The hike: The McKinley Lake hike can be a wet one, but there are two fee cabins for overnighters. The first, McKinley Trail Cabin, is just 250 feet from the trailhead, and the second, McKinley Lake Cabin, is 2.2 miles away at the north end of the lake. Both are available under the Forest Service reservation-and-fee system (see Appendix 2). Campsites are limited.

The trail meets the shoreline of McKinley Lake in just two places: the southern lobe of the lake at Mile 1, and the cove at the upper end of the lake by the McKinley Lake Cabin. The cabin is nestled into the woods just above the lake. This end of the lake is full of spawning red salmon by late July, and bears may be nearby looking for a fish dinner.

Beyond the cabin is what's left of the Lucky Strike Mine, which must have been named before the results were in. Though over 100 claims were staked and about $200,000 spent on development, the mine yielded only 16 ounces of gold and 9 ounces of silver. Rusting machinery, pipe, tram track, and a collapsed tunnel are the most obvious artifacts near the trail, and lesser-used paths branch back into the forest where the mine once operated. Take care exploring around the shafts, and don't drink any water from the mine area—it may be contaminated with heavy metals.

Like several of Cordova's hikes, this trail is improved with boardwalk and log corduroy over wet places. Here and on other Cordova trails the

MCKINLEY LAKE

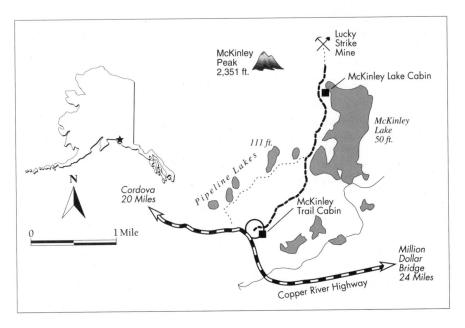

Forest Service has covered wood surfaces with fishing net recycled from Cordova's fishing fleet for better traction.

An alternate route to or from McKinley Lake is the Pipeline Lakes Trail, which is *very* wet and a mile longer than the McKinley Lake Trail. This hike isn't recommended without rubber boots and a real passion for the venerable Alaska sport of muskeg slogging. If any of the trail markers are down, the route may be a bit difficult to follow in a place or two, so keep an eye on where you are on the topographic maps you've brought with you. There is a bit of history here, too—the lakes were a source of water for the trains that ran from Cordova to the Kennecott Copper Mine on the Copper River and Northwestern Railway from 1911 to 1938.

Fishing. McKinley Lake supports salmon, cutthroat trout, and Dolly Varden. The outlet stream, a 0.5-mile bushwhack from the trail, offers the best fishing. Red salmon cruise up the stream in late June and early July, and there is a silver salmon run in September.

Trip summary:	A half-day or overnight hike to Saddlebag Lake and a view of Saddlebag Glacier.
Distance:	3 miles one way.
Special features:	Rain forest and Saddlebag Glacier.
Location:	25 miles east of Cordova.
Difficulty:	Easy.
Trail type:	More developed.
Total elevation gain:	200 feet in.
Best season:	May through October.
Maps:	USGS Cordova B-3 and B-4 (trail not shown), Forest Service leaflet *Saddlebag Glacier Trail*; Trails Illustrated *Prince William Sound East*.
Manager:	Chugach National Forest, Cordova Ranger District.

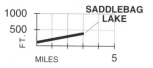

Saddlebag Lake and Saddlebag Glacier in the rain, July.

SADDLEBAG GLACIER

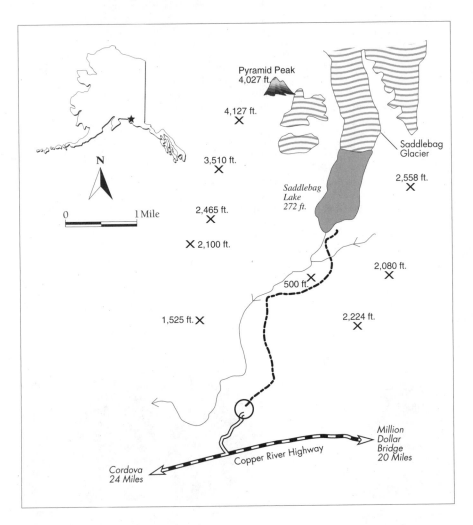

Pyramid Peak
4,027 ft.

4,127 ft.
X

3,510 ft.
X

Saddlebag
Glacier

N

2,558 ft.
X

0   1 Mile

2,465 ft.
X

*Saddlebag
Lake
272 ft.*

X 2,100 ft.

2,080 ft.
X

500 ft. X

1,525 ft. X

2,224 ft.
X

*Million
Dollar
Bridge
20 Miles*

Copper River Highway

*Cordova
24 Miles*

Finding the trailhead: Drive about 24.8 miles east of Cordova on the Copper River Highway and turn north on a firewood cutting road. Continue about a mile to the trailhead.

The hike: The locals call this trail Cordova's Portage Glacier (Hike 22) without the RVs, visitor center or crowds. The mass of Saddlebag Glacier's blue ice in the distance, a beautiful lake with floating icebergs and bergy bits, green mountainsides, waterfalls, and jagged peaks make a spectacular view at the end of this easy half-day hike. Mountain goats may be feeding high on the slopes.

The first half of the Saddlebag trail winds through Sitka spruce rain forest, with mosses hanging thickly from tree branches, bright green lichen on tree trunks, knee-high ferns and a sea of devil's club; the second half of the hike is grassy and brushy with alder and cottonwood. Sing to those potential bears in the woods.

The tread is relatively dry (for Cordova, of course), so some mountain bikers use the trail. There is one unbridged stream crossing, but a series of large rocks placed in the shallow stream make for easy rock hopping. The trail ends on a gravel beach with a great view of the valley and the glacier. It's possible to camp here at lower water levels.

Shorter hikes. Hike a mile or so out to get a taste of Cordova's rain forest.

62   CHILDS GLACIER

Trip summary:	A shorter day hike along the lip of the Copper River, across from the Childs Glacier.
Distance:	0.8 mile between two parking areas in the Childs Glacier Recreation Area.
Special features:	The Copper River and Childs Glacier. Watch for dangerous waves caused by glacial ice calving into the river.
Location:	48 miles east of Cordova.
Difficulty:	Easy.
Trail type:	More developed, partially accessible.
Total elevation gain:	Essentially flat.
Best season:	June through October.
Maps:	USGS Cordova C-2 and C-3; Forest Service leaflet *Childs Glacier Trail*; Trails Illustrated *Prince William Sound East*.
Manager:	Chugach National Forest, Cordova Ranger District.

Finding the trailhead: Drive 48 miles east of Cordova on the Copper River Highway, and turn left into the parking area just before the Million Dollar Bridge. (Railroaders built the bridge over the Copper River in 1910 for the Copper River and Northwestern line to the Kennecott Copper Mine.) Park either in the area by the bridge-viewing platform immediately after the turnoff, or in the large car park at the Childs Glacier viewing area about a mile farther on the access road. The trail connects the two parking areas.

The hike: It's big, it's dirty, and it's powerful. The Copper River, Alaska's fourth largest river, drains parts of four of the world's most glaciated mountain ranges. The short Childs Glacier Trail runs along the Copper where it narrows into a channel only 0.25 mile wide as it meets the Childs Glacier. This meeting of river and glacier is one of the most awesome sights in Alaska.

CHILDS GLACIER

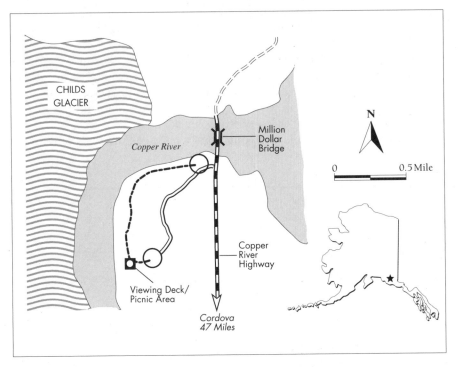

The Copper River, undercutting the face of the Childs Glacier.

The cracking and booming of the glacier are the first sounds hikers hear when they leave their vehicles. The glacier's face is 300 feet high and runs along the river for about 2 miles. Advancing 500 feet a year on average, the glacier dumps about 700 million cubic feet of ice into the river each summer, when the river rises high enough to undercut the base of the glacier. Huge icefalls crash into the silty water and send waves across the river; about a dozen a year are big enough to clear the river's high bank, sometimes stranding salmon on dry land. A sign at the viewing area reminds fish fans that taking these salmon home is illegal.

The trail connects the Million Dollar bridge area and the glacier viewing area to the south. The viewing area has several picnic tables and shelters and a 15-foot high viewing deck that offers the best in glacier watching. As you watch the glacier calving, think about the experience of two visitors a few years back who were hurled into the trees by a giant wave while they stood on the bank. Water lapped at the feet of people standing on the deck. Be ready to get away from the bank quickly if you see a big chunk of ice calve.

The trail was built as fully accessible, but now the river has eroded a section in the southern quarter. The north section is still accessible, but is near the river bank, so who knows when the Copper may claim it too.

Return to your vehicle by backtracking on the trail or by taking the road.

TRIPS IN THE INTERIOR

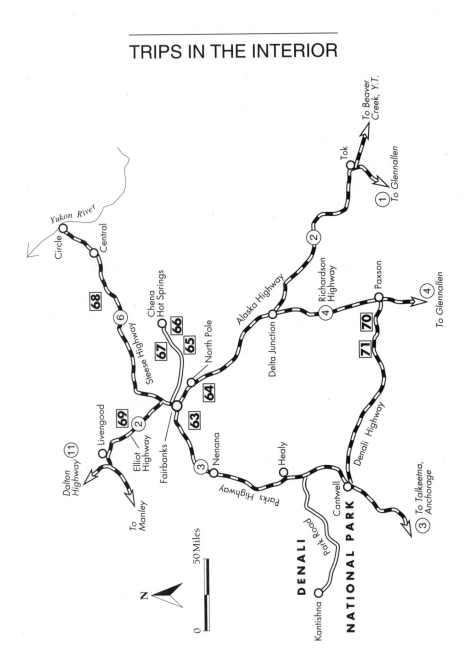

DENALI NATIONAL PARK AND PRESERVE

Denali National Park and Preserve is a 150-mile swath of parkland along the Alaska Range, between the Nenana River and the Kichatna Mountains. Spilling well over the range to the north, the park also includes major rivers—the Teklanika, Toklat, and Kantishna—that drain north into the Yukon River basin. The Outer Range in the northeast, the Kantishna Hills in the northcentral, and a huge expanse of boreal forest in the northwest part of the park complete the geography. Altogether, the park/preserve covers about 6 million acres, the size of Massachusetts.

The park's anchor is the central mountain massif topped by Mount McKinley (Denali), the tallest mountain in North America at 20,320 feet. Relatively few people get to the top of the mountain, but many more sample the backcountry north of the peak, where hikers enjoy alpine mountains, swift rivers, wildflowers, and wildlife.

The park is accessible via the Parks Highway (240 miles north of Anchorage and 120 miles south of Fairbanks) and the 90-mile park road that parallels the north side of the range. Most Denali visitors reach the interior of the park by traveling at least part of the park road. The road corridor, the most intensively visited and managed park area in the state, gives hikers a rare degree of easy access to Alaska's mountain wilderness.

Denali and the south side of the Alaska Range.

DENALI NATIONAL PARK AND PRESERVE
PARK ROAD CORRIDOR

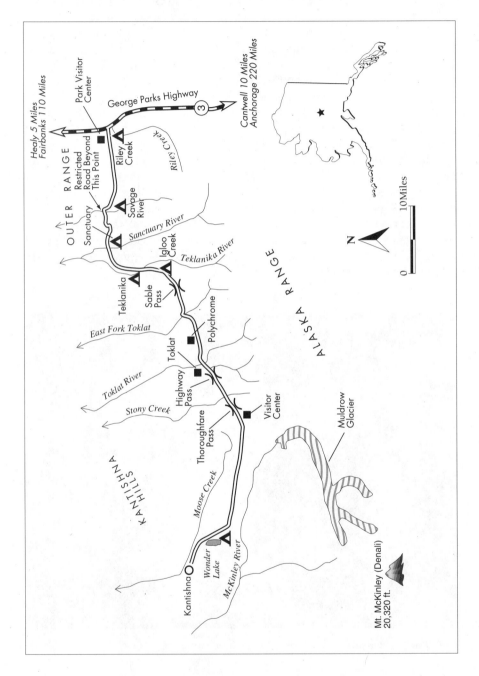

No developed trails cross the backcountry. A few shorter trails exist in the front country near the park entrance, and the Park Service is considering building new trails in the entrance area and along the road corridor. Most hiking opportunities in the park involve cross-country hiking in the backcountry.

Introduce yourself to Denali by reading the park newspaper, *Denali Alpenglow.*

PARK ENTRANCE TRAILS

Horseshoe Lake, a day hike to an oxbow lake and a beaver dam and lodge near the Nenana River, is an easy hike of 0.7 mile one way. The trailhead is 1.2 miles west of the park entrance via the park road.. The trailhead is on the right, just west of the railroad tracks.

Mount Healy Overlook is a day hike to two viewpoints of the Alaska Range, the higher one on the alpine ridge below Mount Healy. The lower viewpoint, an easy hike, is 1 mile one way, and the Healy Ridge viewpoint, a moderate, rocky hike, is 2.5 miles one way. The trail begins in the Denali Park Hotel guest parking area, off the park road about 1.5 miles from the park entrance.

The Morino Loop Trail, 1.3 miles and easy, connects the Denali Park Hotel with the Morino Campground.

The Taiga Loop Trail, also 1.3 miles and easy, forms a loop between the Denali Park Hotel, the park road, and the boreal forest, or taiga, along Horseshoe Creek.

The Rock Creek Trail, 2.3 miles one way and moderate, connects the Denali Park Hotel with park headquarters. It's possible to loop back to the hotel on the Roadside Trail, 1.8 miles one way.

PROPOSED NEW TRAILS

ENTRANCE AREA

Riley Creek Trail, a 1-mile, accessible loop trail in Riley Creek Campground.

Triple Lakes Trail, about 4 miles one way, from Riley Creek Campground to three small lakes above Riley Creek.

PARK INTERIOR

Savage River: A trail system at about Mile 14 of the park road, with a very short loop trail, a 2-mile loop trail, and a 1.5-mile trail to the alpine ridge to the east. Visitors can drive private vehicles on the park road as far as Savage River.

Primrose trails: a very short loop trail south of the road, and a trail to Primrose Ridge to the north, at about park road Mile 18.

Toklat: a very short loop trail at Mile 53.

Eielson Visitor Center: a 3-mile loop trail to the ridge to the north at park road Mile 66.

Wonder Lake trails: Two very short trails at Wonder Lake, 85 miles from the park entrance, and an upgrade of the hiker-made McKinley Bar route that extends 2 miles from the Wonder Lake Campground road to McKinley River.

THE PARK BACKCOUNTRY

There are literally hundreds of cross-country hiking possibilities in the park's backcountry. No guidebook can begin to do the area justice by describing specific hikes, and this approach would conflict with park policy anyway. Park managers have taken the approach of not recommending specific hikes, hoping that as a result, hikers will spread out over the landscape in small parties, leaving the park unscarred for future visitors. What follows here is a trip-planning guide for hikers who want to take a hiking trip into the Denali backcountry.

THE PARK ROAD

From Memorial Day to mid-September, the only way into the park past Mile 14 on the park road (Savage River) is by public bus, for a fee. There are shuttle buses for day visitors, and camper buses for overnight visitors. You can reserve bus tickets and campsites at developed campgrounds by phone, beginning in January, or in person at the visitor center within two days of your trip into the park. Only a portion of the available slots are offered for phone reservation (see Appendix 1 for reservation information).

In May, the park road is usually opened in stages, the schedule depending on the winter snowpack and spring weather. Until Memorial Day, some stretches of the road may be open to private cars. Check with the park on conditions at the time—the road situation changes from day to day in May. In mid-September, the park opens the road to private vehicles by lottery. Apply to the park in July for a lottery permit for September.

A few people travel the road by mountain bike.

BACKPACKING THE BACKCOUNTRY

Backpacking in Denali's backcountry involves a slug of logistics at the park visitor center because of requirements imposed to keep the hoards of visitors from loving the park's fragile tundra to death. Park managers have carved the backcountry up into 43 units and established a permit system with quotas for overnight visitors. There are no permit requirements for day hikers.

Backpackers have to get in touch with the terrain in Denali's trailless backcountry, following streambeds and ridgelines, practicing route-finding skills, and crossing unbridged streams safely. For more information, see the introductory section, "Hiking in Alaska."

GETTING A PERMIT

Head for the backcountry desk in the park's visitor center. NPS issues permits only one day in advance of your trip, and requires that overnighters use bear-resistant food containers, which the park supplies. Hikers plan their own trips, using the information at the desk. You can buy USGS topo maps for your hike at the Alaska Natural History Association shop in the visitor center. The steps for getting a permit, in order, are as follows:

1. **Visit the Backcountry Simulator** to brush up on wilderness safety and low impact techniques.

2. Figure out where to go. **Check the quota board** behind the backcountry desk to see which units are open. Then, to choose among them, **look over the Backcountry Unit Descriptions and the topographic maps** that show the unit boundaries. The Backcountry Unit Descriptions, which list features and routes in each unit, are the best information on Denali hiking available. For a multi-day trip, you may have to change units during your hike, so check out the units adjacent to your top choices, too.

3. **Ask a ranger** at the desk to issue you a permit for your chosen unit(s).

4. **Buy a ticket for the camper bus.** You might be a bit frazzled by your experience at the visitor center, but persevere; there's some good backcountry out there once you actually make it into the park.

DAY HIKING FROM THE PARK ROAD

There are several options for day hiking in the interior of the park. Either pick out a hike yourself from the Backcountry Unit Descriptions and topographic maps, or join one of the Discovery Hikes. A "Disco" hike is a half day, moderate to moderately strenuous, ranger-led day hike to a backcountry destination. Register up to two days in advance at the visitor center. There are also easy, guided walks at Toklat and the Eielson Visitor Center.

Day hikers can take a shuttle bus into the park, go hiking, and return to the park entrance by bus later the same day. Alternatively, camp one or more nights at a campground on the park road, take a shuttle bus to your hike, and return to your campground by bus that evening. Visitors can stay in park campgrounds a total of fourteen days a year.

FAIRBANKS

Fairbanks, Alaska's largest Interior city, is better known for its rivers and winter trails than its summer hiking trails. The best hiking near the city is on the rolling, high, bareback ridges between the Tanana and Yukon Rivers, in the Steese and White Mountain areas north of town, and the Chena River area to the east.

---

63 CREAMER'S FIELD

Trip summary:	Three shorter interpretive trails at Creamer's Field, an 1,800-acre migratory waterfowl refuge.
Distances:	Seasonal Wetland Trail: 0.5 mile one way.
	Boreal Forest Trail: 1.4 mile loop.
	Farm Road Trail: 0.3 mile one way.
Special features:	Birding, interpretive trails, naturalist-led hikes, a visitor center, and a piece of Fairbanks history. Creamer's buildings are on the National Register of Historic Places.
Location:	On College Road in Fairbanks.
Difficulty:	Easy.
Trail type:	Seasonal Wetland Trail: accessible.
	Boreal Forest and Farm Road trails: more developed. The Farmhouse Visitor Center is accessible.
Total elevation gain:	Essentially none.
Best season:	May through September.
Maps:	Trail maps are available at the trailhead kiosk and the Farmhouse Visitor Center.
Manager:	Alaska Department of Fish and Game.

Finding the trailhead: Creamer's Field is located on College Road in Fairbanks, about halfway between University Avenue and the Steese Highway, just east of the Tanana Valley Fairgrounds. From University Avenue and College Road, drive east on College Road about 2 miles, past the Fairgrounds, to the traffic light at Danby Street. Turn left, or north, and follow the road around the Alaska Fish and Game headquarters to the refuge.

From the east, take the Steese to College Road, turn west and drive about 1.6 miles to the access road to Creamer's. The access road is about 0.1 mile east of the traffic light at Danby Street.

Creamer's is on the city's Red Line bus route.

The hikes: Creamer's Field offers short hikes in the heart of Fairbanks, great migratory bird viewing in spring and fall, and a chance to explore a bit in the forests and wetlands of Interior Alaska. Creamer's is a historic dairy that operated until 1966 (see sidebar), and the old farmhouse has been

CREAMER'S FIELD

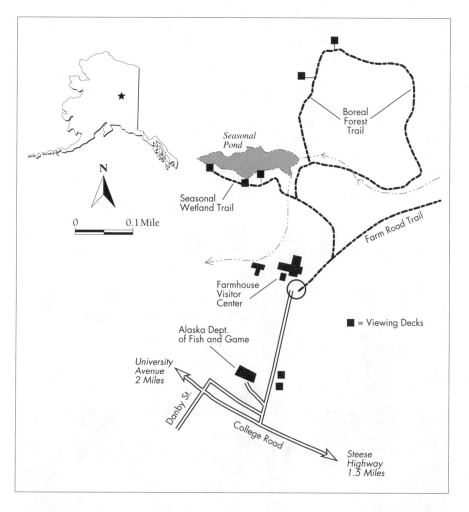

Seasonal Pond

Boreal Forest Trail

Seasonal Wetland Trail

Farm Road Trail

Farmhouse Visitor Center

Alaska Dept. of Fish and Game

University Avenue 2 Miles

Danby St.

College Road

Steese Highway 1.5 Miles

N

0   0.1 Mile

■ = Viewing Decks

renovated as the refuge's visitor center. From June 1 to September 1, the visitor center is open, and local naturalists lead walks several times a week.

In spring and fall Creamer's attracts great flocks of migratory birds like geese, ducks, cranes, and plovers, which stop to rest and feed here on their long journeys between summer and winter grounds. Some of the birds, including a group of about 100 young sandhill cranes, remain on the refuge all summer. The first of the migratory birds, usually Canada geese, arrive in mid-April. The height of the spring migration is from mid-April to mid-May, and mid-August to mid-September is the height of the fall migration. During spring and fall, as many as 800 cranes a day stop at Creamer's.

Seasonal Wetland Trail. This graded trail leads to three small viewing decks by a seasonal wetland. Interpretive signs explain the wetland and its seasonal wildlife.

Boreal Forest Trail. A one-mile loop that splits off from the Seasonal Wetland Trail about 0.2 mile from the visitor center, this trail meanders through a lowland forest with a long section of boardwalk. The forest is typical of Alaska's Interior, with white and black spruce, tamarack, paper birch, balsam poplar, aspen, and some tree-sized willows. A short side trail leads to a 12-foot-high viewing tower that overlooks a low-growing birch forest. Ask for the trail guide for this walk. There is another short side trail with a viewing deck at the edge of a logged and burned demonstration area.

Farm Road Trail. Just as it sounds, this old dirt road winds through fields and patches of forest. Take binoculars, and look and listen for migratory waterfowl.

Please, no bikes, and pets are allowed only on leash or under voice control. To keep from disturbing nesting and resting birds, don't wander off the trails into the fields.

The historic farmhouse at Creamer's Field in Fairbanks.

A Family Named Creamer and a Subarctic Dairy

The dairy history of Creamer's Field goes back to Alaska's gold rush era. Just after the turn of the 20th century, a couple named Hinckley hauled three cows up the Yukon and Tanana Rivers to the new town of Fairbanks and started a dairy. Charlie and Anna Creamer, who first came north in the Klondike gold rush, bought the Hinckleys' dairy in 1928—with a name like Creamer (pronounced like it's spelled), what else could they do? Dairying in the subarctic had its challenges, like feeding the cows over the long winter (answer: grow three tons of hay and grain per cow) and keeping the milk from freezing in the delivery truck (a wood stove did the trick).

The natural meadows next to the dairy had apparently always attracted migrating birds, but when the Creamers turned the meadows into grain fields and pasture, the birds must have cheered them on. In the spring and fall, the birds could stop over and eat their fill of the leftover oats and barley from the fields. The return of the geese to Creamer's has always marked the coming of spring in Fairbanks, and when the dairy folded in 1966, the community pitched in to help Fish and Game buy the fields to protect them as bird habitat.

And how do the birds fare now that the cows are gone? They get special barley plantings for their dining pleasure.

Trip summary:	A shorter day hike on an interpretive loop trail along the Chena River.
Distance:	1.5 to 2.5 miles.
Special features:	A trail guide, good views, lush forest, wildflowers. There is a day use fee.
Location:	20 miles east of Fairbanks in the Chena Lake Recreation Area.
Difficulty:	Easy.
Trail type:	Accessible.
Total elevation gain:	Essentially none.
Best season:	June through September.
Maps:	Use the trail booklet *Chena River Nature Trail*, available at the entrance station and trailhead.
Manager:	Fairbanks North Star Borough.

CHENA RIVER NATURE TRAIL

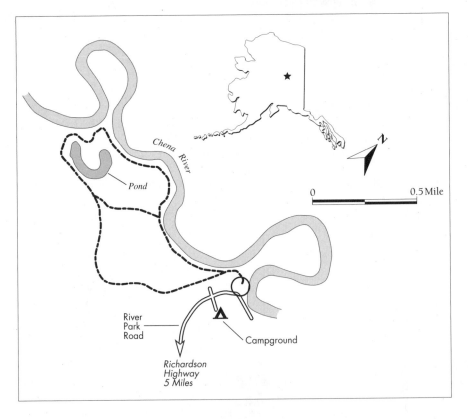

Rose shrubs can be six feet tall along the Chena River Nature Trail.

Finding the trailhead: From the intersection of Airport Way and the Steese Expressway at the southeast edge of Fairbanks, drive about 14 miles east on the Richardson Highway past the town of North Pole to Laurance Road. Turn left toward the Chena Lake Recreation Area, and drive about 5 more miles, stopping to buy a day pass at the entrance station on the way, to the turnoff to the River Park; turn left. At the second left on the River Park Road, in about 0.7 mile, turn into the trailhead parking area. There are restrooms and water at the trailhead.

The hike: The Chena River Nature Trail is a pleasant stroll through the boreal forest along the Chena River, in the River Park section of the Chena Lake Recreation Area. The recreation area is the site of a flood control dam on the Chena, and is loaded with the usual damsite amenities: campgrounds, picnic sites, horseshoe pits, volleyball and basketball courts, boating and swimming areas, and a bike trail.

The nature trail, though, is in a quiet spot along the river. It's an easy walk on a graded gravel bed, so lightweight shoes are fine. The trail guide interprets the natural history of the Chena, river dynamics, plant succession, and the Interior's boreal forest.

The section along the river passes through birch forest with a lush green understory of wild rose, horsetail, and tall grasses. By mid-summer, you may have to look up to see the tops of some of the rose bushes. Circling back from the river, the trail passes by an oxbow pond and through stands of willow trees, a mixed spruce/birch forest, and a black spruce bog. The entire loop is about 2.5 miles long; for the 1.5-mile option, take the cutoff trail to the left just past the #3 interpretive post.

In early summer, keep an eye out for migratory songbirds, and in mid-August, look for chum salmon spawning in the river.

65 GRANITE TORS

Trip summary:	A longer day or overnight trip on a loop trail to an alpine ridge topped with granite pinnacles and towers.
Distance:	A 15-mile loop.
Special features:	Great views, scenic granite outcrops, a rock climbing area for experienced climbers, and a trail shelter. Limited water on the trail.
Location:	45 miles east of Fairbanks in the Chena River State Recreation Area.
Difficulty:	Moderately strenuous.
Trail type:	More developed at lower elevations; less developed in the alpine tundra.
Total elevation gain:	About 2,700 feet.
Best season:	June to mid-September.
Maps:	USGS Big Delta D-5; Alaska State Parks leaflet *Granite Tors Trail*.
Manager:	Alaska State Parks, Northern Area.

Key points:

Starting East of Rock Creek		Starting West of Rock Creek
0.0	Trailhead	15.0
4.0	Knob 2,211 feet	11.0
5.5	North Tors side trail	9.5
7.0	Trail shelter	8.0
8.0	Plain of Monuments	7.0
10.0	The Lizard's Eye	5.0
15.0	Trailhead	0.0

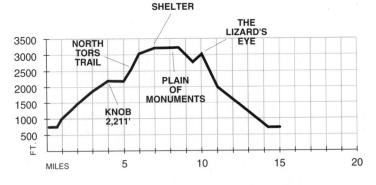

GRANITE TORS

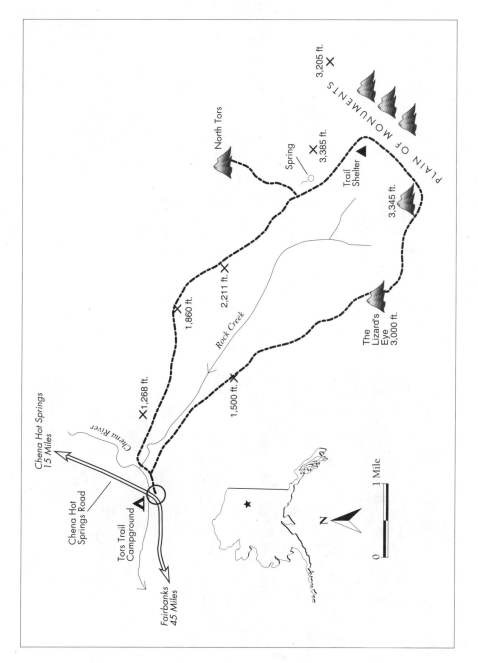

Finding the trailhead: From Airport Way and the Steese Highway in Fairbanks, drive about 5 miles north on the Steese to Chena Hot Springs Road. Turn east and drive 40 miles to the Tors Trail Campground on the left. Park in the day use area by the river. Walk back out to the main road, cross the bridge over the river to the west, and find the trailhead on the south side of the road below the guard rail. Take care crossing the road, especially with kids.

The hike: The Granite Tors are granite towers, pinnacles, and slabs that crown the alpine ridge at the head of Rock Creek, southwest of the Chena River. (A *tor* is a large, isolated outcrop of rock). The Plain of Monuments, about midway on the hike, is Alaska's natural Stonehenge. There are scattered tors west of the Plain of Monuments, including the Lizard's Eye, a tor with a round opening near the top. A side trail a bit less than a mile long leads to the North Tors, a group of tors north of Rock Creek.

This hike is a rare breed in Alaska—a loop trail that returns exactly to its starting point. The trail loops around the Rock Creek drainage. The forks of the trail to the east and west sides of the creek divide about 0.25 mile from the trailhead.

For the shortest hike to a tor, take the west fork to the Lizard's Eye, about 5 miles from the trailhead, but if you're set on walking the entire loop, the east fork is probably the place to start. Hiking this direction is a more gradual climb—there is one very steep section of the trail, with a 500-foot elevation change, a mile below the Lizard's Eye, and it's downhill if you start from the east.

Above treeline on the Granite Tors Trail.

250

The Plain of Monuments, Alaska's Stonehenge, on the Granite Tors Trail.

About five miles of the trail is alpine, marked with rock cairns and wooden tripods. Watch the weather; it can change from sunny, shorts weather to cold, blowing rain and fog quickly, making the route across the high country hard to find.

Water is scarce. The only source on the trail above treeline is a small, intermittent spring about 500 feet above the North Tors side trail intersection. Be sure to boil or filter any surface water you use for drinking or cooking. Consider carrying all your water from town or from the campground.

The tors invite exploring, but they can be dangerous climbing for inexperienced and unequipped parties, so stay within the limits of your skills and experience.

Some optional hikes to consider besides the entire 15-mile loop are as follows:

Take the east trail to Knob 2211, an out-and-back hike to a good view of the alpine ridge and the distant tors, 4 miles one way.

Follow the east trail to the North Tors, about 6 miles one way.

Hike the west trail to the Lizard's Eye, 5 miles one way.

The trail shelter, at the east edge of the alpine area on the hike, is for emergency use—no reservation, no fee. The trail is open to foot traffic only.

Shorter hikes. See the optional hikes above, or try a short walk, about a mile one way, up either trail fork. The east trail crosses Rock Creek and threads through lush spruce/birch forest, passing the edge of a beaver pond. The west trail runs along a continuous boardwalk through black spruce wetlands before it begins climbing.

Trip summary:	A shorter day hike to Angel Rocks, a rugged group of granite walls and towers, or a longer day or overnight traverse between Angel Rocks and Chena Hot Springs.
Distance:	Angel Rocks: 1.7 miles one way on an out-and-back hike, or a 4-mile loop via a rough, steep trail. Angel Rocks-Chena Hot Springs traverse: 8.3 miles.
Special features:	Angel Rocks: granite outcrops, good views, and a rock climbing area for experienced and equipped climbers. Traverse: an alpine ridge with fine views and a trail shelter.
Location:	55 miles east of Fairbanks in the Chena River State Recreation Area.
Difficulty:	Angel Rocks: moderate. Traverse: moderately strenuous.
Trail type:	More developed lower on the Angel Rocks Trail and the Chena Hot Springs trails; less developed near Angel Rocks; a route across the alpine tops.
Total elevation gain:	Angel Rocks: 750 feet. Traverse: about 2,000 feet.
Best season:	June through mid-September.
Maps:	USGS Circle A-5, Alaska State Parks leaflet _Angel Rocks Trail_, and the Chena Hot Springs trail leaflet _Hiking/Cross-Country Ski Trails and Snowmachine Area_.
Manager:	Alaska State Parks, Northern Area, and Chena Hot Springs.

Key points:
1.7 Angel Rocks summit
3.5 Traverse high point, 2,800 feet
5.0 Trail shelter
6.7 Bear Paw Butte trail junction
8.3 Chena Hot Springs

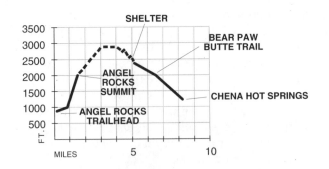

ANGEL ROCKS

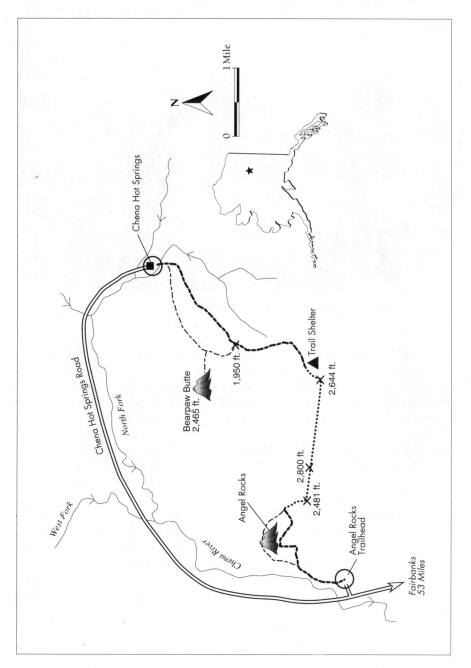

The alpine ridge between Angel Rocks and Chena Hot Springs.

Finding the trailhead: From Airport Way and the Steese Highway in Fairbanks, drive about 5 miles north on the Steese to Chena Hot Springs Road. Turn east and drive 49 miles to the Angel Rocks Trailhead on the right. Chena Hot Springs, the other end of the traverse, is at the end of the Chena road, 7.5 miles beyond the Angel Rocks Trailhead.

The hikes: The granite Angel Rocks shoot up out of the forest on the hillside above the Chena River, and offer plenty of cracks and crevices to explore and good views to enjoy. The area around the rocks is a pleasant scene of granite, aspen, and spruce.

It's a steep, somewhat rough trail, but this is a much easier hike to see a tor landscape than the hike to the Granite Tors (Hike 65). Keep an eye on the kids, though; there are some steep drops here, and the trail that loops through the rocks and back down to the river is steep and rough.

For a longer hike, try the traverse to Chena Hot Springs over the 2,800-foot alpine ridge to the east of Angel Rocks. You'll need to shuttle a car or bicycle to the hot springs or arrange for a ride back to the trailhead. Between Angel Rocks and the Chena Hot Springs trails, the route is unimproved except for scattered rock cairns to mark the way. Be sure to have a topographic map, compass, warm clothes, and rain gear for the traverse, and be prepared to turn back if weather moves in and the visibility deteriorates.

The Angel Rocks Trail is open to foot traffic only, and open fires are prohibited.

254

Angel Rocks. The trail first parallels the North Fork of the Chena, and then begins to climb, reaching a small granite outcrop with a view of the rocks in about a mile. The path skirts several of the rocks, with side trails leading to good views. (Be careful of the exposure, and don't try climbing unless you're equipped and experienced.) Please stay on the switchbacks; steeper paths erode easily with hiker traffic.

The trail flattens out and splits behind the rocks, at about 1,750 feet elevation. Take a left to explore the upper rocks; the right fork leads up to one more granite tower, to the ridge above and, eventually, to Chena Hot Springs. For the shortest return to the trailhead, explore around the rocks and then retrace your steps from the trail junction behind the rocks back down the hill.

Alternatively, follow the left fork through the rocks and continue steeply down to the valley bottom. Then turn south along a small slough and follow it back to the main trail. Taking the left fork adds about 0.5 mile to the hike.

Angel Rocks-Chena Hot Springs. From the trail junction behind Angel Rocks, follow the trail up the ridge to the last granite tower. Above the tower, the trail becomes rougher. Cairns lead into a forested saddle, at which point the route of travel changes from southeast to east. Follow this rough route and some cairns across the saddle and up to the 2,800-foot summit, the high point of the hike. The route continues east along this alpine ridge crest. Savor the views of the Alaska Range and the nearby peaks of the Tanana Hills if it's a clear day. Look east to Far Mountain, at 4,694 feet the highest peak in the area, and west to Chena Dome, 4,421 feet.

A bit over a mile from the first point on the alpine ridge, at the last rocky alpine bump, the route turns northeast through brush and small trees toward Point 2,644. After a couple of more bumps, the route drops into a forested saddle at 2,450 feet elevation and picks up the Overlook Trail from Chena Hot Springs. About 100 feet to the right, or east, of the trail is the trail shelter, for emergency use—no reservation, no fee required.

Continue down the Overlook Trail, passing the trail to Bear Paw Butte at 6.7 miles. At about 7.5 miles, take a left onto the Hillside Cutoff. The trail begins to get wetter here, and the cutoff is higher and drier. At about 8.1 miles, the cutoff trail deadends into a dirt road. Take the road to the right, about 0.2 mile to the bottom of the hill and onto the resort grounds.

Break out the swim suit and head for the spring-fed hot pool, tubs, and spas. Besides the usual lodge amenities, including rooms, meals and a bar, there is also a three-dimensional relief model of the area in the lodge by the breakfast counter.

Shorter hikes. Besides the hike to Angel Rocks, Chena Hot Springs has an easy trail system for short walks. Stay on the higher trails like the Hillside Cutoff, the Ridge Trail, and the Overlook Trail; the lower trails in the Spring Creek valley are cross-country ski trails and can be quite wet in summer. The resort plans to begin offering guided hikes; if you are interested ask for a schedule.

Trip summary:	A two to four day loop hike on alpine ridges that circle the Angel Creek watershed.
Distance:	A 30-mile loop.
Special features:	Alpine rambling, great views, and wildflowers.
Location:	55 miles east of Fairbanks in the Chena River State Recreation Area.
Difficulty:	Strenuous.
Trail type:	An alpine route with more developed trail approaches.
Total elevation gain:	About 8,500 feet.
Best season:	June through early September; water availability best in June.
Maps:	USGS Circle A-5 and A-6; Big Delta D-5 (route not shown); Alaska State Parks leaflet *Chena Dome Trail*.
Manager:	Alaska State Parks, Northern Area.

Key points:

From Mile 50.5 trailhead

1.0	Overlook of Angel Creek
3.0	Rock outcrop viewpoint, treeline
4.5	Ridgeline, 3,700 feet
10.0	Chena Dome, 4,421 feet
17.0	Trail shelter, 2,750 feet
23.0	Angel Creek route
27.0	Rocky opening; begin final descent
30.0	Mile 49.1 trailhead

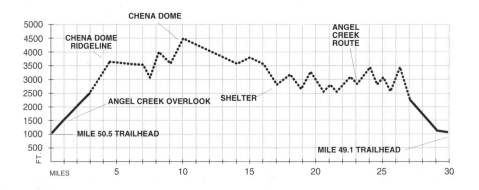

Finding the trailhead: The two trailheads are at Miles 50.5 and 49.1 of Chena Hot Springs Road east of Fairbanks. From Airport Way and the Steese Highway in Fairbanks, drive about 5 miles north on the Steese to Chena Hot Springs Road and turn east. The Chena Dome trailheads are on the left (west) side of the road, just beyond the Angel Rocks Trailhead.

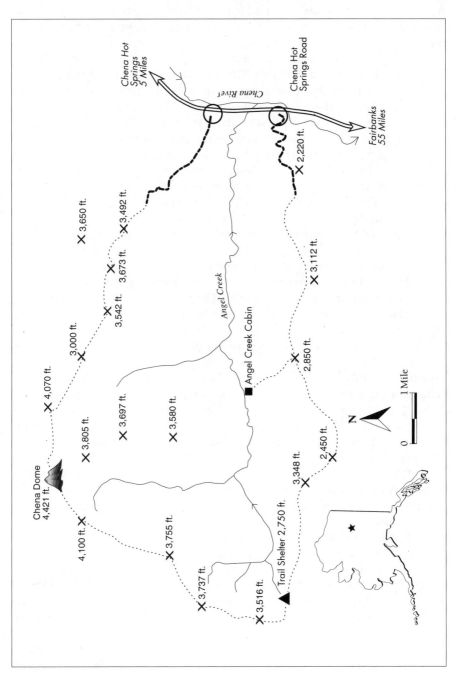

The hike: A hike for true animals, the Chena Dome Trail loops around the Angel Creek watershed on an alpine ridgeline with views that go on forever. About three miles of developed trail lead to the ridgeline from either trailhead, and from there the hike is an alpine route marked with rock cairns and mileage posts.

June and July are the flower months on this hike; August is the berry month. Look for migratory birds like plovers and surfbirds nesting on the tundra, and for resident ptarmigan in the high country too. Stay alert for bears, especially in the wooded saddles where visibility is limited. The trail is open to bicycling and horseback riding, but isn't really suitable for either beyond treeline. Open fires are prohibited; there isn't much wood anyway.

The park recommends starting the hike at the upper (north) trailhead, at Mile 50.5 of Chena Hot Springs Road. Starting from the north side spreads out the total amount of climbing (a whopping 8,500 feet) more evenly over the whole hike. Hiking the south side involves an incredible amount of climbing and dipping between peaks and saddles, and starting there means doing most of the climbing in the first half of the hike, when packs are heaviest.

The route is very steep in places, and especially on the south side, somewhat difficult to follow in spots. A topo map, the State Parks leaflet, and a compass are required gear for the hike. Carry a good tent, decent rain gear, warm clothes, and extra food; if the weather turns, it could be nasty on the exposed ridge.

Water is scarce on the ridgetops, so the best advice is to carry as much as possible and replenish at every opportunity. Many of the low saddles on the hike hold water in small tundra ponds either early in the summer or after rain. The most reliable water appears to be snowbanks and pools about Mile 12, and tundra ponds and a gully that may hold snow just past Mile 20. Taking the hike before the summer solstice is probably the best advice for finding ample water. There is no reliable water near the trail shelter.

A brief trail log follows.

Mile 1. Angel Creek valley viewpoint, from an opening next to the trail.

Mile 3. A rock outcrop with a fine view at treeline.

Mile 4.5. The ridgeline at 3,700 feet; views of the entire route open up, with Chena Dome straight ahead.

Mile 7. A low saddle, possible water in small pools.

Mile 8.5. Wreckage from a military plane crash from the 1950s.

Mile 10. Chena Dome, 4,421 feet, the hike's high point, with a radio relay station on top. Look south to the Alaska Range and northwest to the White Mountains; all around are the Tanana Hills. After the route drops off the peak, ridge rambling heaven begins—for the next six miles, it's a nearly flat ridge run.

Mile 17. Emergency trail shelter (no reservation, no fee), in a wooded, 2,750-foot saddle. The trail finishes curling around the upper end of Angel Creek and heads east. Past the cabin, it's peaks and saddles for the next 8 miles or so to the east, with some major ups and downs.

A tundra camp on the Chena Dome hike.

Mile 21. Change in direction. The trail turns northeast across a low, wooded saddle and regains the high ridge on the other side. This part of the route may be a bit difficult to follow, especially in bad weather.

Mile 23. A marked route off the ridge into the Angel Creek valley, a bad-weather bail-off route, in a 2,850-foot saddle. There is a fee cabin in the valley bottom, and a trail that leads out to the main road, but it's a wet ATV trail.

Mile 27. A rocky opening at 2,250 feet. Rock cairns mark the trail as it drops off the ridge to the northeast, beginning its descent of switchbacks to the trailhead.

Mile 30. The south trailhead, Mile 49.1 of Chena Hot Springs Road.

Other possible hikes from the north trailhead:
Point 3,700. A long, out-and-back day hike to the 3,700-foot ridge with the first panoramic view of the route and the Angel Creek drainage, 4.5 miles one way with 2,700 feet of climbing.

Chena Dome. An out-and-back, overnight hike to Chena Dome, 10 miles one way, with the only possible water on the way at Mile 7. It takes 5,000 feet of climbing to get there, but the ridge walking is superb.

Shorter hikes. From the north trailhead, hike 1 mile one way to the first viewpoint, or 3 miles one way to the rocky viewpoint at treeline.

Trip summary:	A two to four day alpine ridge traverse on a high divide south of the Yukon River.
Distance:	A 27-mile traverse.
Special features:	High tundra hiking, wildflowers, panoramic views, two trail shelters.
Location:	100 miles northeast of Fairbanks in the Steese National Conservation Area.
Difficulty:	Strenuous.
Trail type:	More developed trail lower; a marked route with sections of constructed trail higher.
Total elevation gain:	About 5,500 feet from Eagle Summit Trailhead and 6,000 feet from Twelvemile Summit Trailhead.
Best season:	June to early September; water availability best in June.
Maps:	USGS Circle B-3, B-4, C-3, and C-4; Bureau of Land Management brochure *Pinnell Mountain National Recreation Trail.*
Manager:	Bureau of Land Management, Northern District.

Key points:

From Eagle Summit Trailhead

4.0	Peak 4,351
6.0	Porcupine Dome
9.0	Pinnell Mountain (4,934 feet)
10.0	Ptarmigan Creek Trail Shelter
14.5	Swamp Saddle (3,450 feet)
18.0	North Fork Trail Shelter
22.0	Table Mountain (4,472 feet)
27.0	Twelvemile Summit Trailhead

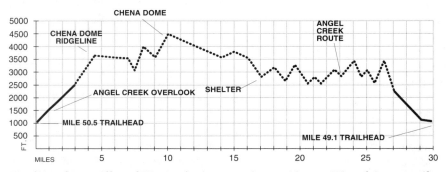

Finding the trailhead: From the intersection at Airport Way, drive 11 miles north of Fairbanks on the Steese Expressway to the intersection of the Steese and Elliot Highways. Turn east onto the Steese (signed as Alaska Route 6). The Twelvemile Summit Trailhead is another 75 miles from the intersection, and the Eagle Summit Trailhead, the recommended starting point, is 96 miles away.

PINNELL MOUNTAIN

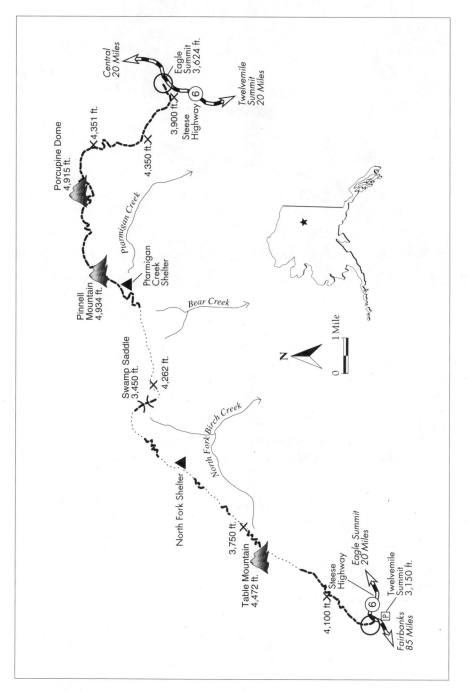

Central
20 Miles

Eagle Summit
3,624 ft.

Twelvemile
Summit
20 Miles

4,351 ft.

3,900 ft.

Steese
Highway 6

Porcupine Dome
4,915 ft.

4,350 ft.

Ptarmigan Creek

Ptarmigan
Creek
Shelter

Pinnell
Mountain
4,934 ft.

Bear Creek

Swamp Saddle
3,450 ft.

4,262 ft.

North Fork Birch Creek

N

0   1 Mile

North Fork Shelter

3,750 ft.

Table Mountain
4,472 ft.

Eagle Summit
20 Miles

Steese
Highway

Twelvemile
Summit
3,150 ft.

4,100 ft.

6   P

Fairbanks
85 Miles

North Fork Trail Shelter, Pinnell Mountain National Recreation Trail.

The Steese is a partially-paved state highway with limited services, so start the trip with a full gas tank and a good spare tire. There are campgrounds along the road, and there is a small emergency shelter at Eagle Summit.

The hike: The premier long hike in the Fairbanks area, the Pinnell Mountain Trail is a National Recreation Trail for good reason. It traverses the highest ridge in the neighborhood, so it offers nearly continuous panoramic views, and fine wildlife and wildflowers. This is the highest of the Fairbanks area's ridge trails, ranging between 3,000 and 5,000 feet in elevation.

Migratory birds like lesser golden-plovers, Lapland longspurs, and surf-birds nest in the high tundra along the trail, and alpine wildflowers put on a show in June and July—look for lousewort, moss campion, mountain avens, alpine azalea, forget-me-not, oxytrope, frigid shooting star, roseroot, Parry's wallflower, and windflower, to name some of the species that carpet the miles of tundra. Plenty of open slopes make it easy to scan for wildlife; hikers sometimes spot wolves, bears, caribou, or wolverines from the trail. Marmots, pikas, and ptarmigan are common.

The trail near Eagle Summit is also a good place to see the midnight sun a few days before and after the summer solstice, which usually falls on June 21. The sun skims but doesn't dip below the horizon from this vantage point.

There are developed trail approaches at each end of the hike, boardwalk across swampy areas, and bench-cut switchbacks in some steep areas, but the Pinnell Trail is mainly a route marked with cairns and mileposts. The trail's first 8 miles or so are in excellent shape, and though it's a bit rougher beyond, it's still adequately marked.

Bring along topo maps, the BLM brochure, a compass, and foul weather gear and clothing. These high ridges catch a lot of weather, and high winds, rain, and snow can hit anytime. Clouds and fog can obscure the trail markers, so be prepared for route-finding with map and compass. In the event of really bad weather, hikers can take any of several ridges back down to the Steese Highway. The quickest route into the trees is from the North Fork Shelter, Mile 18, down to a mining road on the North Fork of Birch Creek and out to the Steese.

Two small, enclosed log shelters at about Miles 10 and 18 are available on a no-fee, first come-first served basis. They have no heat and no established water supply. Several lower saddles on the ridge offer some protection from the weather and make good campsites. There is no firewood here, so don't forget the camp stove, and by all means remember the bug dope.

By mid-summer, water near the trail may be scarce. The best bets for water are low saddles (from seeps, snow-melt pools, and tundra ponds), and north-facing slopes (from snow patches). The section of the trail through a low saddle at about Mile 20, at the bottom of the climb to Table Mountain, passes within 0.25 mile or so of an upper tributary stream of the North Fork of Birch Creek. Following the stream downhill is probably the hike's best bet for running water in the dry part of the year.

In other places, you may have to descend a long way to find water. Carry as much as possible and refill at every opportunity. Boil or filter all surface water, and to protect water quality as much as possible, dispose of wash water and human waste below and well away from any possible water source.

Shorter hikes. Take a short hike to good views from either trailhead, or try a longer day hike. Eagle Summit is the higher trailhead, so the views get better faster from there. Some possible destinations:

- **From Twelvemile Summit**

Point 4,100 feet: a bit over 2 miles one way and a 1,000 feet climb. The summit is a short off-trail climb.

Table Mountain (4,472 feet): 5 miles one way and a 1,700 feet climb.

- **From Eagle Summit**

Point 3,900: The first hill above the trailhead, 0.5 mile one way and a 300-foot climb.

Peak 4,350: 2.5 miles one way and a 700-foot climb. At about Mile 2, where the trail curls around the ridge below the peak, climb away from the trail to the southwest to the summit.

Peak 4,351: 4 miles one way and a 1,000-foot climb.

Gold Fever in the Yukon Hills

The rolling mountain ridges north and east of Fairbanks, a small sliver of Alaska that stretches up the Yukon River into the Yukon Territory, are a complex stew of ancient rocks. They're also a storehouse of the metal that brought European-Americans to the state a century ago: gold! The first gold strikes in the Yukon and Interior Alaska were here, and miners still work the hills for gold.

These high, rounded hills are a "crystalline terrane" to geologists, meaning that they're formed from crystalline, metamorphic rocks like schist and gneiss. These old rocks, in the range of 600 million years old, are cut with much younger intrusions of magma that cooled into granite. Recent research has shown that the gold in the rocks is hydrothermal, that is, left in the rock by blazing hot water that welled up from deeper in the earth roughly 90 million years ago.

In the Fairbanks and Circle areas, the gold washed out over millions of years from the rock grouping called the Birch Creek schist, and prospectors discovered it in flakes and nuggets in the streambeds that run through the hills. Birch Creek was the site of the 1890s gold stampede that made Circle, the tiny town at the end of the Steese Highway, into the "Paris of the North" for a few brief years. Birch Creek runs through the valley south and east of the Pinnell Mountain ridgeline.

Trip summary:	A half-day hike on the Summit Trail to a viewpoint on Wickersham Dome, or a two to four day trip to Beaver Creek.
Distance:	Wickersham Dome: 3.5 miles one way. Birch Creek: 20 miles one way.
Special features:	Alpine tundra and views; Beaver Creek, a national wild river; fee cabins.
Location:	40 miles northwest of Fairbanks in the White Mountains National Recreation Area.
Difficulty:	Wickersham Dome: moderate. Beaver Creek: strenuous.
Trail type:	More developed.
Total elevation gain:	Wickersham Dome: about 900 feet in and 100 feet out. Beaver Creek: about 1,800 feet in and 2,700 feet out.
Best season:	June through September.
Maps:	USGS Livengood A-3, B-2, B-3; Bureau of Land Management leaflet *Summit Trail*; BLM *White Mountains National Recreation Area Winter Trails Map*.
Manager:	Bureau of Land Management, Northern District Office.

Key points:

1.0   Point 2,660
2.0   Ski Trail junction
3.5   North side of Wickersham Dome
10.0   Trail high point, 3,100 feet
18.0   Wickersham Creek Trail
20.0   Beaver Creek

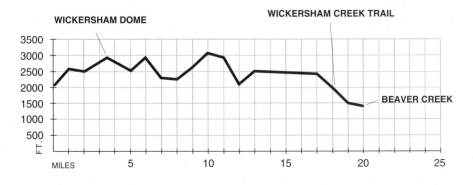

Finding the trailhead: From the intersection at Airport Way, drive 11 miles north of Fairbanks on the Steese Expressway to the intersection of the Steese and Elliott Highways. Continue north, straight ahead, on the Elliott Highway

SUMMIT TRAIL

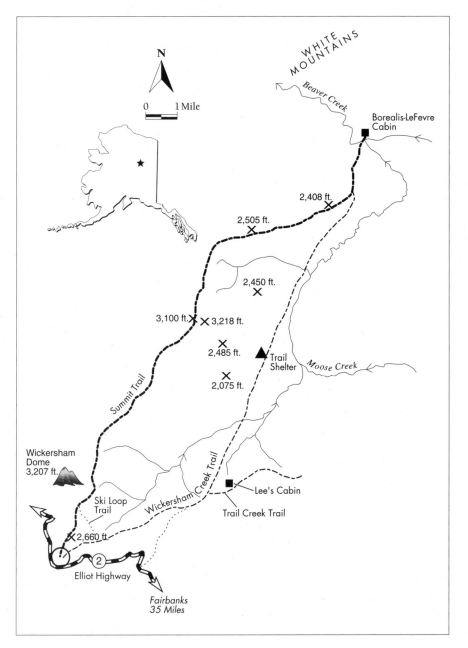

A Knob with a view, near Wickersham Dome on the Summit Trail.

(signed as Alaska Route 2) another 28 miles to the Wickersham Dome Trailhead on the right.

The hike: The White Mountains National Recreation Area is well known for its winter trails and cabins, but most of the NRA's trails are too wet for summer use. The Summit Trail is one of the few trails dry enough for summer hiking. The path follows a fairly dry ridgeline to Wickersham Dome and beyond, and eventually drops to Beaver Creek, a hike of 20 miles one way. The shorter trip to the north side of Wickersham Dome leads to distant views of the White Mountains, the rugged peaks in the heart of the recreation area. In season, there is good berry picking along the trail.

Wickersham Dome. From the parking area, take the trail out of the north end of the parking area (the left side as you face away from the highway; a second trail, the Wickersham Creek Trail, is straight ahead, bearing east). It climbs gradually through sparse spruce and brushy dwarf birch, reaching a 2,660-foot alpine knob in about a mile. After crossing a wet, forested saddle on boardwalk, pass by the Ski Loop Trail junction at about 2 miles. The ski trail leads back to the Wickersham Creek Trail, but it's deep in water and muck in the summer.

Above treeline again on the slope of Wickersham Dome, find a summer blueberry and wildflower bonanza, with tiny gardens of alpine azalea and other flowers. There is a communication tower on the top of the dome, but the high points on the north side afford good views as well. At the high point on the trail, roughly 2,900 feet elevation, head off-trail to the west for the best views, to one of the small knobs that rise 200 feet or so above the elevation of the trail.

Beaver Creek. A strenuous trip of 20 miles one way, the hike to Beaver Creek climbs and descends along the ridge beyond Wickersham Dome. Most of the wet areas on the hike are boardwalked. The trail reaches its high point, 3,100 feet, at Mile 10, and at Mile 13 begins the long descent to the creek. The last two miles of the hike are on the Wickersham Creek Trail. The hike ends at Beaver Creek, a national wild river, about 3 miles above the "Big Bend". At the bend, the creek turns sharply northeast around the White Mountains.

The Borealis-LeFevre Cabin is across Beaver Creek from the end of the trail. The creek, though, may be uncrossable at higher water levels. Early summer high water usually subsides by mid-June. Look up or down the creek for the best crossing spot for the water level. It's possible to make a loop by returning on the Wickersham Creek Trail, but it may be too wet for some hikers' tastes.

Lee's Cabin. An easy/moderate hike of 7 miles one way on the Wickersham Creek and Trail Creek Trails leads to Lee's Cabin, another BLM fee cabin. The Wickersham Creek Trail leaves the east end of the Wickersham Dome parking area. Follow it 6 miles to the intersection with the Trail Creek Trail, and take the latter trail another mile to the cabin. These trails are open to all-terrain vehicles, but are hikeable to Lee's Cabin. Though this hike isn't particularly scenic, the cabin and its view make a decent overnight trip. There is no surface water at the cabin, but there is a rain catchment supply that should be boiled or filtered before using.

For reservations for the Borealis-LeFevre Cabin and Lee's Cabin, contact BLM in Fairbanks (see Appendix 2).

DENALI HIGHWAY

The Denali Highway is an all-weather gravel road that connects the Parks Highway at Cantwell, south of Denali National Park, with the Richardson Highway at Paxson, north of Glennallen. It was the access road to Denali National Park before the Parks Highway was built.

The highway, which crosses many miles of alpine tundra, is open only in summer. With views, great examples of glacial geology, fishable lakes and streams, and several campgrounds, the Denali is a good remote road to explore. Pick up the BLM brochure *Denali Highway* before your trip. Few services are offered, so fill up the gas tank and make sure the spare tire is in good shape before starting out.

The eastern end of the highway cuts through the Tangle Lakes Archeological District, which features one of the densest concentrations of prehistoric artifacts in the North American subarctic. Ancient hunters left behind over four hundred sites where stone chips and ancient campfires tell of caribou hunts going back ten thousand years.

Several trails off the highway east of Paxson, many of them wide, muddy and rutted from off-road vehicles, are less than attractive as hiking trails. However, the mountains and tundra away from the ORVs make great hiking.

70 LANDMARK GAP LAKE

Trip summary:	A half-day or overnight hike on an off-road vehicle trail to a scenic lake in the Amphitheater Mountains, with off-trail hiking from the end of the vehicle trail.
Distance:	2.5 miles one way to the south shore of the lake, with several side trips possible from the lake.
Special features:	A beautiful glacial lake, alpine country, fishing. The trail to the lake is a wide, sometimes muddy multiple-use trail for off-road vehicles, mountain bikes, and hikers.
Location:	On the Denali Highway 25 miles west of Paxson.
Difficulty:	Easy.
Trail type:	More developed to the lake; routes and cross-country beyond.
Total elevation gain:	About 100 feet.
Best season:	Late June through early September.
Maps:	USGS Mount Hayes A-5, BLM *Trail Map and Guide to the Tangle Lakes National Register District.*
Manager:	Bureau of Land Management, Glennallen District.

Finding the trailhead: The trailhead is on the north side of the Denali Highway, about 25 miles west of Paxson and 12 miles east of Maclaren Summit. See the introduction to this section for information on the Denali Highway.

LANDMARK GAP LAKE

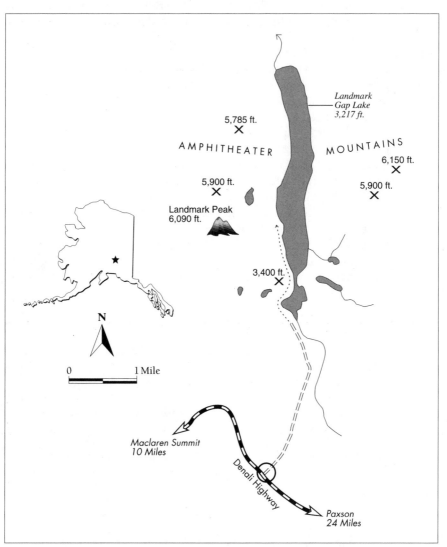

The hike: The Amphitheater Mountains, a group of outlier peaks of the Alaska Range north of the Denali Highway, are just too tempting for a hiker to pass by. One of the finest spots in the Amphitheater range is Landmark Gap Lake, 2.5 miles from the highway on the Landmark Gap Trail North.

The trail is a bad dirt road with a rock base and several mudholes. It isn't a pretty sight, but the destination certainly is. Landmark Gap Lake is nearly 4 miles long, a narrow finger of water filling a glacially-carved gap in the Amphitheater Mountains. Visible through the gap are glaciated Alaska Range peaks, including Mount Moffit (13,020 feet) and McGinnis Peak (11,400 feet).

From the end of the road/trail on the south shore of the lake, a foot path continues around to the west shore and wanders a couple of miles up the lake, fading eventually to a game trail. Good campsites mark the first mile of the lake and the knobs above it. The 3,400-foot knob on the southwest edge of the lake makes a great viewpoint. Those with a lot of energy can hike up to Landmark Peak (6,090 feet) on the mountain ridge west of the lake, or hike through the gap to the north side of the Amphitheaters.
Fishing. Anglers can fish for grayling and lake trout in the lake.

71 MACLAREN SUMMIT

Trip summary:	A variety of day or overnight hikes on the rolling divide east of the Maclaren River.
Distance:	Up to 5 miles one way.
Special features:	Panoramic views, glacial features, small lakes and ponds.
Location:	On the Denali Highway 37 miles west of Paxson.
Difficulty:	Easy.
Trail type:	Less developed trail and cross-country.
Total elevation gain:	About 200-300 feet, depending on destination.
Best season:	Late June through early September.
Maps:	USGS Mount Hayes A-5, BLM *Trail Map and Guide to the Tangle Lakes National Register District*.
Manager:	Bureau of Land Management, Glennallen District.

Finding the trailhead: The trailhead is on the north side of the Denali Highway at Maclaren Summit, 37 miles west of Paxson and 98 miles east of Cantwell. See the introduction to this section for information on the Denali Highway.

The hike: A wide-open tundra ramble with exhilarating views, the Maclaren Summit hike begins at the second-highest highway summit in Alaska. A little-used two-track vehicle trail leads north across a tundra plateau. The track, and the hike, follows an esker, a winding, stony ridge left on the landscape by a stream flowing inside a glacier that once covered the area. The stream, confined by ice walls, left glacial debris in a long mound that now stands out above the surrounding land.

Stay on the vehicle track until it veers away and down to the right. Leave the track and keep following the ridge cross country, bearing a bit left, or west, from the track, staying between the lake-dotted High Valley to the

MACLAREN SUMMIT

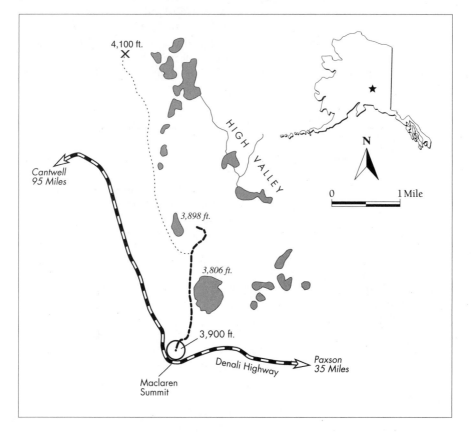

4,100 ft.
X

Cantwell
95 Miles

HIGH VALLEY

N

0   1 Mile

3,898 ft.

3,806 ft.

3,900 ft.

Denali Highway

Paxson
35 Miles

Maclaren
Summit

east and the slope break down to the Maclaren River to the west. The lakes, the Amphitheater Mountains, the Maclaren River, and the Alaska Range's peaks and glaciers make a fine panorama.

The easy walking continues to good lunch or camp spots near a number of lakes and ponds. Almost anywhere on the ridge makes a good destination. For a longer hike, continue out to the 4,100-foot high point about 5 miles out the ridge.

This ridge is a major geographic feature, dividing the Southcentral coast drainage of the Susitna River from the Interior drainage of the Delta, Tanana and Yukon Rivers. If you think it's odd that a piece of country south of the Alaska Range drains into the Interior, you're right. The Delta's cutting power is the culprit—the river slices all the way through the range from south to north.

The trail, open to mountain bikes and motorized vehicles, is rarely used by either.

SOUTHEAST ALASKA

TRIPS IN SOUTHEAST

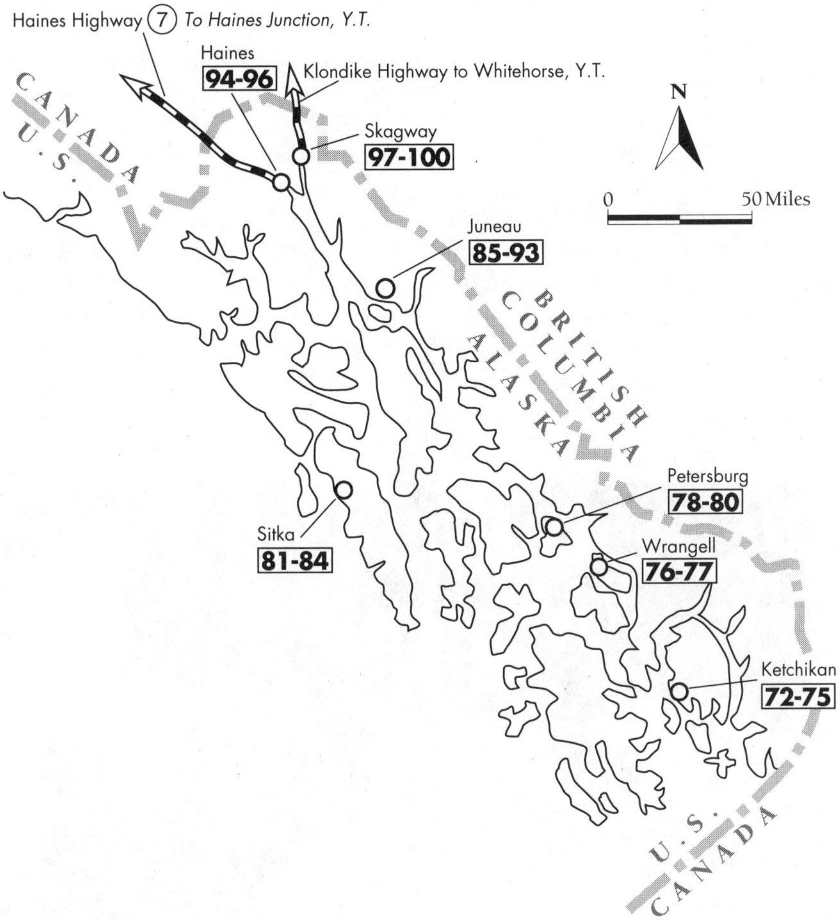

Haines Highway (7) *To Haines Junction, Y.T.*

Haines
94-96 Klondike Highway to Whitehorse, Y.T.

Skagway
97-100

N

0   50 Miles

Juneau
85-93

CANADA
U. S.

BRITISH COLUMBIA
ALASKA

Petersburg
78-80

Sitka
81-84

Wrangell
76-77

Ketchikan
72-75

U. S.
CANADA

KETCHIKAN

Ketchikan, Alaska's fourth largest city, lies on the southwest corner of Revillagigedo ("Revilla") Island, where it basks in over 13 feet of rain a year. Ketchikan is so far south, it's nearer to Seattle than Anchorage. Accessible only by air or sea, the city is the first Alaska state ferry stop on the trip up from the south.

Ketchikan locals have a plan to build new trails and upgrade some of the local hiking routes over the next few years as money becomes available, but for now the city has fewer nearby hiking trails than the other larger Alaska cities.

Besides the trails described here, try the **Connell Lake Trail** on Ward Lake Road (2 miles one way when rebuilt as the Forest Service plans) and for a short, easy walk, the trail at **Totem Bight State Historical Park** 10 miles north of town on the North Tongass Highway (0.3 mile, an interpretive trail with Tlingit and Haida totem poles).

The Forest Service's **Misty Fjords National Monument**, 50 miles east of Ketchikan and accessible by tour boat or floatplane, is a beautiful, wild area that's well-known for sea kayaking, but it also features some fine trails to mountain lakes, including Punchbowl Lake (Rudyerd Bay Trailhead, 0.9 mile, trail shelter), Nooya Lake (Rudyerd Bay Trailhead, 0.8 mile, trail shelter) Winstanley Lake (Behm Canal Trailhead, 2.5 miles, trail shelter), and Humpback Lake (Mink Bay/ Boca de Quadra Trailhead, 3 miles).

The boardwalk trails in Southeast can be as slick as slug slime when wet.

Trip summary:	A half-day hike to Deer Mountain, a longer day hike to Blue Lake, or a two to three day traverse on alpine ridges across Revilla Island to Silvis Lakes.
Distance:	Deer Mountain: 2.5 miles one way. Blue Lake: 4.5 miles one way. Traverse: 14 miles.
Special features:	Mountain scenery and an alpine traverse; a trail shelter below Deer Mountain. Travelers without cars can walk to the trailhead from downtown Ketchikan.
Location:	A mile southeast of downtown Ketchikan.
Difficulty:	Deer Mountain: moderately strenuous. Traverse: strenuous.
Trail type:	Deer Mountain: more developed trail. Traverse: more developed trail lower; a less developed trail/route on the alpine ridges.
Total elevation gain:	Deer Mountain: 2,600 feet. Traverse: 4,700 feet.
Best season:	Deer Mountain: June through September. Traverse: Mid-June through mid-September.
Maps:	USGS Ketchikan B-5; USFS leaflet *Deer Mountain Trail.*
Manager:	Tongass National Forest, Ketchikan Ranger District.

Key points:

Deer Mountain Day Hike		**Deer Mountain-Silvis Lakes Traverse**	
1.0	Viewpoint	2.2	Deer Mountain spur trail
2.0	Viewpoint	2.4	Deer Mountain Shelter
2.2	Deer Mountain spur trail	4.5	Blue Lake
2.5	Deer Mountain summit	5.5	Northbird Peak
		7.5	John Mountain spur trail
		9.0	Mahoney Mountain spur trail
		11.0	Upper Silvis Lake outlet stream
		13.0	Lower Silvis Lake outlet stream
		14.0	South Tongass Highway

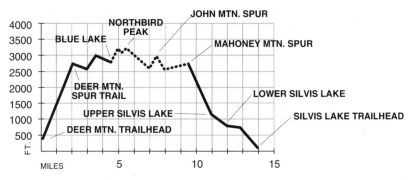

DEER MOUNTAIN

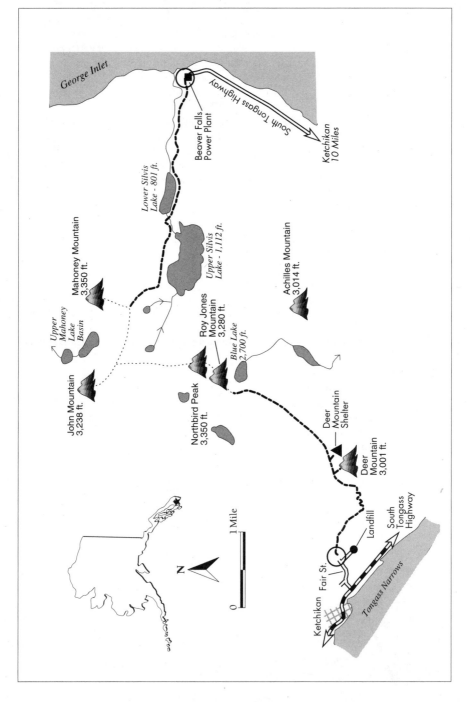

George Inlet

South Tongass Highway

Ketchikan
10 Miles

Beaver Falls
Power Plant

Lower Silvis
Lake - 801 ft.

Upper Silvis
Lake - 1,112 ft.

Mahoney Mountain
3,350 ft.

Achilles Mountain
3,014 ft.

Upper
Mahoney
Lake
Basin

Roy Jones
Mountain
3,280 ft.

Blue Lake
2,700 ft.

John Mountain
3,238 ft.

Northbird Peak
3,350 ft.

Deer
Mountain
Shelter

Deer
Mountain
3,001 ft.

Landfill

South
Tongass
Highway

1 Mile

N

Ketchikan   Fair St.

Tongass Narrows

0

Finding the trailheads: Deer Mountain. From the Southeast Alaska Visitor Center (SEAVC, at the corner of Main and Mill by the city dock), travel east and south on Mill and Stedman streets, the main route through town, 0.4 mile to Deermount Street. Turn left (east) and continue 0.3 mile to Fair Street; turn right and follow Fair 0.4 mile to the top of the hill. Cross Nordstrom Drive, which leads to the right to the landfill, and turn right into the trailhead parking area about 100 feet beyond the intersection. "Hiker" signs lead to the trailhead.

Silvis Lakes. From SEAVC, follow Mill and Stedman streets east and south through Ketchikan. The route becomes the South Tongass Highway; follow it 13 miles to the end of the road at the Beaver Falls Power Plant. Park down the hill by the first buildings and walk up the gated, graveled road 50 feet away.

The hike: Popular with both locals and visitors, the Deer Mountain Trail climbs a 3,001-foot peak above Ketchikan with a panoramic view of mountain peaks, forests, islands, and ocean. It's a good hike for travelers, as the trailhead is a walk of only a mile from downtown Ketchikan. Take your rain gear even if it's sunny; Ketchikan is one of the wettest places in Southeast, and the weather changes quickly.

The traverse across the island on the Deer Mountain-John Mountain alpine ridgeline is a fine high-country ramble. The ridge is so close to the ocean that it's possible to smell the salt air while hiking through alpine heather on the mountain tops. True animal hikers can make it in one extremely long day, but mere mortals should plan on two days, and if the weather is fine, you might even want to spend a third day in the high country.

Early summer snow is a safety concern on both the day hike and the traverse. Deep snow lingers until mid-June, and some snow stays on the ground most of the summer. The steep sidehill trail below Deer Mountain is prone to snowslides early in the season, and hikers need to exercise caution to avoid slipping and sliding off the trail or falling through a wind-formed cornice. Be prepared to turn back if you encounter dangerous snow conditions. On the traverse, it's possible to lose the trail markers in deep snow, and some steep, narrow spots on the ridge may be tricky or dangerous in snow. Consider carrying an ice ax if doing the trip early in the summer.

Deer Mountain summit. The trail to the summit climbs steadily up a moderate grade through hemlock and cedar forest. There are some fine rock and log steps on the lower trail, and many switchbacks on the way. There are viewpoints at about one and two miles, but by far the best is from the peak. Above the second viewpoint, the trail traverses an open subalpine slope with good views north, across Ketchikan Lake. Take the spur trail to the summit at 2.2 miles; 0.2 mile farther on the main trail is the spur to the shelter, which sits in the saddle northwest of and below the summit. Continue to Blue Lake, 4.5 miles from the trailhead, for a longer hike and a taste of the alpine country.

High above Ketchikan on the Deer Mountain Trail, June.

Deer Mountain-Silvis Lakes Traverse. The traverse stays high in alpine country for eight miles, from Deer Mountain to below Mahoney Mountain. Be prepared for bad weather and poor visibility; take along a topo map and compass, warm and waterproof clothing, and a good tent if tackling the hike. Beyond Blue Lake, the trail is less defined, a marked route with some sections of tread.

The best overnight spots are the Deer Mountain shelter, Blue Lake, the upper part of the Upper Mahoney Lake basin between John and Mahoney mountains, and a number of partially protected spots along the ridge. The spur trails to John and Mahoney mountains make great side trips.

Silvis Lakes Trail. The hike to the Silvis Lakes and on to Mahoney Mountain follows the Beaver Falls power project road for about 2.5 miles to the powerhouse on Lower Silvis Lake, where it becomes a foot trail. The top of Mahoney Mountain is 6 miles one way and about 3,300 feet elevation gain from the Silvis Lakes trailhead.

With the road, dams, powerhouse, pipeline, and fluctuating lake levels, the Silvis Lakes Trail doesn't have a great natural destination, but the hike is pleasant enough, with the smell of cedar in the air and red-rocky Mahoney Mountain looking impressive above the lower lake.

Shorter hikes. The two-mile viewpoint on the Deer Mountain Trail and the two-mile hike to Lower Silvis Lake are the best shorter hikes.

Fishing. There are a few rainbow trout in the Silvis Lakes.

The Southeast Alaska Forests

Southeast Alaska's Tongass National Forest is the biggest national forest in the country, and Southeast's forests, together with the forests of coastal British Columbia and the U.S. Pacific Northwest, make up the largest area of temperate rain forest on earth. Western hemlock is the most common tree in Southeast, making up about 70 percent of the forest, but the less common Sitka spruce, which can grow to 8 feet in diameter and live 700 years, is more famous as the Alaska state tree. That's a pretty big honor for a tree that grows in less than a quarter of the area of the state.

The high-volume, old-growth stands of forest dominated by Sitka spruce get most of the attention from conservationists and loggers, though they make up only about 500,000 acres of the 5.4 million acres of forest on the Tongass considered "commercial." About half these stands are now off-limits to loggers in wilderness or wildlife habitat conservation areas.

Less common in the rain forest are the cedars: western redcedar, which grows only about as far north as Petersburg, and yellow-cedar, which is more common in northern Southeast. Feathery mountain hemlock replaces western hemlock in the "montane" forests near treeline, and lodgepole pine, locally called shore pine, grows on the edges of wet meadows and muskegs in acid soils.

In northern Southeast, near Haines and Skagway, the climate is much drier. Subalpine fir, paper birch and granite mountains give the area a completely different look from the rest of Southeast.

Trip summary:	A shorter day hike around Ward Lake.
Distance:	A 1.3-mile loop.
Special features:	Interpretive signs, wildlife, fishing, old-growth forest, campgrounds, and picnic areas; a very popular local trail.
Location:	8 miles north of Ketchikan on Ward Lake Road.
Difficulty:	Easy.
Trail type:	More developed.
Total elevation gain:	About 50 feet.
Best season:	March through November.
Maps:	USGS Ketchikan B-6 (NE); USFS leaflet *Ward Lake Nature Trail.*
Manager:	Tongass National Forest, Ketchikan Ranger District.

Finding the trailhead: Drive (or bicycle) 7 miles north of the center of Ketchikan on the North Tongass Highway and turn right on Ward Lake Road. Join the trail at the far end of the Signal Creek Campground (0.7 mile from the highway), at the Grassy Point Picnic Area (1.1 miles), or at the Ward Lake Picnic Area (1.3 miles).

WARD LAKE NATURE TRAIL

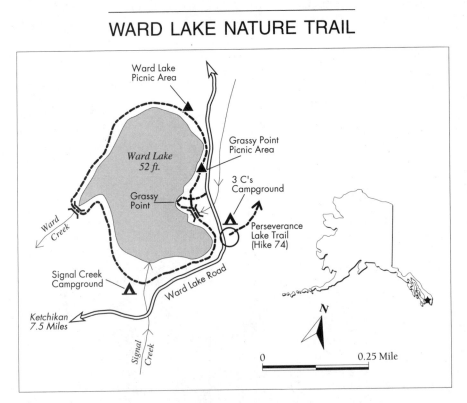

When the new Ward Lake Bypass Road is complete, access to the campground, picnic areas, and trail will change—watch for signs.

The hike: Although this is Ketchikan's most popular trail, it's still possible to enjoy the quiet of an old-growth forest and hear and glimpse wildlife on this short walk. The trail skirts the shoreline around Ward Lake, elevation 52 feet. On the east side of the lake, the trail connects picnic areas and campgrounds near the road; the west side is away from the road, and quieter. The bridge over the lake's outlet stream, a short walk from the west side of the Signal Creek Campground, offers a good view of the lake and the rocky stream.

Giant spruces and hemlocks line the trail, many with huge root buttresses. Salmonberry, wood violets, dogwood, huckleberry, mosses, ferns, and other plants thrive in the understory, and forest birds like thrushes, winter wrens, and Steller's jays are common. Salmon spawn in Ward Creek in late summer and fall. Hikers commonly see deer, beaver, and red squirrels. Swans, geese, ducks, and loons all use the lake in spring and early summer.

Interpretive signs along the trail describe the ancient forest. If it's raining, stay dry under one of the covered picnic shelters on the east side of the lake, at Ward Lake and Grassy Point picnic areas.

Fishing. Pink, red, and silver salmon, steelhead, Dolly Varden, and cutthroat trout use Ward Creek and Ward Lake at different times of the spring, summer, and fall. Check current regulations before wetting a line.

74 *PERSEVERANCE LAKE*

Trip summary:	A shorter day or overnight trip to mile-long Perseverance Lake.
Distance:	2.3 miles one way.
Special features:	Forest and lake scenery, fishing.
Location:	8 miles north of Ketchikan.
Difficulty:	Moderate.
Trail type:	More developed.
Total elevation gain:	500 feet in, 100 feet out.
Best season:	March through November.
Maps:	USGS Ketchikan B-6 (NE) and B-5 (NW); USFS leaflet *Perseverance Lake*.
Manager:	Tongass National Forest, Ketchikan Ranger District.

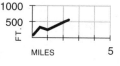

PERSEVERANCE LAKE

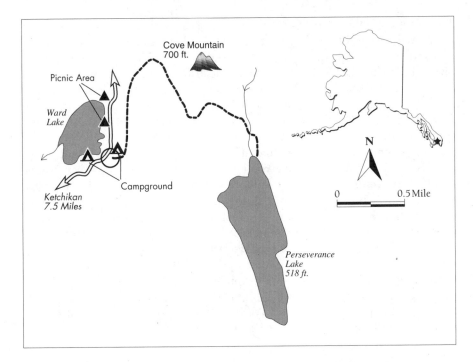

Finding the trailhead: Drive (or bicycle) 7 miles north of the center of Ketchikan on the North Tongass Highway and turn right on Ward Lake Road. The trail begins a mile from the highway, on the right. The current parking area is on the left, about 200 feet beyond the trailhead and across from the entrance to the Three C's Campground.

When the new Ward Lake Bypass Road is complete, access to the campground and trail will change—watch for signs.

The hike: It doesn't take too much perseverance to reach Perseverance Lake these days, what with 0.5 mile of wide, gravel tread and almost 2 miles of "step and run" boardwalk making up the trail. The boardwalk is covered with roofing material for better traction, but keep in mind that the boards can be slick if it's wet or icy.

The hike meanders across a landscape of ancient forest, small streams, wet meadows, and muskeg. About 0.2 mile from the lake, a bridge crosses Ward Creek, the lake's outlet stream. A big log jam by the outlet and several rocks, meadows, and points on the edge of the lake make good casting spots for anglers; otherwise the lakeshore is fairly thick with vegetation. It's tough

The log-strewn outlet stream of Perseverance Lake.

to get very far around the lake without serious brush-bashing, so most hikers stay close to the end of the trail at the north end of the lake. The Forest Service plans to build a trail around the lake when time and money allow. **Fishing.** Fishing for brook and rainbow trout is decent most of the spring, summer, and fall.

Trip summary:	A tidewater, river, and lake trail that can be done as a longer day or overnight hike, or be turned into a trip of several days of fishing and wildlife watching.
Distance:	6 miles one way from the Naha Bay dock to Heckman Lake.
Special features:	A saltwater lagoon, a beautiful Southeast river, two lakes, two fee cabins, wildlife, and fishing. Access is by boat or floatplane.
Location:	25 miles north of Ketchikan; 10 miles north of the end of the Ketchikan road system.
Difficulty:	Easy/moderate.
Trail type:	More developed.
Total elevation gain:	About 400 feet.
Best season:	April through October.
Maps:	USGS Ketchikan C-5; USFS leaflet *Naha River Trail*.
Manager:	Tongass National Forest, Ketchikan Ranger District.

Key points:

2.0   East end of Roosevelt Lagoon
2.5   Naha River picnic shelter
4.0   Jordan Lake cabin
6.0   Heckman Lake cabin

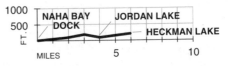

Finding the trailhead: The trail runs between tidewater in Naha Bay and the northwest end of Heckman Lake. Hikers can be dropped off or picked up via floatplane at either the Naha Bay saltwater dock or Heckman Lake (see Appendix 3 for air taxi information). Access by boat is to the saltwater dock.

At this writing it's difficult to find a water taxi that will take hikers to the Naha; other boat alternatives are renting a skiff at Knudson Cove, 15 miles north of town on the North Tongass Highway, or renting a kayak in Ketchikan. It's possible for experienced kayakers to paddle at high slack tide through the tide race at the mouth of Roosevelt Lagoon and on through the lagoon to the lower Naha River, but remember that the narrow slot at the west end of the lagoon becomes a dangerous chute of roaring whitewater when the tide is changing.

The hike: The Naha River Trail features a saltwater lagoon, a fine river with waterfalls and cascades, good fishing, two lakes, and a Forest Service fee cabin with a skiff and oars at each of the lakes. The trail stays near water for most of its length.

The river's lake-dominated watershed is one of the richest aquatic environments anywhere, providing homes for a terrific variety of fish. Besides

NAHA RIVER

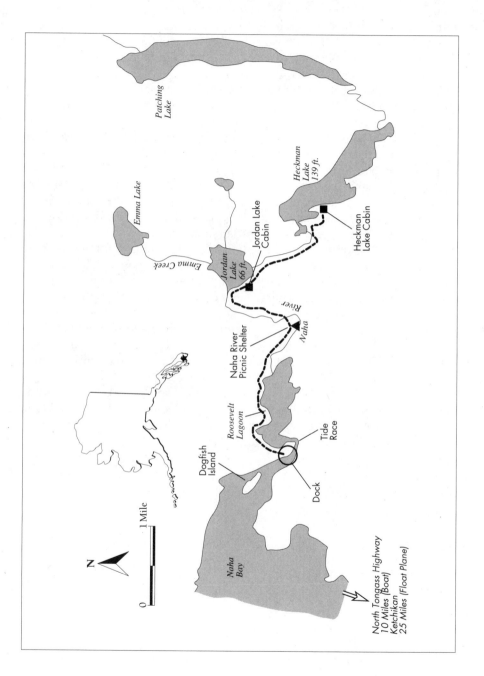

the two lakes on the trail, there are five other significant lakes in the watershed. Grayling and trophy-sized cutthroat trout inhabit the high mountain lakes. The lower river and the lakes on the trail support Dolly Varden and cutthroat trout, mid-summer to fall runs of four species of salmon, and abundant spring and fall steelhead runs. Two areas of falls/cascades, at about Miles 2.5 and 5.5 of the trail, offer good fishing (for both people and black bears, so be on your best bear country behavior).

The lower part of the trail features Roosevelt Lagoon, a tidal lagoon frequented by waterfowl and shorebirds. Lots of local anglers use the lower river, especially on weekends, so hikers who want maximum solitude should plan to spend most of their time on the upper part of the trail. Just below the Forest Service picnic shelter at Mile 2.5 is a private camp, labeled Orton Ranch on the USGS map.

The trail is planked across wetter areas. The first 2.5 miles are essentially flat, with a bit more climbing on the upper trail near the lakes. Jordan Lake is only 66 feet above sea level, and Heckman Lake is 139 feet elevation.

The Forest Service fee cabins at Jordan Lake (Mile 4) and Heckman Lake (Mile 6) offer the best overnight options. See Appendix 2 for reservation information. Tent camping is possible, but there are no established sites. Hikers frequently see deer, black bear, and waterfowl, including trumpeter swans, and the old-growth spruce/hemlock/cedar forest along the river is impressive.

Shorter hikes. Hikers wanting maximum solitude could plan a floatplane dropoff and pickup at Heckman Lake, and spend their time on the Naha between Heckman and Jordan Lakes. It's 2 miles one way between the lakes.

Fishing. The premier fishing on the Naha is for spring and fall steelhead, but anglers can fish for Dollies and cutthroat all spring, summer, and fall. From July through September, the river hosts runs of silver, pink, red, and chum salmon.

WRANGELL

Wrangell is a small, friendly town that at least for now is a bit off the beaten path of industrial, cruise ship tourism. It's another Southeast town that's accessible only by air or water. The portion of the Tongass National Forest south of town has a forest management road system like the Pacific slope forests of Oregon and Washington, and makes a good area for a vacation of car camping, fishing, and short hikes. Most trails here have to be surfaced because of the wet ground.

Besides the two trails described below, also try the 0.4-mile trail to **Mount Dewey**, the northernmost green bump above town, accessible from downtown by car (Front Street to St. Michael, left on Reid, right on Mission, and left on Third) or foot (Front Street to McKinnon, up the McKinnon staircase, left on Third and around a right curve to the trailhead). For a short walk to another small lake, try the 0.1-mile of partially-planked trail to **Highbush Lake** (it has a rowboat), 28 miles south of Wrangell on the Zimovia Highway and Forest Roads 6265 and 50040. Purchase the Forest Service's *Wrangell Island Road Guide* for exploring the National Forest roads, trails and lakes south of town.

Wrangell also has several remote Forest Service trails accessible only by boat or floatplane.

The Wrangell waterfront and Zimovia Strait from Mount Dewey.

Trip summary:	A shorter day trip to a waterfall on Rainbow Creek, or a longer day or overnight hike to Shoemaker Bay Overlook on the ridge south of Institute Creek.
Distance:	0.5 mile one way to Rainbow Falls; 3.4 miles one way to Shoemaker Bay Overlook.
Special features:	Waterfalls, a ridgetop view of the Wrangell area, a trail shelter. The trail is almost entirely surfaced with logs and planks. The Forest Service is also planning a new trail to Institute Creek from the north end of Wrangell.
Location:	5 miles south of Wrangell.
Difficulty:	Moderate to Rainbow Falls; moderately strenuous to the overlook.
Trail type:	More developed.
Total elevation gain:	Rainbow Falls: 500 feet. Overlook: 1,600 feet in, 100 feet out.
Best season:	Falls: March through October. Overlook: Mid-May through September.
Maps:	USGS Petersburg B-2 (NE), B-1 (NW).
Manager:	Tongass National Forest, Wrangell Ranger District.

Key points:
0.5   Rainbow Falls, lower viewing deck
0.7   Rainbow Falls, upper viewing deck
2.5   Institute Creek bridge
3.4   Shoemaker Bay Overlook

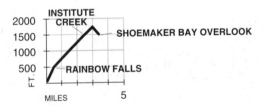

Finding the trailhead: The trailhead is on the Zimovia Highway south of Wrangell, 5 miles south of the state ferry dock. Look for the trail on the east (left) side of the highway, across from the Shoemaker Bay Recreation Area (small boat harbor, camp/picnic/parking area). There is a trailhead parking area on the west side of the highway. For travelers without cars, taking a taxi or rental bike to the trailhead are viable options.

The hike: The Rainbow Falls Trail is a short, steep hike to see Rainbow Creek in freefall in a lush hemlock forest. A longer hike continues up Institute Creek beyond the falls to a trail shelter and camp/picnic area on the ridgetop overlooking Shoemaker Bay and Zimovia Strait.

RAINBOW FALLS AND INSTITUTE CREEK

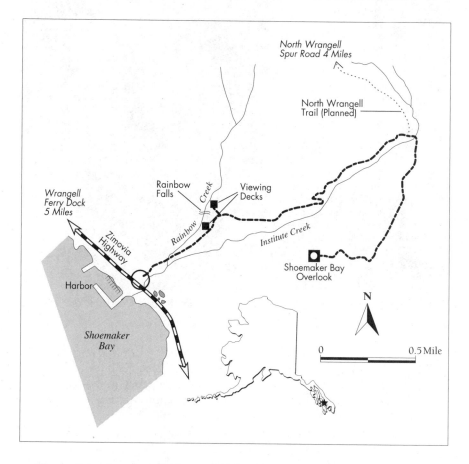

The trail is almost entirely surfaced with stairs, log steps, and "step and run" boardwalk. A masochistic Forest Service employee has even counted the steps, calculating 1,849 stairsteps, mostly on treated lumber, to the Shoemaker Bay Overlook. If this is your first boardwalk hike, keep in mind that all the stairstepping can be tough on hikers with knee or hip injuries.

Rainbow Falls. Staircases, log steps, and boardwalk steps make up the 500-foot climb to Rainbow Falls. Bring a lunch to eat on one of the two viewing decks, one below the falls at 0.5 mile and one above at 0.7 mile. The better view of the falls is from the lower deck.

Shoemaker Bay Overlook. The trail beyond Rainbow Falls follows Institute Creek (named for the defunct Wrangell Institute, a former Bureau of Indian Affairs school on the Zimovia Highway), passing a falls-and-cascades section on a set of switchbacks. Above the switchbacks, the trail emerges from hemlock/cedar forest into a series of wet meadows fringed with yellow-cedar, spruce, and shore pine. The trail crosses Institute Creek and curls around to the west, traversing more meadows on the way to the overlook.

Shoemaker Bay Overlook at the end of the Rainbow Falls/Institute Creek Trail.

The trail shelter, an open, three-sided shelter, sleeps about four. These are high, wet meadows, so there are few if any decent tent sites nearby. Plenty of insects are possible, so bring some mosquito netting if you plan to sleep in the shelter. A picnic table, outhouse, and fire pit round out the amenities. Be careful with kids; there is a cliff beyond the picnic table and a pole fence.

This small recreation area offers a scenic spot for a long lunch or overnight. There is no water at the overlook; besides small trickles and ponds between Institute Creek and the shelter, the best water source is Institute Creek at the trail bridge. If you'll need water at the shelter, bring a container for collecting some, and boil or filter it.

North Wrangell Trail. The Forest Service is planning a new trail to connect north Wrangell with the Institute Creek Trail. The North Wrangell Trail will be about 4.5 miles long, with the trailhead at the end of the North Wrangell spur road, about two miles from the Forest Service office. Ask at the office about the current status of the trail. The trail will traverse the high ridge north of Institute Creek, and two more trail shelters are planned. When completed, this trail system will be suitable for a two-to-three day trip just outside Wrangell.

Trip summary:	A shorter day or overnight hike to a forested lake.
Distance:	0.6 mile one way.
Special features:	A trail shelter and rowboat, wildlife, fair trout fishing.
Location:	28 miles south of Wrangell.
Difficulty:	Easy.
Trail type:	More developed.
Total elevation gain:	150 feet out.
Best season:	March through November.
Maps:	USGS Petersburg B-1.
Manager:	Tongass National Forest, Wrangell Ranger District.

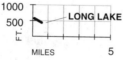

Finding the trailhead: Drive 25 miles south of Wrangell on the Zimovia Highway and its extension, Forest Road 6265. Turn south (right) on Road 6270 and continue 2.7 miles. Turn south (right) on Road 6271, and drive

LONG LAKE

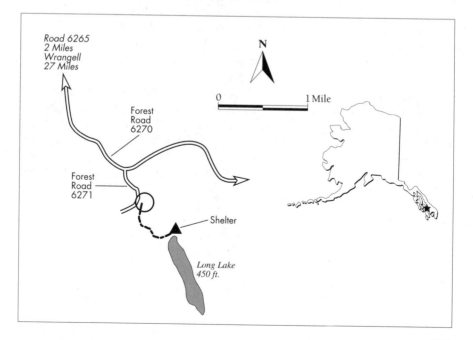

another 0.4 mile to the trailhead. The Forest roads are single lane with turn-outs—use caution and be prepared to yield to oncoming traffic.

The hike: Long Lake, a skinny, mile-long lake, is a quick trip off the Forest Service's Wrangell Island road system. Another Southeast hike where your feet don't even have to touch ground, the trail is entirely planked and bridged, mostly across wet meadows, with two sets of log stairs thrown in for good measure. The walk also features a short section of dark, mossy hemlock forest and small, bouldery creeks.

At the end of the trail, the three-sided trail shelter will sleep about four campers. A rowboat, fire pit, outhouse, and picnic table round out the amenities. Life vests for the boat are the hiker's responsibility.

Watch for beaver on the lake, and waterfowl and shorebirds around the lake and in nearby wetlands. Don't forget the insect repellent, and a length of mosquito netting to cover your head isn't a bad idea for sleeping in a sleeping bag in the open shelter. There is a very limited area suitable for tenting on the lakeshore near the shelter.

Look for the line of old boardwalk parallel to Road 6271 near the trailhead. The trail used to extend about a mile from Road 6270 before contractors built Road 6271 as a spur logging road.

Fishing. Fishing is fair for smaller cutthroat trout.

PETERSBURG

Petersburg, Alaska's Norwegian heritage capital, is the town that fish built—not with hammer and nails, but just about as effectively. The town's economy revolves almost completely around fishing, and most of the nearby trails lead to fishing holes. The Forest Service's *Mitkof Island Road Guide* map is a big help for finding your way around the island. The road system is confined to the island. The only access to Petersburg from the outside world is by air or water; it's on the state ferry route.

In addition to the three trails below, try the **Raven Trail**, a 4-mile trail that begins behind the airport and ends at a recreation cabin in high, wet meadows above Petersburg. Across the Wrangell Narrows (same trailhead as Hike 80), try the steep, 4-mile trail to the top of **Petersburg Mountain**. For a more remote trip, try the spectacular **Cascade Creek** *Trail*, 4 miles long, to waterfalls, lakes, and cabins northeast of Petersburg in Thomas Bay. Access is by water taxi or floatplane.

Trip summary:	Shorter day to half-day hikes, or a possible overnight trip, to a group of small lakes on the Three Lakes trail system. The Ideal Cove Trail leads from the lakes to the coast.
Distance:	A variety of hikes, from 0.3 mile one way to a loop hike of nearly 7 miles, is possible. About 4 miles of trails connect the lakes in a "figure 8." The Ideal Cove Trail is about 1 mile long, one way.
Special features:	Forested lakes, each with a picnic table and rowboat; a trail shelter at Shelter Lake; fishing; coast hiking and camping. You'll need waterproof boots for the Ideal Cove Trail.
Location:	27 miles south of Petersburg.
Difficulty:	Three Lakes: easy. Three Lakes with a side trip to Ideal Cove: moderate.
Trail type:	Three Lakes: more developed (entirely planked). Ideal Cove: less developed and wet, with minimal maintenance.
Total elevation gain:	50 to 300 feet, depending on the route chosen.
Best season:	Mid-April to mid-October.
Maps:	USGS Petersburg C-3 (NE) and C-2.
Manager:	Tongass National Forest, Petersburg Ranger District.

Finding the trailhead: Follow the Mitkof Highway 21 miles south of Petersburg to Three Lakes Loop Road (signed) and turn left (east). The three trailheads are 6.3 miles (Crane Lake), 6.7 miles (Hill Lake), and 7.2 miles (Sand Lake) from the Mitkof Highway. The Three Lakes Loop Road is a winding, single-lane gravel road with turnouts; drive with caution.

The hikes: The Three Lakes Loop trail system—three trailheads and four miles of boardwalk—connects Sand, Hill, and Crane lakes and the smaller Shelter Lake. The three larger lakes get their names from the sandhill cranes that stop here on their migrations. The Ideal Cove Trail, an old, unmaintained but passable Civilian Conservation Corps trail, leads down Hill Creek to the coast of Frederick Sound.

Three Lakes. Sand, Hill, and Crane lakes each have a small recreation area with a wooden platform, picnic table, and rowboat. There is a refurbished, CCC-era three-sided trail shelter at Shelter Lake. All the lakes are at about 150 feet elevation.

The entire Three Lakes area consists of wet forest and meadow, so tenting isn't a good option, except possibly setting up a free-standing tent on one of the platforms. Flowers and berries are abundant. The bogs bloom early, with shooting star, marsh marigold, bog orchid, and other flowers.

There are several possibilities for hiking the Three Lakes Loop. The shortest hike is to pick one of the Three Lakes and hike there, no more than 0.4

THREE LAKES AND IDEAL COVE

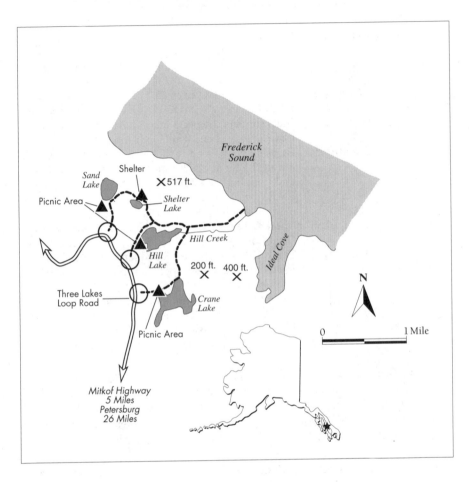

mile one way. A two-lake loop is about 2.5 miles round trip, including a short road walk back to the trailhead you started from. A long loop touching all the lakes is about 2.8 miles plus a 0.9-mile road walk. Leave a second vehicle or a bicycle for the shuttle if you don't want to walk the road.

Ideal Cove Trail. Just below Hill Lake, at the bridge over Hill Creek, is the junction with the less developed Ideal Cove Trail. About a mile one way, this old CCC trail to the coast of Frederick Sound is now a bit rough and muddy, so waterproof boots (e.g., rubber boots) are the footwear of choice.

The trail was the access to Three Lakes before the Mitkof Highway was built in the early 1970s; the lakes were once known as the Ideal Lakes. After the highway was built, Forest Service and youth program crews gradually built the trail system around the lakes, and use and maintenance of the Ideal Cove Trail tailed off.

Hill Lake, Three Lakes Trail.

The trail follows Hill Creek and reaches the coast at the mouth of the creek. Ideal Cove, mostly State land with a private cabin, is around the next point to the south, but the ideal campsites are to the north. Hike 0.5 mile beyond the end of the trail along the coast to the next point. Find campsites in the forest back of the point, and a small stream for water just around the point. Plan to hike the coastline no higher than mid-tide.

Doing this side trip to the coast from the Three Lakes loop can yield up to a 6.7-mile round-trip hike, the longest possible hike on this trail system.

Fishing. The Three Lakes offer decent cutthroat trout and Dolly Varden fishing.

Trip summary:	A shorter day hike on a low-elevation trail along Ohmer Creek.
Distance:	1 mile one way.
Special features:	Old-growth spruce forest, a pretty creek, a beaver pond, fair fishing. The trail is across the creek from the Ohmer Creek Campground.
Location:	22 miles south of Petersburg.
Difficulty:	Easy.
Trail type:	Accessible to less developed.
Total elevation gain:	Insignificant.
Best season:	Mid-April to mid-October.
Maps:	USGS Petersburg C-3 (SE) (trail not shown).
Manager:	Tongass National Forest, Petersburg Ranger District.

Key points:
0.2   End of accessible section along Ohmer Creek
0.5   Floating bridge across beaver pond
0.7   Forest/wet meadow edge
1.0   Snake Ridge Road

Finding the trailhead: Follow the Mitkof Highway 22 miles south of Petersburg to the trailhead on the west (right) side of the highway, just north of the Ohmer Creek bridge. The entrance to the Ohmer Creek Campground is south of the creek.

The hike: The Ohmer Creek Trail is a short, easy hike in three distinct sections: an accessible section along the creek, a boardwalk section across a beaver pond and wet meadows, and a less developed section through forest. The creek's brown stain, from the acidic muskegs and wet meadows that make up a sizeable part of its drainage basin, doesn't stop the fish from loving Ohmer Creek—most of the trout and salmon species found in the Petersburg area use the stream at one time or another during the year, peaking with salmon runs in late summer and fall.

The section nearest the highway is accessible, following the creek closely for 0.2 mile. The wide, compacted gravel path meanders through a rich bottomland forest of giant Sitka spruce. At 0.1 mile the hike passes the confluence of two forks of the creek, one swift and shallow, the other deep and slow. The trail crosses Woodpecker Cove Road and continues along the creek; there is parking at the crossing.

The second section of the trail begins at about 0.2 mile, where the trail bends away from the creek on boardwalk. The boardwalk continues about 0.5 mile, crossing a floating bridge over a broad, open beaver pond full of floating pond lilies. Beyond the bridge, two short spur trails lead to the

OHMER CREEK

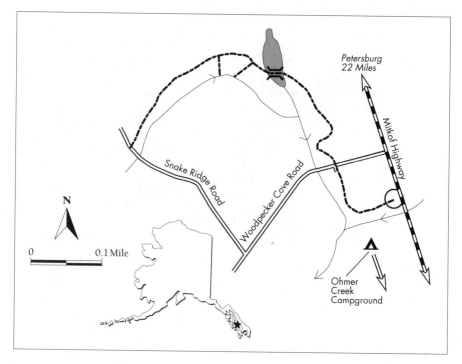

stream for fishing, looking for salmon, or just enjoying the creek. The planked trail leads across a pine-fringed wet meadow.

At the end of the meadow, the trail climbs a short set of steps into the forest. The last 0.3 mile of the hike is over natural, sometimes wet, tread, and traverses through forest away from the creek. The trail ends at Snake Ridge Road.

There are several options for hiking the trail:
- Take a short walk on the first section along the creek and return, about 0.4 mile total.
- Hike to the beaver pond and first spur trail to the creek and return, 1 mile total. This is a great family hike if you have smaller children who can manage a mile under their own power.
- Stroll to the end of the meadow and return, 1.4 miles.
- Hike the trail and return via the Snake Ridge and Woodpecker Cove roads, about 1.8 miles total.
- Hike to the end of the trail and return the same way, 2 miles.

Fishing. Fishing is fair to good for cutthroat trout, Dolly Varden, and silver and pink salmon in late summer and fall, the creek's peak fish time. There are also spring steelhead and early summer king salmon runs.

Trip summary:	A two to three day hike up Petersburg Creek to Petersburg Lake, partially in the Petersburg Creek-Duncan Salt Chuck Wilderness.
Distance:	10.3 miles one way.
Special features:	Forests, meadows, a large lake, stream and lake fishing, a fee cabin. The trailhead is a mile across the Wrangell Narrows from Petersburg, accessible by water taxi or sea kayak.
Location:	On Kupreanof Island, a mile west of Petersburg.
Difficulty:	Moderate.
Trail type:	More developed.
Total elevation gain:	About 500 feet in and 400 feet out.
Best season:	Mid-April to mid-October.
Maps:	USGS Petersburg D-3 (SW) and D-4 (SE).
Manager:	Tongass National Forest, Petersburg Ranger District.

Key points:
0.8   Petersburg Creek
3.0   Cabin Creek
4.4   High tide Trailhead
4.5   Wilderness boundary
7.0   Shaky Frank Creek
7.5   Pine bog
9.5   South Fork Creek
10.3   Petersburg Lake Cabin

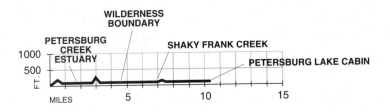

Finding the trailhead: The hike begins at the Kupreanof state dock, a mile west of the Petersburg waterfront and accessible by water taxi or sea kayak. The dock is a 5-minute water taxi ride from Petersburg (see Appendix 3 for water taxi information). There is also a high tide trailhead suitable for small boats 4.4 miles up the trail. Skiffs need a tide of at least 14 feet, and kayaks, about 12 feet, to make it all the way there. The hike along the lower creek, though, is highly recommended, so don't despair if you can't get to the high tide trailhead.

The hike: The Petersburg Lake Trail is one of only a very few longer, low-elevation hikes in Southeast Alaska. The hike's diversity is pretty remarkable,

PETERSBURG LAKE

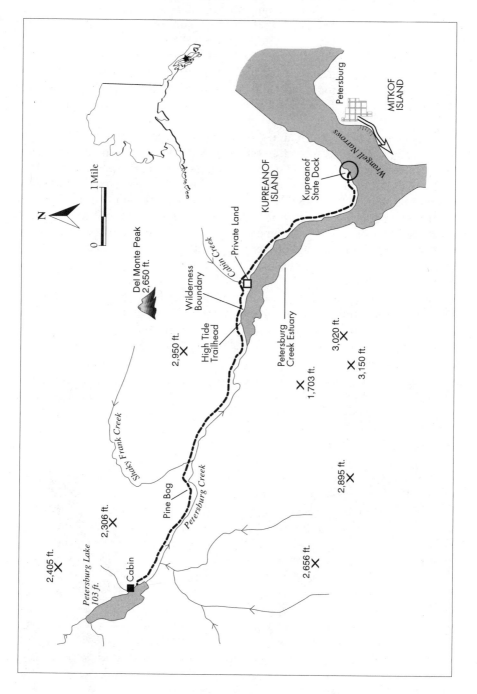

considering that the net elevation gain is only 100 feet. The creek, wildflower meadows, old-growth forests, and mile-long Petersburg Lake make this a premier hike. At the lake, there is a fee cabin and a rowboat for the cabin occupants to use (it's available to anyone when the cabin isn't occupied). See Appendix 2 for cabin reservation details.

The trip offers good fishing and a chance to see swans and other waterfowl, eagles, black bears, and forest birds. Four species of salmon, spring and fall steelhead, cutthroat trout, and Dolly Varden use the lake and stream. Eagles and bears are especially plentiful when the salmon are thick in late summer and fall.

The creek changes personalities several times on the way to the lake. It's a wide, slow, meandering stream in the estuary, or tidally influenced section; a swift, rocky creek; a dark stream in deep forest with pretty pools and riffles; and a slow, deep, marsh-fringed stream flowing out of the lake. The fork that enters from the south at 9.5 miles is actually a larger stream.

The lower trail jogs out of the forest now and then onto the strip of coastal meadow along the estuary. The meadows are thick with wildflowers in summer. The forest in this reach of the valley is deep and mossy, like something out of Tolkien. Mini-forests of skunk cabbage line the boardwalk trail (see *Our Friend the Skunk Cabbage* below).

The trail passes tall spruce stumps, all that's left of giant trees cut with crosscut saws, mainly in the 1910s, for building Petersburg and its canneries. Still visible on some of the stumps are the cuts for springboards, the platforms sawyers stood on to make their cuts above the trees' massive root buttresses.

Lower Petersburg Creek in an intermittent mist.

Petersburg Lake Cabin.

Just before Mile 3 is the only significant climb on the hike, a quick up and down to avoid a piece of private land. At 4.5 miles, the trail enters the Petersburg Creek-Duncan Salt Chuck Wilderness. Between the wilderness boundary and Shaky Frank Creek, the hike crosses three beaver dams. Two are bridged and one is not; the undeveloped crossing is straightforward enough, though you might get your feet wet. It may take a minute to find the trail on the far side of the pond.

Just beyond Shaky Frank Creek is a 0.5 mile-long muskeg bordered by lodgepole pine. Del Monte Peak is visible to the east. Take care on a few high log bridges in this upper section of the trail.

The developed trail ends at the cabin, by a small stream on the lakeshore. The cabin is also accessible by a short floatplane trip from Petersburg, so non-hikers use the cabin as well. Across the lake are the 3,600-foot alpine summits of Portage Mountain.

The two landslides on the trail, about Miles 3 and 10, cut loose on the same day: October 26, 1993. The upper slide partially dammed Petersburg Lake, raising the lake level. The creek is gradually cutting through the dam and lowering the lake level, but the flooding has left a band of dead trees around the perimeter of the lake. The trail does some fancy footwork across down logs through this slide. This and other log work by the Petersburg trail crew would make the Civilian Conservation Corps crews of the 1930s happy to see their skills being carried on.

Much of the area is wet, so tent camping is fairly limited. A few possibilities are the meadows on the lower creek (in dry weather), sand bars on the middle reach, and a few possible sites in the brushy forest by the lake. Waterproof boots are the preferred footgear except during extended periods of dry weather.

Shorter hikes. A day hike on the lower trail, up to 4.5 miles one way, makes a good jaunt for exploring the estuary and coastal meadows.

Fishing. Of the many fishing opportunities, the Department of Fish and Game notes the spring steelhead and fall silver salmon runs as highlights.

Our Friend the Skunk Cabbage

The skunk cabbage's wet forest habitat may be less than glamorous, but this is a plant with charisma. Its thick, shiny leaves, growing to four or five feet long, make it impossible to miss on Southeast trails, and its banana-yellow, leaf-like "spathes" that pop out of the mud in March are the first sign of the Southeast spring.

The spathe opens to reveal a prominent floral spike, which blossoms with hundreds of tiny flowers. The pollen these flowers shed is responsible for the slightly skunky odor that gives the plant its name and its undeserved reputation.

For humans, skunk cabbage is inedible without careful preparation, but animals love it. Bears, deer, and Canada geese eat the leaves and roots, and Steller's jays munch on the seeds. In traditional times Southeast Alaska's Native people roasted the roots to destroy the irritating chemical, and ground them into flour.

Skunk cabbage in all its glory.

SITKA

Sitka, Southeast's third largest city, is the only major Southeast community on the outer Pacific coast. Like most Southeast towns, Sitka is accessible only by air or water. Sitka's main claim to historic fame is its past as the capital of Russian America, back when the tsar claimed Alaska. Sitka is just a small freckle of civilization on big, wild, mountainous Baranof Island.

For other hikes around Sitka, consider two remote hikes on Kruzof Island, the island topped by the Mount Edgecumbe volcano, ten miles to the west across Sitka Sound. Access to these hikes is by charter boat or floatplane. The moderately strenuous **Mount Edgecumbe Trail** leads to the top of the peak, about 7 miles one way, from Fred's Creek Cabin (fee and reservation required). There is a trail shelter about 4 miles up the trail.

A Southeast Sitka spruce grove.

For an easier hike, walk across the island from Mud Bay to the **Shelikof Cabin** (another fee cabin) on the outer coast. The 7-mile hike follows the Kruzof Island Road and the Shelikof Trail.

On the road system, try the steep, rarely maintained trail to the top of **Mount Verstovia**, 2.5 miles one way. The trailhead is two miles southeast of Sitka on the main road, Sawmill Creek Road, in an unlikely spot next to a bar and grill. The popular, easy/moderate, more developed **Beaver Lake Trail**, 1 mile one way, is 7 miles south of Sitka. The trail leads from the Sawmill Creek Campground to forested Beaver Lake, and continues 0.2 mile along the lakeshore to half a dozen plank platforms for grayling fishing or picnicking. Finally, there's the one-mile trail to **Thimbleberry and Heart lakes**, 4 miles east of Sitka on Sawmill Creek Road.

81 INDIAN RIVER

Trip summary:	A longer day or overnight hike on a low-elevation forest trail up Indian River to Indian River Falls.
Distance:	4 miles one way.
Special features:	A pretty, clearwater stream, deep forest, and a waterfall. The trailhead is within easy walking distance of downtown Sitka.
Location:	A mile east of downtown Sitka.
Difficulty:	Moderate.
Trail type:	More developed; the last mile is a little rougher.
Total elevation gain:	About 650 feet.
Best season:	Mid-April through October.
Maps:	USGS Sitka A-4 (SW).
Manager:	Tongass National Forest, Sitka Ranger District.

Key points:

0.5   Muskeg viewpoint
1.5   Forks of Indian River
3.0   Billy Creek
4.0   Indian River Falls

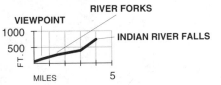

Finding the trailhead: Follow Sawmill Creek Road about 0.6 mile south from the intersection of Sawmill and Lake Street to Indian River Road, by the State Trooper Training Academy, on the left (north) side of the road. Follow Indian River Road about 0.3 mile to a gate; park your car here if driving. Walk straight ahead, about 0.2 mile, to the trailhead at the end of the closed city waterworks road.

The hike: Indian River is as good a low-elevation, forest-and-stream hike as there is in Southeast. The small river is a beautiful clearwater stream full of rocky riffles, deep green pools, and bouldery rapids. The hike features several crossings of forks of the river and its tributaries, all over bridges.

INDIAN RIVER

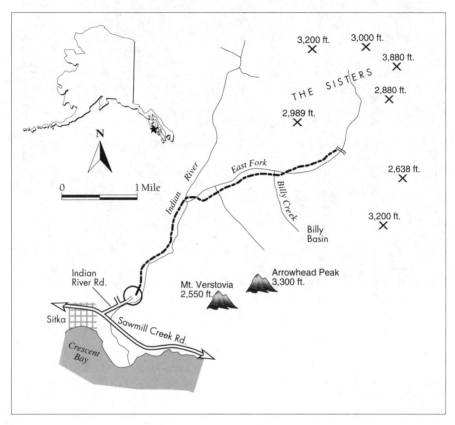

The forest is the signature spruce-hemlock-cedar forest of Southeast, with cathedral-like, open, mossy pockets of giant Sitka spruce. Wood thrushes, Steller's jays, and winter wrens are common, and runs of silver, pink, and chum salmon make their way up the river in late summer and fall. Hikers sometimes see deer and bears in the valley.

At 0.5 mile, a muskeg opening on the left side of the trail provides a view up the valley to The Sisters, the alpine peaks that split the two forks of Indian River. The trail's grade is very gradual, with the steepest section in the last mile from the last river crossing to the falls. The maintained trail ends at the east fork of the river just below the falls. Several places to camp dot the trail, with established sites in the first mile, at the river forks, and at the falls.

Inveterate local bushwhackers take a couple of cross-country trips from the trail: one to Billy Basin, which once hummed with the activity of a mine and ore mill, and another to the subalpine basin about 1.5 miles up the river beyond the end of the trail.

Indian River Falls.

Shorter hikes. Head for the muskeg viewpoint, 0.5 mile one way, or the river forks, 1.5 mile one way.

Fishing. The river is closed to all salmon fishing, but anglers can take a shot at landing Dolly Varden. The Dolly fishing is best in early spring and from mid-summer through fall.

82 *SITKA NATIONAL HISTORICAL PARK*

Trip summary:	Two shorter, day loop hikes in a small national historic park that features Russian America's history and Southeast Alaska Native history and art.
Distances:	West Loop to Shiskeenue fort site: 1 mile loop. East Loop to Russian Memorial: 0.7 mile loop.
Special features:	An outdoor museum of Southeast Alaska Native totem poles, the site of the Battle of Sitka, forests, salmon viewing on Indian River. A popular walk; day use only, and pets on leash only.
Location:	In Sitka, a mile east of downtown, adjacent to Sheldon Jackson College.
Difficulty:	Easy.
Trail type:	Accessible.
Total elevation gain:	Insignificant.
Best season:	March through November.
Maps:	USGS Sitka A-4 (SW) (trails not shown); NPS brochure; NPS trail map.
Manager:	Sitka National Historic Park.

Finding the trailhead: From Lake and Lincoln in downtown Sitka, travel east on Lincoln, past the small boat harbor and Sheldon Jackson College, about 0.6 mile to the park visitor center. Be sure to stop in at the center to see the interpretive displays.

Most people walk the West Loop counter-clockwise, beginning on the west (sea, or right) side of the visitor center; to walk it clockwise, or to cross the Indian River bridge for the most direct route to the East Loop, stroll east out of the parking area, to the left of the visitor center. There is also a trailhead for the East Loop on Sawmill Creek Road, about 0.2 mile southeast of the Indian River bridge.

The hike: Sitka National Historic Park, Alaska's oldest national park, commemorates the 1804 Battle of Sitka, when a force of Russians and Aleuts drove away the local Tlingit people and established Sitka as the capital of Russian America. Shiskeenue, the site of the fort the Tlingits defended against the Russian invaders, is on the West Loop.

The West Loop also meanders through an outdoor display of Southeast Alaska Native totem poles. The carved cedar poles were collected and brought to Sitka in the early 1900s. Many of them are Haida poles from Prince of Wales Island, an island in southern Southeast Alaska. They are no longer in their cultural context, but are preserved as in a museum. The booklet *Carved History*, available in the park bookstore, is a guide to the poles in the park. A Southeast Alaska Native cultural center in the visitor center offers demonstrations of wood carving and other Native arts.

SITKA NATIONAL HISTORIC PARK

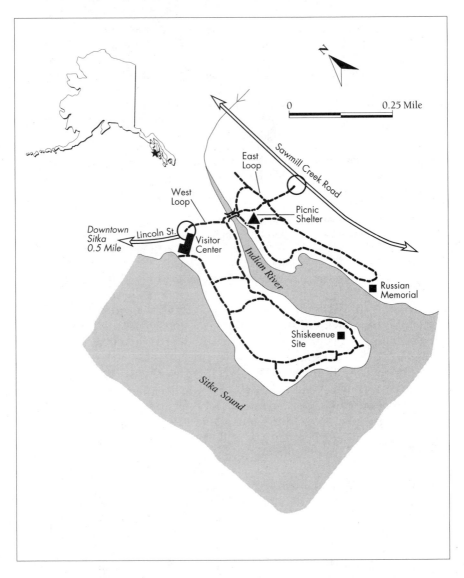

0.25 Mile

East Loop

Sawmill Creek Road

West Loop

Picnic Shelter

Downtown Sitka 0.5 Mile

Lincoln St.

Visitor Center

Indian River

Russian Memorial

Shiskeenue Site

Sitka Sound

The park trails are more of a stroll than a hike. They're a good, undemanding introduction to the look, smell, and feel of Southeast's water-and-forest environment, as well as a showcase of local history and Native culture. The park offers naturalist-led walks in summer.

West Loop. Starting the 1-mile West Loop on the sea side of the visitor center, the trail leads into the forest and through the park's collection of totem poles to the fort site. The site of the Tlingit stronghold is a broad opening in the forest on the point of land at the mouth of Indian River. Past

The West Loop, Sitka National Historic Park.

the fort, the trail circles back along Indian River to the visitor center. There are several points along the first half of the loop where visitors can step out onto the stony beach a few yards off the trail and drink in the view of Sitka Sound.

Near the end of the loop, a bridge spans Indian River, leading to the East Loop. In late summer and fall, the river runs thick with the salmon that once were the Tlingits' main food supply. Now the river is closed to all salmon fishing to protect fish stocks.

East Loop. The 0.7-mile East Loop features picnic tables, a picnic shelter that's a good place to duck in out of the frequent Sitka rain, and the Russian Memorial, a restored Russian cross in honor of the Russian sailors who died in the Battle of Sitka.

The Ten-Cent Treatise on Totems

Totem poles, those tall, elaborately carved cedar poles, are one of the most striking art forms imaginable. Crests of human and animal figures, stacked one on top of another, are a window into a different reality—who can look at the figure of a grinning orca, with a tiny human face as the blowhole, without being pulled into the Tlingit and Haida world for just an instant?

These Northwest Coast Native creations are part history, part literature, and part art. It's commonly thought that they developed from family histories carved into the house posts that supported the traditional Northwest Coast communal homes.

The poles generally tell a story—of a family, a legend, or an event—but only the characters of the story are discernible from the pole alone. The Tlingit erected poles as monuments or to mark grave sites, to describe special events or visions, or to ridicule someone for not repaying a debt, sort of an artsy way of turning the person's name over to the collection agency of public opinion. Wealthy Tlingits would also commission totem artists to carve poles for special events like potlatches, public celebrations of feasting and gift-giving.

Totem carving has seen a revival in recent years, and the poles are again common in Southeast and other parts of Alaska. Sitka National Historic Park and Totem Bight State Historical Park north of Ketchikan offer beautiful short hikes to see totem poles in their natural environment.

83 STARRIGAVAN BAY

Trip summary:	Two shorter day-hiking trails in the Starrigavan Recreation Area. The trails can be hiked as a loop, returning to your starting point on lightly-traveled roads.
Distances:	Estuary Life Trail: 0.25 mile one way. Forest & Muskeg Trail: 0.75 mile one way. Estuary Life/Forest & Muskeg Loop: 1.4 mile loop.
Special features:	Birding, salmon viewing, saltwater meadows, rain forest, an interpretive brochure, and an adjacent campground.
Location:	7.5 miles north of Sitka, at the north end of the Sitka road system.
Difficulty:	Easy.
Trail type:	Estuary Life: accessible. Forest & Muskeg: more developed.
Total elevation gain:	Estuary Life: insignificant. Forest & Muskeg: 100 feet.
Best season:	March through November.
Maps:	USGS Sitka A-5 (trails not shown); Forest Service/State Parks map/brochure *Starrigavan Recreation Area*.
Manager:	Tongass National Forest, Sitka Ranger District, and Alaska State Parks, Southeast Area.

Finding the trailhead: From downtown Sitka, drive west and north from the corner of Sawmill Creek Blvd. and Lake Street. Sawmill Creek becomes Halibut Point Road; follow it to the recreation area, about 7.5 miles from town and just past the state ferry terminal. The Starrigavan Campground and the three trailheads are all within a mile of the terminal.

The hikes: These two trails, a cooperative project of Tongass National Forest and Alaska State Parks, are short, easy hikes adjacent to the Starrigavan Campground at the north end of Sitka's road system. Both are interpretive trails. You'll need the park/forest brochure, available at the trailheads, to get the most out of the hikes.

The Forest Service sponsors interpretive hikes in the summer. There are also plans for another trail here, a 1.25-mile loop trail to Mosquito Cove, west of the Starrigavan Campground'a bay side.

There are three trailheads. **The Forest & Muskeg Trailhead** is at the south end of the recreation area, across from the Old Sitka boat ramp, and **The Estuary Life Trailhead** is farther north, just south of the turnoff to the two campgrounds. A short path connects the Starrigavan Campground's estuary side with the Estuary Life Trail.

The third trailhead is at the meeting of the trails on Nelson Logging Road (signed as Road 7578), 0.3 mile off Halibut Point Road. The parking area is

STARRIGAVAN BAY

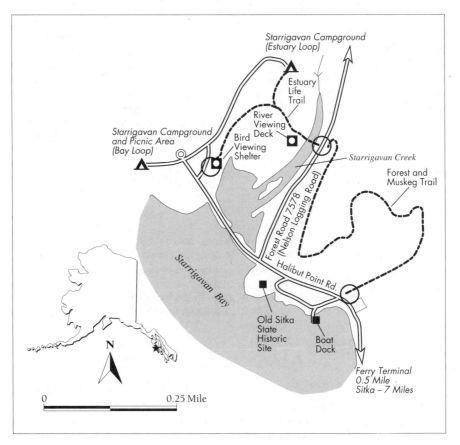

on the right, across the road from the footbridge to the Estuary Life Trail. The Forest & Muskeg Trail leads up the hill behind the parking area.

Hiking the two trails as a 1.4 mile loop is simple; just return to your starting point by following Halibut Point Road, a distance of 0.4 mile on the road.

Estuary Life Trail. The Estuary Life Trail, entirely boardwalk, features a bird viewing shelter and a river viewing deck. From the Halibut Point Road trailhead, it's just a few feet to the birding shelter, which overlooks Starrigavan Creek's estuary. Estuaries are biologically rich areas where streams meet the sea, exchanging salt and fresh water in rhythm with the tides. Waterfowl like mergansers and great blue herons use the estuary year-round, and many other species of birds can be seen here too.

Beyond the bird viewing shelter, the trail leads through forest and tall grass meadows, passing the connecting path to the Starrigavan Campground's estuary loop. The river-viewing deck overlooks the shallow stream. Spawning

The stream viewing deck on Starrigavan Creek's Estuary Life Trail.

salmon crowd the creek in late summer and fall (pinks in August and September, and silvers in September and October). The creek is closed to all salmon fishing.

The trail ends at Nelson Logging Road, just beyond a footbridge over the stream. The north end of the Forest & Muskeg Trail is just across the road. **Forest & Muskeg Trail.** The trail leads through hemlock, spruce, and cedar forest, pine wetlands, and muskeg. The theme of this section of the interpretive brochure is the biology of northern Southeast Alaska's forests and muskegs. The cedar here is Alaska, or yellow cedar, the only cedar that grows this far north. The trail winds along boardwalk and gravel tread, climbing gradually into muskeg openings with fine views of the mountains at the heart of Baranof Island.

Trip summary:	A longer forest and alpine hike above Sitka. The trail can be hiked as a day or overnight traverse, or as an out-and-back hike from either trailhead.
Distance:	6.25 miles.
Special features:	Subalpine and alpine hiking, views, and a trail shelter on an alpine ridge.
Location:	On the high ridge above Sitka.
Difficulty:	Moderate from Harbor Mountain Trailhead; moderately strenuous from Gavan Hill Trailhead.
Trail type:	More developed.
Total elevation gain:	800 feet from Harbor Mountain; 2,700 feet from Gavan Hill.
Best season:	Mid-June through September.
Maps:	USGS Sitka A-4 (SW) and A-5 (SE) (trail not shown).
Manager:	Tongass National Forest, Sitka Ranger District.

Key points:

Harbor Mountain Trailhead		Gavan Hill Trailhead
0.0	Harbor Mtn. Trailhead	6.25
1.25	Harbor Mtn. ridge	5.0
2.5	Trail shelter	3.75
3.25	Gavan Hill Overlook	3.0
5.25	Sitka viewpoint	1.0
6.25	Gavan Hill Trailhead	0.0

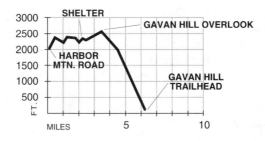

Finding the trailheads: Harbor Mountain Trailhead. Follow Halibut Point Road north about 4 miles from the intersection of Lake Street and Sawmill Creek Blvd. in Sitka (Sawmill Creek becomes Halibut Point Road). Turn right on Harbor Mountain Road and follow it a bit over 5 miles to the trailhead. Harbor Mountain Road, a narrow, winding gravel road with pullouts, isn't suitable for RVs or trailers. The Harbor Mountain trailhead is in subalpine country at 2,000 feet elevation.

Gavan Hill Trailhead. From Lake Street and Sawmill Creek Blvd., travel east 0.2 mile on Sawmill and turn left on Baranof Street. Follow Baranof 0.2

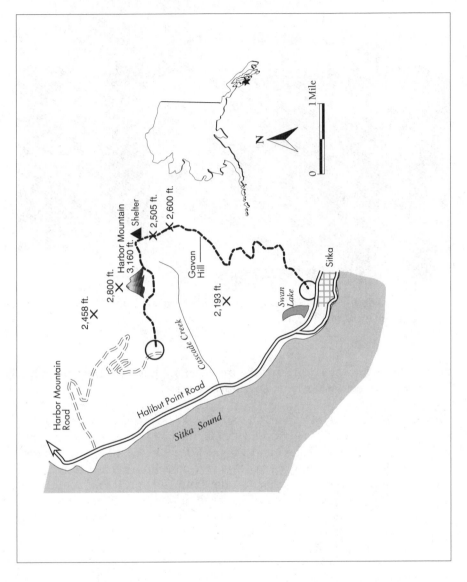

Weather closing in, Gavan Hill ridge. In the background is the Harbor Mountain/Gavan Hill trail shelter.

mile to the end of the street; find the trailhead on the right. The Gavan Hill Trailhead is an easy walk from downtown Sitka.

The hike: The Harbor Mountain-Gavan Hill hike traverses the open ridgeline above Sitka, skirting Cascade Creek's watershed and providing great views of Sitka Sound, Kruzof Island and Mount Edgecumbe, Sitka, and Baranof Island's wild, snowy summit peaks. A side trip to climb Harbor Mountain's first peak, a fine wildflower slope on the south side of the mountain, and stretches of alpine heather around the head of Cascade Creek are some of the hike's highlights. Eagles ride thermals above the subalpine ridge, and deer use the high country in summer.

A small, enclosed trail shelter (no reservation, no fee) in the saddle connecting the Harbor Mountain and Gavan Hill ridges is the best overnight spot. The shelter has a commanding view, and the knob behind it has an even better view of the dark, rugged peaks that form the backbone of Baranof Island.

Most of the spots suitable for pitching a tent on the ridge are exposed sites. The weather can change dramatically at this elevation so be prepared for rain, cold winds, and poor visibility. The trail is well-defined, but may be difficult to follow in places when still snow-covered early in summer. Please don't build campfires in this easily-damaged subalpine zone. There

316

is no water on the high ridges after the snowpack melts, typically by mid-summer.

From the Harbor Mountain Trailhead, 0.2 mile of boardwalk switchbacks climb to the ridge west of Harbor Mountain. Subalpine vegetation mixes with montane forests in this northern section of the hike. At 1.5 miles the trail connects with the Harbor Mountain summit ridge. A steep trail leads toward the first peak, but there's no easy route to the true summit.

Beyond, the hike passes stunted, twisted hemlocks as it curls around the south side of Harbor Mountain into subalpine and alpine terrain. Past the shelter at 2.5 miles, the trail crosses the flat, open summit of Gavan Hill, a fine overlook, and descends on boardwalk and stairsteps into the forest, eventually reaching the Baranof Street Trailhead. A mile above the trailhead is a good view of Sitka's south side.

Shorter hikes. On the Gavan Hill side, the Mile 1 viewpoint is a decent destination. Travelers without vehicles may want to try the trail to the Gavan Hill Overlook, a steep 3 miles one way, but easily accessible by foot from town. At Harbor Mountain, there are decent views just 0.2 mile up the trail, and a jaunt to Harbor Mountain's south summit is about 2 miles one way.

JUNEAU

Juneau, Alaska's capital and third largest city, has the most extensive trail system in Southeast. Travelers could easily spend two weeks on the Juneau trails. Like most of Southeast, the only thing missing is a trail hike of several days. As Juneau was the first major gold-mining area in the state, most of the trails near Juneau originated as mining roads, trails, or tramways.

Besides the trails covered in detail here, try the **Amalga Trail** to Eagle Lake and Eagle Glacier (7.5 miles one way, fee cabin, Glacier Highway Mile 28.4) and the **Peterson Lake Trail** (4.3 miles one way, fee cabin, Glacier Highway Mile 24) north of Juneau. South of Juneau are the **Sheep Creek Trail**, featuring mining history and great spring birding (3 miles one way, Thane Road Mile 4) and the **Bishop Point Trail** along the coast (8 miles one way, end of Thane Road, Mile 5.5).

On Douglas Island are the **Mount Jumbo** (also called Mount Bradley) Trail (3 miles one way to the peak, trailhead next door to 401 Fifth Street in Douglas), and the **Treadwell Ditch Trail**, a good spring and fall hike that runs along the east slope of the island (12 miles one way, access on Eaglecrest Ski Area Road and on the Dan Moller Trail, Hike 90).

From downtown Juneau, try the **Mount Roberts Trail** (3.5 miles one way starting from the staircase at the east end of Sixth Street) to Gastineau Peak and the route to Mount Roberts. A tourist tramway runs from Juneau's dock area to the trail at the 1,700-foot level.

Trip summary:	Half-day to longer day hikes into the subalpine and alpine basins of Gold and Granite Creeks, or an overnight trip to the alpine headwaters of Granite Creek.
Distances:	3 miles one way to the end of the Perseverance Trail on Gold Creek; up to 4.5 miles one way to the alpine headwater basin of Granite Creek; or an 11-mile round trip to the headwaters of both streams.
Special features:	Subalpine and alpine basins, mountain streams, mining history. The trailhead is accessible by foot from downtown Juneau.
Location:	1.5 miles east of downtown Juneau.
Difficulty:	Perseverance Trail: easy to moderate. Granite Creek: moderate to moderately strenuous.
Trail type:	A more developed trail, except that the last mile up Granite Creek is a less developed trail/route.
Total elevation gain:	Perseverance: 800 feet. Granite Creek: 1,400 feet to the lower basin, 1,900 feet to the upper basin.
Best season:	Perseverance Trail: Mid-May through early October. Granite Creek: mid-June through September.
Maps:	USGS Juneau B-2 (SE) and B-1 (SW); *Perseverance Trail* brochure.
Manager:	Alaska State Parks, Southeast Area.

Key points:

	Perseverance Trail		Granite Creek via Perseverance Trail
1.0	Mount Juneau Trail/Ebner Falls	2.0	Granite Creek Trail
2.0	Granite Creek Trail	3.5	Lower basin
3.0	Lurvey Falls/trail end	4.5	Upper basin

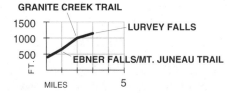

Finding the trailhead: From Egan Drive and Main Street in downtown Juneau, travel up Main Street, and turn right on 6th and left on Gold. Jog right on 8th and left onto Basin Road, and follow it to the trailhead at the end of the road, about 1.5 miles from Egan and Main. The roads to the trailhead are extremely steep and narrow (one of the reasons Juneau is called "a little San Francisco"), so if you drive, drive slowly and be prepared to yield to pedestrians and other vehicles.

PESERVERANCE TRAIL AND GRANITE CREEK
• MOUNT JUNEAU

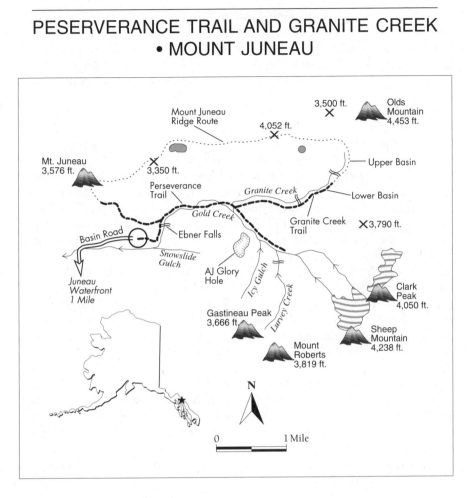

If you walk from downtown, add the 1.5 mile uphill hike to the distances quoted above.

The hike: These trails up the high mountain valleys of Gold and Granite Creeks are close to town and popular. The Gold Creek valley is the site of the 1880 gold discovery that led to the founding of Juneau. Great mountain scenery, mining remains, alpine basins in Granite Creek, and acres of wild-flowers are the highlights of the trails.

Hikers, runners, and mountain bikers all use the wide, graded Perseverance Trail, which is the old wagon road to the Perseverance Mine, first traveled in 1889. The steeper Granite Creek Trail is hiking country. Landslides occasionally close the Perserverance Trail near the trailhead.

The mining history begins with the Ebner Mine adit only a few feet up the Perseverance Trail. Visible from the trail are remains of two of the three biggest mines in Juneau's early days, the AJ (Alaska Juneau) and the

Perseverance. Mining may come again to the valley: Granite Creek and the nearby mountains are all staked as mining claims.

Perseverance Trail. The first mile of the trail offers great views of the AJ Mine Portal Camp, Snowslide Gulch, and Gold Creek's Ebner Falls. The steep trail to Mount Juneau begins across from the spur trail to the top of Ebner Falls at Mile 1 (see Hike 86).

Above Ebner Falls, the old wagon road follows close by foaming, bouldery Gold Creek, crossing it three times on the way to the end of the trail just beyond Lurvey Falls. The trail ends in the Silver Bow Basin, where the Perseverance Mine operated from the 1880s to the 1920s.

The AJ Glory Hole, off the trail via a spur path that's a bit of an alder bash, is a major hole in the ground that yielded millions of dollars in gold. Take care if you choose to go see the hole; the fractures along the cliff edge are a good warning. The sheer sides of the 800-foot hole are visible from the trail. A tunnel connected the workings in the hole with the rest of the mine complex farther down the valley.

Granite Creek. Turn left about 2 miles out the Perseverance Trail to hike the Granite Creek Trail. At the very beginning of the trail is a steep rock pitch that is the roughest part of the trail. The lower Granite Creek Basin is about 1.5 miles up the trail, at the top of Granite Creek's lower cascades. Another mile of less developed trail/route leads past another set of cascades into the creek's high headwater basin, below the 4,453-foot dome of Olds Mountain.

There are plenty of good campsites in the two basins among rock slabs, snow patches, marmots, and heather. From the upper basin, a climb of Olds Mountain is possible but quite a project, and hikers can also take a jaunt up into a land of alpine knobs and basins on the way to the Mount Juneau ridge to the west (Hike 86).

Shorter hikes. The 1 mile, one-way hike to Ebner Falls leads to some great scenery on Gold Creek.

Trip summary:	A steep half-day hike to Mount Juneau, or a longer

See Map on Page 319

day or overnight loop hike on the Mount Juneau ridge to Granite Creek, returning to the trailhead via the Gold Creek and Perseverance Trails.

Distance:	Mount Juneau: 3 miles one way.
	Mount Juneau ridge loop: a 12-mile loop.
Special features:	Alpine ridge rambling, incredible views, wildflowers. Allow at least ten hours for the loop hike.
Location:	1.5 miles east of downtown Juneau.
Difficulty:	Mount Juneau: moderately strenuous.
	Mount Juneau ridge loop: strenuous.
Trail type:	More developed lower, but mainly a less developed trail/route. Snow stays on parts of the ridge route most of the summer.
Total elevation gain:	Mount Juneau: 3,000 feet.
	Mount Juneau ridge loop: 3,900 feet.
Best season:	Late June to mid-September.
Maps:	USGS Juneau B-2 (SE) and B-1 (SW); *Perseverance Trail* brochure.
Manager:	Alaska State Parks, Southeast Area.

Key points:

1.0	Mount Juneau Trail
3.0	Mount Juneau summit
6.0	Peak 4,052
7.5	Head of Granite Creek
10.0	Perseverance Trail
12.0	Perseverance Trailhead

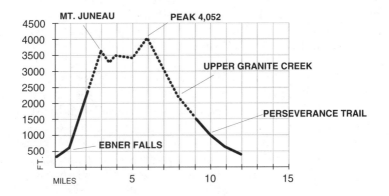

The Mount Juneau ridge loop near Granite Creek.

Finding the trailhead: Access to the Mount Juneau Trail is via the Perseverance Trailhead above downtown Juneau. See Hike 85, "Finding the trailhead."

The hike: The Mount Juneau hike is a relatively short and very steep trail, 3 miles one way, to the 3,576-foot peak and the high country behind Juneau. The reward at the top is a panoramic view of mountains, ocean, snow, and ice.

If you've got the energy and the luxury of a day or more of fair weather, Mount Juneau could be just the beginning of the alpine fun. The 12-mile ridge loop continues east from the peak along an alpine ridge to upper Granite Creek, returning to the trailhead via the Granite Creek and Perseverance trails.

If you're prepared for wind and weather, camping is possible in the upper basin of Granite Creek, and even on the ridgetop. Be sure to carry the topo map and a compass for this hike. If visibility and weather deteriorate, this ridge jaunt could become a survival march really quickly.

Mount Juneau. The steep trail climbs via switchbacks through brush and patches of Sitka spruce, leveling off about halfway to the peak as it crosses an open sideslope below the peak and above Gold Creek and Juneau. The last stage of the climb is straight up a steep, subalpine mountainside. The steep grade and small, loose rocks present a bit of a hazard, especially coming down; a walking staff is a big help.

The last part of the climb, now on an alpine slope, parallels an old tramline that ends on the peak. At the top the view is magnificent. Snowy mainland peaks stretch forever to the east, and the Inside Passage, Admiralty Island, and the Chilkat and Fairweather ranges lie in full view to the west, all the way to Glacier Bay. The only detraction is the collection of junk buildings, container vans and tram equipment that litters the mountaintop. Just walk out the ridge a bit to get away from the mess.

Mount Juneau ridge loop. From Mount Juneau, it's about 4.5 miles of ridge running to the headwaters of Granite Creek and the trail/route down Granite Creek. There is no constructed tread on the ridge, but there is a hiker-made path or rock cairns much of the way. Experienced ridge runners will find this ramble relatively easy, with no big drops and climbs on the ridge, and continuously amazing views. To the north is Blackerby Ridge and its high points, Cairn Peak and Observation Peak. To the south, the Mount Roberts/Sheep Mountain ridge separates Gold Creek from Sheep Creek.

Near Granite Creek, the route becomes less obvious—take the lower, inner ridge off Peak 4,052, not the higher ridge toward Olds Mountain. Don't descend from the ridge until you can see the route into the Granite Creek basin down fairly moderate slopes. Starting down too soon leads to slopes too steep to descend safely.

Snow stays on the ridge all summer, but by early July a snowfree route usually appears on all the steep sections. Travel early in summer may require an ice ax. Don't step out onto the cornices that overhang the north edge of the ridge.

Once in Granite Creek, follow the trails down the Granite and Gold Creek valleys to the trailhead. See Hike 85 for more information on the Perseverance and Granite Creek trails.

87 DAN MOLLER TRAIL

Trip summary:	A half-day hike or overnight up Kowee Creek to Dan Moller Cabin, and off-trail hiking into higher country above the cabin.
Distance:	3 miles one way.
Special features:	Meadows, a subalpine basin, a fee cabin.
Location:	On Douglas Island, a mile west of Juneau.
Difficulty:	Moderately strenuous.
Trail type:	More developed trail to the cabin; a route to the upper basin and ridgeline.
Total elevation gain:	1,700 feet to the cabin.
Best season:	Late May through October.
Maps:	USGS Juneau B-2 (SE).
Manager:	Tongass National Forest, Juneau Ranger District.

Key points:

0.6 Zahn Bench viewpoint
0.75 Treadwell Ditch Trail
3.0 Dan Moller Cabin

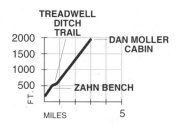

The subalpine basin above Dan Moller Cabin.

DAN MOLLER TRAIL

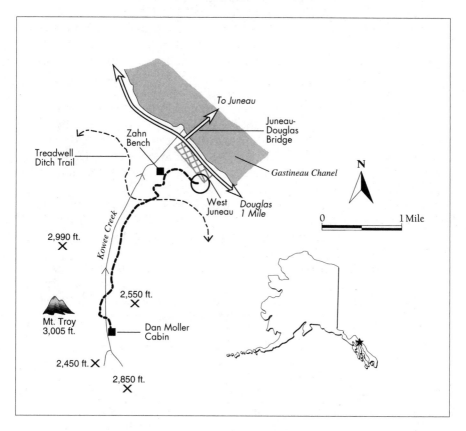

Finding the trailhead: From Egan Drive and 10th Street in Juneau, take the Juneau-Douglas bridge west across Gastineau Channel and bear left toward Douglas. Take the first right turn on Cordova Street, follow the left curve at the end of Cordova onto Pioneer Avenue in 0.2 mile, and find the trailhead on the right in another 0.2 mile, nestled between houses in a residential area.

Travelers without cars can take the Juneau-Douglas city bus to the corner of the Douglas Highway and Cordova Street, and walk 0.4 mile to the trailhead.

The hike: The Dan Moller Trail, a boardwalk trail, is a good antidote for the rain forest claustrophobia that can strike hikers who have been in Southeast too long. The hike follows the course of Kowee Creek, meandering along a string of wet meadows that come alive with wildflowers early in summer. There's a view of forests and mountains nearly everywhere except for a short stretch or two in the trees, and the trail is close enough to the creek that hikers can hear it singing away on its run to Gastineau Channel.

The hike passes the Zahn Bench viewpoint in 20 minutes or so, and shortly after, the intersection with the Treadwell Ditch Trail. Continue through meadow and forest, and in the last 0.5 mile of the trail, notice the cooler air, mountain hemlock forest, and brushy slopes of Southeast's montane zone.

The large cabin, popular as a ski cabin in winter, is on a cleared knoll above the creek. See Appendix 2 for reservation information. The easiest way to water is to take the trail behind the cabin to the creek. There aren't many spots dry and level enough for tents nearby.

The planked trail ends behind the cabin, but it's a pretty hike across wet ground up to the basin at the head of the left fork of Kowee Creek. From the basin, it's about a 500-foot climb in less than a mile up the slope to the lowest point on the ridgeline above. The ridge above Kowee Creek is the crest of Douglas Island, with views of Juneau, Mount Jumbo, and Admiralty Island.

Several hikeable peaks rise to either side of the saddle above Kowee Creek, including Peak 2,850 and Mount Troy, 3,005 feet. On those rare clear Juneau days, this is a relatively easy way to spend a spell on Juneau's fine mountaintops.

The cable towers in the upper basin reveal the remains of Juneau's ski hill before it was moved farther north on Douglas Island to Eaglecrest.

Shorter hikes. Take the 0.6-mile walk to the Zahn Bench, a viewpoint "for those who like a comfortable seat and a good view," as the plaque says.

Trip summary:	A variety of shorter and longer day hikes, beginning from the Mendenhall Glacier Visitor Center, a Forest Service visitor center near Alaska's southernmost road-accessible glacier.
Distance/Difficulty/ Total elevation gain:	Photo Point Trail: 0.3 mile one way; Easy; essentially no elevation gain. Trail of Time: 0.5 mile nature loop; Easy; Less than 100 feet. Moraine Ecology Trail: 1.5 mile loop; Easy; Less than 100 feet. East Glacier Loop Trail: 4 mile loop; Moderate; 600 feet. Nugget Creek Trail: 3.5 miles one way; Moderate; 1,200 feet. East Glacier/Nugget Creek loop: 8 mile loop; Moderate; 1,500 feet.
Special features:	Mendenhall Lake and Glacier, Nugget Creek Falls, successional and old-growth forests, an interpretive trail, and a visitor center with displays, books, and videos on glaciers and glacial landscapes.
Location:	13 miles north of Juneau.
Trail type:	Photo Point Trail: accessible. Other trails: more developed.
Best season:	April to mid-November for the Trail of Time, Photo Point and Moraine Ecology Trails; May to mid-October for East Glacier and Nugget Creek.
Maps:	USGS Juneau B-2 (NW); Forest Service *Mendenhall Glacier* brochure.
Manager:	Tongass National Forest, Juneau Ranger District.

Finding the trailhead: From downtown Juneau, drive 9 miles north on Egan Drive/Glacier Highway to the south junction with the Mendenhall Loop Road. Turn right (east) on the Loop Road. Continue straight ahead on the Loop Road and Mendenhall Glacier Road about 3.6 miles to the visitor center.

The visitor center is also accessible by private shuttle from the cruise ship dock area in downtown Juneau (see Appendix 3), or by the city's Mendenhall Valley bus and a 1.5-mile walk from the closest bus stop, at Mendenhall Loop Road and Mendenhall Glacier Road.

The hikes: The Mendenhall Glacier Visitor Center, set on a hill on the south shore of Mendenhall Lake, was the Forest Service's first visitor center, built in the 1960s. The focus is the glacier, Alaska's southernmost road-accessible chunk of blue ice, not to mention Alaska's only suburban glacier.

MENDENHALL GLACIER VISITOR CENTER TRAILS

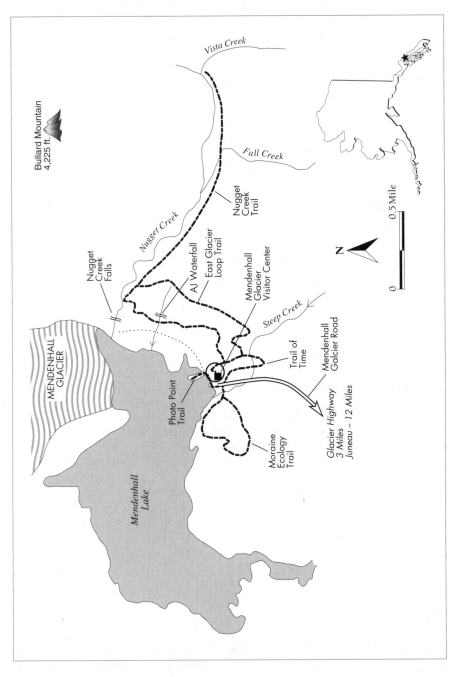

The top of Nugget Creek Falls, on the East Glacier Loop Trail.

The glacier flows 12 miles off the Juneau Icefield and terminates on the floor of the Mendenhall Valley, the home of a Juneau bedroom community.

The lake and glacier are one of Juneau's main destinations for cruise ship tourists, but these folks don't venture much beyond the visitor center and the Photo Point Trail. The variety of hikes and the ease of access from Juneau and the Mendenhall Valley make the shorter trails here very popular. Be sure to check out the displays in the center. Forest Service naturalists offer short, guided hikes daily in summer.

Photo Point Trail. This paved, accessible trail, 0.3 mile one way, leads to a rocky point that juts out into Mendenhall Lake and provides good views of the glacier and Nugget Creek Falls. Branching off from the Photo Point Trail, the informal East Lakeshore Trail leads about 0.5 mile to the base of Nugget Creek Falls, a roaring torrent that falls onto the outwash gravels in front of the glacier. The Forest Service plans to upgrade this trail. Avoid the lake's shoreline early in summer to protect nesting birds.

Trail of Time. The Trail of Time is a 0.5-mile, self-guided interpretive trail. Ask for the guide pamphlet at the visitor center or at the kiosk in the parking area. The pamphlet explains the glacier's advances, retreats, and the landscape left behind after the ice's most recent retreat.

Start the hike behind the visitor center. About halfway around the loop, you'll see a small day use trail shelter, built in the 1930s by the Civilian Conservation Corps, a good spot for a rest or lunch on a rainy day. Two bridges cross Steep Creek at the south end of the trail. The trail ends on the Mendenhall Glacier Road, across from the lower parking area.

Moraine Ecology Trail. The Moraine Ecology Trail, a 1.5 mile-loop, begins in the lower parking area and circles across the low, forested, pond-dotted moraine in front of Mendenhall Lake. Trail signing is sparse at this writing. The Forest Service plans to build a new, short, salmon-viewing trail along Steep Creek, link it to the Moraine Ecology Trail, and produce a trail guide or signs for the two trails.

East Glacier Loop Trail. The East Glacier Loop Trail, 3.5 miles long, begins 0.1 mile from the visitor center along the Trail of Time. It climbs the steep slope east of the visitor center, dips into the Nugget Creek valley, and circles back to the Trail of Time. Hiking the loop involves hiking most of the Trail of Time as well, so the entire hike is almost 4 miles long.

The forest of cottonwood, alder, and spruce on the lower slope is young; this area has only been out from under the ice since the 1930s. A short spur trail in the first mile leads to the AJ Waterfall, created by water that runs through a tunnel from Nugget Creek. Until the 1940s, the tunnel supplied water to a hydroelectric plant for the Treadwell and AJ Mines.

The AJ falls, though, are just a warmup for the view at 1.25 miles. The trail looks down on roaring Nugget Creek Falls, which falls 300 feet out of the Lower Basin of Nugget Creek to lake level. There's also a view of the face of the Mendenhall Glacier.

At 1.5 miles, the East Glacier Trail intersects the Nugget Creek Trail, which continues up Nugget Creek about 2 miles. East Glacier climbs away from the creek, into older spruce-hemlock forest not affected by the glacier in recent times. The trail passes the remains of an ore car rail line, crosses a rock ledge, and begins a slow descent to the Trail of Time, which it meets at the trail shelter by the upper Steep Creek bridge.

Nugget Creek Trail. The Nugget Creek Trail, 2 miles one way, begins 1.5 miles out the East Glacier Loop Trail, and deadends at Vista Creek by a defunct trail shelter. Camping here isn't too grand, but there is a place to pitch a tent along the creek above the shelter site, in the trees.

Mainly a forest trail above the glacier's trimming influence, Nugget Creek is a pretty hike with no great destination. There is one viewpoint—a view of Bullard Mountain from a brushy draw a few minutes from trail's end. A rough route extends up the valley from Vista Creek; there are two more basins above in the 4-mile ascent to the Nugget Creek Glacier.

East Glacier/Nugget Creek loop. The longest possible hike near the visitor center, about 8 miles, combines the Trail of Time, East Glacier, and Nugget Creek Trails. This hike involves adding the out-and-back trip up the Nugget Creek valley to the East Glacier Loop.

Trip summary:	A half-day or longer hike along the west side of Mendenhall Lake and the Mendenhall Glacier to an outstanding viewpoint above the glacier.
Distances:	1 mile to lower overlook, 3.25 miles to the West Glacier overlook point.
Special features:	Views of blue ice and snowy alpine peaks. Access to the glacier for experienced and equipped glacier travelers, and access to a strenuous route to the summit of McGinnis Mountain.
Location:	13 miles north of Juneau.
Difficulty:	Moderate.
Trail type:	Mainly a more developed trail; less developed and rougher just before the Mile 3 outcrop, and a partially marked route beyond.
Total elevation gain:	About 1,300 feet.
Best season:	Late May through September.
Maps:	USGS Juneau B-2 (NW).
Manager:	Tongass National Forest, Juneau Ranger District.

Key points:

1.0	Lower overlook
2.0	Avalanche Creek
3.0	Rock outcrop; end of maintained trail
3.25	West Glacier overlook point

Finding the trailhead: From downtown Juneau, drive 9 miles north on Egan Drive/Glacier Highway to the south junction with the Mendenhall Loop Road. Turn right (east) on the Loop Road and follow it about 3.7 miles to Montana Creek Road (on the way, turn left at a signed intersection for the Loop Road, just over 2 miles from Egan Drive). Turn right onto Montana Creek Road, and in about 0.3 mile, bear right on Mendenhall Lake Road toward Mendenhall Campground. Drive about 0.7 mile, passing the campground, to the trailhead at the end of the road.

From the ferry terminal, turn onto the north side of the Loop Road at Glacier Highway Mile 12, drive about 2.5 miles to Montana Creek Road, turn left and continue to the trailhead.

WEST GLACIER

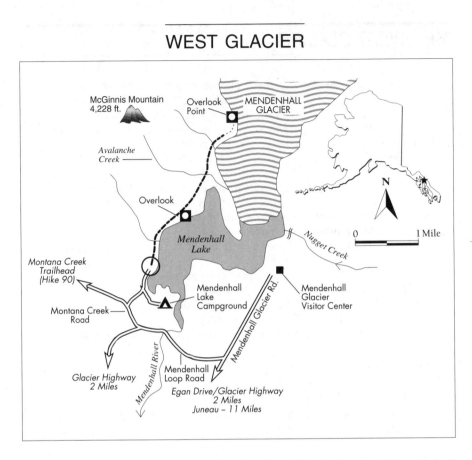

Public transit to the campground and trailhead is via the city's Mendenhall Valley bus, which stops at the intersection of Montana Creek Road and the Loop Road. It's a 1-mile walk to the trailhead from the bus stop.

The hike: The West Glacier hike follows the west side of Mendenhall Lake and Mendenhall Glacier, mainly through brushy woods of alder and cottonwood, to several viewpoints above the valley. The final destination, though, the West Glacier overlook point, allows hikers to see into the hall of the mountain king, a land of peaks and ice. This is a beauty of an area, but be prepared for frequent helicopter noise; the glacier is a prime destination for air tours.

The trail begins to climb in about a mile, crossing several tumbling mountain streams that spill off the slope of McGinnis Mountain, elevation 4,228 feet, the alpine peak west of the glacier. There are several rock outcrops with great views, and the scenery improves as the trail climbs.

The viewing bench on the rock outcrop at one mile is the first overlook, and the last and best is the West Glacier overlook, a point of rock directly above the glacier and a bit beyond the end of the maintained trail.

At about 2 miles cross an avalanche stream that falls directly off McGinnis Mountain. The creek has been wiped clean of vegetation by snowslides off

Overlooking the Mendenhall Glacier and Mendenhall Lake on the West Glacier Trail.

the mountain. Above the glacier now, hikers can look out over blue ice, green forests, and snowy peaks, with the white froth of Nugget Creek Falls in the distance across the glacier.

The trail is a bit rougher over rocks as it approaches the block of bare rock at 3 miles. The obvious trail ends on this outcrop. Discover the best views, though, around the corner at the West Glacier overlook, a lower point about 0.25 mile away on a route marked with a few cairns. Follow the faint but discernible route carefully, up and then back down the rocky shoulder to a point directly above the glacier. The view takes in miles of ice, dark peaks, and a dozen or so waterfalls.

The brushy woods along the trail is a "successional" forest that has pioneered the new land that emerged after the glacier's retreat in the 1930s. Eventually spruce trees will grow up and shade out the cottonwood and alder, and hemlock seedlings will sprout under the spruce canopy, unless the glacier comes back and cleans the slope again first.

McGinnis Mountain. A rough route leads up to McGinnis Mountain on the long spur ridge above the outcrop at the end of the trail. The 4-mile route is strenuous, somewhat hard to find, and suitable for experienced hiker/scramblers only. The best months for heading up McGinnis are July and August.

Shorter hikes. Hike one mile one way to the lower viewpoint, at about 250 feet elevation.

Trip summary:	A longer day or overnight traverse from Montana Creek to Windfall Lake, or a short day/overnight hike to Windfall Lake along Herbert River.
Distance:	Montana/Windfall traverse: 11 miles. Windfall Lake from the Windfall Lake (north) trailhead: 3.25 miles one way.
Special features:	A fine creek walk, forests, wetlands, a large lake, and fishing.
Location:	15 miles north of Juneau.
Difficulty:	Traverse: moderate. Windfall Lake from north trailhead: easy.
Trail type:	More developed.
Total elevation gain:	Traverse: 700 feet. Windfall Lake: 100 feet.
Best season:	May through October.
Maps:	USGS Juneau B-2 (NW), B-3 (NE), and C-3 (SE).
Manager:	Tongass National Forest, Juneau Ranger District.

Key points:

**Montana Creek/
Windfall Lake Traverse**

1.0	Closed road ends
3.0	Upper Montana Creek bridge
4.0	Montana/Windfall Creek summit
6.0	Windfall Creek bridge
8.0	Windfall Lake spur trail
8.5	Upper Herbert River crossing
11.0	Windfall Lake (north) Trailhead

Windfall Lake

2.5	Upper Herbert River crossing
3.0	Windfall Lake spur trail
3.25	Windfall Lake

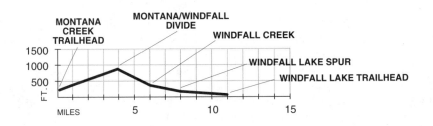

Finding the trailheads: Montana Creek (south). About 9 miles north of Juneau on Egan Drive/Glacier Highway, turn right (east) on Mendenhall Loop Road. Just over 2 miles from the highway, turn left at a signed intersection for the Loop Road, and continue to Montana Creek Road, a total of about 3.7 miles from the highway. Turn right up Montana Creek Road and follow it 2 miles to the end of the road and the beginning of the hike.

MONTANA CREEK AND WINDFALL LAKE

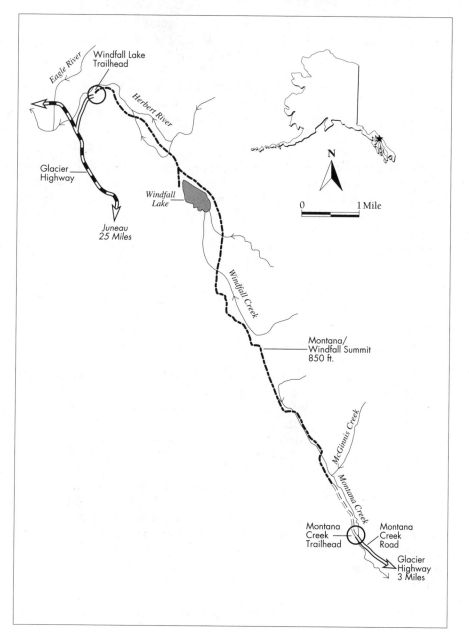

Eagle River

Windfall Lake
Trailhead

Herbert River

Glacier
Highway

Windfall
Lake

Juneau
25 Miles

N

0   1 Mile

Windfall Creek

Montana/
Windfall Summit
850 ft.

McGinnis Creek

Montana Creek

Montana
Creek
Trailhead

Montana
Creek
Road

Glacier
Highway
3 Miles

Travelers without cars can take the Mendenhall Valley city bus as far as the intersection of the Loop Road and Montana Creek Road, 2 miles from the trailhead.

If traveling from the ferry terminal or other points to the north, turn east at the north junction of the Loop Road, Mile 12 of the Glacier Highway, drive 2.5 miles to Montana Creek Road, turn left, and continue to the trailhead.

Windfall Lake (north). Drive to Mile 27 of the Glacier Highway north of Juneau, 0.1 mile south of the Herbert River bridge. Turn right onto the access road and follow it about a mile to the trailhead.

The hikes: The hike from the Montana Creek trailhead to Windfall Lake, the only overnight trail traverse near Juneau, features lush forest, pretty creeks, meadows, and wetlands, and half mile-long Windfall Lake. The best camping is at Windfall Lake, which is an easy, popular hike from the north trailhead and a good family overnight hike. The trail is planked across wet sections.

Montana Creek to Windfall Lake. The first mile of the hike is along the closed Montana Creek Road. The trail begins at the end of the road, near the confluence of Montana and McGinnis creeks. Entering the forest, the path follows Montana Creek through its narrow, v-shaped valley. The trail stays close by the creek for nearly 2 miles, requiring some fancy trailwork like steep staircases and anchored tread across caved-in sections of the bank.

After crossing the creek, the hike leads to the low divide between Montana and Windfall creeks, in a broad, wet meadow at 850 feet elevation. On the Windfall Creek side, the trail stays high above the deeply-incised creek until the valley widens at Mile 5 of the hike. Crossing the creek on a bridge, hikers walk into a fantasy forest of gnarled spruces with moss-hung limbs and ranks of tall devil's club.

Windfall Lake to the north trailhead. The south end of the lake is an extensive wetland, and a bird paradise. The best access to the lake is via a plank spur trail at the north end. It's about 0.25 mile to the lake from the spur trail junction, and another 0.2 mile more to the best campsites on a dry point of land between two small coves. There used to be a cabin here, and the Forest Service is considering building a new cabin at the lake.

Below the lake, the trail meets the Herbert River and follows the silty glacial stream to the trailhead, crossing and recrossing its south channel. Look for bald eagles along the river.

Fishing. The lake supports Dolly Varden and cutthroat trout, and silver, pink, and red salmon during spawning runs. Windfall Creek and Herbert River below the lake are closed to fishing in June and July to protect returning red salmon.

Trip summary:	Half-day hikes to Spaulding Meadows and the John Muir Cabin on connecting trails, or an overnight trip to the cabin.
Distance:	3 miles to Spaulding Meadows and 3 miles to the John Muir Cabin. The trails divide about 0.8 mile from the trailhead.
Special features:	Meadows, mountain views, a fee cabin. The area is too wet for comfortable tent camping.
Location:	About 13 miles north of Juneau, at Auke Bay.
Difficulty:	Moderate.
Trail type:	More developed, except the upper section of Spaulding Meadows Trail is less developed, rougher, and wet.
Total elevation gain:	Spaulding Meadows: 1,600 feet. John Muir Cabin: 1,500 feet.
Best season:	May through October.
Maps:	USGS Juneau B-2 (NW) and B-3 (NE).
Manager:	Tongass National Forest, Juneau Ranger District.

Key points:

	Spaulding Trail			Auke Nu Trail
0.8	Auke Nu Trail junction		0.8	Spaulding Trail junction
3.0	Spaulding Meadows		1.0	Waydelich Creek
			2.8	Auke Nu Creek
			3.0	John Muir Cabin

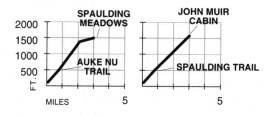

Finding the trailhead: Look for the trailhead on the north side of Glacier Highway, about 13 miles north of Juneau and 0.3 mile west of the Auke Bay Post Office. The city's Mendenhall Valley bus stops 0.5 mile east of the trailhead at the intersection of the highway and Mendenhall Loop Road.

The hikes: The Spaulding and Auke Nu trails share the first 0.8 mile, and then divide to different destinations. Spaulding leads to meadows on the high ground between Waydelich (that's "waddly" in Juneau-ese) and Lake Creeks, with a view of the peaks west of Mendenhall Glacier. The Auke Nu Trail climbs gradually toward the back side of Auke Mountain and the John

SPAULDING AND AUKE NU TRAILS

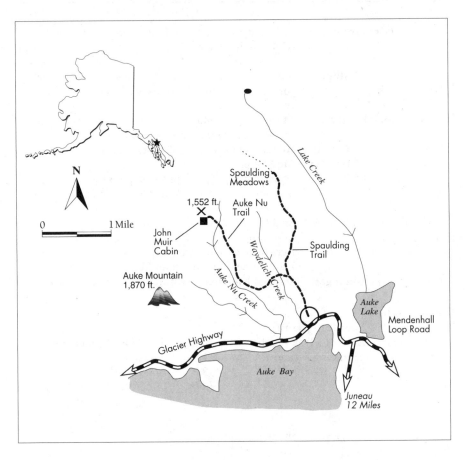

Muir Cabin, which is on the crest of a 1,550-foot knob near the head of Auke Nu Creek.

Hiking options include a shorter day hike to one of the destinations, a longer day hike that takes in both trails, or an overnight to the Muir cabin (reservation and fee required; see Appendix 2). Berry bushes grow in the neighborhood, and bears are fairly common. The trails are popular Nordic ski trails during Juneau's winter.

Spaulding Trail. The Spaulding Trail follows the route of an old corduroy log road to mining claims first staked in 1908. Victor Spaulding found a body of ore by tunneling through the moss and earth, but he never developed a mine. Hikers who explore around the meadows may find the remains of a cabin and prospect trenches.

The meadows and the views of the snow-covered peaks to the east, though, are the main event. Most of the trail remains relatively dry or planked until

The view from Spaulding Meadows.

the final stretch before the meadows, which may be wet enough to soak your boots.

Auke Nu Trail. The Auke Nu Trail crosses Waydelich Creek and climbs gradually on the east side of Auke Nu Creek, finally crossing the creek about 0.2 mile below the cabin. The creek is the best fresh water supply for overnighters at the cabin. Be sure to filter, boil, or treat the water. Juneau volunteers built this large, solid cabin as a Juneau centennial project in 1980.

Trip summary:	A half-day or overnight hike up the Herbert River to the Herbert Glacier.
Distance:	4 miles one way to the end of the maintained trail on the glacier's outwash plain; another mile of off-trail scrambling to the source of the river at the glacier.
Special features:	Lush forest and Herbert Glacier.
Location:	27.5 miles north of Juneau.
Difficulty:	Easy to the end of the trail; moderate to the river's source.
Condition:	More developed trail to the outwash plain; a route to the river's source.
Total elevation gain:	200 feet in, 100 feet out; another 300 feet to the river's source.
Best season:	Mid-May through October.
Maps:	USGS Juneau C-3 (SE).
Manager:	Tongass National Forest, Juneau Ranger District.

Finding the trailhead: Drive to Mile 27.5 of the Glacier Highway north of Juneau. The trailhead is on the right, 0.2 mile north of the Herbert River bridge.

The hike: Deep forest, a large river, a glacial "beach," bedrock and blue ice make a fine setting for this 4-mile trail up the Herbert River. The maintained trail ends on the Herbert Glacier's outwash plain, with Herbert Glacier in the distance. Lucky hikers might see a wild goat or two in the mountains above the glacier.

The lower part of the trail traverses the floor of the Herbert and Eagle River valleys, passing through a forest of Sitka spruce and, underneath the spruce, a mini-forest of devil's club and fern. The trail brushes up against the river twice in the first 1.5 miles, and then bears away from the stream and skirts a series of rocky, rolling hills.

At about 2.5 miles look for a small pond where you may see a duck or two, and at about 3.5 miles pass a beaver pond. In another 0.5 mile, the trail emerges onto the open outwash plain with part of the glacier visible ahead, still about 0.5 mile away. For folks who want a closer look, it's possible to scramble around to the river's source as it thunders out of the glacier.

The least brushy route follows the river up and bears left as the river curves to the north along the face of the glacier. A detour onto the rocky moraine is necessary; don't even think about trying to cross the river. Negotiating the moraine requires a little freelance scrambling, but the general direction of the route is obvious. The river's source is about a mile from the end of the trail. It's best to stay off the glacier unless you know what you're doing.

HERBERT GLACIER

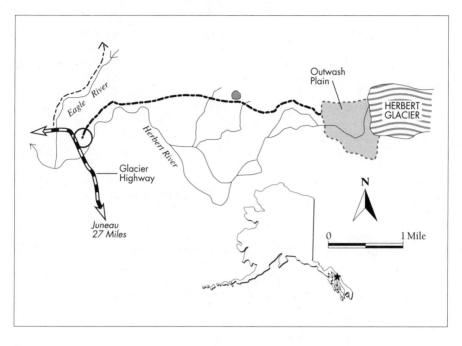

The sandbars and outwash in the last 0.5 mile of the trail are probably the best campsites on the hike.

Shorter hikes. The first 1.5 miles of the trail is a pleasant forest and river walk.

Trip summary:	A shorter day or overnight hike in the forest along Cowee Creek to the coast at Berner's Bay. The hike ends at Point Bridget, the point of land that separates Berner's Bay from Lynn Canal.
Distance:	3.5 miles one way to Point Bridget.
Special features:	Wildflower meadows, old-growth forest, coastal scenery and wildlife, two fee cabins, and salmon runs in late summer and fall.
Location:	39 miles north of Juneau, near the north end of the Juneau road system.
Difficulty:	Easy.
Trail type:	More developed trail to Blue Mussel Cabin at Mile 3.4; then a 0.1 mile hike over a stony/bouldery beach to Point Bridget.
Total elevation gain:	About 50 feet in, 250 feet out.
Best season:	April through mid-November.
Maps:	USGS Juneau C-3 (NW) (trail not shown); Alaska State Parks brochure *Point Bridget State Park*.
Manager:	Alaska State Parks, Southeast Area.

Key points:
  0.5   Cowee Creek Meadows
  2.1   Cowee Meadow Cabin
  2.4   Berm Beach
  3.4   Blue Mussel Cabin
  3.5   Point Bridget

Finding the trailhead: The trailhead is 39 miles north of Juneau on the Glacier Highway, on the left (north) side of the road, about a mile beyond the North Bridget Cove Trailhead.

The hike: A short, nearly flat hike with a lot of variety and two fee cabins for overnighters, Point Bridget is a great trip for beginning hikers and families. Kids, and adults too, will find plenty to keep them busy, exploring old-growth forest, wildflower meadows, stony beaches, and small creeks. In the wildlife department, Point Bridget hikers may see deer, geese, rafts of sea ducks, whales, sea lions, seals, and, beginning in late July, salmon runs in Cowee Creek (and maybe bears, too, so make plenty of noise on the trail, especially when the fish are running).

Cowee Meadows Cabin, at 2.1 miles, is in the meadow by Echoing Creek. The Blue Mussel Cabin, 3.4 miles from the trailhead, is on the coast just inside Point Bridget. A tiny creek runs by the cabin, and there's even a wood-fired sauna. See Appendix 2 for cabin reservation information.

Tent camping is possible in the drier parts of Cowee Meadows (the meadows roughly beyond the first mile of the trail are in the state park; check the brochure map to be sure you're on public land). There are also good tent

POINT BRIDGET

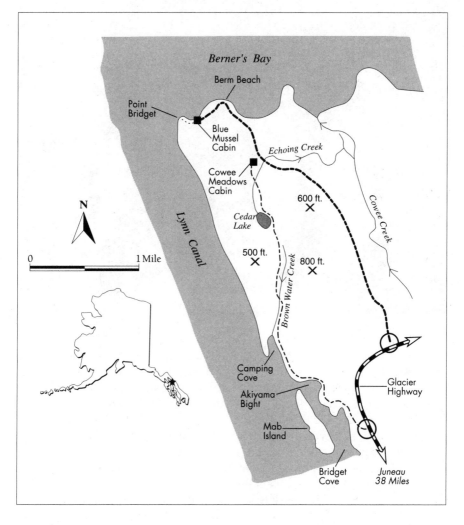

Berner's Bay

Berm Beach

Point Bridget

Blue Mussel Cabin

Echoing Creek

Cowee Meadows Cabin

Cowee Creek

600 ft. ✕

Cedar Lake

Lynn Canal

0 — 1 Mile

N

500 ft. ✕

800 ft. ✕

Brown Water Creek

Camping Cove

Akiyama Bight

Glacier Highway

Mab Island

Bridget Cove

Juneau 38 Miles

sites in the trees behind Berm Beach, at about 2.5 miles, with the nearest water from Echoing Creek, back by the Cowee Meadows Cabin.

The hike begins as a boardwalk through muskeg and forest, and reaches the upper end of Cowhee Meadows in about 0.5 mile. Then the trail skirts the meadows on the west, just inside the forest, to the Cowee Meadows Cabin. This forest/meadow edge is a good place to look and listen for a variety of birds and other wildlife. The drier parts of the meadow put on a wildflower show earlier in summer, practically swimming in shooting stars, lupine, chocolate lilies, irises, and other flowers.

At Echoing Creek, behind Cowee Meadows Cabin, a 0.7-mile, less developed, and minimally maintained trail leads to Cedar Lake, a small lake set in yellow cedars. The trail climbs about 300 feet to the lake.

343

Berm Beach on the Point Bridget Trail.

Beyond Echoing Creek and the cabin, the Point Bridget Trail continues to Berm Beach and its fine wildflower meadow. The beach is rocky, but holds some tidepool treasures. A minus tide is best for exploring the intertidal zone.

Beyond Berm Beach, the trail climbs the bluff into the forest. Just before it drops back down to the Blue Mussel Cabin, a short side trail leads to a small opening on the bluff with a picnic table. It's a good spot to take a break, have lunch, and look out over the ocean. Hikers might see whales, sea lions, and seals, and in late spring and early summer there will more than likely be at least one big raft of scoters, an abundant sea duck.

Shortly, the main trail dips down to the beach and the cabin. A rougher trail continues out the bluff to the forest on Point Bridget, but the easiest way to get to the point is by rock-hopping 0.1 mile along the beach.

Cedar Lake-North Bridget Cove Trails. The less developed, minimally marked and maintained Cedar Lake and North Bridget Cove trails form a loop of sorts with the more developed Point Bridget Trail. From the Cowee Meadows Cabin, it's about 0.7 mile to Cedar Lake, 2.2 miles to Camping Cove, and 4.2 miles to the North Bridget Trailhead on the Glacier Highway. From here, it's a mile north to the Point Bridget Trailhead. The trails form roughly a 9-mile loop, rated moderate for difficulty, with camping at Camping Cove, Akiyama Bight, and North Bridget Cove.

Fishing. Cowee Creek hosts Dolly Varden and cutthroat trout and runs of pink and silver salmon. Check the regulations before wetting a line.

HAINES

Haines, a small town in northern Southeast Alaska, is a state ferry stop, and has the best (and except for Skagway, the only) road connection to the rest of the state. There are no national parks or forests near Haines, so the small trail system here is entirely a volunteer and Alaska State Park effort.

94 MOUNT RIPINSKY AND 7 MILE SADDLE

Trip summary:	Longer day hikes, or an overnight trip in decent weather, on the high mountain ridge just north of Haines.
Distances:	Mount Ripinsky via Young Road trailhead: 3.8 miles one way.
	Peak 3,920 via 7 Mile trailhead: 3.2 miles one way.
	Mount Ripinsky-7 Mile Saddle traverse: 10 miles.
Special features:	An alpine ridge hike; sweeping views. Allow at least 8-10 hours for the day hike across the ridge.
Location:	The prominent mountain ridge above Haines.
Difficulty:	Shorter hikes from either end: moderately strenuous. Traverse: strenuous.
Trail type:	Young Road to 7 Mile Saddle: less developed.
	7 Mile to 7 Mile Saddle: more developed.
Total elevation gain:	Young Road-Mount Ripinsky: 3,200 feet.
	7 Mile to Peak 3,920: 3,900 feet.
	Traverse: About 4,800 feet from 7 Mile, 4,500 feet from Young Road.
Best season:	Late June to mid-September.
Maps:	USGS Skagway A-2 (NE) and B-2 (SE and SW).
Manager:	Haines State Forest, Haines volunteers.

Key points:

Young Road		7 Mile
0.0	Young Road Trailhead	10.0
2.5	Upper Johnson Creek	7.5
3.4	Mount Ripinsky, SE summit	6.6
3.8	Mount Ripinsky, NW summit	6.2
5.3	Jones Gap	4.7
6.8	Peak 3,920	3.2
8.1	7 Mile Saddle	1.9
10.0	7 Mile Trailhead	0.0

MOUNT RIPINSKY AND 7 MILE SADDLE

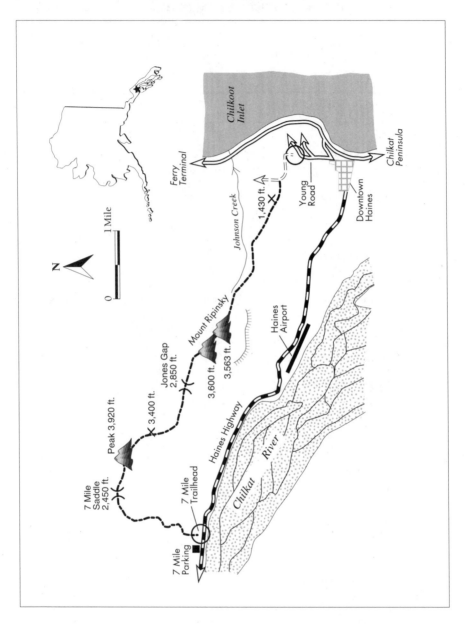

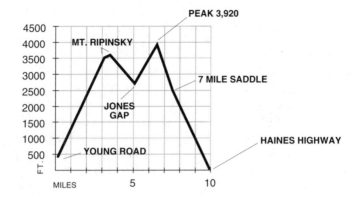

Finding the trailheads: Young Road Trailhead. As of this writing, the Young Road Trailhead is not well marked. From downtown Haines, follow 2nd Avenue uphill (north) from 2nd and Main. In 0.3 mile, continue straight ahead on Young Road where the main road angles right toward the ferry terminal. In another 0.3 mile, continue straight ahead again as Bjornstad Street angles right.

A mile from Main Street, at the crest of the road, look to the left for a steep, rough road to a watertank and radio relay station. If driving, park off the main road and walk up the road past the tank, bear right on the utility right-of-way, and follow it 0.4 mile to the point where it begins to descend. The trail begins on the left.

7 Mile Trailhead. Look for the trail sign and boardwalk trail at Mile 6.8 of the Haines Highway, northwest of Haines, on the north (mountain) side of the road. Park 0.1 mile west, at Mile 6.9, in the parking area on the north side of the road.

Shuttle distance between the trailheads is about nine miles, so a bicycle is a reasonable shuttle vehicle—there are bikes for rent in Haines.

The hikes: Mount Ripinsky, the peak at the top of the vertical rock wall north of Haines, is the first of a string of alpine summits that divide the Chilkat and Chilkoot River watersheds. The ridge ramble in the Takshanuk Mountains between Ripinsky, Peak 3,920, and 7 Mile Saddle is the only high-elevation trail hike near Haines.

The ridge can be heavy with snow until late June or early July. If traveling earlier, bring an ice ax and snowshoes and pay attention to avalanche danger. The route can be easy to lose in early summer snow and in bad weather, so carry topo maps and a compass, and be prepared to backtrack if necessary.

Hikers can choose between an out-and-back hike from one of the trailheads and, for the whole banana, the 10-mile traverse between the trailheads. The 7 Mile Trail is a better trail and climbs into the high country more quickly. Young Road, though, only a mile from downtown, is the easier access for travelers without cars.

347

The traverse between the two trailheads is a strenuous, very long day or overnight hike. Doing the traverse from Young Road saves about 300 feet of elevation gain, but walking north to south from 7 Mile may be a bit more scenic, with constant mountain and ocean views.

Mount Ripinsky Trail (Young Road). The trail climbs through a deep hemlock forest into alpine country, passing the headwaters of Johnson Creek before climbing to Ripinsky's southeast summit, elevation 3,563 feet. The northwest summit, 3,610 feet, is about 0.4 mile farther.

7 Mile Saddle Trail. The hike to the ridgeline is all business: steep, with many switchbacks, up a dry hillside of lodgepole pine and birch, past huge Sitka spruce trees, by tumbling streams, and through subalpine meadows and mountain hemlock thickets near treeline. Peak 3,920 is a steep climb from 7 Mile Saddle.

Mount Ripinsky/Peak 3,920 Ridge. The trail across the top of the ridge is marked intermittently with cairns and some stakes, but is easy enough to follow. Wolverines have chewed up many of the stakes from the original trail marking. Between the peaks, the route dips to 2,850 feet in Jones Gap, making a healthy climb no matter which way you're hiking.

The ridge is generally dry after all the snow is gone, by about mid-July. Camping is possible, with water nearby, near 7 Mile Saddle and on upper Johnson Creek. In *really* good weather, consider camping high on the ridge.

95 MOUNT RILEY

Trip summary:	Half-day and longer day hikes to the summit of Mount Riley, the 1,760-foot high point on the Chilkat Peninsula south of Haines. A shorter, easy side trip leads to the Chilkoot Inlet coast at Kelgaya Bay.
Distances:	Mount Riley: 2.8 miles from Mud Bay Road or 4 miles from Beach Road, or a 7-mile traverse between the two trailheads.
Special features:	Forest hikes and good views from the summit.
Location:	3 miles south of Haines.
Difficulty:	Moderate.
Trail type:	Generally more developed with a few rough spots; less developed near Mount Riley's summit.
Total elevation gain:	1,500 feet from Mud Bay Road; 1,600 feet from Beach Road.
Best season:	Late May through September.
Maps:	USGS Skagway A-2 (NE) and A-1 (NW).
Manager:	Alaska State Parks, Haines Ranger Station.

MOUNT RILEY

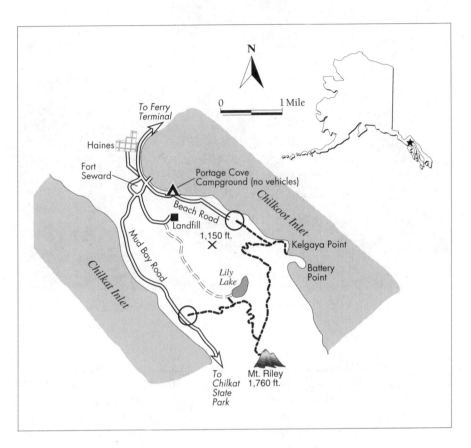

Key points:

From Mud Bay Road

1.1	Lily Lake spur trail
2.6	Junction: trail to Beach Rd.
2.8	Mount Riley summit

From Beach Road

0.9	Trail to Kelgaya Bay
2.2	Mount Riley ridge
3.8	Mount Riley/Mud Bay Trail
4.0	Mount Riley summit

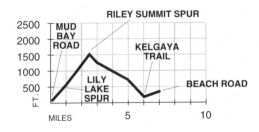

The Chilkat Peninsula, Haines, and Mount Ripinsky from the summit of Mount Riley.

Finding the trailheads: Mud Bay Road. From the Haines Post Office, near the end of the Haines Highway in Haines, drive southeast and take the first right turn in 0.1 mile. From here, it's 3 miles on Mud Bay Road to the trailhead. The road takes one left and two right jogs; just follow the signs. The parking area is on the right, and the trail begins on the left side of the road.

Beach Road. From the post office, drive southeast along the waterfront; the Haines Highway becomes Beach Road. Pass the Portage Cove Campground (no motor vehicles allowed), climb a hill, and follow the road through a subdivision to the trailhead at the end of the road, about 2 miles from the post office.

The hike: Mount Riley, at 1,760 feet elevation, is the highest point on the Chilkat Penisula. The peak, a rock outcrop in a sea of forest, offers sweeping views of Haines, Chilkat and Chilkoot Inlets, Taiya Inlet, and Lynn Canal, and the glaciated mountains all around. The Mount Riley Trail from Mud Bay Road is the shortest and most direct route to the top.

A longer route to the summit, the Battery Point/Riley Summit Trail from the end of Beach Road, is more varied and scenic. About a mile from the trailhead, a short side trail leads to the coast of Chilkoot Inlet, to Kelgaya Beach, and Kelgaya Point.

Mount Riley Trail from Mud Bay Road. The shorter hike from Mud Bay Road begins as a flat trail, but soon becomes a tangle of steep switchbacks through an open forest of spruce and hemlock. Near the peak, the trail reaches a marshy opening, crosses it on boardwalk, and meets the Riley Summit Trail from Beach Road. From here, it's 0.2 mile to the summit.

Riley Summit from Beach Road. The hike to Mount Riley from Beach Road climbs from the Battery Point junction to the ridgeline north of Mount Riley and continues to the peak. Below the ridgeline, the trail passes through coastal forest with huge rock outcrops. The ridgeline itself is a north-facing slope that may hold snow well into June.

Mount Riley Traverse. The Haines State Park ranger recommends starting the 7-mile traverse from Mud Bay Road. Road distance between the two trailheads is only 5 miles, so a bicycle can be used as a shuttle vehicle.

Lily Lake Road. This 4.5-mile hike to Mount Riley makes a good loop option for hikers without cars. Combining this hike with the trail from Beach Road forms a loop of sorts from the Fort Seward/Portage Cove area in the south part of Haines.

Follow FAA Road from behind Fort Seward's Officers Row (the row of big frame houses above the square) about a mile to the road closure, and continue about 2 miles on the Lily Lake water facility road to the intersection with the Mount Riley Trail from Mud Bay Road. Take the trail about 1.5 miles to the summit.

Kelgaya Bay. The hike to the coast at Kelgaya Bay is a shorter day or overnight trip. Though this trail is often referred to as the Battery Point trail, the developed trail ends at Kelgaya Point, the point north of Battery Point. From the Beach Road trailhead, hike 0.9 mile and turn left at the trail junction. It's just 0.1 mile to the beach and another 0.2 mile to Kelgaya Point. There are campsites in the forest behind the point. The only source of water is the small creek at the trail junction.

Look for birds like scoters and harlequin ducks, and keep an eye out for marine mammals. Earlier in the summer the coastal meadows bloom with shooting star, lupine, irises, chocolate lilies, and other wildflowers.

Trip summary:	Day or overnight hikes along the coast south of Haines to Seduction Point, at the southern tip of the Chilkat Peninsula. Seduction Point is a longer day hike, but there are coves along the way that make good shorter to half-day destinations.
Distance:	Up to 7 miles one way.
Special features:	Coastal scenery, wildlife. Avoid high tide between the two Twin Coves and between David's Cove and Dalasuga Point. Allow at least eight to ten hours for the round-trip day hike to Seduction Point.
Location:	8 miles south of Haines.
Difficulty:	Easy as far as Kalhagu Cove; moderate to moderately strenuous beyond.
Trail type:	More developed trail to Kalhagu Cove; less developed trail/route beyond. There is no trail between David's Cove and Dalasuga Point, just a scramble over rocks and boulders along the coast.
Total elevation gain:	Kalhagu Cove: about 150 feet in and 350 feet out. Seduction Point: 500 feet in and 700 feet out.
Best season:	May through mid-October.
Maps:	USGS Skagway A-1 and A-2.
Manager:	Chilkat State Park.

Key points:

1.2   Moose Meadows Beach
3.0   Kalhagu (West Twin) Cove
4.5   David's Cove
6.25 Dalasuga Point
6.75 Trail junction
7.0   Viewpoint
7.0   Campsite

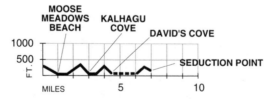

Finding the trailhead: From the Haines Post Office, near the end of the Haines Highway in Haines, drive southeast and take the first right turn onto Mud Bay Road in 0.1 mile. Mud Bay Road takes one left and two right jogs in the first 3 miles; just watch for signs, and drive 6.7 miles on the road to the Chilkat State Park entrance. Turn right at Chilkat State Park, and drive

SEDUCTION POINT

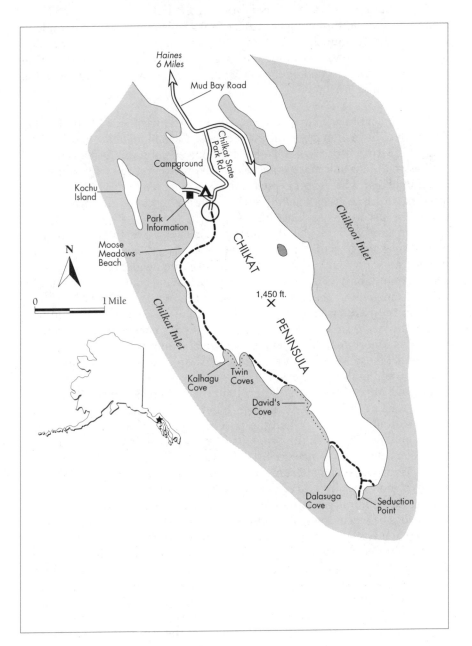

about 1.6 miles to a fork in the road. Take the left fork into the trailhead parking area.

The right fork leads to the campground in 0.1 mile, and to the homey log cabin information station/viewing deck in 0.4 mile. Beyond the station look for the park boat launch, an alternate beginning for the hike. At lower tide levels, it's possible to hike along the coast to meet the trail at Moose Meadows Beach. This is a good option early in the year when the first mile of the trail may still be icy.

The hike: The hike follows the coastline on the west side of the Chilkat Peninsula to Seduction Point, the point of land that splits Chilkat and Chilkoot Inlets. The trip features coastal meadows, rugged points, and small coves, as well as good bird and marine mammal viewing. If you're lucky, you might see humpback whales, orcas, sea lions, seals, or porpoises. Also look for large paper birch trees on the bluffs above the ocean; Dalasuga Point in particular has a fine grove of birches.

It's an easy, well-traveled trail as far as Kalhagu Cove, the western of the Twin Coves, and relatively easy as far as David's Cove. Beyond David's, private land and rough topography force hikers to negotiate a rough, rocky section of the coast. Check tide tables before leaving, and avoid high tide on this section and the beach section between the two Twin Coves.

From the parking area, the trail leads about a mile downhill through forest, crosses a small stream, and emerges on a coastal meadow known locally as Moose Meadows. The meadows are full of wildflowers in summer, and Moose Meadows Beach is a great spot to watch for shorebirds, seabirds, and marine mammals.

Beyond Moose Meadows the trail alternates between beach and forest before a climb and descent through blueberry patches and deep, mossy forest to Kalhagu Cove. When the trail emerges on the Kalhagu beach, it disappears briefly. Walk the beach and find the trail on the far side of the cove. Repeat this sequence at East Twin Cove.

At David's Cove, an old campsite in a meadow near the bend in the cove makes a good stopping place. To go farther, curl around the beach and begin the scramble through the jumble of rocks, boulders, outcrops, and storm-tossed logs between David's and Dalasuga Coves. The scramble can be treacherous when wet—stay high to avoid the slickest rocks.

Just before reaching Dalasuga Point, look for the trail leading uphill onto a grassy bluff. Once on the bluff, bear left—the faint path on the right wanders out to a viewpoint on the bluff. The trail from here is rarely traveled and may be difficult to follow in places. In about 0.5 mile the trail splits. The right fork leads to a view from Seduction Point, and the left drops down to a campsite (carry water) in the cove east of the point.

Allow at least ten hours if doing the entire trip as a day hike. There are possible campsites at most of the coves and several small streams for collecting water, but only Moose Meadows and David's Cove have campsites close to fresh water.

Expect to see and hear some low-elevation air traffic on the hike. This is a fine hike, and could be one of the premier trails in Southeast if trail conditions could be improved beyond David's Cove.

Shorter hikes. The easy hike to Moose Meadows, 1.2 miles one way, makes a great short day hike, family hike, or overnight.

SKAGWAY

Skagway, a small town at the head of Alaska's Inside Passage, is and always has been a tourist town, beginning with the Klondike gold rush of 1898. It's easily the most pedestrian-friendly town in the state; all the local trails are easy for travelers without cars to reach. Skagway is accessible by road from the Yukon and British Columbia, or by road and ferry from Haines.

This northern reach of Southeast Alaska is the driest outpost in the wettest region of the state. Granite mountains and trees like subalpine fir and lodgepole pine give the Skagway area a very different look from the rest of Southeast.

97 *LAUGHTON GLACIER*

Trip summary:	A half-day or overnight hike up the upper Skagway River to the Laughton Glacier.
Distance:	1.5 miles to the Laughton Glacier Cabin; 2.5 miles to the glacier.
Special features:	Laughton Glacier, subalpine fir forest, a fee cabin. The trailhead is not accessible by road; it is a flag stop on the White Pass and Yukon Route Railroad.
Location:	14 miles north of Skagway on the WP&YR Railroad.
Difficulty:	Easy to the cabin, moderate to the glacier.
Trail type:	More developed trail to the cabin; a route following Laughton Creek to the glacier.
Total elevation gain:	About 200 feet to the cabin and 1,000 feet to the glacier.
Best season:	Mid-June to mid-September.
Maps:	USGS Skagway C-1 (SE); cooperative city map *Skagway Trail Map.*
Manager:	Tongass National Forest, Juneau Ranger District.

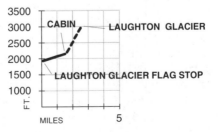

355

LAUGHTON GLACIER

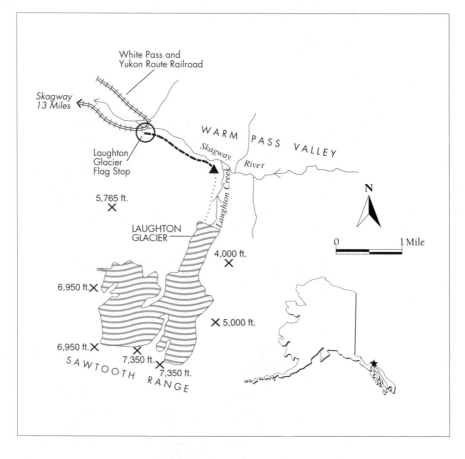

Finding the trailhead: The trailhead is the Laughton Glacier Flag Stop at White Pass and Yukon Route Railroad Mile 14; there is no road access. The train depot is on 2nd Avenue in downtown Skagway, just east of Broadway and the National Park Service visitor center. All flag stops must be ticketed at least a day in advance. Check with WP&YR (see Appendix 3) for a current schedule.

The hike: The highlight of the Laughton Glacier hike is the awesome view of the glacier's five fingers of ice spilling off the jagged, dark peaks of the Sawtooth Range. The Laughton, a valley glacier in the upper watershed of the Skagway River, has recently retreated, leaving a denuded trim line on each side of the valley that contrasts starkly with the evergreen forest above the glacier's recent path.

The hike follows the roaring river through a band of sweetly aromatic subalpine fir forest for 1.5 miles to the Forest Service's Laughton Glacier

356

The craggy fingers of Laughton Glacier and the Sawtooth Range.

Cabin. This upper valley of the Skagway River is known as Warm Pass Valley. A historic gold rush trail to Atlin, B.C., crosses the pass at the head of the valley.

The route to the glacier turns up the north-facing Laughton Glacier valley, beginning as a well-beaten path from the cabin. Hike over the rocky outwash plain, staying in the streambed or close by the creek. The fairly evident route stays on the west side of the creek, marked occasionally by rock cairns. In about a mile, the route peters out as it reaches a huge boulder pile in front of the rocky face of the glacier. Murky streams pour out from under the glacier. Don't approach any overhanging ice.

To see more, climb around the boulder field to the right (west) and hike farther along the margin of the ice. It's about another mile to the end of the valley, in a glacier-filled basin below the five crevassed, whipped-cream fingers of nearly vertical ice. Hike onto the glacier at your own risk.

There are a few tent sites in the trees near the cabin, at the confluence of the river and Laughton Creek. See Appendix 2 for cabin reservation information.

Denver Glacier. Another WP&YR flag stop, the Denver Glacier trailhead is at railroad mile 6. The trail is a rougher hike, 3.5 miles one way, to the moraine below the Denver Glacier. There is a Forest Service fee cabin, actually a renovated railroad car, on the railroad siding at the trailhead.

Trip summary:	A 3-5 day traverse through the Coast Mountains and "the longest museum in the world," from Alaska's coast to Lake Bennett in the interior of British Columbia. The hike follows the route of the Klondike gold rush of 1898.
Distance:	A 33-mile traverse.
Special features:	Forests, streams, lakes, alpine country, and the most historical hike in Alaska. Lake Bennett, at the north end of the trail, is not on a road, so hikers must use one of several alternate means of getting back to civilization. See "Finding the trailheads" below. Firearms are prohibited on the Chilkoot Trail. Permits are required. Parks Canada plans to begin limiting the number of hikers and charging a fee for using the trail on the Canadian side. Details had not been worked out by the time this book went to press, but hikers will be able to obtain permits and pay fees in Skagway. See Appendix 1 for Parks Canada's address and phone number.
Location:	Trailheads are at Dyea (dy ee'), 9 miles northwest of Skagway; Log Cabin; 27 miles north of Skagway; and Lake Bennett.
Difficulty:	Moderately strenuous.
Trail type:	More developed trail, with boulder hopping above Sheep Camp and on the Golden Stairs. Snowfields remain near the pass all summer.
Total elevation gain:	About 4,500 feet from Dyea to Bennett, the usual direction, or about 2,500 feet from Bennett to Dyea.
Best season:	Late June to mid-September.
Maps:	USGS Skagway C-1 (SW, NW) and Canadian topo maps White Pass (104 M/11), Homan Lake (104 M/14), and Tushi Lake (104 M/15). Most hikers use the National Park Service's map, *A Hiker's Guide to the Chilkoot Trail*.
Manager:	Klondike Gold Rush National Historical Park; Parks Canada, Chilkoot Trail National Historic Site.

Key points:

5.0 Finnegan's Point*
7.5 Canyon City*
10.5 Pleasant Camp*
11.5 Sheep Camp*
12.0 Sheep Camp ranger station/historic site
16.0 The Scales
16.5 Chilkoot Pass
20.5 Happy Camp*
23.0 Deep Lake*
26.0 Lake Lindeman*
29.0 Bare Loon Lake*
29.25 Log Cabin Cutoff Trail
33.0 Lake Bennett*
     * = Designated camp areas.

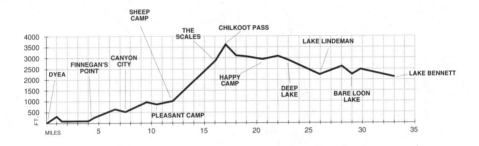

Finding the trailheads: Dyea and Log Cabin are road-accessible, while Bennett, at the end of the trail, is accessible, depending on what services are being offered in a particular year, by boat, train, or hiking. Shuttle vans from Skagway provide transportation to the Dyea and Log Cabin trailheads. See Appendix 3 for transportation information, and check with the Park Service visitor center at 2nd and Broadway in Skagway for up-to-date information before your hike.

Dyea. To reach the Dyea trailhead, drive just over 2 miles north of Skagway's 2nd Avenue on State Street/Klondike Highway to Dyea Road. Turn left and continue about 7 miles to the trailhead on the right side of the road, just before the Taiya River bridge. Trailhead parking and a ranger station are both currently located 0.4 mile before the trailhead.

Log Cabin. Drive 27 miles north of Skagway on the Klondike Highway, about 5 miles north of the Canadian customs station at Fraser. The parking area is on the left side of the highway.

Lake Bennett. Bennett, the end of the trail, is intermittently a railroad stop on the White Pass and Yukon Route Railroad, which runs to and from Skagway. There is also boat service from Bennett to Carcross, Y.T., where hikers can catch scheduled buses to Skagway or Whitehorse, Y.T. The Log Cabin Cutoff Trail, at Mile 29.25 of the hike, is a spur trail that leads to the

CHILKOOT PASS

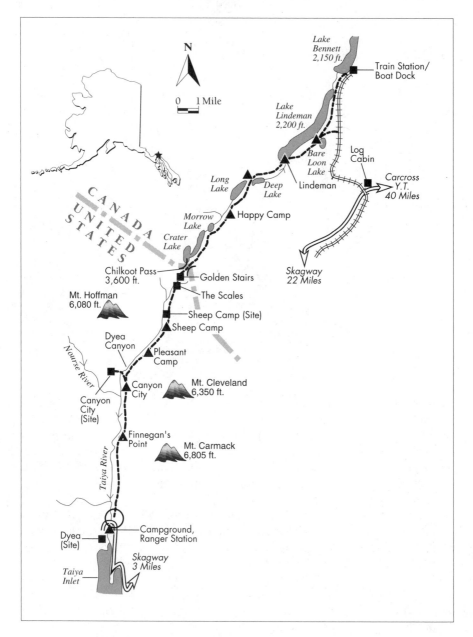

Hikers at the top of the Golden Stairs, Chilkoot Trail.

railroad tracks. Some hikers walk the tracks, a total of eight miles, to the Klondike Highway at Log Cabin, then take a bus or shuttle van from there. If the train is running, taking it is an easier and safer option than hiking the tracks.

The hike: An outdoor museum, a beautiful hike, and the only long trail traverse in Southeast Alaska, the Chilkoot Trail attracts hikers from all over the world. The hike is amazingly diverse, including coastal and interior forests, a large river, a snowy mountain basin, rocky country above treeline, sparkling alpine streams, and huge lakes.

Large numbers of hikers, designated campsites, cooking shelters, and ranger stations make this, well, not exactly a *wilderness* hike, but there are compensations—a chance to meet hikers from all over the country and the world, and the experience of hiking through an "outdoor museum" of artifacts from the gold rush. Please leave all the artifacts in place, and take photos for your memories. The peak season of use is mid-July to mid-August. If you think there are a lot of hikers on the trail now, you should have been there in 1898.

The "historically correct" direction is south to north, from Dyea to Lake Bennett, but the hike is equally fine from north to south, and even a little easier starting at either Bennett or Log Cabin. With Parks Canada imposing a fee on hikers crossing the pass (as was planned as this book went to press), some hikers may be tempted to do the trip as an out-and-back hike from Dyea to the pass.

Hikers must camp in the designated camp areas. Each camp includes a toilet, several tent sites, and a pole or cache for protecting food from bears. Most also have small shelters. Please build fires only in the stoves in the shelters; cook in the shelters or at least 300 feet from any campsite; hang or cache your food when in camp; and bring a good tent—the small shelters are for cooking and warming only. Keeping bears from developing a taste for hikers' food is a big concern here.

The hike may seem tame with all these amenities, but the weather in the high country can be just as nasty and unforgiving as anywhere else in Alaska. Between Sheep Camp and Deep Lake is a long, difficult ten miles of alpine hiking. Some Chilkoot trekkers bring cotton clothes and marginal rain gear, which could make the trip miserable if not dangerous in poor weather.

Dyea to Sheep Camp. The lower part of the trail follows the Taiya River valley through coastal forest. It stays low for the first 5 miles except for some brief climbing. Parts of this section of trail follow an old logging road. Finnegan's Point, the site of a short-lived toll road during the gold rush, is the first camp area on the trail.

Canyon City grew up at the mouth of the Taiya River canyon. The "city" had electric lights and was the lower terminal of a tram line for hauling supplies over the pass. The camp area now lies in a cottonwood flat by the river, next to a small, cascading creek. The historic townsite is across the river, about 0.5 mile beyond the camp area, but not much is left standing.

The river between Canyon City and Pleasant Camp is a crashing, bouldery stream in a deep canyon. For camping, Pleasant Camp is usually not as crowded as Sheep Camp.

Sheep Camp is in the last mile of forest before the subalpine and alpine section of the hike begins. Most hikers camp here because it's the last camp area before the pass, and the next day is a long day to Happy Camp or Deep Lake, the next designated camps. A ranger station and the historic townsite are about 0.5 mile up the trail.

Sheep Camp to Lake Lindeman. Above Sheep Camp, the mountain wonderland begins. Waterfalls tumble down sheer granite faces, and cottonwoods splintered by avalanches are a reminder of the 1898 snowslide that killed about sixty stampeders.

Above treeline, Long Hill leads to The Scales, where tram operators weighed their loads before hoisting them over the pass. Tram towers and piles of cable and equipment remain here, the most concentrated group of artifacts on the trail. From The Scales, it's a boulder-field climb up the Golden Stairs (men carved snow steps here in 1898) to a great view of the Taiya River valley, and a short hike farther leads to the pass and the Parks Canada warden cabin and warming shelter. Welcome to Canada.

Snow stays near the pass and in the Crater Lake basin north of the pass most of the summer. The hike follows a valley of lakes and cascading streams all the way to Lindeman. Between the camps at Happy Camp and Deep Lake, the trail climbs the ridge east of Long Lake. Happy Camp is an alpine camp, and Deep Lake is at treeline.

The trail descends to forested Lake Lindeman west of a sheer-walled gorge carved by Deep Lake's outlet stream.

Lindeman to Bennett. There are two camp areas, a Parks Canada camp, and an interpretive tent at Lake Lindeman. Some years the wardens lead guided hikes to the Lindeman City townsite. The historic Lindeman cemetery is above the trail.

Leaving Lindeman, the trail follows a granite, piney ridge to Bare Loon Lake (campsite, no shelter). In another 0.25 mile, the spur trail to the railroad tracks and Log Cabin forks right. The final miles of the hike are soft and sandy. Near the north end of Lake Lindeman is a private cabin, and off the trail between the lake and Lake Bennett is Lindeman Rapids, which claimed several stampeders' outfits and a few lives in the spring of 1898.

The historic church at Bennett is the only gold-rush era building still standing on the trail. The train station and boat dock are just around the corner of the lake to the east.

The Rush of '98

"All Fool's Day, and most all the fools are here" is how one man's diary describes the stampede on the Chilkoot Trail during the Klondike gold rush. It was April 1, 1898, just two days before avalanches killed about sixty people below Chilkoot Pass. The uninhabited peaks rang with voices as the thousands of stampeders plodded back and forth through the heavy snow, carrying enough supplies through the pass to last a year of prospecting.

The stampede to the Klondike began in July of 1897, when the steamship Portland landed in Seattle with two tons of gold from the Klondike, a river in the nearly-unknown Yukon. The Seattle Post-Intelligencer immediately printed a special edition, plastering it with the screaming headline "Gold! Gold! Gold! Gold!" Practically overnight, salesmen were hawking supplies, guidebooks and maps to the flood of would-be prospectors, and dubious-looking boats began hauling the stampeders north.

Most of them ended up at the head of Alaska's Inside Passage, where two passes, White Pass and Chilkoot Pass, connected the sea with the headwaters of the Yukon. The Chilkoot Trail, the shorter and more popular, led 33 miles through the mountains to Lakes Lindeman and Bennett, where stampeders built boats to float the remaining 550 miles to the Klondike. Instant wilderness cities popped up along the trail and by the lakes, but after just one year, the rush was over, and the trail was deserted by 1899.

By summer, 30,000 stampeders had reached the new gold rush town of Dawson, but they were too late; all of the good ground had already been staked. Before they had even left the West Coast, prospectors who were already in the Yukon and Alaska had sprinted to the Klondike and staked their claims. Soon most of the newcomers melted away, either back south or on to new gold strikes in Alaska.

Trip summary:	Hikes to mountain lakes above Skagway: Lower Dewey Lake is a shorter day hike, and Upper Dewey is a longer day or overnight hike. Devil's Punch Bowl, a smaller alpine lake, is a side trip from Upper Dewey.
Distances:	Lower Dewey Lake: 0.6 mile one way.
	Upper Dewey Lake: 3 miles one way.
Special features:	Lakes, alpine country, and a trail shelter at Upper Dewey Lake. No camping at Lower Dewey Lake without a City of Skagway permit.
Location:	Above downtown Skagway.
Difficulty:	Lower lake: easy.
	Upper lake: moderately strenuous.
Trail type:	Lower lake: more developed.
	Upper lake: less developed, very steep and slow hiking in places.
Total elevation gain:	Lower lake: 500 feet.
	Upper lake: 3,100 feet.
Best season:	Lower lake: mid-May through early October.
	Upper lake: mid-June to mid-September.
Maps:	USGS Skagway B-1 (NW); cooperative city map *Skagway Trail Map.*
Manager:	City of Skagway and Tongass National Forest, Juneau Ranger District.

Key points:
    0.5 Sturgill's Landing (Hike 100) trail junction to right
    0.6 Lower Dewey Lake Loop Trail and lake access
    0.7 Upper Dewey Lake Trail to right
    3.0 Upper Dewey Lake
    4.2 Devil's Punch Bowl

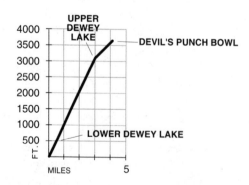

DEWEY LAKES AND STURGILL'S LANDING

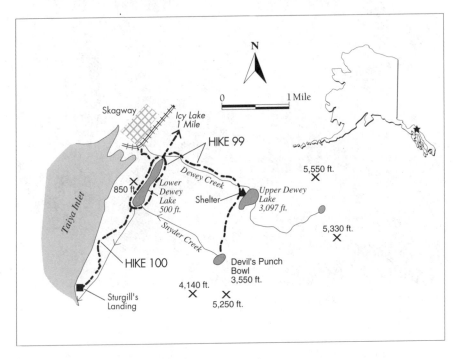

Finding the trailhead: In downtown Skagway, follow 2nd Avenue east from the Park Service visitor center for 3 blocks. If driving, park near here on the street or in the lot east of the railroad station on 2nd Avenue. On foot, turn left along the railroad siding just before 2nd Avenue crosses the tracks. In 0.1 mile, cross the tracks (watch for trains!) to the trailhead.

The hike: There are two Dewey Lakes, and they are two very different hikes. Lower Dewey Lake lies in the trees 500 feet above downtown Skagway, and the 0.6-mile trail is easy if a bit steep. Upper Dewey Lake, in a subalpine basin at 3,097 feet elevation, is a longer, very steep haul up the mountain slope above the lower lake.

From the trailhead, follow marked switchbacks about 0.5 mile up to a trail junction near Lower Dewey Lake. The trail to Sturgill's Landing forks right here. 0.1 mile farther are a spur trail to the lower lake and a fork to the Lower Dewey Lake Loop Trail. Continue straight ahead another 0.1 mile and turn right at a marked junction for Upper Dewey Lake.

Lower Dewey Lake. The lower lake, long and narrow, lies in a slot in the bench above the city. For the quickest and easiest access to the lake, continue straight ahead at the first trail junction at 0.5 mile and turn right to the shoreline in 0.1 mile. The loop trail leads about two miles around the lake.

Upper Dewey Lake Trail shelter.

Picnic sites dot several points around the lake. Camping is legal here only with a permit from the City of Skagway (see Appendix 1).

Upper Dewey Lake. The trail to the upper lake climbs very steeply along the course of cascading Dewey Creek. The grade eases to a normal climb about a third of the way up, and there are some wet, eroded sections beyond. Just below the lake, the forest opens into subalpine stands of mountain hemlock and subalpine fir and crosses the creek on a footbridge.

The lake is just below treeline in a classic cirque, or glacial basin, below steep, rocky slopes, and peaks. The trail shelter is a log cabin, a little rough inside but well-weatherproofed. There are also campsites on the lake.

Hiking around the lake is easy and scenic, and there is a good side trip up into the basin above the lake. Sheer rock walls rim the basin, and a waterfall tumbles down from above.

Devil's Punch Bowl. A less developed trail/route leads from Upper Dewey Lake to Devil's Punch Bowl, an icy lake in an alpine cirque. Bear right about 100 feet beyond the Upper Dewey Cabin to find the path. Marked with rock cairns, the route leads through stunted mountain hemlocks, boulders, and alpine tundra across the ridge to the south to Devil's Punch Bowl. The lake's shoreline is rugged and not too inviting for camping. The best views on the Dewey Lakes trip are from the high point on the Devil's Punch Bowl Trail.

Fishing. There are a few small trout in Lower Dewey Lake.

Trip summary:	A half-day or overnight hike to Sturgill's Landing, the site See Map on Page 365 of an early Skagway wood camp, on the coast of Taiya Inlet.
Distance:	3.5 miles one way.
Special features:	Coastal scenery and wildlife, Lower Dewey Lake, and a "magic" forest.
Location:	Southeast of downtown Skagway.
Difficulty:	Moderate.
Trail type:	More developed to Lower Dewey Lake, less developed beyond. The final stretch of the trail is rocky and steep.
Total elevation gain:	500 feet in, 500 feet out.
Best season:	Mid-May to early October.
Maps:	USGS Skagway B-1 (NW); cooperative city map *Skagway Trail Map*.
Manager:	City of Skagway and Tongass National Forest, Juneau Ranger District.

Key points:

0.5   Upper Dewey Lake Trail junction (Hike 99)
1.5   South end of Lower Dewey Lake
3.5   Sturgill's Landing

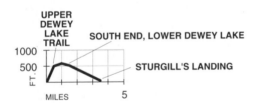

Finding the trailhead: In downtown Skagway, follow 2nd Avenue east from the Park Service visitor center for three blocks. If driving, park near here on the street or in the lot east of the railroad station on 2nd Avenue. On foot, turn left along the railroad siding just before 2nd Avenue crosses the tracks. In 0.1 mile, cross the tracks (watch for trains!) to the trailhead.

The hike: Sturgill's Landing is in a small rocky cove on Taiya Inlet. Sturgill's was a wood camp in Skagway's earlier days. Equipment from the woodcutting operation can still be seen along the trail and in the cove. The mountains and glaciers across the fjord make a fine view, and hikers may be lucky enough to see marine mammals in the cove.

There is a small Forest Service camp and picnic area above the log-strewn beach, with tables, fire pits, an outhouse, and a very few tent spots nestled among the rocks, pines, and spruces. A small creek empties into the cove just east of the camp/picnic area.

Follow the trail from Skagway toward Lower Dewey Lake, and turn right at the intersection in 0.5 mile, at the top of the climb. Follow the west side of the Lower Dewey Lake Loop Trail to the end of the lake, about 1.5 miles from the trailhead. Continue straight ahead beyond the lake toward Sturgill's.

The trail tunnels through sections of densely-clustered hemlock forest that locals call the "magic forest." Toward the end of the hike, the trail becomes steep, rocky, and poorly defined, but the destination is obvious. Take care with children on this final stretch. Once in sight of the cove, bear right to find the camp/picnic area.

OFF THE BEATEN PATH: DISCOVERING WILDERNESS ALASKA

Traveler, there is no path; paths are made by walking.

-Spanish proverb.

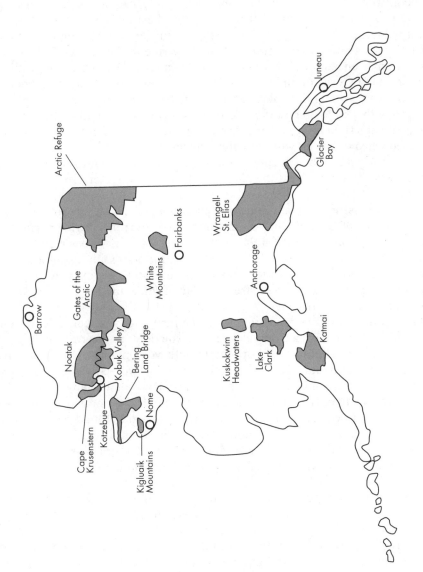

This section offers brief descriptions of a few of the remote hiking areas in the state. There are no trails or other facilities in most of these areas. You'll need to carefully plan your own route from the hundreds of possible hikes by studying topographic maps and gathering information from public land managers and from air taxi operators who fly into the areas. The topographic maps listed under each entry are from the U.S. Geological Survey's 1:250,000-scale series.

Discovering Alaska this way, on your own initiative and taking complete responsibility for your own experience and safety, can be the experience of a lifetime. For many, a guided trip may be the best introduction to Alaska's real wilderness. Contact park and refuge managers (see Appendix 1) for a list of guides and air taxi companies that operate in their areas. It's best to be an experienced trail hiker and do at least a few of the alpine ridge hikes in the state before attempting a fly-in trip into a remote wilderness area.

There are several possibilities for remote trips, ranging from a two-week march with a 60-to-80 pound pack to a base camp and day hikes in a choice spot. What's right for you depends on how much ground you want to cover and how heavy a pack you are willing to carry.

There are a number of considerations for taking trips into remote, trailless areas. Be sure to read the *Hiking in Alaska* introductory section to this guide.

Stream crossings. Stream courses that don't even show up as perennial streams on USGS maps can become uncrossable torrents during periods of heavy rain. Leave yourself a way out in case you can't cross a stream on your route, and ask for advice from someone familiar with the area if your route involves crossing a larger stream or river. Don't rely entirely on pilots for this information; they see streams from altitude and are not always experienced in river crossings.

Backup plans. Leave your itinerary and a plan with a responsible person, in addition to your air taxi operator, in case you don't return on schedule. Be sure to discuss alternate pickup points with your pilot in case you can't reach your destination. Consider carrying a small two-way radio for ground to air communication in case of unavoidable delays, route changes, or injury.

Planning your route. Cross-country travel is much easier if you can avoid brush and tussocks as much as possible. Tussocks are wet-tundra cottongrass lumps that make hiking slow and difficult. Focus on higher alpine areas; elevations above 3,000 feet are generally free of brush and tussocks. Ridgelines and stream gravel bars make the best hiking routes. Most Alaska off-trail hiking is rugged and difficult, especially for hikers accustomed to hiking on developed trails. For planning purposes and until you know your own pace, count on covering no more than six map miles (one township, the survey squares on 1:250,000 topographic maps) per day on a remote trip.

Leaving a margin of safety. Extra food, a good first aid kit, bear protection, and good clothing and equipment are exponentially more important on a trip into Alaska's true wilderness.

GATES OF THE ARCTIC

Description:	A national park and preserve in the heart of the Brooks Range, America's northernmost mountains.
Location:	In arctic north-central Alaska.
Access:	Air charter from Bettles or Kotzebue, which are served by scheduled air; scheduled air service to Anaktuvuk Pass; or hiking from the Dalton Highway.
Best season:	Mid-June to early September.
USGS maps:	Ambler River, Chandalar, Chandler Lake, Hughes, Killik River, Philip Smith Mountains, Survey Pass, Wiseman.
Manager:	Gates of the Arctic National Park and Preserve.

The area: The Gates of the Arctic is a remote and undeveloped park of 8.5 million acres, most of which has been designated wilderness. Gates is Bob Marshall country; the early Forest Service wilderness crusader's travels here were the beginnings of the movement to designate a wilderness park in the central Brooks Range. Marshall coined the name for the area, for Frigid Crags and Boreal Mountain, two peaks that form a "gate" across the North Fork of the Koyukuk River.

The main ranges in the park are the Endicott Mountains in the eastern part of the park and the Schwatka Mountains in the west. Mount Igikpak,

An unnamed canyon in Gates of the Arctic National Park and Preserve.

elevation 8,510 feet in the Schwatka Mountains, is the highest point in the park.

The higher parts of the ranges and the north slope are arctic tundra, while the lower valleys on the south side are forested. The park is rugged, mountainous, and millions of grass tussocks make hiking with a heavy pack slow and difficult. There are glaciers only at the highest elevations, so most high passes are glacier-free, and the park's streams run clear except during high water.

The park's many wild valleys and mountains make great hiking. The upper watersheds of the Koyukuk, John, Alatna, and Kobuk south of the range, the Itkillik, Anaktuvuk, Chandler and Killik north of the range, and the Noatak flowing west offer an incredible variety of arctic and alpine tundra rambling. A number of lakes in the park make good dropoff and pickup points for chartered aircraft.

Park headquarters are in Fairbanks, and there are ranger stations at Bettles, Anaktuvuk Pass, and Coldfoot. Call or stop by one of the offices before your trip to check on current conditions.

ARCTIC NATIONAL WILDLIFE REFUGE

Description:	A huge, remote wildlife refuge extending from the south side of the Brooks Range to the Arctic Coast.
Location:	In the arctic northeast corner of Alaska.
Access:	Air charter from Fort Yukon or Kaktovik, both of which are on scheduled air routes from Fairbanks.
Best season:	Mid-June to early September.
USGS maps:	Arctic, Barter Island, Black River, Chandalar, Christian, Coleen, Demarcation Point, Flaxman Island, Mount Michelson, Philip Smith Mountains, Sagavanirktok, Table Mountain.
Manager:	Arctic National Wildlife Refuge.

The area: Made a household word by the debate over oil development on the coastal plain, the Arctic Refuge extends across the Brooks Range from the forested south slope to the Arctic Ocean. It is the only protected area in the United States that spans the whole range of subarctic and arctic ecosystems.

The highest peaks, around 9,000 feet elevation, and the only significant mountain glaciation in the entire Brooks Range lie in the Romanzof and Franklin Mountains at the heart of the refuge. A smaller but dramatic flanking range, the Sadlerochit Mountains, lies on an east-west axis north of the main ranges. The northwest corner of the refuge includes parts of the Philip Smith Mountains.

North of the range, several swift, braided rivers flow north to the ocean through the country's only protected expanse of arctic tundra plain. The rivers have lyrical names like Ivishak, Okpilak, Aichilik, Kongakut, Jago, and Hulahula, which was named by Hawaiian whalers in the 1890s. The Porcupine caribou herd migrates through the mountains and along the coast on both sides of the international border, calving on the coastal plain from late May to mid-June.

There are only a few lakes in this section of the Brooks Range. Tundra airstrips and gravel bar landing areas are fairly widespread, though, for hiking access.

WRANGELL-ST. ELIAS

Description:	Alaska's largest mountain-and-glacier wilderness, and the largest national park in the U.S., encompassing four major mountain ranges.
Location:	Southcentral Alaska, east of Glennallen.
Access:	By road, via the McCarthy and Nabesna Roads (See Hikes 54-57); by air charter from McCarthy, Glennallen, Nabesna, Tok, or Cordova.
Best season:	June to mid-September, depending on elevation.
USGS maps:	Bering Glacier, Cordova, Gulkana, Icy Bay, McCarthy, Mount St. Elias, Nabesna, Valdez, Yakutat.
Manager:	Wrangell-St. Elias National Park and Preserve.

The area: Wrangell-St. Elias is a huge, diverse park and preserve that, together with Glacier Bay National Park and national and provincial parks in Canada, make up the largest protected area in the world. Four major mountain ranges converge here. The variety of geology and mountain landscapes in the park is outstanding.

The Wrangell and St. Elias mountains are high, glaciated ranges that form a mountain wall across the center of the park/preserve, broken only by a gap along the Chitina and White Rivers. The Wrangells are volcanoes, while the St. Elias is a coastal range featuring some of the continent's highest peaks, including Mount Logan. Logan, across the border in Canada, is second in height only to Denali in North America. Mount St. Elias, 18,008 feet, is the highest point in the park.

In the north end of the park/preserve the Mentasta and Nutzotin mountains form the eastern end of the Alaska Range. The Chugach Mountains rise along the southern coast of the park.

On the north, or Interior, side of the Wrangell-St. Elias chain, tundra and forest extend down to the upper Copper River valley. On the south slope, moisture from the Gulf of Alaska feeds the ranges' massive glaciers and icefields.

There are many good fly-in hiking routes in the park/preserve. Charter aircraft can fly backpackers to a number of ridgetop landing areas, stream gravel bars, and airstrips left from the area's mining days. Ask for ideas at the park visitor center in Copper Center. There are also park ranger stations at Chitina, Slana, and Yakutat.

One trip-planning consideration is the Dall sheep hunting season in parts of Wrangell-St. Elias, beginning in early to mid-August.

KATMAI

Description:	A national park and preserve created around the Valley of Ten Thousand Smokes, the valley buried in ash by the 1912 Katmai eruption.
Location:	Southwest Alaska, at the north end of the Alaska Peninsula, east of King Salmon.
Access:	Scheduled air to King Salmon and then scheduled float plane to Brooks Camp in the park; or air charter from King Salmon or Kodiak to remote locations in the park.
Best season:	June through mid-September.
USGS maps:	Afognak, Iliamna, Karluk, Mount Katmai, Naknek.
Manager:	Katmai National Park and Preserve.

The area: Katmai covers 4 million acres in a swath across the Aleutian Range, from the coast to the lakes region west of the crest of the range. It is a land of steaming volcanoes, large lakes and rivers, a wild Pacific coastline, and a healthy population of brown bears. The volcanoes in the range are active. The spectacular 1912 eruption of Novarupta, a vent on the side of Mount Katmai, buried the Ukak Valley under 700 feet of ash and pumice, creating the Valley of Ten Thousand Smokes.

The Valley and its environs—Knife Creek, Windy Creek, the Buttress Range, Novarupta, and Katmai Pass—are the most common backpacking destinations in the park. A concession-operated shuttle bus (fee) carries hikers and sightseers over the 23-mile road from Brooks Camp to the Three Forks overlook above the valley. There is no developed trail, but visitors can hike down into the valley from the overlook.

Some of the peaks at the head of the Valley can be climbed without crossing glaciers, but others require glacier-travel equipment and experience. High winds and sudden weather changes streaking through Katmai Pass from Shelikof Strait can make backpacking here a challenge.

Brooks Camp includes a lodge, a campground, and a small store, and bear-viewing platforms near the mouth of Brooks River and a short walk away at Brooks Falls. A trail leads from the campground about four miles to Dumpling Mountain, which overlooks the entire Brooks and Naknek Lake area.

There are other, more remote hiking destinations as well, including the Walatka Mountains in the northern part of the park. Backpacking permits are recommended; pick one up at park headquarters in King Salmon or the visitor center at Brooks Camp. Anywhere you visit in Katmai, be prepared for the park's most charismatic inhabitants, its brown bears. Pick up the required bear-resistant food container for your backpack trip at King Salmon or Brooks Camp.

LAKE CLARK

Description:	A park and preserve in the Aleutian and Alaska Ranges west of Cook Inlet.
Location:	In Southcentral Alaska, across Cook Inlet from Anchorage and the Kenai Peninsula.
Access:	Seat-rate fares on flights from Anchorage to Port Alsworth or Iliamna and then air charter from there into the park; or air charter from Anchorage or Kenai.
Best season:	Mid-June to mid-September.
USGS maps:	Lake Clark, Lime Hills, Iliamna, Kenai, Seldovia, Tyonek.
Manager:	Lake Clark National Park and Preserve.

The area: The 4-million acre Lake Clark National Park and Preserve includes Pacific coastline, glacier-covered volcanoes, wild rivers, huge blue-green lakes, precipitous granite peaks, plenty of wilderness hiking country, and some of Alaska's finest mountain scenery. Mount Redoubt and Mount Iliamna, the park's two 10,000-foot plus volcanoes, are visible from Anchorage. Lake Clark is a forty-mile-long lake west of the mountain chain.

There are many good hiking routes in the park/preserve. Air charters to the string of big lakes in the western foothills, especially Telequana, Turquoise, and Twin Lakes, provide the best hiking access. From the lakes, there are routes into and through the Alaska Range. There are a number of routes that involve glacier travel, which is for the experienced and equipped only. The "Telequana Trail," a historic route between Lake Clark and Telequana Lake, is not a developed trail.

The lakes in the northwest part of the park/preserve are within the preserve and open to hunting during the late summer and fall.

The field headquarters for the park/preserve are at Port Alsworth on Lake Clark. A short developed trail leads to Tanalian Falls at Port Alsworth.

KUSKOKWIM HEADWATERS

Description:	A section of the Alaska Range between Denali and Lake Clark National Parks, at the headwaters of the South Fork of the Kuskokwim River.
Location:	In Southcentral Alaska, 100 miles northwest of Anchorage.
Access:	Air charter from Anchorage or McGrath.
Best season:	Late June to early September.
USGS maps:	McGrath, Lime Hills.
Manager:	State of Alaska, Division of Land.

The area: Despite being the second-longest river in Alaska, the Kuskokwim River is relatively unknown. At the headwaters of the Kuskokwim's South Fork and the Big and Stony rivers is a section of the Alaska Range that is not designated parkland, but is wild, beautiful, and undiscovered country. The Revelation Mountains, a spectacular range of peaks with names like Mount Mausolus, Babel Tower, The Apocalypse, and Golgotha, lie northwest of the main divide. Access is somewhat difficult, but a few strips and small lakes provide aircraft landing spots.

WHITE MOUNTAINS

Description:	Limestone peaks and high, rolling ridges in the heart of the million-acre White Mountains National Recreation Area.
Location:	In the Interior, north of Fairbanks.
Access:	The Steese Highway and Nome Creek Road.
Best season:	June through mid-September.
USGS maps:	Circle, Livengood.
Manager:	Bureau of Land Management, Northern District Office.

The area: Mount Prindle, elevation 5,286 feet, and Rocky Mountain, 5,062 feet, are the prominent peaks in the White Mountains, a range that stands out above the surrounding Yukon-Tanana uplands between Beaver Creek and the Yukon River. The best access is from the trailhead on Nome Creek, at the upstream end of the new Nome Creek Road. There is good dry tundra hiking above about 3,500 feet on long and challenging wilderness hiking routes into the heart of the range.

NORTHWEST ALASKA

Description:	A few accessible hiking areas in the remote northwest corner of Alaska.
Location:	Western and Arctic Alaska, in the vicinity of Nome and Kotzebue.
Access:	Mainly air charter from Nome or Kotzebue. Scheduled air service runs to Nome and Kotzebue from Anchorage and Fairbanks.
Best season:	June through mid-September for lower elevations; mid-June to early September for higher elevations.
USGS maps:	See below.
Manager:	National Park Service, with the exception of the Kigluaik Mountains area, which is managed by the Bureau of Land Management, Northern District.

The areas: In the **Bering Land Bridge National Preserve** near Nome is remote hiking terrain on ridges near the Continental Divide, among granite pinnacles set in arctic tundra. The preserve is used extensively by local people for subsistence hunting and fishing. Access is by charter flight from Nome; see USGS maps *Bendeleben* and *Kotzebue*.

Cape Krusenstern National Monument, on the cape just northwest of Kotzebue, records about 6,000 years of human history in a series of over one hundred beach ridges formed by sea level fluctuations. Behind the beaches limestone hills back a maze of lagoons. The beaches and hills make the best hiking. People from Kotzebue and nearby villages own parcels of land on the cape and use the area for subsistence hunting and fishing, so please respect private property and traditional uses. Access is by a short charter flight from Kotzebue; see USGS maps *Kotzebue* and *Noatak*.

Kobuk Valley National Park and Noatak National Preserve, east and northeast of Kotzebue, are best known for their namesake rivers. These NPS areas also include some remote hiking country in the Baird and De Long Mountains, the westernmost ranges of the Brooks Range that enclose the Noatak basin. Extensive areas of sand dunes south of the Kobuk River can be explored on foot. See USGS maps *Baird Mountains, De Long mountains, Misheguk Mountain, Ambler River,* and *Howard Pass*.

The Kigluaik Mountains, a small, alpine range of sawtooth peaks north of Nome can be explored from Nome's road system. See USGS maps *Nome, Teller, Bendeleben,* and *Solomon*.

GLACIER BAY

Description:	A park and preserve set among mountains, fjords, and tidewater glaciers.
Location:	In Southeast Alaska, northwest of Juneau.
Access:	Scheduled air or private ferry to Gustavus from Juneau and Haines, and bus from the airport to the park headquarters at Bartlett Cove. A tour boat run by the park concessioner drops off and picks up backpackers, kayakers, and campers at three points in the upper Bay, the heart of the park/preserve.
Best season:	Late May to mid-September.
USGS maps:	Juneau, Mount Fairweather, Skagway, Yakutat.
Manager:	Glacier Bay National Park and Preserve.

The area: Glacier Bay, the southernmost of Alaska's spectacular meetings of glacier and sea, splits into long fingers that extend into the jumble of wild mountains near the Alaska/British Columbia border. Retreating glaciers have exposed the bay only in the last two hundred years, and now the blue ice is over 60 miles up the bay.

The land in Glacier Bay, scraped clean by the ice and then exposed by its retreat, is being recolonized by plant life. Visitors see the stages of plant succession here from oldest to youngest as they travel up the bay, including rain forest, cottonwoods, alder and willow brush, fireweed and dryas, moss and algae, and, nearest the ice, bare earth and rock. Bears use the coast extensively, and marine mammal sightings are common, especially of humpback whales.

Glacier Bay is mainly a cruise ship and tour boat park. Only a tiny percentage of the visitors to the park actually set foot in the backcountry, and those who do spend the vast majority of their time within 100 yards of the coast.

Backcountry hiking in the park requires a permit and a backcountry orientation session. Hiking is logistically difficult. The tour boat drops kayakers, hikers, and campers at only three locations up the bay. For most, this means that only shorter hikes, up to two to three days, are feasible. There are no trails in the park backcountry, so hikers have to follow the terrain—coastline, stream beds, ridges, and glacial moraines. Areas farther up the bay have been exposed more recently, so are more open country and better hiking.

True animal hikers could string together a real hiking expedition by carrying a backpack raft for crossing rivers and paddling around headlands. Taking a kayak multiplies the hiking options significantly. You can bring your own (folding by commercial jet, or hard shell by private ferry), or rent one at Bartlett Cove (not cheap).

There are three frontcountry trails in the Bartlett Cove area near park headquarters and the Glacier Bay Lodge. The Forest Trail, a mile long, is partially accessible. Park naturalists lead daily interpretive hikes on the trail in summer. The Bartlett River Trail, 2 miles one way, leads to a tidal meadow on the river through spruce/hemlock forest. The rougher Bartlett Lake Trail, 4 miles one way, splits off from the Bartlett River Trail. The walk-in campground at Bartlett Cove is the only accommodation in the park other than the lodge.

APPENDIX 1: INFORMATION SOURCES

Alaska Public Lands Information Centers

Anchorage:
605 West 4th Avenue
Anchorage, AK 99501
(907) 271-2737

Fairbanks:
250 Cushman St., Suite 1A
Fairbanks, AK 99701
(907) 456-0527

Southeast Alaska (Ketchikan):
50 Main Street
Ketchikan, AK 99901
(907) 228-6214

Alaska Department of Fish and Game

Creamer's Field Migratory Waterfowl
    Refuge
1300 College Road
Fairbanks, Alaska 99701
(907) 459-7200

Alaska State Parks

Kenai Peninsula Area
Morgan's Landing, Mile 85 Sterling
    Highway
P.O. Box 1247
Soldotna, AK 99669
(907) 262-5581

Kachemak Bay State Park
Winter: c/o Kenai Peninsula Area
Summer: P.O. Box 3248
Mile 168.5 Sterling Highway
Homer, AK 99603
(907) 235-7024

Chugach State Park
Potter Section House
HC 52 Box 8999
Indian, AK 99540
(907) 345-5014

Alaska State Parks (cont'd)

Matanuska-Susitna/Valdez/Copper
    River Area
Mile 0.7 Bogard Road
HC 32 Box 6706
Wasilla, AK 99687
(907) 745-3975

Northern Area
3700 Airport Way
Fairbanks, AK 99709
(907) 451-2695

Southeast Area
400 Willoughby Ave., 3rd Floor
Juneau, AK 99801
(907) 465-4563

Haines Ranger Station (Chilkat State
    Park)
221 Main Street, #25
Haines, AK 99827
(907) 766-2292

Arctic National Wildlife Refuge

101 12th Avenue, Room 266
Fairbanks, AK 99701
(907) 456-0250

Bering Land Bridge National Preserve

P.O. Box 220
Nome, AK 99762
(907) 443-2522

Bureau of Land Management

Anchorage District Office
6881 Abbott Loop Road
Anchorage, AK 99507
(907) 267-1246

Glennallen District Office
Box 147
Glennallen, AK 99588
(907) 822-3217

Bureau of Land Management (cont'd)

Northern District Office
1150 University Avenue
Fairbanks, AK 99709
(907) 474-2250
(907) 474-2372 (trail condition recording)

Center for Alaskan Coastal Studies

P.O. Box 2225
Homer, AK 99603
(907) 235-6667

Day tour operator:
Rainbow Tours
Cannery Row, Homer Spit
P.O. Box 1526
Homer, AK 99603
(907) 235-7272

Chena Hot Springs

Mile 56.5, Chena Hot Springs Road
P.O. Box 73340
Fairbanks, AK 99707
(907) 452-7867
(800) 478-4681 in Alaska

Chugach National Forest

Seward Ranger District
334 Fourth Avenue
P.O. Box 390
Seward, AK 99664
(907) 224-3374

Glacier Ranger District
Mile 0.3 Alyeska Highway
P.O. Box 129
Girdwood, AK 99587
(907) 783-3242

Cordova Ranger District
612 Second Street
P.O. Box 280
Cordova, AK 99574
(907) 424-7661

Denali National Park

P.O. Box 9
Denali NP, AK 99755
(907) 683-2294
(800) 622-7275 (toll-free reservation line)
(907) 272-7275 (Anchorage reservation line)

Fairbanks North Star Borough

Chena Lakes Recreation Area
P.O. Box 71267
Fairbanks, AK 99709
(907) 488-1655

Gates of the Arctic National Park/ Preserve

P.O. Box 74680
Fairbanks, AK 99707
(907) 456-0281
or
Bettles Ranger Station
Box 26030
Bettles, AK 99726
(907) 692-5494

Glacier Bay National Park/Preserve

Box 140
Gustavus, AK 99826
(907) 697-2230

Kachemak Heritage Land Trust

395 E. Pioneer Avenue
P.O. Box 2400
Homer, AK 99603
(907) 235-5263

Katmai National Park/Preserve

P.O. Box 7
King Salmon, AK 99613
(907) 246-3305

Kenai National Wildlife Refuge

Ski Hill Road Visitor Center
Mile 58 Sterling Highway Visitor
   Contact Station
Box 2139
Soldotna, AK 99669
(907) 262-7021

Klondike Gold Rush National Historical Park

2nd and Broadway
P.O. Box 517
Skagway, AK 99840
(907) 983-2921

Lake Clark National Park/Preserve

4230 University Drive, Suite 311
Anchorage, AK 99508
(907) 271-3751

Field headquarters:
1 Park Place
Port Alsworth, AK 99653
(907) 781-2218

Matanuska-Susitna Borough

Recreation Services Division
350 East Dahlia Avenue
Palmer, AK 99645
(907) 745-9631

Northwest Areas, National Park Service

(Kobuk Valley, Cape Krusenstern, Noatak)
P.O. Box 1029
Kotzebue, AK 99752
(907) 442-3890

Mountaineering Club of Alaska

P.O. Box 102937
Anchorage, AK 99510

Parks Canada

Chilkoot Trail National Historic Site
300 Main Street, Room 205
Whitehorse, Y.T. Y1A 2B5
(406) 667-3910

Sitka National Historic Park

P.O. Box 738
106 Metlakatla Street
Sitka, AK 99835
(907) 747-6281

Skagway, City of

East end of 7th Avenue
P.O. Box 518
Skagway, AK 99840
(907) 983-2232

Tongass National Forest

Ketchikan Ranger District
3031 Tongass Avenue
Ketchikan, AK 99901
(907) 225-2148

Tongass National Forest (cont'd)

Wrangell Ranger District
525 Bennett Street
Wrangell, AK 99929
(907) 874-2323

Petersburg Forest Service Visitor
Information Center
First and Fram Streets
P.O. Box 649
Petersburg, AK 99833
(907) 772-4636

Petersburg Ranger District
2nd Floor, Post Office Building
P.O. Box 1328
Petersburg, AK 99833
(907) 772-3871

Sitka Ranger District
201 Katlian Street, Suite 109
Sitka, AK 99835
(907) 747-4220

Forest Service Information Center
Centennial Hall
101 Egan Drive
Juneau, AK 99801
(907) 586-8751
(800) 478-8737 (in Alaska)

Juneau Ranger District
8465 Old Dairy Road
Juneau, AK 99801
(907) 586-8800

Mendenhall Glacier Visitor Center
Mile 3.6, Mendenhall Glacier Road
(907) 789-0097

Skagway Visitor Contact Station
(summer)
2nd and Spring
P.O. Box 554
Skagway, AK 99840
(907) 983-3088

Wrangell-St. Elias National Park/Preserve

Mile 105.5 Old Richardson Highway
P.O. Box 439
Copper Center, AK 99573
(907) 822-5234

APPENDIX 2: CABIN RESERVATIONS

State and federal agencies maintain over two hundred public-use cabins in Alaska. The cabins are rustic; most have bunks, a table and benches or chairs, a few shelves, a wood or fuel-oil stove for heat (the fuel supply is the occupants' responsibility), and an outhouse. Typical cabins sleep four to six people; some are larger.

Chugach and Tongass National Forests

For information on National Forest cabins, contact the Anchorage and Ketchikan branches of the Alaska Public Lands Information Center, the visitor information center in Juneau, or any Forest Service office (see Appendix 1 for a list of Forest Service offices). For reservations, call the toll-free telephone reservation service.

Alaska Public Lands Information Center
605 West 4th Avenue
Anchorage, AK 99501
(907) 271-2737

Southeast Alaska Visitor Center
50 Main Street
Ketchikan, AK 99901
(907) 228-6214

Forest Service Information Center
Centennial Hall
101 Egan Drive
Juneau, AK 99801
(907) 586-8751
(800) 478-8737 (in Alaska)
Toll-free reservation line:
(800) 280-2267

Alaska State Parks

Reservations for cabins in units of the Alaska State Park system (state parks, state recreation areas, state historical parks) may be made at the Department of Natural Resources Public Information Center in Anchorage, or at the nearest State Park office (see Appendix 1 for a list of offices that manage trails covered in this guidebook).

Department of Natural Resources
Public Information Center
3601 C Street, Suite 200
Anchorage, AK 99503
(907) 269-8400

Bureau of Land Management

BLM cabins in the White Mountains National Recreation Area may be reserved through the BLM office in Fairbanks:

Bureau of Land Management
1150 University Avenue
Fairbanks, AK 99709
(907) 474-2250

APPENDIX 3: TRANSPORTATION AND OUTFITTING

This appendix is a list of transportation suppliers and outfitters as noted in the text for specific trips. Air and water taxi operators change from year to year, so for current information, contact local visitor information bureaus or the manager of the area you wish to visit.

Southcentral:

Regional transportation: Cordova
Alaska Marine Highway System
P.O. Box 25535
Juneau, AK 99802
(800) 642-0066
(907) 272-4482 (Anchorage)
(907) 424-7333 (Cordova)

Hikes 17-18: Kachemak Bay State Park
Kachemak Bay Water Taxi
Slip A-1, Homer Harbor
P.O. Box 1234
Homer, AK 99603
(907) 399-3333

Hike 23: Portage Pass
Alaska Railroad
Passenger Services Dept.
P.O. Box 107500
Anchorage, AK 99510
(907) 265-2494
(907) 265-2607 (Portage-Whittier recording)

Hike 48: Red Shirt Lake
Canoe rentals (reservations necessary):
Tippecanoe Rentals
South Rolly Campground, Nancy Lakes Parkway
 or Mile 66.6, Parks Highway
P.O. Box 1175
Willow, AK 99688
(907) 495-6688

Southeast:

Regional transportation: all Southeast communities in the guidebook.
Alaska Marine Highway System
P.O. Box 25535
Juneau, AK 99802
(800) 642-0066

Hike 78: Naha River
Floatplane charters:
Island Wings
P.O. Box 7432
Ketchikan, AK 99901
(907) 225-2444

Hike 80: Petersburg Lake
Water taxi:
Alaska Fish Tales
P.O. Box 2036
Petersburg, AK 99833
(907) 772-3377

Hike 88: Mendenhall Visitor Center Trails
Glacier Express shuttle van (Marine Park to Mendenhall Glacier):
Alaska Native Tours
3235 Hospital Drive
Juneau, AK 99801
(907) 463-3231

Hike 97: Laughton Glacier
White Pass and Yukon Route Railroad
2nd and Broadway
P.O. Box 435
Skagway, AK 99840
(800) 343-7373
(907) 983-2217

Southeast (cont'd):

Hike 98: Chilkoot Pass
Shuttle van:
Chilkoot Express
7th and Broadway
P.O. Box 543
Skagway, AK 99840
(907) 983-2512

Boat:
Chilkoot Water Charters
General Delivery
Carcross, YT
Y0B1T0 Canada
(403) 821-3209

Rail:
White Pass and Yukon Route Railroad
2nd and Broadway
P.O. Box 435
Skagway, AK 99840
(800) 343-7373
(907) 983-2217

Glacier Bay National Park and Preserve

Gustavus-Bartlett Cove shuttle and tour boats into the park backcountry:
Glacier Bay Lodge
(summer)
Bartlett Cove
Gustavus, AK 99826
(907) 697-2225
(winter)
520 Pike Street Suite 1610
Seattle, WA 98101
(800) 622-2042
(206) 623-7110

Private ferry to Gustavus from Juneau:
Auk Nu Tours
76 Egan Drive
Juneau, AK 99801
(800) 820-2628

APPENDIX 4: FURTHER READING

Bears

Alaska Public Lands Information Centers. *Bear Facts: The Essentials of Traveling in Bear Country* (brochure).
Herrero, Stephen. *Bear Attacks: Their Causes and Avoidance*. Lyons and Burford, 1985.

Ecology

O'Clair, Rita M., Robert H. Armstrong and Richard Carstensen. *The Nature of Southeast Alaska: A Guide to Plants, Animals, and Habitats*. Alaska Northwest Books, 1992.

Family Hiking

Ross, Cindy. *Kids in the Wilds*. The Mountaineers, 1996.

First Aid and Wilderness Medicine

Lentz, Martha, et. al. *Mountaineering First Aid*. The Mountaineers, 1990.
Wilkerson, James, ed. *Medicine for Mountaineering*. The Mountaineers, 1992.

Fish

Alaska Department of Fish and Game, *Sport Fishing Alaska* (brochure).
Armstrong, Robert H. *Alaska's Fish: A Guide to Selected Species*. Alaska Northwest Books, 1996.
Limeres, Rene and Gunnar Pedersen, *Alaska Fishing*. Foghorn Press, 1995.
Swensen, Evan. *Fishing Alaska*. Falcon Press, 1992.

Map and Compass

Hjellstrom, Bjorn. *Be Expert with Map and Compass*. Collier Books, 1994.

Map Atlas

DeLorme Mapping. *Alaska Atlas & Gazetteer*. 1992.

National Parks, Forests and Refuges

Simmerman, Nancy L. *Alaska's Parklands*. The Mountaineers, 1983.

Native Peoples

Langdon, Steve. *The Native People of Alaska*. Greatland Graphics, 1993.

Plants

Hall, Judy K. *Native Plants of Southeast Alaska*. Windy Ridge Publishing Company, 1995.
Parker, Harriette. *Alaska Mushrooms*. Alaska Northwest Books, 1994.
Pojar, Jim and Andy MacKinnon. *Plants of the Pacific Northwest Coast*. Lone Pine Publishing Company, 1994.
Pratt, Verna. *Field Guide to Alaskan Wildflowers*. Alaskakrafts, 1989.
Pratt, Verna and Frank. *Wildflowers of Denali National Park*. Alaskakrafts, 1993.
Schofield, Janice J. *Alaska Wild Plants*. Alaska Northwest Books, 1993.
Trelawny, John. *Wildflowers of the Yukon*. Alaska and Northwest Canada. Sono Nis Press, 1988.
University of Alaska. *Wild, Edible and Poisonous Plants of Alaska*. Cooperative Extension Service, University of Alaska, 1985.
Viereck, Leslie and Elbert Little. *Alaska Trees and Shrubs*. University of Alaska Press, 1972.

Road Guides

Molvar, Erik. *Scenic Driving Alaska and the Yukon*. Falcon Press, 1996.
Vernon Publications. *The Milepost* (updated annually).

Wilderness Safety and Minimum-Impact Wilderness Use

Harmon, Will. *Wild Country Companion*. Falcon Press, 1994.

Wildlife

Alaska Department of Fish and Game. *Wildlife Notebook Series*. 1994.
Alaska Geographic Society. *Alaska Mammals*. 1981.
Armstrong, Robert H. *Guide to the Birds of Alaska*. Alaska Northwest Books, 4th ed., 1995.
Smith, Dave. *Alaska's Mammals: A Guide to Selected Species*. Alaska Northwest Books, 1995.
Sydeman, Michelle and Annabel Lund. *Alaska Wildlife Viewing Guide*. Falcon Press, 1996.

APPENDIX 5: SAMPLE BACKPACKING CHECKLIST

Use this list as a sample equipment checklist for backpacking. Plan the gear you bring based on your needs, the specific hike, a weather forecast, and the remoteness of the area you're visiting.

- ☐ Pack, pack cover
- ☐ Wool or synthetic layered clothing
- ☐ Synthetic hat, gloves, neck gaiter, socks
- ☐ Waterproof rain gear, rain hat, umbrella
- ☐ Hiking boots, camp shoes, neoprene booties for stream crossings
- ☐ Hiking staff
- ☐ Your FalconGuide

- ☐ Tent and ground cloth
- ☐ Tarp and line
- ☐ Sleeping bag and pad

- ☐ Cook stove, fuel, repair kit
- ☐ Cook kit, mugs, bowls, utensils
- ☐ Waterproof matches, lighters, fire starter, candles
- ☐ Pocket knife
- ☐ Lightweight, high-calorie food
- ☐ Extra food in case of delays or weather
- ☐ Water bottles
- ☐ Water bag or other container
- ☐ Filter or other water treatment method

- ☐ Fanny pack or other small bag for day hikes
- ☐ Fishing gear, license, and regulations
- ☐ Camera, film, binoculars
- ☐ Personal toiletries
- ☐ Book, journal, pencil
- ☐ Watch
- ☐ Flares
- ☐ Two-way radio

- ☐ First aid kit
- ☐ Sunglasses, sun hat, sunscreen, lip balm
- ☐ Bug repellent, headnet, bug jacket
- ☐ Trowel, toilet paper
- ☐ Stuff sacks, line for hanging food
- ☐ Bear repellent or firearm
- ☐ Compass, maps
- ☐ Flashlight and batteries (optional in mid-summer)

- ☐ Small repair kit for tent, pack, and clothing, including duct tape
- ☐ Plastic or nylon bags for keeping clothing, camera, and other items dry
- ☐ Garbage bags

ABOUT THE AUTHOR

Author Dean Littlepage wore out hiking boots all over the West before moving to Alaska in 1982. Since then he has hiked, skied, and paddled more than 5,000 miles in Alaska's backcountry. Between trips he has worked on trails in every way from swinging a pulaski to planning systems of trails, including a stint as manager of the Iditarod National Historic Trail.

Giving up all hope of a regular paycheck, Dean shifted gears to freelance writing and exhibit planning, specializing in history, travel, and the outdoors. He has recently curated a major exhibit on the Alaska gold rush era for the Anchorage Museum of History and Art, written a book on the gold rush called *The Alaska Gold Rush*, and co-authored a guidebook to the Yukon River.

His other main interests are in local non-profit education and conservation groups. He chaired the original planning group that began the development of Alaska's first environmental education center, and he has served on the boards of directors of several non-profits, including the Alaska Natural History Association and Friends of Chugach State Park. Dean is a founder and director of the Great Land Trust, a Southcentral Alaska land conservation trust.

All packed up for a two-week wilderness ramble.
DIEDRA BOHN PHOTO.

get
FALCON GUIDED

Falcon Press Publishing has **FALCON** GUIDES to hiking, mountain biking, rock climbing, walking, scenic driving, fishing, rockhounding, paddling, birding, wildlife viewing, and camping. Here are a few titles currently available, but this list grows every year. If you would like a free catalog with an undated list of available titles, call FALCON at the toll-free number at the bottom of this page.

HIKING GUIDES

Hiking Alaska
Hiking Alberta
Hiking Arizona
Hiking Arizona's Cactus Country
Hiking Northern Arizona
Hiking the Beartooths
Hiking Big Bend National Park
Hiking California
Hiking California's Desert Parks
Hiking Carlsbad Caverns
  and Guadalupe National Parks
Hiking Colorado
Hiking the Columbia River Gorge
Hiking Florida
Hiking Georgia
Hiking Glacier & Waterton Lakes National Parks
Hiking Grand Canyon National Park
Hiking Hot Springs
  in the Pacific Northwest
Hiking Idaho
Hiking Maine
Hiking Michigan
Hiking Minnesota
Hiking Montana
Hiker's Guide to Nevada
Hiking New Hampshire
Hiking New Mexico
Hiking New York

Hiking North Carolina
Hiking Olympic National Park
Hiking Oregon
Hiking Oregon's Eagle Cap Wilderness
Hiking Oregon's Three Sisters Country
Hiking South Dakota's Black Hills Country
Hiking Southern New England
Hiking Tennessee
Hiking Texas
Hiking Utah
Hiking Utah's Summits
Hiking Vermont
Hiking Virginia
Hiking Washington
Hiking Wyoming
Hiking Wyoming's Wind River Range
Hiking Yellowstone National Park
Hiking Zion & Bryce Canyon National Parks
Exploring Canyonlands & Arches National Parks:
  A Hiking & Backcountry Driving Guide
Trail Guide to Bob Marshall Country
Wild Country Companion
Wild Montana

BEST EASY DAY HIKES

Yellowstone National Park
Canyonlands and Arches National Parks

■ *To order any of these books, check with your local bookseller or call FALCON at 1-800-582-2665*

388

FALCON™